The English Language series

Series Editors: David Britain and
Rebecca Clift

The Vocabulary of World English

STEPHAN GRAMLEY

Senior Lecturer in English, University of Bielefeld, Germany

A member of the Hodder Headline Group
LONDON
Co-published in the United States of America by
Oxford University Press Inc., New York

First published in Great Britain in 2001 by
Arnold, a member of the Hodder Headline Group,
338 Euston Road, London NW1 3BH

http://www.arnoldpublishers.com

Co-published in the United States of America by
Oxford University Press Inc.,
198 Madison Avenue, New York, NY10016

British Library Cataloguing in Publication Data
A catalogue record for this book is available from the British Library

Library of Congress Cataloging-in-Publication Data
A catalog record for this book is available from the Library of Congress

ISBN 0 340 74071 X (hb)
ISBN 0 340 74072 8 (pb)

1 2 3 4 5 6 7 8 9 10

Production Editor: Rada Radojicic
Production Controller: Bryan Eccleshall
Cover Design: Mousemat Design

Typeset in 10pt Times by J&L Composition Ltd, Filey, North Yorkshire
Printed and bound in Malta by Gutenberg Press

What do you think about this book? Or any other Arnold title?
Please send your comments to feedback.arnold@hodder.co.uk

To Hedda with thanks for her patience and love
and to Chris, Vivian and Felix for their interest and help

Contents

Preface   xi

1   Studying the Variety in the Vocabulary of English   1
1.1 Basic assumptions   1
     1.1.1 The unity and variety of English   1
     1.1.2 Standard English (StE) and General English (GenE)   2
1.2 The lexicon of English   4
1.3 Words   4
     1.3.1 Meaning, comparing meaning, change of meaning   5
     1.3.2 The study of words   6
     1.3.3 Words in their linguistic, social, and pragmatic contexts   6
1.4 The mental lexicon, dictionaries, and other resources   6
     1.4.1 The mental lexicon   7
     1.4.2 Dictionaries   8
     1.4.3 Special dictionaries   12
     1.4.4 Thesauruses   13
     1.4.5 Encyclopedias   16

2   English in the British Isles: The Sources of Words and the
     Meaning of Meaning   18
2.0 Introduction   18
2.1 The sources of English vocabulary   19
     2.1.1 The Old English (OE) period   19
     2.1.2 The Middle English (ME) period   21
     2.1.3 The personal pronoun system of OE and ME   22
     2.1.4 The Modern English (ModE) period   24
2.2 Meaning   28
     2.2.1 Iconic meaning   28
     2.2.2 Reference, or meaning as denotation   29
     2.2.3 The representational (mentalist) approach   33
     2.2.4 The use theory of meaning   42
2.3 Summary   45

3	English in America: How to Compare Meaning and Vocabulary	47
3.1	How to compare vocabulary	47
	3.1.1 The semiotic triangle	47
	3.1.2 A typology for comparison	50
3.2	Comparison from the point of view of the referent	51
	3.2.1 Analogues: national institutions	57
3.3	Comparisons from the perspective of the word	59
	3.3.1 Same word, 'same thing': prototypes and semantic features	59
	3.3.2 Same word, same concept and food prototypes	60
	3.3.3 Same word, similar concept	61
	3.3.4 Same word, different concept (tautonyms)	64
	3.3.5 Lexical gaps	67
3.4	The perspective of the concept	67
	3.4.1 Same concept, same word plus different word	67
	3.4.2 Same concept, different words (synonyms)	70
	3.4.3 International variation in the area of food and cooking	71
	3.4.4 Conceptual gaps	72
3.5	Complex lexical combinations: phrasal verbs; collocations; idioms	73
	3.5.1 Collocations	73
	3.5.2 Idioms	74
3.6	Prepositions	77
	3.6.1 Grammatical prepositions	77
	3.6.2 Lexical prepositions	79
3.8	Summary	84
4	English in the Southern Hemisphere: Vocabulary Change	85
4.0	Introduction	85
4.1	Vocabulary change in southern hemisphere English	85
4.2	Loss of vocabulary	86
4.3	New vocabulary	87
	4.3.1 Borrowing	88
	4.3.2 Word formation	91
4.4	Standard and non-standard	98
	4.4.1 Words from other varieties of English as a resource	98
	4.4.2 Aboriginal English	99
4.5	Meaning change	99
	4.5.1 Denotation: Semantic broadening and narrowing	99
	4.5.2 Connotation: amelioration and pejoration	104
4.6	Taboo words and euphemisms	105
4.7	Summary	111
5	Whose English? English as a Second, Foreign, or International Language	112
5.0	Introduction	112

5.1 Languages in contact   112
    5.1.1 Language status   113
    5.1.2 English as a second language   114
5.2 ESL in Africa and Asia   121
    5.2.1 Africa   121
    5.2.2 Asia   125
5.3 User and use   128
    5.3.1 Dialects   128
    5.3.2 Diatypes   129
5.4 Summary   133

6   The New Englishes: Linguistic Dimensions of Vocabulary Difference 135
6.0 Introduction   135
6.1 Expanding the Vocabulary of English   135
    6.1.1 West Africa   136
    6.1.2 South Asia   137
    6.1.3 Borrowing   137
    6.1.4 Coining new words and expressions   137
    6.1.5 Semantic shift   142
6.2 Cultural differences in connotation   143
6.3 Fixed expressions: proverbs and idioms   147
    6.3.1 Proverbs   147
    6.3.2 What proverbs are used, by whom, and why   149
    6.3.3 Idioms   151
6.4 English against a differing linguistic background   153
    6.4.1 Grammatical differences: The system of personal pronouns   153
    6.4.2 The use of *yes* and *no*, and tag questions   158
6.5 Summary   164

7   English in Action: Social Dimensions of Vocabulary Differences   165
7.0 Introduction   165
7.1 Politeness   165
7.2 Vocatives and modes of address   167
    7.2.1 Motivation for using vocatives   167
    7.2.2 Kinship terms   170
    7.2.3 Names and titles   174
    7.2.4 Differences according to social features   179
7.3 Communicative strategies   187
    7.3.1 Speech acts   187
    7.3.2 Pragmatic idioms   191
7.4 Summary   197

8   International English: How Native and Non-Native Speakers
    Use Words   198

8.0   Introduction   198
8.1   Style   198
      8.1.1   Style in regional varieties of English   199
      8.1.2   Formulaic language   200
      8.1.3   Formulaic texts   201
      8.1.4   Class and style   204
      8.1.5   Jargon   206
8.2   Group language and slang   207
8.3   Non-native speaker varieties   215
      8.3.1   English in Dutch   216
      8.3.2   English in Spanish   219
      8.3.3   Code-switching and code-mixing   221
8.4   International English   223
      8.4.1   Internet English   223
      8.4.2   Youth culture   228
      8.4.3   English for Special/Specific Purposes (ESP)   232
8.5   Summary   239

9   Convergence or Divergence?   240
9.1   English in one global world   240
9.2   Linguistic relativity   241
9.3   Voices speaking for convergence, for divergence   243

Solutions to the Exercises   245

Comments on the Projects   278

Dictionaries, Thesauruses and Encyclopedias   283

Bibliography   287

Glossary and Index   297

Preface

This is a book about vocabulary. It is intended for anyone, particularly college and university students, with little or no previous knowledge of linguistics, the study of language. It presupposes that its readers are interested in English words and want to learn about them. The book pursues and intertwines four different sets of goals. First, it looks at the vocabulary of a wide variety of exemplary areas drawn from basic semantic fields ranging from 'Life and Living Things' to 'Entertainment, Sports, and Games' and much more. At the same time it pays special attention to words in numerous kinds of English, its geographical-national varieties, but also those determined by age, gender, ethnicity, function, field, and style. Furthermore, the most important areas of linguistics which touch on words are introduced. Most central to this is lexicology, meaning, and word formation, but also some lexical aspects of grammar as well as brief and periph-eral forays into pronunciation and spelling. Finally, since this book is intended to be an introduction, a great deal of emphasis is placed on exercises and projects which are intended to familiarize the book's users with resources and techniques that are helpful in the study of vocabulary. An extensive bibliography and a glossary of over 400 terms, which also serves as an index, is included. In pursu-ing these goals it is also hoped that the study of English in its lexical variety will widen horizons and lead to greater tolerance for other people's English – English which is different from our own.

This is a book about vocabulary, but it is not a dictionary, and it contains only relatively few exemplary word lists. It is about vocabulary in two senses. First, it looks at the ways in which the vocabulary of the various types of English has acquired its inventories of words, that is, how the process of the accretion of words (but with only a passing mention of loss) takes place. To do this we repeat-edly return to three processes.

The first of these is to look at where English words come from, which involves a survey of the earliest sources of English words (especially Chapter 2), but also of a variety of instances of borrowing (throughout the whole of the book). Secondly, there is the question of change of meaning, or semantic shift (especially Chapter 3). The third process is that of word formation, which includes what, in the field of lexical morphology, is called derivation and compounding (especially Chapter 4).

The second sense in which we will be looking at the vocabulary of English is from the point of view of three important 'background' factors. The first of these has to do with the ways in which English has interacted with differing linguistic backgrounds. Today this is most evident where English is used as a second language by speakers of other languages (especially Chapter 6). One of the most widespread sources of divergence and change in vocabulary is the varying social features of its speakers, whether of age, class, gender, ethnicity, or something else (see especially Chapter 7). The final background point is that of how the language is used, and includes formulaic language and texts, group language, and field- and medium-determined use (see Chapter 8).

Some 20 years ago Ferguson and Heath posed some questions about American English (1981: p. xxxi) which can be rephrased to ask today about World English. How has English changed in the world? How did it become dominant? How uniform is it? And is it becoming more or less so? Furthermore, what is public policy like in regard to language? How widely shared are the ways of talking of English users, and do they cut across linguistic and cultural boundaries? A start toward answering these questions is suggested in numerous passages in this volume. This is, so to speak, the external approach to English (see Fig. 1.1).

In this book we want to examine the worldwide vocabulary of English from several distinct internal points of view as well. This we want to do by exploring the area of *lexicology*,[1] i.e. the study of the words of a language (see below § 1.2 on the *lexicon*) and related areas of linguistics (see Fig. 1.3). We will also take a look at some of the more grammatical aspects of vocabulary, for example the personal pronouns of English. Throughout we will present numerous and, we hope, helpful examples and case studies of a variety of interesting topics chosen with an eye to their intrinsic interest to the reader as well as for the principles they illustrate (see Fig. 1.2 for an overview of the areas). However, we have also set a wide range of exercises and projects which will require students and readers to pursue a number of the themes and word fields on their own. Indeed, quite a few of the themes will remain very one-sided if the exercises are ignored (assuming that you do not look ahead to the suggested solutions).

ORGANIZATION OF THE BOOK

The book is divided into nine chapters. Chapter 1 explains the scope of the book in more detail and provides an introduction to important resources in the study of English (dictionaries, thesauruses, encyclopedias). Chapters 2–4 and 6–8 each deal with one particular 'type' of English (native or first language, second language, foreign language, and international). Chapter 5 gives an introduction to use and user categories and some aspects of language contact.

In addition, each chapter pursues a particular question which is important for the study of the lexicon: resources (1), the sources or words and meaning (2), comparison of meanings and of words (3), change in vocabulary and in meaning

---

1 Words in bold italics are defined in the glossary.

(4), language contact, variation according to user and use (5), the influence of the linguistic (6) and social background (7), and pragmatic aspects of vocabulary and language use (7 and 8). Throughout the book a variety of lexical-semantic fields are used to do this. Furthermore, lexical topics such as phrasal verbs, collocations, modes of address, idioms, taboo words, euphemisms, antonomasia, toponyms and eponyms are treated, as are lexical aspects of grammar such as pronouns, prepositions, and auxiliary verbs and such morphological topics as word formation.

Case studies

A number of the areas treated have been given special treatment in the form of what are called case studies. For example, Chapter 2 contains, among others, case studies of the influence of Irish English and of (British) schools and universities, and Chapter 3 includes case studies of units of measure and of bakery products, all intended to provide examples of how a lexical field is made up in a particular variety of English while extending the national-regional perspective outward to the corresponding fields in other national-regional varieties.

Exercises and projects

A variety of exercises will help the reader and student to apply the concepts discussed and show the importance of using resources such as dictionaries of various kinds. Interspersed with the exercises are also projects, i.e. suggestions for open-ended research on local or contrasting vocabulary use. While a key is given to the exercises, the projects, by nature, cannot be supplied with answers. Nor is it expected that anyone will undertake all the projects; but they do offer useful starting points for term papers and term projects. I have assigned them to students and have found them to be the foundation for stimulating work. In a number of cases the results of my own and my students' investigations will be given as suggestive of the type of findings that can be garnered in this way.

Glossary and literature

This book is intended for introductory work in language study, and for that reason we have tried to use 'plain language' (cf. §8.1.5 on the 'Plain English' movement). Of course, this does not excuse the writer or the readers from the necessity of making use of the terms of the field. Throughout the book technical terms have been set in bold and italic when they first occur in a given chapter, which is a cue that they can be found in the glossary at the end. The glossary itself contains cross-references to the chapters and sections where the terms are used and therefore serves simultaneously as an index.

THANKS

Finally, thanks are due to a number of people, especially several of my colleagues, most especially Konrad Sprengel and Käthe Henke, who read all or large parts of the book in manuscript form, making helpful suggestions and pointing out embarrassing mistakes. Mike Pätzold cooperated with me in an early phase of this book, which was originally intended to be a cooperative effort. His ideas about the overall concept and his helpful suggestions about exemplary material and resources were invaluable. We also taught a seminar together in which we used material and concepts from parts of this book. Thanks, too, to the students who let me use them as subjects and who carried out some of the projects suggested in the book.

The series editors, Dave Britain and Rebecca Clift offered comments at various stages in the composition of this book, and if I did not follow all their suggestions, the fault is mine. Finally, I would like to thank everyone at Arnold, but particularly Christina Wipf Perry, Emma Heyworth-Dunn, and Sarah Barrett, who supported me with their very professional advice and procedures.

Studying the Variety in the Vocabulary of English

The . . . spread of English as a global language ha[s] been seen to mark the threshold of the Modern English period. (Traugott 1972: 162f.)

1.1 BASIC ASSUMPTIONS

Underlying this book are two basic theses about the English language. The more general one is that English is a single language used in many parts of the world often with very different social functions, but that it is one language and that its users can employ it to communicate with each other. This does not mean that communication is always unproblematic; and that is the substance of the second hypothesis: English varies, sometimes enormously, depending on such factors as where it is spoken, who speaks it, and on what occasion.

1.1.1 The unity and variety of English

You, the reader, should bear in mind that English is a single language, and the very fact that this book is written in English – albeit with some idiosyncratic and/or local characteristics of the author – should itself be reminder enough. There are, of course, slightly differing national conventions of spelling and a few minor regional grammar differences, but the basic unity of English may be pre-supposed and will not be the centre of our attention.

'Unity does not, of course, mean identity' (Svejcer 1978:16). Consequently, we will be looking at the variety within this unity. In principle, this will take two major forms in this book. One will be to look at variety according to place. For the most part, place will be understood in a very straightforward physical-geographical sense. That is, we will be interested in how the vocabulary of English differs in the British Isles, North America, the Caribbean, Australia, New Zealand, and South Africa (Chapters 2–4), all places where English is well established as a *first language* (*ENL* = English as a Native Language). But we will also explore the language in places where it is a *second language* (*ESL* = English as a Second Language): East Africa, West Africa, and parts of Southern Africa as well as South and Southeast Asia and the Philippines (Chapters 5 and 6). Here we turn particularly to aspects of language contact as well as social and prag-matic aspects of vocabulary and language use. Without wanting to strain the place dimension too much, we will also consider a few examples of how English has interacted as a *foreign language* (*EFL* = English as a Foreign Language) with a few of its close European and American neighbours (Dutch, French, German, Spanish) (in parts of Chapter 8). In any case we want to expand the view of English beyond the more usual Anglo-American perspective.

However, place is not just physical-geographical. It is also virtual (so we will look at English on the Internet), social (so class, gender, race and ethnicity are significant factors), and functional (so the purpose the language is used for is also a part of its variation). See Fig. 1.1.

1.1.2 Standard English (StE) and General English (GenE)

So far we have used the term 'English' as if we are all in agreement about what this means. Despite all the variety just outlined, there will be a need to limit what we feel it is feasible to look at. One possibility is to consider restricting ourselves to *Standard English (StE)*. Just what this is is difficult to define exactly, but many people will agree that it is the kind of English which is used by speakers with at least a moderate degree of education. This is, of course, potentially a restriction of our range of observation to the English of the higher socio-economic classes. One result of this is that the scope of StE may tendentially be drawn too narrowly to include (at least some sorts of) slang as well as vulgar and taboo expressions.

Since the intention behind the choice of StE is *not* to filter English socially – indeed, both slang and vulgar or taboo expressions are included – it would

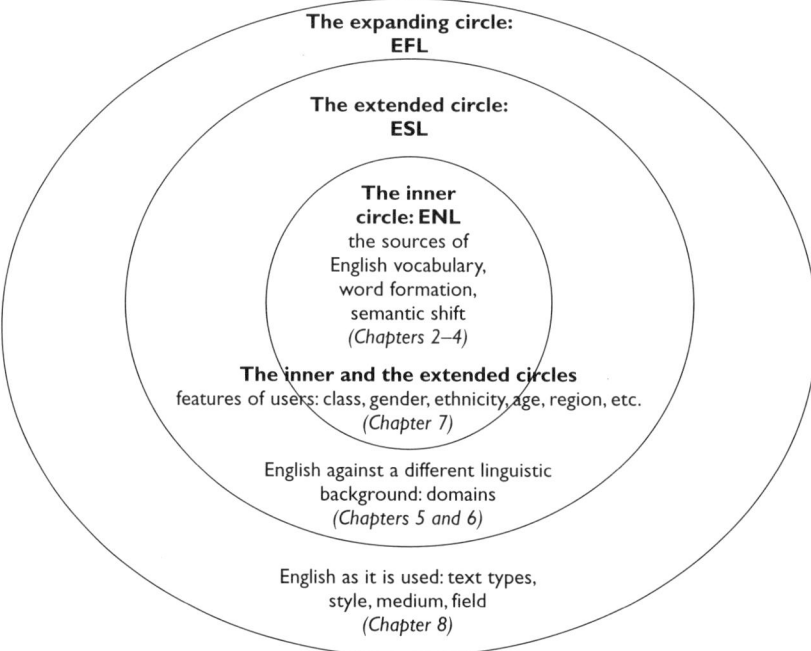

The expanding circle:
EFL

The extended circle:
ESL

The inner circle: ENL
the sources of English vocabulary, word formation, semantic shift
(Chapters 2–4)

The inner and the extended circles
features of users: class, gender, ethnicity, age, region, etc.
(Chapter 7)

English against a different linguistic background: domains
(Chapters 5 and 6)

English as it is used: text types, style, medium, field
(Chapter 8)

Fig. 1.1. An external view of English (after Kachru 1985)

perhaps be more appropriate to speak of a restriction to **General English (GenE)** (cf. Wells 1982: 2f.). This useful term refers to English usage wider than StE, though explicitly not including obvious local and regional dialects. We will, in other words, want to include the usage of speakers whose English is easily intelligible to StE speakers, but which may diverge in regard to a number of more or less stigmatized grammatical forms, such as third person *don't* (*it don't work*) and lexically restricted regionalisms like *spigot* ('tap, faucet'). Although it is far from easy to know where to draw the line, by going beyond StE we hope to incorporate material diverse enough to avoid blatant classism.

In adopting GenE as the label for our observations we want to emphasize that this includes both **written English** and **spoken English**. English in its printed form is relatively unitary throughout the world and closely associated with StE. Furthermore, written StE English has been codified in grammar books, dictionaries, and manuals of style. For this reason many people who are new to the study of language have a tendency to identify English with the written language and with StE. Yet it also includes the spoken language, especially what is called **colloquial English**. Certainly, spoken English is much more diverse than written English. We are likely to hear (and speak) it in both its standard and various of its non-standard guises.

What both Standard and General English do not include is what Wells (1982: 4ff.) has called the **traditional dialects**, those local varieties of English in England and Scotland (and transplanted to a few parts of Ireland and North America) which represent independent and more or less parallel developments from the period of Old English (450/550–1150) onward. Such varieties differ, often dramatically, from StE in pronunciation, grammar, and of course vocabulary. The Scottish (and Northern English) word *brig* ('bridge') or the Appalachian word *lief* ('gladly' as in *I'd as lief go as not*) are examples. We will include such words only where they have been borrowed into (local) GenE. This is the case with such Southern American regionalisms as *fixin'* ('preparing') or *carry* ('transport') as in *Pa's fixin' to carry me to town*.

Another case which is marginal to our observations is that of severely restricted localisms borrowed both from foreign languages and from English **creoles**. Speakers of StE with a Pennsylvania Dutch (= German) background will recognize and use words like *rut(s)chy*, as in *Don't be so rutschy* ('squirmy, unable to sit still', especially of children) or *spritz*, as in *The grapefruit spritzes* ('squirt', as when grapefruit segments are dug out). English speakers in places where StE is in a **continuum** (a series of gradually different varieties stretching from the low or non-standard extreme to StE) will be inclined, especially in the appropriate social constellation of familiarity and relaxation, to use creole words in what is otherwise StE. They may replace StE *eat* with the Jamaican Creole word *nyam* (Grimshaw 1971: 437), as in *We ben a nyam* ('We were eating').

1.2 THE LEXICON OF ENGLISH

The vocabulary of a language, the totality of its words, is called its **lexicon**. The complete vocabulary of any language is large. And a language with as much regional and social variation as English contains not only an enormous number of words but also numerous differences in word inventories between user groups. This poses a practical problem. Since we cannot look at everything and since long lists of differences are uninspiring, we must decide on what to deal with. The solution is the choice of a general cultural-world perspective that includes some of what we consider to be the major areas of human endeavour/activity.

To provide a basis for our choice we have taken the divisions adopted in the *Lexicon of Contemporary English* (McArthur 1981). This reference work categorizes the vocabulary of English in the fourteen broad areas listed in bold in the boxes below (see Fig. 1.2). To each of the categories we have added the section numbers of the passages below where they have been treated at some length.

1.3 WORDS

In treating the subjects listed above we will be looking at both **lexical words** and **grammatical** (or **form**) **words**. The former refer to reality in our physical and mental worlds and consist chiefly of nouns, verbs, and adjectives; the latter express relationships within the language itself and include conjunctions, pronouns, prepositions, articles.[1]

The term used for both lexical and grammatical words is **lexeme**, which is the designation for the kind of item which is listed in a dictionary (a dictionary **entry** or **headword** is called a **lemma**). A lexeme is abstract; it is conceptual. As a result it is not important how it is represented, i.e. as sound or as a set of written symbols. And the writing can be script or print; the print can be all small (lower-case) letters or capitals or, indeed, some mixture of the two. Whenever we want to refer to a particular instance of a lexical or grammatical word, we can use the term **word form**. When it is written, a word form is customarily distinguished by being both preceded and followed by a blank space.

Lexemes need not be single word forms. That is, both *perambulator* (one word form) and *baby carriage* (two word forms, a **complex** or **multi-word item**) are single lexemes. Where a lexeme has more than one distinct meaning we can talk about each combination of the lexeme and a particular meaning as a **lexical unit**. For example, *pudding* is one lexeme, but at least two different lexical units, one of which is the relationship between *pudding* and the meaning 'a kind of food held

---

1 The term **word** by itself is sometimes used to refer to any grammatical or lexical word in whatever form it takes. For example, *a* and *an* are the same word (the indefinite article); and *go, goes, going, went*, and *gone* are all the same word (= lexeme) even though each is used in a grammatically different way and includes a form (*went*) from a different root.

Life and living things: plants and animals (2.2.1.1; 4.3, 4.6.5)

The body: its functions and welfare: parts of the body (4.6.4–6);
appearance (8.2.1-2; 8.1.3; 8.4.1.1,8.2.6)

People and the family: political, social institutions (2.1.2.1.; 2.2.2; 3.2.6–7;
4.5.4); religion (2.1.2.1); ethnic designations and slurs (4.6.2–5; 7.2.3.2); Maori
social life (4.3.2.1); solidarity and kinship (7.2); matrimony (8.1.3; 8.4.1.1);
social class (8.1.4; 8.2); military (2.1.2.1; 8.2.3; Case study 8.11)

Buildings, houses, the home, clothes, belongings, and personal care:
the bush (4.3.3.1–3); settling the land (4.5.2–3); topography (Case study 8.5)

Food, drink, and farming: bakery products, the eating day, foods
(3.3; 4.3.2.1; 6.1.1; 8.3.2); cowboy culture (Case study 8.5)

Feelings, emotions, attitudes, and sensations:
Puritan attitudes (6.3.1); politeness (7.1); power and solidarity (7.2);
apologies, compliments, thanks (7.3.2.4–11); words for others (8.2.4–5, 8.2.4.7);
emotions (8.4.1.4)

Thought and communication, language and grammar: *passim*

Substances, materials, objects, and equipment: substances (8.4.3.1)

Arts and crafts, science and technology, industry and education:
art (2.1.2.1); education (2.1.2.1; 2.2.3); cooking utensils (3.6.4); school
(8.2.4); the Internet (8.4.1); science and technology (8.4.3.1)

Numbers, measurement, money, and commerce: 3.2.1–5
trade and shipping (2.1.2.2); numbers, units of measure (8.4.3.1)

Entertainment, sports, and games: baseball (1.4.5); fashion and
clothing (2.1.2.1; 8.3.2); music (Case study 8.10)

Space and time: colour (6.2)

Movement, location, travel, and transport: transportation
(4.5.5–6); greetings, leavetaking (7.3.2.1–3); air traffic control (Case study 8.12)

Fig. 1.2. An encyclopedic view of English: the semantic areas of English

together in a bowl or cloth and cooked by boiling or steaming'. The other
lexical unit is *pudding* and the meaning 'sweet course at the end of a meal' (see
Chapter 3).

1.3.1 Meaning, comparing meaning, change of meaning

In order to talk coherently about words we need to be able to talk about meaning, and this is a theme we will be dealing with in Chapter 2. However, since we
are also looking at numerous varieties of English, it will be necessary to explore

the ways in which comparisons in meaning and vocabulary can be made from one language variety to another (Chapter 3). In Chapter 4 we will go one step further and talk about how words and meanings change (borrowing, word formation, semantic shift).

1.3.2 The study of words

Among the goals pursued in this book one of the most central is the study of the vocabulary of English (*lexicology*). In introducing this discipline we try to view vocabulary within the larger context of the language as a whole. For this reason vocabulary is seen in connection with other areas within the study of language, as Figure 1.3 attempts to show (the numbers in small print refer to the most important sections in which the particular areas are dealt with).

1.3.3 Words in their linguistic, social, and pragmatic contexts

As we leave Chapters 2–4, we move on to areas in which English is used against a non-English linguistic background such as is the case in East and West Africa and parts of Southern Africa and South and Southeast Asia (Chapters 5 and 6). The English spoken in such places is a second language variety for most people, and it is used to reflect cultures and values which English may, originally, have been ill-equipped to express. How users of the language have dealt with these problems will interest us, as well as why they have chosen the solutions they have. Chapter 7 addresses some of the ways in which the social and cultural background of its users affects English, both native and non-native.

Chapter 8 looks at lexical developments in areas where English is for some a native language, for others a second language, and for yet others a foreign language. We will look at some of the interesting things that happen to the vocabulary of English as it appears in a few other languages, such as Dutch, German, French, or Spanish. Or English in international user groups: young people's language and technical terminologies (where vagueness and ambiguity can be life-threatening).

The final chapter is a general discussion of the question of divergence and convergence. Is English developing into local varieties which, in the long term, may become mutually unintelligible (much as Latin mutated into French, Spanish, Italian, Catalan, Romanian, etc.)? Or is English maintaining 'unity in diversity'?

1.4 THE MENTAL LEXICON, DICTIONARIES, AND OTHER RESOURCES

Throughout this book you will be asked to do exercises and to work on projects. In order to carry them out successfully it will be necessary for you to draw on a wide range of reference works which are the products of *lexicography*. The present section serves as an introduction to them. For the most part you will be directed toward dictionaries, of which there is an enormous number of many kinds, serving all sorts of purposes. What dictionaries share is their orientation toward the word.

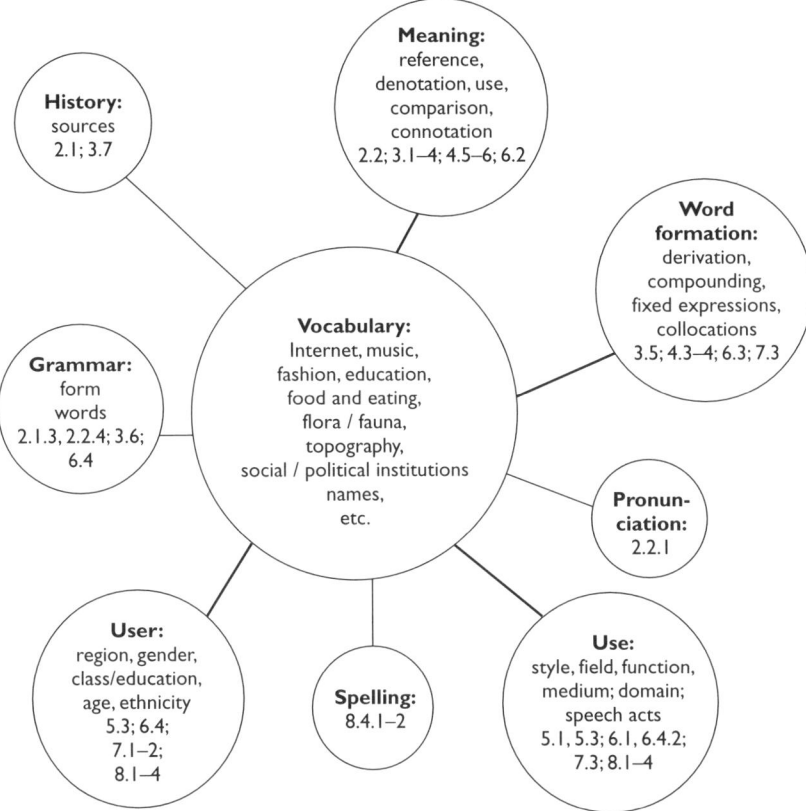

Fig. 1.3. An internal view of English

Another, second type of reference book is the thesaurus, which is organized according to meanings. The third and final type of resource is the encyclopedia, which gives information about the 'real world'. These three approaches reflect the three points of the ***semiotic triangle***, which is introduced in §3.1.1.

1.4.1 The mental lexicon

We pointed out above that the word *lexicon* is used to refer to the collectivity of words and morphemes in a given language. It is also used to designate a type of book, for example the *Lexicon of Contemporary English* (McArthur 1981), also mentioned above. A third prominent meaning of lexicon is that of the ***mental lexicon*** (or semantic memory) of any given individual, including his or her encyclopedic knowledge of the world. The way we store items is surely not alpha-betical – even though spellings may have an influence on memory. Rather, it seems much more likely that we associate linguistic with non-linguistic know-ledge so as to build up categories or fields of words and things. Within the fields we make finer and finer distinctions. How this may look will be dealt with in connection with meaning, (especially §2.2). The fields themselves may be organized as networks of overlapping similarities in meaning, or as hierarchies of features of meaning or they may be grouped around prototypical concepts or, indeed, some combination of these.

Brain dysfunction of one or another type, especially **aphasias**, indicate that other types of organization are also present. Words sometimes come out wrong even among people who do not suffer from aphasia. This can involve replacing one word with another on the basis of phonological similarity, as when we produce *sympathy* when we mean *symphony*. There can be 'blends' of two words, as when *flustered* and *frustrated* gives us *flustrated*. Or we can produce **spoonerisms**, in which words in a phrase are exchanged (*Work is the curse of the drinking class*) or sounds are exchanged (for example, the foreigner who thanked his American host for helping him get to know '*the American lay of wife*').

Association tests, as well as aphasias and slips of the type just quoted, indicate that storage may well be governed by a variety of principles. Links between words may be via *coordination* (*car–truck–bus–train*; *right–wrong*), *collocation* (a *confirmed bachelor*; *dogs bark*), *superordination* (*birds* are *animals*; *chairs* are *furniture*), or by synonymy (*ghost–spirit–spook*). It is not clear how, in the end, the mental lexicon is structured.

1.4.2 Dictionaries

Dictionaries are human artefacts. Their principles of organization can be explained explicitly. They are books which contain lists of the words of a language about which they provide information of various sorts. In this section we will review some of the many types of dictionary with a view to describing what kind of information they give and how it is organized.

1.4.2.1 Printed or electronic?

When you look for a dictionary to use, you may well have one or more at your disposal on your bookshelf. If not, you can make a trip to the library, and you will surely have to do this to get hold of some of those recommended as aids to the exercises in this book. Increasingly, however, dictionaries and other reference works are also available on the Internet or in the form of CD-ROMs. Some of the Internet resources are free, but quite a few demand a fee. A useful starting point is <http://www.dictionary.com>.

1.4.2.2 Monolingual or bilingual?

The major difference between these two types of dictionary is that an English monolingual dictionary will give its information (definitions, etc.) in English, while a bilingual one uses an English entry for which foreign language translations are offered by way of definition (and of course vice versa: FL entry + English translation equivalents). Bilingual dictionaries are often less helpful than they might be because they do not offer enough context to tell one meaning of a word from another. If *greed* is given as German *Gier*, *Habgier*, *Habsucht*, or *Geiz*, how is the user to know when to use which German word? And of course, not every occurrence of these four German words can be realized by the English word *greed*. There simply is seldom, if ever, a one-to-one relationship between words in different languages.

1.4.2.3 ENL, ESL, or EFL user?

Monolingual dictionaries also differ considerably from each other. We can distinguish such major unabridged ones as *Webster's Third New International Dictionary of the English Language* (1971) or *The Random House Dictionary of the English Language* (1987). Most native-speaker students will be more likely to have a middle-sized one-volume **desk dictionary**. Note, however, that quite a few dictionaries cater to use and users of a particular regional-national variety of English (see Table 1.1). Non-native speakers will benefit more from a **learner's dictionary** (see Table 1.2).

A dictionary intended for a native speaker usually makes different assumptions from those of one intended for non-native speakers. A typical monolingual native speaker desk dictionary such as the *Random House Webster's College Dictionary* (RHWCD) defines *greed* as 'excessive or rapacious desire, esp. for wealth or possessions; avarice; covetousness'. Some of the words in the definition may force the user to look further to find out what *rapacious*, *avarice*, and *covetousness* mean. Here is where a monolingual learner's dictionary, intended for non-native speakers, is helpful. The *Longman Dictionary of Contemporary English* (*LDOCE*) defines its entries by using a limited 'defining vocabulary' of approximately 2000 common words. *Greed* is defined as follows: 'a strong desire to have a lot of something, esp. food, money, or power, often in a way that is selfish or unfair to other people'. Needless to say, none of the words used here is likely to set off a further search.

1.4.2.4 Context and collocation

One of the important further distinctions between bilingual or monolingual native-speaker and monolingual learner's dictionaries is the use or lack of use of example sentences which offer illustrations of typical context and **collocations**. Neither of the first two types give examples of how *greed* is used, while the *LDOCE* continues its definition with the example sentence:

> *It was pure greed that made me finish all those chocolates! | The speculators' greed (for profit) has left several small investors penniless.*

1.4.2.5 Basic or extended?

Learner's dictionaries obviously have several decisive advantages over native-speaker dictionaries. The latter are not, however, without their own advantages. Chief among these is that the number of entries is typically much greater. They

Table 1.1. Desk dictionaries

AmE
American Heritage College Dictionary, 3rd edn (1993)
Encarta World English Dictionary (1999)
Merriam-Webster's Collegiate Dictionary, 10th edn (1993)
Random House Webster's College Dictionary, 2nd edn (1997)
Webster's New World College Dictionary, 3rd edn (1997)
BrE
Chambers Dictionary (1993)
Collins English Dictionary, 4th edn (1998)
Concise Oxford Dictionary of Current English, 10th edn (1999)
Longman Dictionary of the English Language, 2nd edn (1991)
AusE
Australian Concise Oxford Dictionary (1987)
Australian National Dictionary (1988)
Macquarie Dictionary (1981)
NZE
Heinemann New Zealand Dictionary (1989)
New Zealand Dictionary (1994)
SingE
Times–Chambers Essential English Dictionary, 2nd edn (1997)

Table 1.2. Learner's dictionaries

Cambridge International Dictionary of English (1995)
Collins COBUILD English Dictionary, 2nd edn (1995)
Longman Dictionary of Contemporary English, 3rd edn (1995)
NTC's American English Learner's Dictionary (1998)
Oxford Advanced Learner's Dictionary of Current English, 6th edn (2000)

list more learned and technical words and are more likely to include biographical and geographical entries. That is, they are more encyclopedic in their approach.[2] While *greed* in the *LDOCE* is preceded by *Greco-* (a combining form) and the same page includes the adjectives *Grecian* and *Greek*, the *RHWCD* is preceded by

---

2 But note that the *Longman Dictionary of English Language and Culture* (2nd edn, 1998), a learner's dictionary, does so as well.

Greece (a geographical entry), then the archaic word *gree²*, then the Scottish word *gree¹*, then *Greco-Roman*, and only then *Greco-*, itself preceded by the biographical entry *Greco* [. . .] *El* (the artist).

Before going on to a review of some of the more specialized dictionaries and other reference works, let us have a look at the kind of information you can find in a monolingual dictionary. A typical entry will be structured in the following way.

1. **Headwords** or **entries** consist not only of simple words, but may also be prefixes and suffixes. Furthermore, abbreviations, geographical and biographical names, chemical formulas, common foreign expressions, and multi-word entries will be found in varying degrees.

2. **Spelling variants** are given together with the headword, e.g. *defence* (BrE) and *defense* (AmE). The syllable structure is indicated, e.g. *de-fence*. Capitalization is indicated as between *congress* (any meeting) and *Congress* (the American institution)

3. **Pronunciation** is indicated using various systems of transcription. Learner's dictionaries use symbols from the ***IPA (International Phonetic Alphabet)*** and give both ***RP*** ('***Received Pronunciation***' sometimes referred to as 'Oxford English'), and ***General American*** pronunciations, e.g. /ˈkɒngres/ and /ˈkɑːngrəs/ respectively. Monolingual native-speaker dictionaries will follow the standard of the country they are oriented toward.

4. **Grammatical information** includes the part of speech (or word class, e.g. noun, transitive verb). Inflectional forms are given, esp. irregular ones (e.g. plural: *criterion, -ria* or past tense and past participle: *know, knew, known*).

5. **Usage labels** are added where needed. They may cover regional (e.g. *chiefly British*; *dialect*), style (*slang*; *informal*), area (*Nautical*; *Law*), currency (*obsolete, archaic*).

6. **Definitions** are structured (numbered) so as to distinguish the various meanings of a (***polysemous***) word. More than one entry is used to distinguish between ***homonyms*** such as *lie* 'to recline' and *lie* 'to make an untrue statement'. Dictionaries vary on the practice of, for example, giving nouns and verbs with the same lexical kernel separate entries, e.g. *lie* (noun) and *lie* (verb).

    Definitions are variously supported by examples of use in sentences (see discussion above), diagrams, illustrations, maps, and tables.

    Common idioms and expressions containing the headword are added, e.g. under *hell* we may find *come hell or high water*.

7. **References to related words** may be given, e.g. under *hedgehog* a reference to *porcupine*.

8. **Related forms** are added. For example, under *fringe* we find *fringeless, fringe-like*, and *fringy*.

9. **Usage notes** are added in more and more dictionaries to distinguish between words with similar or overlapping meanings including stylistic level and social connotation (e.g. *help* vs. *assist* vs. *aid*).

10. *Etymologies* are given in monolingual native speaker dictionaries, but not in learner's dictionaries.

1.4.3 Special dictionaries

1.4.3.1 Historical or contemporary?

The *Oxford English Dictionary* (*OED*) (see Table 1.3) traces back words to their first written use and tries to provide at least one quotation showing the word's use in each of the subsequent centuries. A whole series of historical dictionaries of numerous national varieties of English has also been produced. There are other dictionaries which are historical only in the sense of being very old. Perhaps the most venerable of these are Samuel Johnson's *Dictionary of the English Language* (1755) and Noah Webster's *An American Dictionary of the English Language* (1828).

1.4.3.2 General or special?

So far we have been assuming that a dictionary is general in scope, i.e. that it lists the most common words in a language or a variety. Within the framework of this book it will also be convenient to draw on more specific types of dictionary. Especially interesting are dictionaries of regional vocabulary (see Table 1.4).

There are, of course, numerous 'sub-varieties' of English, each prospectively with its own dictionary. Table 1.5 gives a further sampling (restricted to one title for each).

Some dictionaries concentrate on listing certain types of entry such as *abbreviations*, clichés, colloquialisms, *dialect* words, *ESP*, *euphemisms*, *hard words*, *idioms*, *names*, new words, *phrasal verbs*, phrases and quotations, *proverbs*, *slang*, etc. (see Table 1.6). Another way of specializing is to deal with some particular aspect of the language. Thus we find dictionaries of spelling, pronunciation,

---

Table 1.3. Historical dictionaries

The Australian National Dictionary: A Dictionary of Australianisms in Historical Perspective (1988)

A Dictionary of American English on Historical Principles (1944)

Dictionary of Canadianisms on Historical Principles (1967)

A Dictionary of South African English on Historical Principles (1996)

A New English Dictionary on Historical Principles, a.k.a. *Oxford English Dictionary* (1884–1928) (plus supplements)

The Oxford English Dictionary, 2nd edn (1989)

The Shorter Oxford English Dictionary on Historical Principles, 3rd rev. edn (1978)

Table 1.4. Dictionaries of regional varieties

Africanisms in Afro-American Language Varieties (1993)

The Compact Scottish National Dictionary (1986)

A Concise Ulster Dictionary (1996)

Dictionary of Africanisms (1982)

Dictionary of American Regional English, vols. i and ii (up to H) (1985, 1991, 1996)

Dictionary of Americanisms (1951)

Dictionary of Bahamian English (1982)

Dictionary of Caribbean English Usage (1996)

A Dictionary of Jamaican English (1980)

Dictionary of Prince Edward Island English (1988)

A Dictionary of South African English, 4th edn (1991)

Longman Dictionary of American English (1997)

The Orkney Dictionary (1996)

The Shetland Dictionary (1979)

Tassie Terms: A Glossary of Tasmanian Words (1995)

Words Apart: A Dictionary of Northern Ireland English (1990)

Words from the West: A Glossary of Western Australian Terms (1994)

Table 1.5. Dictionaries of 'sub-varieties' (examples)

Creoles	*A Krio-English Dictionary* (1980)
Dialects	*The Concise Scots Dictionary* (1985)
English for Special Purposes	*Webster's New World Dictionary of Media and Communications* (1996)

grammar, etymology, or usage (see Table 1.7). Further reference works may be distinguished by the way the entries are organized. Among the dictionaries, we might mention reverse dictionaries, which list entries by the final element of a word. Organization by meaning or by field is covered not by dictionaries, but by thesauruses and the like (see below, §1.4.4). Tables 1.6 and 1.7 cite a single example of each of the types just mentioned.

1.4.4 Thesauruses

A *thesaurus* (< Greek for 'treasure') is basically a dictionary of **synonyms**. Words which share some element of meaning are grouped together. Other names for what is basically a thesaurus (or a combination of dictionary and

Table 1.6. Dictionaries by class of entry (examples)

Abbreviations	*Acronymania: A Celebratory Roundup of Nomenclature Yielding Mischief: Abbreviations, Neologisms, Initialisms, Acronyms!* (1993)
Allusions	*And Now for Something Completely Different: Dictionary of Allusions in British English* (1997)
Clichés	*A Dictionary of Clichés* (1996)
Collocations	*The BBI Dictionary of English Word Combinations*, 2nd edn (1997)
Colloquialisms	*A Dictionary of Australian Colloquialisms*, 4th edn (1996)
Euphemisms	*Euphemisms: Over 3,000 Ways to Avoid Being Rude or Giving Offence* (1993)
Foreign words and phrases	*The Oxford Dictionary of Foreign Words and Phrases* (1997)
Hard words	*Dictionary of Confusing Words and Meanings* (1985)
Idioms	*Idioms: Their Meanings and Origins* (1996)
Names	*The Guinness Book of British Place Names* (1993)
New words	*The Oxford Dictionary of New Words* (1997)
Phrasal verbs	*Cambridge International Dictionary of Phrasal Verbs* (1997)
Phrases and quotations	*NTC's Dictionary of Quotations* (1994)
Proverbs	*Random House Dictionary of Popular Proverbs and Sayings* (2000)
Slang	*Slang: The Authoritative Topic-by-Topic Dictionary of American Lingoes from All Walks of Life* (1998)

Table 1.7. Dictionaries by linguistic level (examples)

Etymology	*The Barnhart Dictionary of Etymology* (1988)
Grammar	*Oxford Guide to English Grammar* (1994)
Pronunciation	*Longman Pronunciation Dictionary*, 2nd edn (2000)
Spelling	*The Oxford Spelling Dictionary* (1995)
Usage	*21st Century Manual of Style* (1993)

thesaurus) are **word finder**, **word or language activator**, **word menu**. The best known of the thesauruses is the one published by P.M. Roget in 1852 as the result of his own project to increase his powers of expression. It has appeared in numerous editions since then.

Table 1.8. The structure of *Roget's Thesaurus*

I. ABSTRACT RELATIONS	5. Results of reasoning
1. Existence	6. Extension of thought
2. Relation	7. Creative thought
3. Quantity	Division II. Communication of ideas:
4. Order	1. Nature of ideas communicated
5. Number	2. Modes of communicating
6. Time	3. Means of communicating ideas
7. Change	
8. Causation	V. VOLITION
	Division I. Individual volition:
II. SPACE	1. Volition in general
1. Space in general	2. Prospective volition
2. Dimensions	3. Voluntary action
3. Form	4. Antagonism
4. Motion	5. Results of action
III. MATTER	Division II. Intersocial volition:
1. Matter in general	1. General
2. Inorganic matter	2. Special
3. Organic matter	3. Conditional
	4. Possessive relations
IV. INTELLECT	
Division I. Formation of ideas:	VI. AFFECTIONS
1. General	1. Affections generally
2. Precursory conditions and	2. Personal
operations	3. Sympathetic
3. Materials for reasoning	4. Moral
4. Reasoning processes	5. Religion

The organization is not alphabetical. Instead, we find words divided and sub-divided into categories such as those shown in Table 1.8. These are then further divided into a total of 990 heads or topics which 'subsume pretty adequately the whole range of ideas that the vocabulary is normally used to express' (Preface, p. vii).

If we want to find synonyms of *greed*, for example, we look this word up in the alphabetical index at the end and find, as it turns out, references to four of the 990 topics, viz. *rapacity* 786 n. [= noun], *avarice* 816 n., *selfishness* 932 n., and *gluttony* 947 n. In the meaning of 'avarice' (part of intersocial volition: possessive relations) *greed* appears in the group

> *avarice*, cupidity, acquisitiveness, possessiveness, monopoly; money-grubbing, mercenariness, venality, hireling character (*Roget's Thesaurus*)

This group appears after one headed by *parsimony*, and it is followed by one headed by *niggard*. All three of these are grouped together as nouns. They, as a whole, are followed by groups of adjectives and verbs from the same word field. The whole is entitled '816. Parsimony'.

The divisions used in *Roget's Thesaurus* are not so convincing that they could not be made differently. Certainly, there are no linguistic grounds for them. For the purposes of this book we have found it more useful to refer to the categories used by McArthur in his learner's thesaurus, the *Longman Lexicon of Contemporary English* (*LLCE*). This is because each of McArthur's 14 semantic areas, except perhaps the final one ('General and abstract terms'), is relatively concrete. The 14 are themselves made up of sub-themes or super-sets, and these then are subdivided into lexical sets. If you look up *greed* in the index you find its pronunciation given in IPA symbols, and you find it labelled *n* for noun. The index gives only one reference number for *greed*: F181. F stands for 'Feelings, emotions, attitudes, and sensations'; 181 falls in the section F170–F189, 'Kindness and unkindness'. F181 contains only three items: *greed*, *avarice*, and *miser*. Consequently, we find that *LLCE* is less comprehensive than *Roget*: there is no entry for *cupidity*, *acquisitiveness*, *possessiveness*, *money-grubbing*, *mercenariness*, *venality*, or *hireling character*, though *monopoly* does show up elsewhere.

What is perhaps the greatest disadvantage of the traditional thesaurus is its failure to offer definitions or otherwise to distinguish between the items offered under a given head. Here we find one of the main improvements in *LLCE* as compared with *Roget*, for the former offers a short definition (using the Longman defining vocabulary) of each entry plus an example sentence. It also supplies further grammatical information, namely that *greed* is an uncountable noun (U) and that if it is followed by a preposition, the preposition will be *for*:

> **greed** [U (*for*)] a strong desire to obtain a lot or more than what is right, esp of food, money, or power: *He had a greed for gold.*

Usage labels are also supplied where appropriate.

Some groups consist not of synonyms, but of **antonyms** (e.g. L14 has the converses *up* and *down*). Other lexical sets are **meronymous**, i.e. they give the typical parts of a whole. M100 (part of M, 'Movement, location, travel, and transport', sections M90–M119, 'Vehicles and transport on land'), for instance, consists of a drawing of a car with its parts labelled.

1.4.5 Encyclopedias

A final type of reference work is the **encyclopedia** or an encyclopedic reference book, which shares aspects of both the dictionary and the thesaurus. As in the dictionary, the usual principle of order is alphabetical according to headword. The entries themselves are not linguistic items, but thematic areas of knowledge. Although this is reminiscent of a thesaurus, a word like *greed* is not entered at all in an encyclopedia; to find it, you would have to relate it to *avarice*, to know that this is one of the seven deadly sins, and to look there.

Despite the tremendous difference between the kind of information given in a dictionary and an encyclopedia, both types of knowledge are necessary if we are to use a language appropriately. We have to know what the common noun *greed* means, but if we want to count as well educated we would also do well to know the cultural implications of *greed*, be it as a theological concept or as the name of a popular movie. A language does not consist solely of dictionary items; it is also full of references to specific things (people, dates, events, ideologies, institutions, social attitudes, etc.). In order to communicate competently with fellow users of English we simply must have encyclopedic knowledge. This is what is understood by **cultural literacy**. An American, whether a baseball fan or not, will know its expressions: the idioms, idiomatic expressions, and figurative language originally taken from baseball but often used in general colloquial speech, such as *batting order* 'the order in which people act or take their turn' or *to take the field* 'to begin a campaign'.

> Baseball has provided the following collection of idiomatic expressions, most of which have a very distinctly American flavour about them: *to play* (*political, economic,* etc.) *hard ball* 'to be serious about s.th.', *to touch base* 'to keep in contact', *not to get to first base with s.o.* 'to be unsuccessful with s.o.', *to pinch hit for s.o.* 'to stand in for s.o.', *to ground out/fly out/foul out/strike out* 'to fail', *to have a/one/two strikes against you* 'to be at a disadvantage', *to play in/to make the big leagues* 'to work/be with important, powerful people', *a double play* 'two successes in one move', *a rain check* 'postponement', *a grand slam* (also tennis and bridge) 'a smashing success or victory', *a blooper* 'a mistake or failure', *a doubleheader* 'a combined event with lots to offer', *batting average* 'a person's performance', *over the fence* or *out of the ball park* 'a successful move or phenomenal feat', *out in left field* 'remote, out of touch, unrealistic', *off base* 'wrong'. (Gramley and Pätzold 1992: 364)

Cultural literacy means more than handling metaphors like those in the quotation above; it also means knowing who the baseball player Babe Ruth was, or at least enough to understand that someone who is called, say, *the Babe Ruth of tennis* must be pretty good.

How much of this kind of knowledge gets into a dictionary is very uncertain. The *Longman Dictionary of English Language and Culture* is an attempt to include the encyclopedic with the linguistic, but as a learner's dictionary it remains very limited. *Britain: An Official Handbook* is useful but puts emphasis on the institutional and stays firmly within a British framework. As a result there is a definite need for reference works which interpret between cultures. A good example is David Grote's *British English for American Readers: A Dictionary of the Language, Customs, and Places of British Life and Literature* (1992), which was extremely useful when I was writing parts of Chapters 2 (on the British educational system) and 3 (on food and baking in America). There is a definite need for more books of this nature.

2 English in the British Isles: The Sources of Words and the Meaning of Meaning

> What's in a name? That which we call a rose
> By any other name would smell as sweet.
>
> (Shakespeare, *Romeo and Juliet*)

2.0 INTRODUCTION

We will begin our exploration of the vocabulary of English by looking at where its words come from (§2.1). Then we will try to see how we can characterize their meanings, i.e. we will try to see 'what's in a name'. It will be useful to examine meaning because this will give us a basis for making comparisons of vocabulary, which will be one of the subjects of Chapter 3. We will be guided in this project by three major and different approaches. The first is *reference* (or *denotation*) (§2.2.2), the second, *representational meaning* (§2.2.3), and the third, *use* (§2.2.4). Each has its advantages, but each also has some drawbacks, as we will see.

Two perspectives on vocabulary, from the meaning side and from the side of *word form*, will accompany us throughout this book, for every lexeme inevitably consists of both these sides, form and meaning, something which has often been expressed in the diagrams shown in Fig. 2.1, originally advanced by the linguist Ferdinand de Saussure (1972: 67) to explain the relationship between the concept (in his example, 'tree') and the word form (for him, the Latin word *arbor*). The point is that every abstract word (*lexeme*) consists of the sounds or letters that make up its form and the concept or meaning that is associated with this form. This two-sided approach will, however, be modified in §3.1.1.

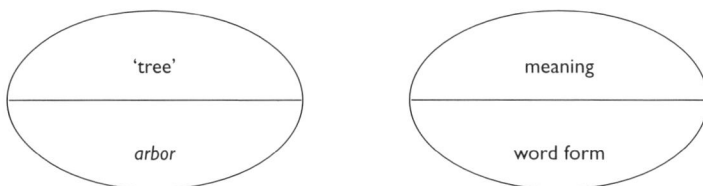

Fig. 2.1. The Saussurean 'egg'

2.1 THE SOURCES OF ENGLISH VOCABULARY

What is today English itself started off as a variety of West Germanic (a set of related dialects spoken in northwestern continental Europe from approx. 500 BC on), which was itself a variety of the **Indo-European** family of languages.[1] Presumably the ancestry of English could be followed further back in time. The chain of inclusion into ever fewer ancestral families could proceed to the point where we end up with one single family 'World'.[2]

Geographical and social divisions within mankind have led to divisions in language. In one community one set of forms and structures used in pronunciation, in grammar, and in vocabulary came to be favoured over the set used in another group. In this way, over sometimes longer and sometimes shorter periods of time, varieties came into existence – be they separate languages, dialects, or social or stylistic variations within the 'same' language – sometimes to continue their existence, sometimes to disappear again.

What this means for the vocabulary of English is that it started with an Indo-European inventory of words which then developed in one form of Germanic. Perhaps some 35 per cent of the non-technical words of English and the majority of the most common ones are Germanic.

> While this is a minority (and if we could count all the terminology of disciplines like chemistry it would be an even smaller proportion), a much higher percentage of our everyday words come from Germanic.

In the preceding sentence those words are underlined which are of Germanic origin: 27 out of 35, or about 80 per cent.

Where do the others come from? The following paragraphs offer a very short guided tour with comments on the historical background. Baugh and Cable (1993), from which many of the examples in the following have been taken, is a useful and readable history of the English language and should be consulted for more background and detail.

2.1.1 The Old English (OE) period

Old English is the name linguists give to the type(s) of the English language spoken in the period from 450/550 to 1150. In these centuries the speakers of OE were confronted with rival groups speaking languages which often had a lasting effect on the vocabulary of English. The major languages or language groups which had an influence on the development of English are Celtic, Latin, and Old Norse.

---

1 The Indo-European family: Indic languages, Iranian, Armenian, Hellenic, Albanian, Italic, Balto-Slavic, Celtic, and, of course, Germanic (see e.g. Baugh and Cable 1993).
2 Parallel to the search for the universal principles of all human language that is at the centre of much modern linguistic inquiry is the search for the common roots of all human language.

2.1.1.1 Celtic

Great Britain, which was eventually to become the home of English, was inhab-
ited by non-English-speaking Britons, whose language belonged to the Celtic
branch of the Indo-European family. When the West Germanic tribes (Jutes,
Frisians, Saxons, and Angles) invaded the island in the years after the departure
of the Romans in AD 410, they annihilated or assimilated the Celtic-speaking
populations or displaced them to the north and west, where today just under a
fifth of the population of Wales can still speak the Celtic language Welsh and far
fewer speak Scottish Gaelic in Scotland or Irish Gaelic in Ireland.

Because the influence of the Celtic speakers was small in general, the impact
of their languages on English was limited. Numerous place names in England are
ultimately of Celtic origin, for example river names such as *Thames*, *Avon*, *Don*,
Exe and city names such as *Carlisle* and *London*. One of the few common nouns
that stem from this early Celtic period is *crag*. See also Case study 2.1.

2.1.1.2 Latin

Before the Germanic invaders came, the Romans had conquered Britain (43 BC–AD
410) and had transmitted some of their culture and vocabulary to the Britons. A
few words borrowed by the Celts from Latin were passed on to the new Germanic
conquerors. Examples include *cross*, *curse*, and *ass*.

In the period after the Roman troops left Britain the influence of Latin was
much stronger than before. As Anglo-Saxon Britain underwent Christianization,
it came under the strong influence of Latin, the language of Christianity in the
West. This included not only ecclesiastical words (*alms*, *altar*, *angel*, *candle*, *chal-
ice*, *cleric*, *deacon*, *disciple*, *mass*, *minster*, *nun*, *palm*, *priest*, *relic*, *shrift*, *shrine*,
etc.), but also words with a more immediate connection to everyday life such as
belt, *cap*, and *tunic*; *cook*, *crisp*, and *kettle*; *cedar*, *cypress*, and *pine*; *cherry*, *pear*,
and *radish*; *oyster*, *lobster*, and *mussel*; *coriander*, *ginger*, and *parsley*. See also
§2.1.2 and §2.1.4.1.

2.1.1.3 Old Norse

The Roman conquest of England was not the first, nor was it to be the last. After
the Anglo-Saxon invasion the Norsemen or Vikings began raiding England in the
eighth century and eventually the Danes gained the throne in the eleventh century.
The Danes brought their own North Germanic language with them. It was related
to English, but different in many ways as well. Borrowing into English from this
Scandinavian source added some 900 words to the language, sometimes driving
out rival OE words. This also led, among other things, to ***lexical doublets***, words
of the same ultimate origin but with different sound patterns and meanings, such
as *shirt/skirt* and *shuttle/skittle*. In both pairs the /ʃ/ or 'sh' sound is of native origin while the /sk/ combination is of Norse origin. Another example is English *no*
and Nordic *nay* (əʊ/ vs. /eɪ/). In addition, numerous English place names are of
Scandinavian origin, e.g. those ending in *-by*, the Danish word for town or farm
(*Derby*, *Rugby*), or in *-thorpe*, the word for village (*Althorp*, *Linthorpe*).

2.1.2 The Middle English (ME) period

Middle English is generally placed between 1150 and 1500. Although this is the shortest of the three periods English is divided into, it saw massive changes in pronunciation (the **Great Vowel Shift**[3]), grammar (the continuation of the loss of inflections which had already begun in the OE period), and enormous additions to vocabulary from French.

2.1.2.1 French

The eleventh century brought the last military conquest of England, by the Norman French.[4] Since much of the new ruling class spoke French while the common people continued to speak English, it was not so much words for every-day things and activities which entered the language as it was words the new mas-ters were likely to use. This involved fashion, art and literature, and learning. Beyond this French words were taken into English massively in the areas of law and administration as well as the military. The church also provided numerous new additions (see Fig. 2.2).

One of the best-known distinctions which reflects the social class divide between speakers of English and of French is that between the names for animals in the field and the names for their meat on the table, as recounted, for example, in Scott's *Ivanhoe*. The former are native English terms, the latter French in ori-gin. This gives us **semantic doublets** like the following: *cow*/*beef*; *pig, swine*/*pork*, *deer*/*venison*, *calf*/*veal*, *sheep*/*mutton*.

Further (lexical) doublets are due to Norman French vs. Central French (Paris) sources. Norman French gives us words like *capital, cattle*, and *catch*, all with initial /k/ as in the ultimate Latin source. Parallel to this we have the words

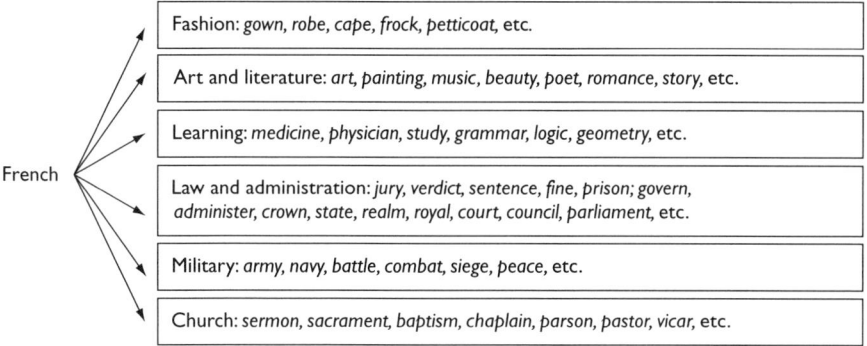

French

Fashion: *gown, robe, cape, frock, petticoat*, etc.

Art and literature: *art, painting, music, beauty, poet, romance, story*, etc.

Learning: *medicine, physician, study, grammar, logic, geometry*, etc.

Law and administration: *jury, verdict, sentence, fine, prison; govern, administer, crown, state, realm, royal, court, council, parliament*, etc.

Military: *army, navy, battle, combat, siege, peace*, etc.

Church: *sermon, sacrament, baptism, chaplain, parson, pastor, vicar*, etc.

Fig. 2.2. The influence of French on English

---

3 The Great Vowel Shift refers to a set of changes in the long vowels of English which took place between the early ME period and the beginning of the ModE period, e.g. /iː/ became /eɪ/ (= ModE /aɪ/ (*tima → time*) and /uː/ became /aʊ/ (*ful → foul*).
4 The name *Norman* also comes from the Northmen (Norse Vikings), who had taken possession of the French coast at Normandy as well.

of Central French origin *chapter*, *chattel*, and *chase*, which show **palatalization** of /k/ to /tʃ/ ('ch'). Other doublets determined in part by the pronunciation differences between Norman French and Central French are the /w/ vs. /g/ distinctions as in *ward/guard* or *warranty/guarantee*. All in all, so many new words entered English from French that English often seems, lexically speaking, to be more a Romance than a Germanic language.

2.1.2.2 Dutch and Scots

The relations between England and its neighbours to the north and east were not always peaceable, but they were long-standing, and large numbers of people moved to and fro. Because Dutch (as well as Flemish and Low German) and Scots are closely related Germanic languages, borrowing came easily. In the case of Dutch it was perhaps in the area of trade and shipping that the most influence can be observed: *groat*, *guilder*, and *dollar*; *deck*, *boom*, *bowsprit*; *keel*, *wake*, *lighter*, *dock*, *freight*. Note also doublets like *skipper* (from Dutch) and *shipper* (native English).

Scots has much the same roots as English, but its pronunciation has developed so differently that we once again find cases of doublets, where one word is a direct development of the southeastern English variety while the other appears in its Scots form and has a generally Scots note to it – cf. *lord* and *laird* or *chest* and *kist*, maybe even ultimately *born* and *bairn* ('child').

2.1.3 The personal pronoun system of OE and ME

Among the borrowings of the OE period we even find that **grammatical** or **form words**, such as some of the **personal pronouns** of English, have been taken over, most prominently *they*, *theirs*, and *them*, which stem from Old Norse and replace the OE pronouns *hie*, *hiera*, *him/hie* (dative/accusative). This may have happened because the OE third person plural pronouns were in danger of being confused with the singular forms (*he*, *his*, *him/hine*). This is a sign of relatively long and intimate relations between speakers of OE and of Old Norse, esp. in the period from 900 to 1100. Tables 2.1 and 2.2 contrast the personal pronoun systems of OE and ME. (Note that the dual is used for two rather than more than two.)

2.1.3.1 Case

The use of grammatical *case* in earlier English was essential and was marked not just on the personal pronouns as it is today (where *I* is the subject case and *me* in the object case) but on adjectives and articles as well ('the good man' is nominative *sē gōda mann*, but accusative *ðone gōdan mann*). As Table 2.1 indicates, there were four cases: the nominative is the present subject case; the genitive, the present possessive; while the dative and accusative (already partly identical in OE) have coalesced to form the present object case.

The continuing loss of case marking can be observed today: the relative pronoun *who* is being used more and more often in place of *whom* when it is a direct object (*the teacher who* (less often: *whom*) *I had for Latin in school*) or when it is

Table 2.1. The personal pronouns of Old English[5]

	Nominative	Genitive	Dative	Accusative	
SINGULAR					
1st person	ic	mīn	mē	mē(c)	'I'
2nd person	ðū	ðīn	ðē	ðē(c)	'you'
3rd person:					
masc.	hē	his	him	hine	'he'
fem.	hēo	hiere	hiere	hīe	'she'
neuter	hit	his	him	hit	'it'
DUAL					
1st person	wit	uncer	unc	unc	'both of us'
2nd person	git	incer	inc	inc	'both of you'
PLURAL					
1st person	wē	user (ūre)	ūs	ūs(ic)	'all of us'
2nd person	gē	ēower	ēow	ēow(ic)	'all of you'
3rd person	hīe	hiera	him	hīe	'they'

Table 2.2. The personal pronouns of Middle English

	Subject	Possessive	Object
SINGULAR			
1st person	I	myn	me
2nd person	thou	thyn	thee
3rd person:			
masc.	he	his(e)	hym
fem.	she	hir(e)	hire
neuter	it	his(e)	it
PLURAL			
1st person	we	oure	vs
2nd person	ye	youre	yow
3rd person	they	hir(e)	hem

the displaced object of a preposition (*the student who* (less often: *whom*) *I gave the assignment to*). In fact *whom* is regularly used only when it comes immediately after prepositions (*To Whom* (*Who) *It May Concern*; *the student to whom* (*who) *I gave the assignment*).

5 There was, of course, considerable variation within the period of OE as well as from region to region. The system outlined is that of taken from Baugh and Cable (1993), and represents the late southern English written variety in the tradition of King Alfred (871–99).

In addition to the final loss of the accusative/dative distinction, the ME system has also lost the old dual. Furthermore, ME shows two important additions: the new phonetically distinctive third person plural pronoun *they* (as mentioned above) and the third person singular feminine *she* have been adopted, perhaps as a reaction to the continuing loss of endings, which were the previous means of distinguishing number and gender.

In a later chapter (Case study 6.5 and § 6.4.1) we will look at two creole systems of personal pronouns (Kriol and early Jamaican Creole) and, finally, the Modern English personal pronoun system.

2.1.4 The Modern English (ModE) period

Modern English dates from about 1500 and runs up to the present. Changes in vocabulary in this period can be attributed more than anything else to expansion: the intellectual expansion of the Renaissance as well as the Age of Discovery, which marked the beginning of imperialism and colonialism on a world scale and the concomitant movement of people from the British Isles and the rest of Europe outward, as well as the immigration of people from the Empire/Commonwealth to the British Isles.

2.1.4.1 Languages of classical learning

Almost as significant as the French influence following the Norman Conquest was the increase in words of Latin or Greek origin. Although this process began in late medieval times, it was with the revival of learning in the Renaissance that classical borrowing really took off. This meant that there were now sometimes *triplets*, where a native English word stands next to one taken from French and another derived from Latin: *kingly*, *royal*, *regal*. As Baugh and Cable (1993: 182) have it:

> The richness of English in synonyms is largely due to the happy mingling of Latin, French, and native elements. It has been said that we have a synonym at each level – popular, literary, and learned. Although this statement must not be pressed too hard, a difference is often apparent, as in … *fast–firm–secure*. . . .

As positive as these new words were for the increased possibilities of expression they offered, they were also accompanied by controversy and were rejected in many cases. Besides enriching the language, they also made certain stylistic registers more inaccessible to the masses and so widened the educational gap between the classes. For many people the semantic relations between everyday words and the corresponding scholarly Latinate words are not immediately evident, but have to be learnt. That is, the association between a verb like *see* and the corresponding adjective *visible* ('able to be seen') must be established. While both of these words are well known, this is not always the case as with pairs like *smell* and *olfactory*. Hence the designation of these non-Germanic items as **hard words**.

Hard words have often been objected to as 'inkhorn' terms, i.e. words felt to be pretentious and/or obscure. Present-day users of English will agree in those cases where the words objected to have not come into common use (e.g. *obtestate* 'to call upon as a witness' or *expend* 'to weigh mentally, to ponder'). However, such now common words as *native*, *fertile*, or *verbosity* were also once the subject of ridicule.

Part of the objection to these new words or **neologisms** lies in their pretentious use, often by the semi-literate. One of the well-known genres of American pioneer life was the frontier boast, which thrived on mock Latinisms meant not to express content so much as to impress listeners (cf. also §3.7).

> The frontiersman, ring-tailed roarer, half horse and half alligator, described himself as *kankarriferous* and *rambunctious*, his lady love as *angeliferous* and *splendiferous*. With consummate ease he could *teetotaciously exfluncticate* his opponent in a *conbobberation*, that is to say a conflict or disturbance, or *ramsquaddle* him *bodaciously*, after which the luckless fellow would *absquatulate*. (Marckwardt 1980: 110)

This tradition was already subject to ridicule in English literature, as in Richard Sheridan's comedy *The Rivals* (1775), in which Mrs Malaprop (whose name gives us the term **malapropism** for the misuse of (usually) hard words) herself put all thought of misuse far from her (but see the words underlined):

> An aspersion upon my parts of speech! Was ever such a brute! Sure, if I reprehend [comprehend] anything in this world, it is the use of my oracular [oral?] tongue and a nice derangement [arrangement] of epitaphs [epigrams].

2.1.4.2 Colonial languages

As the British empire expanded into the – for the British – farthest reaches of the world, it sent its superfluous poor, its criminals, and its middle classes out to settle in the new colonies, dispatching many of its better-off citizens to administer them and the natives they were taking control of. This opening to a wider world brought many British and Irish into contact with non-European cultures and languages, with consequences for the vocabulary of English. In this way words like *bungalow* and *verandah*, *pukka* and *palanquin* (all ultimately from an Indian language) came into English.

2.1.4.3 Immigrant languages

In the twentieth century immigration to Britain from various parts of the Commonwealth, but especially from India and Pakistan, Cyprus, the Caribbean, and East and West Africa, brought people from a non-English cultural background to Great Britain and with them new words to talk about 'new' things. As a result Britons can no longer think of *steel drum bands* and *dreadlocks*, of *dashikis* and *saris*, of *tandoor(i)*, *chutney*, *feta*, or *pita* as exotic.

Exercise 2.1: Doublets

Identify the source of each of the following lexical doublets.

1. anger	angst	7. raid	road
2. belly	bellows	8. scoot	shoot
3. crown	corona	9. school	shul
4. kirk	church	10. shoal	school
5. plane	piano	11. wake	watch
6. loyal	legal		

Resources you might use: a good desk dictionary will usually be adequate, but you might try an etymological dictionary such as *The Barnhart Dictionary of Etymology*.

Case study 2.1: Irish influence on Irish English (IrE)

The ways in which languages affect each other are quite varied. When a foreign word is borrowed, its presence is usually relatively obvious, especially when the lending language is noticeably different, as in the cases of the colonial and immigrant languages referred to above. When, however, the lending language is as much at home in the British Isles as English is and when both languages share what is essentially the same culture, tracing influences may be more difficult. This is the situation we have in **Ulster**, where the interaction between English (and closely related Scots, cf. §2.1.1.1) and Irish has been intimate over a long period of time. In this first case study we will look more specifically at some of the subtleties of this relationship.

Ulster Catholics are more likely to have a **Gaelic** (**Irish**) linguistic background while Ulster Protestants are typically Scots and English in origin. Despite this they share many linguistic items which outsiders might find puzzling. For example, according to the general principle that a short imperative is more likely to appear brusque and unfriendly, we find the following contrast, which native speakers elsewhere can subscribe to as well:

Come in. (*cool reception*)
Come on in. (*warmer*)

Ulster speakers, however, can add a further dimension of warmth by doubling (or quadrupling or sextupling, but not tripling, or quintupling) the preposition:

Och, come on on (on on) in. (*very warm*) (Todd 1984b: 173)

Despite what they share, there are also many expressions which (while under-standable to members of the other speech community) are peculiar to only one of the two groups (see Table 2.3).

One explanation which has been advanced is that the English of Ulster Catholics, drawing perhaps more on Gaelic, may reveal something about the influence of the Irish Gaelic *substratum* on IrE. This question, which is unde-cided, asks, for example, to what extent Gaelic constructions are the models for ones of the type: *to be after* + V-*ing* for something that has been going on, but has recently ended (*He's after singin'* 'has been singing and has just stopped') (Todd 1984b:174).

Some support for the influence of the substratum comes from a look at the language situation among rural speakers of English in Northern Ireland. Todd (1984b; 1989) has found numerous community differences in which Catholic speakers are more likely to use expressions modelled on Gaelic, especially the way the two groups construct idioms. It seems that the Irish mode of using nominal-izations is much more visible in Catholic IrE usage, which centres around nouns and prepositional phrases, while Protestant usage prefers adjectives or verbs. Table 2.4 gives some examples of equivalent expressions.

Table 2.3. Ulster English words (Todd 1989: 341, 347)

SHARED		CATHOLIC (OFTEN GAELIC-DERIVED)	
ark	meal chest	*greeshy*	ashes
dab-han	expert	*moilly*	bald
drouth	thirst	*prockus*	mess, confusion
gawk	stare, stupid person		
hogo	bad smell	PROTESTANT	
fernenst	in front of	*dram*	drink
foother	awkward, clumsy person	*rag*	temper
plump	boil vigorously	*stoor*	dust
scad	scum, discoloration		

Table 2.4. Ulster English expressions (Todd 1989: 352)

Catholic:	She's in bed *wi' the oul' head.*
Protestant:	She's *not well* at all.
Catholic:	I don't like *the look o' that.*
Protestant:	It looked *cankersome.*
Catholic:	Well the *gulpin* (unmannerly person) let *a guldher* (loud shout) *out of him.*
Protestant:	He *shouted and kehoed.*

Exercise 2.2: IrE expressions

The following exercise gives you the opportunity to explore equivalent ways of expressing ideas. The examples listed have been taken (sometimes modified) from Todd (1989) as more typically Irish(-Catholic). They make use of prepositions more than Ulster-Protestant or, indeed, non-Irish speech would.

Find an expression equivalent in meaning in which a preposition is not so central.

Expression	Equivalent
1. His leg's always at him	
2. There's a cuttin' on him	
3. She let a scrake out of her	
4. If he didn't take the legs from in under me	
5. There not a pick on her.	

Sources you might use: Todd (1984b; 1989).

Before leaving this point, we should perhaps also take into consideration Todd's overall evaluation of the linguistic situation: 'In Northern Ireland, it is not so much that the communities do not understand each other's English, but rather that the differences provide a useful means of underlining a speaker's cultural affiliations' (1989: 353).

We will now turn to the other major approach we are using in this book: meaning.

2.2 MEANING

One of the things which we must be sure we understand is that the relationship between word form and meaning is arbitrary. This is one of the important messages contained in Figure 2.1 at the beginning of this chapter. The actual word form which is used to designate any given 'concept' could be anything, any combination of sounds or of letters (or of tactile shapes as in Braille, etc.). There are few exceptions to this principle of *arbitrariness*, and they can be summed up briefly.

2.2.1 Iconic meaning

When a sign contains some feature which resembles what it designates it may be referred to as *iconic*. Since words consist primarily of sounds, *iconic meaning* would be typical of a relationship of (some kind of) similarity between the sound of a word and what it expresses. Two types of words have sounds which are considered by their users to suggest what they mean: onomatopoeic words and words containing sound symbolism. (See also Exercise 8.9 on icons on the Internet; for a critique of iconism, see Eco 1979: 191ff.).

2.2.1.1 Onomatopoeia

Especially prominent among the words which show *onomatopoeia* are animal calls. English speakers normally accept without further thought as self-evident that cats 'say' *meow* and dogs 'say' *bow-wow*. These, too, are rather arbitrary, as we can see from the fact that dogs also go *wuff* and in other languages they may 'say' something very different indeed; for example the crowing of the rooster, despite a shared first consonant, differs considerably while remaining ono-matopoeic within the framework of each of the languages: *cock-a-doodle-doo* (English), *kikeriki* (German), *cocorico* (French).

Exercise 2.3: Animal sounds

In this exercise match up the English onomatopoeic word for an animal call with the animal it is associated with (as in the song 'Old McDonald had a farm') by labelling the boxes left of the animal names with one of the letters a–f. Then complete the boxes to the right with the appropriate letters g–l.

a. baah	❑ bird	❑	g.	glouglou (French)	
b. cluck	❑ chicken	❑	h.	cua cua (Spanish)	
c. neigh	❑ duck	❑	i.	Grunz (German)	
d. oink	❑ horse	❑	j.	Blök (German)	
e. peep	❑ pig	❑	k.	pío pío (Spanish)	
f. quack	❑ sheep	❑	l.	hinnn/hiii-hiii (Spanish)	

Resources you might use: for a–f, a good English desk dictionary; for g–l, moderate-size bilingual dictionaries of French, German, and Spanish.

2.2.1.2 Sound symbolism

Sound symbolism, a.k.a. **phonesthetics** or **phonesthesia**, is the often rather vague association of some idea or feeling with a particular sound or combination of sounds. One example of this is the occurrence of initial /sn-/, which occurs in an astonishingly large number of words which suggest 'nose': *snaffle, snarl, sneer, sneeze, snicker/snigger, sniff, sniffle, snifter, snivel, snob, snook, snoop, snoot(y), snooze, snore, snorkel, snort, snot(ty), snout, snub(-nosed), snuff,* and *snuffle*. Of course, even more words which begin with /sn-/ do not have anything to do with noses (e.g. *snare, sneak, snipe, snow,* or *snug*).

Even though many of the words involved in onomatopoeia and sound symbol-ism belong to the core vocabulary of English, neither are very frequent, and the effect of the sounds used on the meaning associated with even these words is hardly objectively verifiable. All the following approaches to meaning agree in viewing the relationship between the form and the content sides of the word as arbitrary.

2.2.2 Reference, or meaning as denotation

One of the most convincing ways to explain to someone what a word means is to point to what it refers[6] to, its **referent**. Anyone who has learnt a foreign language

---

6 This is a 'naive' approach to reference in which real-world entities are put into relation with words. A more sophisticated understanding of entities is to see them as mental representations (see §2.2.3).

(especially on the spot, i.e. without a bilingual dictionary at hand) knows how useful and efficacious such a procedure is. A word's referential meaning is the thing it denotes.

Suppose someone wanted to know what *Big Ben* means. Now if we were standing at the right place in London, namely at Westminster Abbey, it would be as easy as falling off a log just to point upward and say, 'That's Big Ben'.[7] If we were somewhere else (and this is much more likely), we could point to a picture of it, in a schoolbook, for example, and say, 'That's it.'

Case study 2.2: Names of persons, places, and things

Big Ben is a noun and as such it is the **name** of something, at least according to one traditional definition of the **part of speech** (or **word class**) noun: 'A noun is the name of a person, place, or thing.' (cf. Todd and Hancock 1986: 313, q.v. 'noun'). This is the essence of the reference theory of meaning.

'Name', however, is a deceptive way to paraphrase 'noun'. For there are various sorts of name. One kind of name is the kind used for a whole class of referents, e.g. *clock* for all the clocks in existence or imaginable. In this example the noun *clock* is what is known as a **common noun**. This use of 'name' will be postponed until later in this chapter (see §2.2.3). Instead, we will look at what is probably the more conventional understanding of 'name.' In this sense, a name is a **proper noun** (or **proper name**), for example, *Big Ben*, the name of a particular clock. Or, to take a fictive example which is a fairly good instance of the referential approach to meaning, think about Alice in Wonderland, who is asked what her name means:

> '*Must* a name mean something?' Alice asked doubtfully.
> 'Of course it must,' Humpty-Dumpty said with a short laugh: '*my* name means the shape I am – and a good handsome shape it is, too. With a name like yours, you might be any shape, almost.' (Lewis Carroll. *Through the Looking-Glass*)

Proper nouns are regularly capitalized in spelling and are understood to refer to unique individuals. Because of this uniqueness most proper nouns are restricted in currency. The name of my sister-in-law, for example, is known to only a relatively small group of people. Other names are widely enough current to be counted as a part of a particular variety of English. Examples which Britons will be familar with but non-Britons may have trouble with include *Guy Fawkes*, *the Queen Mum* (persons), *Whitehall*, *Fleet Street*, (*New*) *Scotland Yard* (places), *Private Eye*, *Big Ben* (things), or *the Proms* (occasion). In this sense we may 'often have the feeling that definitions of proper nouns

---

7 Big Ben itself is somewhat vague, since it refers to (a) the bell in the tower at Westminster, (b) the tower itself, or (c) the clock in the tower. It may also refer to the chimes broadcast before the BBC radio news and perhaps much more. We will leave this referential vagueness unresolved.

tell us more about something in the real world than they do about a word' (Blair 1981: 34).

In Great Britain there are numerous instances of proper names which refer not just to a given place but also to the typical activity carried out in that place. *Whitehall*, for instance, is not just the name of a street in London, but also a designation for the British government, which has its offices in or near Whitehall. In this sense *Whitehall* can be in disagreement with *Westminster* (≅ the Parliament) or with *Downing Street* (≅ the Prime Minister) or may regret the unfortunate publicity attracted by *Buckingham Palace* (≅ the Queen/the royal family). Have you noticed that this process of metonymy is especially likely to involve nouns which refer to places (*toponyms*)?

Such uses of place names for institutions or persons, a process involving *metonymy* (the replacement of one term by another which it is associated with – see also Exercise 8.2), is a general phenomenon in language, and in English it has the added fascination of often involving differences from one English-speaking country to another.

Exercise 2.4: Toponyms

In the following, a few expressions of the type just illustrated have been listed, but a number of blanks have been left. See if you can complete them by giving the place name used as a metonym for the function indicated. How hard or easy is it to get the necessary information? Where can you look? Note: not all the blanks can be filled by appropriate toponyms.

UK	USA	Australia
1. the governmental executive (Government or Administration)		
Whitehall	_____	_____
2. the legislative (Parliament or Congress)		
Westminster	_____	_____
3. the head of government (Prime Minister or President)		
Downing Street	_____	_____
4. the head of state		
Buckingham Palace	_____	_____
5. the world of finance		
_____	Wall Street	_____
6. an imaginary remote place		
_____	_____	Bullamakanka

Resources you might use: *Longman Dictionary of English Language and Culture*; *Britain: An Official Handbook*.

Project 2.1: Toponyms

Toponyms (place names) and other proper names are all around us. By their very nature they are usually known only locally. The street I grew up on (Church Street) has a lot of meaning to the people on or near it. But no one really expects a proper name like this, with its particular denotation, to be current very far away. There are, of course, exceptions, such as historical places otherwise unlikely to be more generally familiar, e.g. the (Dublin) *General Post Office, Mafeking, Runnymede, Valley Forge, Waitangi.*

A look at the board of an American as opposed to a British Monopoly set makes clear the significance of the varietal familiarity of place names. Where, for instance, the American version uses American street names for the most expensive properties, *Park Place* and *Boardwalk*, they are called *Park Lane* and *Mayfair* on the British game board.

Make a survey of toponyms in an area you are familiar with and try to determine whether any of them have a more than local meaning. What kind of non-local meaning might this be? How far away would they be known?

2.2.2.1 Criticism of the reference theory: referring and non-referring expressions

Seeing meaning as reference is perhaps best suited for words which refer to unique entities. This is normally the case with proper names, and we have used them widely in presenting this theoretical position. In addition to proper names, there are other definite expressions, e.g. personal pronouns (*I, you, he, she, it,* etc.) and definite noun phrases (*that car over there, this morning,* etc.). They, too, are all also accessible from the perspective of referential meaning.

This procedure of matching names and specific things could be repeated for many other words and phrases in English. But there are a number of shortcomings involved in using it. One of the most obvious weaknesses of the approach via reference is that there are numerous words that do not correspond to objects we can point to in the world around us. This includes among other things:

- non-referring items such as *the, of, and* (articles, prepositions, conjunctions, and the like);
- happenings, centred, for example, around *read, run,* or *understand* ('things' that take place);
- abstract 'things' like *love* or *monarchy* (emotions or concepts).

Non-referring words and expressions which are highly grammatical in nature and sometimes referred to as form words or grammatical words simply do not exist outside language in any referential sense; of course we could refer to the letters on a page or the sounds in a pronunciation, but these are merely the outward expression of a word and have no meaning of their own. Yet non-referring expressions do carry meaning, as we see if we leave such a word out, as in the following with and without the crossed-out grammatical words: ~~The~~ *woman is a kind ~~of~~ friend.* We will look below at a more suitable approach to this sort of meaning (see §2.2.4).

Happenings and abstract 'things', in contrast, are referring expressions. They correspond to some kind of reality outside the language; the difficulty is that you cannot very well point at something and say, 'That's *think* (or that's *monarchy*).' Words of this kind simply do not have easily distinguishable referents even though the referents may be said to exist. Their meanings, too, are best dealt with using a different approach (see §2.2.3).

Our criticism of the referential approach is not complete, however: other difficulties also crop up when we equate a word to its referent. One of these is multiple reference, or the fact that the same 'thing' (the same referent) may be referred to by two or more different words or expressions. My father's name was *Dale*, and that is what my mother called him. But I called him *Dad*. If we accept the reference theory of meaning, this means that *Dale* means 'Dad' and that *Dad* means 'Dale' because both have the same referent. It also means that *Fleet Street* means 'the British press' and that *the (British) press* means 'Fleet Street'. Both examples reveal weaknesses in the reference theory. For *Dale* and *Dad* cannot be used in the same way by the same speaker. Furthermore, while most speakers of English will be able to interpret the expression *the (British) press*, quite a few will have no idea what *Fleet Street* refers to. Another difficulty is that they do not suggest the same thing to different people. Assuming that a speaker knows that *(New) Scotland Yard* has the same referent as *(London) Metropolitan Police*, the latter does not suggest the same thing to a Sherlock Holmes fan and to children playing a popular board game also called Scotland Yard. The connotations, in other words, are very different. *Metropolitan Police* is probably fairly neutral in connotation, while *Scotland Yard* may strike terror into the hearts of (some) criminals or touch off disdain among taxpayers worried about the problems of too little political and juridical oversight.

Obviously, reference is not all there is to meaning. So it is to another aspect of meaning that we now turn: to meaning as mental representation.

2.2.3 The representational (mentalist) approach

A point related to the criticism just elaborated is the fact that a narrow version of the reference theory of meaning requires that there must be an actual referent. Some words have no referents in the real world. Fairy tale beings (gnomes, elves, drolls, dragons, etc.), fantasy creatures (hobbits, golems, etc.), and science fiction aliens and androids (cyborgs, robots, terminators, klingons, gaghs, etc.) all exist only in an imaginary world, but they are so real that we can draw (or recognize) pictures of them; furthermore, actors can dress up like them and play them in movies. One response to this objection is that our imagination is real – at least for each of us. This view, which includes mental reality, is sometimes referred to as representational (because we have models or representations of some world, real or not, in our minds). Inasmuch as we refer to something in our mental reality, representational approaches may also be said to be referential.

The difference between referential and representational approaches to meaning lies in what we believe reality to be. In its most crude form reality is material reality, which means that anything that does not have material existence does not have meaning. In this extreme form at least, the referential theory must be rejected. The opposite (representational) extreme is to see reality as consisting exclusively of concepts in our minds, of ideas (sometimes called idealism). In the sense of idealism we can then think of meaning as concerned not with 'real-world' persons, places, things, feelings, ideas, etc., but with the 'reality' of what we have in our minds and associate with a word.

This split between 'real-world' reality and mental reality is significant when we examine language, for to do justice to language we must recognize that the relationship between the real world and language is far from a one-to-one correspondence. Language does not merely mirror the world, coming up with a word for every class of thing. The classes named somehow have to come into existence, and it is not clear to what extent the classes which we recognize are products of our culture. The BrE distinction between a *bus* (for city-wide transportation) and a *coach* (for overland, long-distance travel) is logical enough, but seems irrelevant to a speaker of AmE, for whom *bus* serves for both. There is no single correct way to categorize the 'real world'. On another level we might make the distinction between a lexicon (a dictionary of a language) and an encyclopedia, a catalogue – and surely always an incomplete one – of 'real-world persons, places, things, feelings, ideas, etc.' (as it was expressed just above). Although parts of this book are somewhat encyclopedic, this is only because looking at information about the 'outside world' is a useful way of comparing English vocabulary in its different varieties.

A novel by Kingsley Amis is set at the college where the central character, Lucky Jim, teaches. The college, or some counterpart of it, may not actually exist somewhere in England, but it certainly comes to exist in the fictional world of Amis's novel. And it comes to exist in the reader's mental reality as well, just as do all the attributes of university life mentioned in it such as the *professors*, the *chairs*, the *Staff Cloakroom*, the *Common Room*, *Abertawe* (University – briefly mentioned, also fictional).

The mentalist approach has the advantage of being usable not only for proper nouns (like *Abertawe* or the *Staff Cloakroom*), but also for common nouns (like *professor* or *chair*) whether real-world or imaginary. If someone wants to know what *Abertawe* (imaginary) or *Oxford* (real-world) means, we can say that it is (the name of) a university in Great Britain, and in the case of Oxford, one which has a long history and a unique reputation. A *chair*, we can say, is a professorship, the position of a professor at a university. A word's meaning is the idea or concept which a speaker associates with it.

2.2.3.1 Proper nouns and common nouns

In distinguishing between the referential and the mentalist approaches to meaning, we have up to now emphasized the difference between proper nouns and common nouns; yet they are not completely different from each other. Each merely has a different 'default setting', i.e. a different kind of meaning which is normal for each. Proper nouns are usually associated with unique entities; common nouns, with whole classes of entities. For example, we assume that there is only one, unique Oxford University; but there are many professors. The former is a case of **constant**, the latter a case of **variable reference**.

This difference is reflected in the fact that typical proper nouns are not accompanied by the article (~~the~~, ~~an~~ Oxford), while most common nouns easily can be (*the/a professor*). Sometimes, however, a common noun is used without the article, namely when it is plural and generic, e.g. *professors*, when it means any and all professors. In the same way a proper noun, while still capitalized, can be used with an article when it is no longer intended to refer to something unique, e.g. *the Oxford University which I mean is a fly-by-night operation out west near Slippery Rock*. In other words, common nouns can sometimes also be construed as having constant (unique) reference (*this university*), and proper ones can, in some cases, be generalized to variable reference.

There are two consequences of this relationship between **proper** and **common nouns**. The first is that proper nouns can serve as a source of new common nouns. The second is that common nouns can be raised to the level of uniqueness and become proper nouns. We will begin with the first case.

When a proper noun becomes generic this process is called **antonomasia**. One way in which this happens is when the name of a particular person (or sometimes place) is used to designate a whole group of similar persons (or places). This involves what are called **eponyms**, which are names of people which have been generalized to whole groups. When James Fenimore Cooper, the nineteenth-century American writer of romances, is called '*the Scott of America*' (after the Scottish writer of romances Sir Walter Scott), we have eponymy and we see that the proper noun *Scott* has been used as a common noun and has a **determiner** such as the definite article.

In other cases, again, proper nouns are generalized even further, so much so that they can not only be used with the article, but may be pluralized and are usually not capitalized any more. For instance, trademarks are occasionally used for products of the same sort from other companies. When facial tissue paper (the kind you use to blow your nose or clean off make-up) is referred to not as *tissues* or *tissue paper* but as *kleenex*, this has happened. *Kleenex* is easily recognized throughout the world. Often, however, this process is much more restricted. The habit of referring to *ball(-point) pens* as *biros* (eponymous for their inventor) in Britain is so relatively restricted that most Americans would have no idea what is meant if someone asked to borrow their biro, unless, of course, the situation made clear what was meant.

It is not only trade names that are raised to generic status; so too are the names of individuals. One of the most (unfortunate) examples of this is the verb *lynch*: it is taken from the name of William Lynch of Pittsylvania, Virginia, who presided over tribunals he instituted without legal authorization around 1776, and is used to refer to the unlawful executions which followed from them.

Exercise 2.5: First exercise on antonomasia

The following is a list of cases of antonomasia. They are all terms which originated in Great Britain or Ireland. In some cases they are known and used outside the British Isles as well. In each case say what the generic (non-antonomastic) expression is (or otherwise define the word). What is its source? Note that this process is not restricted to nouns, but includes verbs created out of nouns as well.

1. to wear a <u>macintosh</u> on a walk
2. to <u>hoover</u> the living room
3. to wear <u>wellies</u> when it rains
4. to <u>boycott</u> non-union products
5. to wear a <u>cardigan</u> on a cool day
6. to <u>bowdlerize</u> a novel
7. to ask a <u>bobby</u> for directions
8. to order a double-decker <u>sandwich</u>

Resources you might use: a good desk dictionary.

Exercise 2.6: Second exercise on antonomasia

A fair number of antonomastic terms are restricted to a particular country for the simple reason that they are drawn from its history and literature. This time, looking at some terms current in the US, give the essence of what each stands for, trace the proper-name background, and give the equivalent in your national-regional variety, if there is one.

1. He's a <u>Benedict Arnold</u>.
2. Just put your <u>John Hancock</u> down on the bottom line.
3. <u>Uncle Sam</u> wants you.
4. Don't count on any support from an <u>Uncle Tom</u> like him.
5. Get the <u>Webster's</u> and see what it says!
6. He's a regular <u>Horatio Alger</u> type millionaire.
7. The seating arrangement is strictly according to <u>(Emily) Post</u>.
8. Don't go in there like a <u>Rambo</u>.

Resources you might use: Flexner and Soukhanov (1997) or, with some luck, a good AmE desk dictionary.

When we move back now to common nouns, we see that they are sometimes raised to the status of proper nouns. This is the case when they are used to refer to one particular instance and in this way become unique, as when I refer to my mother as *Mother*. Such 'new' proper nouns may continue to be treated grammatically like common nouns as far as the use of the article is concerned, but when written they are capitalized to signal the change of status, e.g. the *Staff Cloakroom* mentioned above, namely that unique staff cloakroom found at Lucky Jim's college. Other real-world examples are where *a/the kingdom* becomes *the United Kingdom* or *a/the college* becomes, for instance, *the City College of Dublin.*

Although we have so far concentrated on differences in proper nouns, anyone who has had contact with the different areas in the English-speaking world is very much aware of the fact that common nouns (and more than just nouns) vary from one national variety of English to another. In the following we want to explore this by making a case study of the area of schools and universities. This will serve not only to give us an extended look at the British[8] system of education and the terminology used to describe it but also to remind us that meaning, both referential and representational, is relative to the real-world and mental reality of a given community of speakers and involves a considerable amount of encyclopedic knowledge.

Any comparison in this area will face two very obvious problems. The first is that the British system will correspond only partially to systems used elsewhere in the anglophone world. As a result the same words sometimes refer to very different things. An English *grammar school*, for instance, is an academically oriented secondary school while an American *grammar school* is a primary school. The second is that equivalent or nearly equivalent parts of the system may be labelled with different words. The yearly divisions of a school according to the age or level of the students are called *grades* in the US, but are usually *forms* in BrE and *classes* in both. (For more on the problems of making comparisons between language varieties, see Chapter 3.)

Case study 2.3: The British education system

We might start out by noting that the general similarity of modern societies throughout the world will ensure that the systems of education will resemble each other in broad outline. That is, everywhere states are interested in providing for the qualified teaching of the fundamentals of literacy and selected cultural knowledge, for the vocational training of students, and for the support of basic and applied research. Everywhere this is also reflected in a three-tiered system of primary, secondary, and tertiary (or higher) education. But the similarities disappear as we look deeper.

England and Wales share a broadly similar system of state-supported education. Scotland is basically like England and Wales, but more standardized and with fewer private schools. Northern Ireland has remained somewhat more traditional in its school system.

Pre-School, primary, and secondary education Children enter the system of formal education at the age of 2 at the earliest, which is when some pre-school education begins. Primary school itself runs generally from ages 5 to 11. Secondary school

---

8 There are numerous local and national differences in the 'British system', as England and Wales have different laws and customs from Scotland. Yet the similarities are evident, as they are with Ireland as well. The same goes for the US, where once again there is unity in diversity.

goes on to age 16 for most, but to 18 for young people preparing for higher education.

Pre-school education. This is centred around the *nursery* (a.k.a. *play*) *school*, optional for 2-to-5-year-olds. Such schools are tax-supported, which distinguishes them from the *kindergarten*, the name sometimes used for private, fee-paying nursery schools.

Primary school. *Primary* (a.k.a. *junior*) *school* is the first step in the mandatory educational system. Such schools cater for children aged 5 to 11. A special type of primary school is the *prep(aratory) school*, which is private (i.e. fee-paying) and prepares its pupils for one of the English public schools (see below). The *middle school*, not be confused with the American *middle school*, is a relatively rare name for the last years of primary school (age 8 to 11) and sometimes for early secondary school (11 to 13).

Secondary school. Today *secondary school* is the generic term for schooling between the ages of 11 and 18 throughout the English-speaking world. In the older, more traditional system there were three types of secondary school. One of them was the *grammar school*, offering university preparatory education. It obviously differs from an American grammar school.

Comprehensive schools have been in existence since the 1960s. The idea was to combine all three earlier school types under one roof. They are tax-supported and much like American *junior* and *senior high schools*. Approximately 90 per cent of all students in England and Wales and almost 100 per cent of those in Scotland go to comprehensives and most finish at the minimum leaving age of 16 with the *GCSE* or *General Certificate of Secondary Education* (formerly *O-levels* for *ordinary level* exams), which is regarded as a minimum or, for some, deficient level of education.[9]

Sixth form colleges make up the final years of school. The name comes from the fact that the sixth form follows the five one-year *forms* (= years, AmE *classes/grades*, SAE *standards*) of comprehensive school education. The sixth form lasts two and sometimes more years and prepares for higher education. At the end students are normally examined in three subjects in the *A-levels*, officially known as *GCE Advanced Tests.*

---

9 The quality of education in the comprehensive schools has frequently been criticized and so there has been a fair amount of 'creaming off' of students, in which better-off parents send their children to public schools (see below). Since the large-scale replacement of grammar schools by comprehensives began, many grammar schools have converted to privately run (day) schools in order to retain their more traditional curriculum and a more selective student population. While this movement toward private schooling is largely motivated by class in Great Britain, it is not unlike the flight to private schools in the US, which, however, has drawn much of its support from the desire of parents to avoid racially mixed schools, to escape potential violence, and/or to provide their children with an explicitly religiously oriented school education.

Public schools are private, fee-paying schools for the 13–17+ age group. Six per cent of students in Britain attend such schools, of which there are several hundred, including such famous and prestigious ones as Charterhouse, Eton, Harrow, Roedean, and St Paul's School for Girls. *Private schools* differ from the public schools in that the former can be run for profit.

Higher education *The institutions.* In any given year about 15 per cent of school leavers continue with higher education. Until recently the majority (about 90 per cent) went to *polytechnics,* which provide career-oriented, technical studies. They may be compared to American junior colleges, community colleges, and schools of engineering. In the meantime they have been redesignated as universities.

The alternative to the traditional polytechnics is the *universities*. The traditional universities, Oxford, Cambridge, Trinity (Dublin), and Edinburgh, all have roots in medieval times. Each consists of several *colleges*, and it is at one particular college within the university that students study. There is the anecdote about

> an American traveler to England who visited Oxford University. Confused by the architectural similarity between two of the colleges in Turl Street – Jesus and Lincoln – he exclaimed, 'I can't tell the difference between Lincoln and Jesus!' A passing student remarked that it was the same with all Americans. (Cashman 1984: 2)

It is the university which grants the degree after the student successfully *sits* (i.e. takes) the final exams.

In the Victorian era a number of new universities were founded which included science and engineering in their programmes. They also allowed Nonconformist students (i.e. those not belonging to the Church of England) to study at them. They are often referred to as *redbrick universities* (from their typical architecture). Their organization around colleges is reminiscent of Oxford and Cambridge. In the 1960s, 16 new universities (occasionally called *glass-and-steel*), more American in organization (more regular classes, lectures, testing; fewer *tutorial*s ('weekly meetings between teacher and student(s) to discuss work'), were founded. They comprise various schools (= departments) where students eventually take their final exams.

Administration and teachers At the top of the university there is the *chancellor*, who is its honorary head (often royalty or a prominent public figure), not its work-a-day administrator. Rather, it is the *vice-chancellor* who is the chief administrative officer of a university. A *principal* is the head of a college.[10]

---

10 Cf. the *chancellor* of a state university system in America, under whom work the *presidents* of the various local universities within the system.

At the core of the traditional university are its *colleges* (from *collegium* or community of scholars), whose purpose is study. A *faculty* is, in contrast to the common American use of the word for teaching staff, a collection of related collegiate departments. Today members of colleges, i.e. its academic staff, are its *fellows*. They give lectures, which are not classes with content to be tested. Outside *Oxbridge* (Oxford and Cambridge) colleges are more like American ones with classes and tests.

At the top of the academic staff is the *professor* (often a *senior fellow*), who holds a *chair*. The next in line is the *reader* (both can be compared to an American *full professor*). The designation *don* is not a title, but a name used for senior Oxbridge fellows. The next down is the *lecturer* (not to be confused with an American *lecturer* or *graduate assistant*). Lecturers are divided into *senior lecturers* (American *associate professors*), (plain) *lecturers* (American *assistant professors*) and *assistant lecturers* (American *instructors*).

Students. When students enrol, they *go up* to, for example, Oxford or Cambridge and then *go down* in the university *vacations* or when they graduate. They may look for private accommodation (cf. American plural: *accommodations*) outside the university *halls (of residence)*, what Americans call *dormitories*.

Degrees. As students go through the system they get *marks* (American *grades* or *grade points*) at the end of the *terms* (cf. *semesters, trimesters, quarters*). The final pay-off comes when studies end: namely the *diploma* traditionally granted by the former polytechnics or the *degree* granted by universities. A *BA (Bachelor of Arts)* degree is awarded after three years' study. *Honours* is not simply a good grade (as in the US), but a more intense course. The *MA (Master of Arts)* is given automatically at Oxbridge after a four-year wait and for a fee; elsewhere in England, an additional year of study is required. The doctor's degree continues to be rarer than in the USA.

Exercise 2.7: British and American terms for schools

Each of the following terms is used in both the UK and the USA, but often has a distinctly different meaning. Identify each with the appropriate letters to help define these differences. Remember that British primary schools run from age 5 to 11; American ones go from 6 to 10 and are included in the elementary school (ages 6 to 12/13).

Terms	UK	USA	Features
grammar school			(a) state-run
high school			(b) private or state
kindergarten			(c) private only
middle school			(d) pre-secondary
prep school			(e) secondary
public school			(f) esp. Scottish

Resource you might use: Grote 1992.

Project 2.2: Non-British systems of education

School and university terminology is notoriously variable. For the following sentences establish what the equivalents of the underlined items might be in some other anglophone country you are familiar with.

1. After her A-levels she went up to Oxford where she read Classics.
2. Her tutorials were with a don who once resented girls on the quadrangle.
3. When she went down in the vac, she volunteered at a dig in Italy.
4. She did Greats in 1984 with a first.
5. And then she stayed on for D.Phil. as a prize fellow.

2.2.3.2 Criticism of the representational approach

For all its usefulness – and we will be using this general type of approach throughout this book – there are a number of critical observations that we can make about meaning as mental representation. Most prominently, mental representations suffer from *ambiguity*. For instance, what I mean (i.e. think about) when I (as an American) say 'college' is said against a different institutional-structural background (a four-year institution granting bachelor's degrees) than when a Briton says the word.

Mental images or concepts, even when they are associated with concrete classes of entities like teachers, are characterized by *vagueness* and leave questions open about what kind of teacher (male/female, young/old, strict/sloppy, etc.). Mental images are simply not clear enough, since they are based on individual experience. This means that even from fellow countryperson to fellow countryperson there will be significant differences. For myself a college is first and foremost a small, private, all-male, denominational liberal arts institution with a distinct regional basis. This is certainly not generalizable to the majority of Americans.

Yet the very fact that people do agree on some kernel idea, however vague it may be, means that the representational approach is a valuable one. It seems that speaker groups – whether the group is defined by region/country, gender, age, ethnicity, education/class, or whatever – do share what are called *prototypes*. This is a psychological approach to cognitive classification or structuring which has established that certain (stereo)typical images lie at the centre of lexical concepts such as *public schoolboy* (GB) or *preppie* (USA). Not all public schoolboys are wealthy, privileged, and upper-class, but this kind of prototype may well prevail.

Above and beyond this, mental representations are *not easily testable* since there are always feelings and thoughts associated with one person's ideas which differ from those associated with another's and which are difficult to verbalize. Even more striking is the fact that basing meaning on mental representations means that there is no explicit yardstick available. Who is to say that my concept of, say, *glory* is the correct one? If mine isn't, whose is? Think about what Humpty-Dumpty says when he defends un-birthdays. It's especially nice to get un-birthday presents since we have so many un-birthdays every year:

'And only *one* [day] for birthday presents, you know. There's glory for you!'

'I don't know what you mean by "glory,"' Alice said.

Humpty-Dumpty smiled contemptuously. 'Of course you don't – till I tell you. I meant "there's a nice knock-down argument for you!"'

'But "glory" doesn't mean "a nice knock-down argument,"' Alice objected.

'When *I* use a word,' Humpty-Dumpty said, in rather a scornful tone, 'it means what I choose it to mean – neither more nor less.'

'The question is,' said Alice, 'whether you *can* make words mean so many different things.'

(Lewis Carroll, *Through the Looking-Glass*)

Following the representational theory (and the example of Humpty-Dumpty) it is just possible that some people's ideas, and hence their meanings, might not be merely vague but downright wrong.

As with the reference theory, representational approaches are only useful for referring expressions regardless of whether the referring expressions are unique (proper nouns) or designate classes (common nouns). Just how we might deal with non-referring ones like function words will be our next topic.

2.2.4 The use theory of meaning

One problem with the referential and representational approaches to meaning is that for many words there is no person, thing, concept or whatever in (real-world or mental) reality which clearly corresponds to them. This is especially true of grammatical or form words (such as *the* or *of*). Another major problem is that we do not all think about the same things even when there are real-world ana-logues to the expressions we are using.

However, all words and expressions do have one thing in common: they all have a use. While we can argue about just what, exactly, *use* itself means, we can certainly approach both referring and non-referring expressions in regard to their use. In this sense, a referring expression like *grammar school* is used in Ireland to refer to a school encompassing the final years of secondary education, while it is used in the US to designate elementary-level education. And a non-referring word like the article *the*, which we discussed above in regard to proper and com-mon nouns, is used to specify the noun it precedes: that is, it picks out a specific instance (or instances) of what a noun designates from among all the possible instances that could be associated with this noun. So the class or group of *professors* (generic) becomes specific when we talk about *this/that/the professor* or *these/those/the professors*.

The **definite** and **indefinite articles** are used in a basically similar way wherever English is spoken as a native language. The few differences which crop up are merely incidental, and should certainly not be seen as a sign of systematic differ-ence. For example, both Americans and Britons say that someone is *in/at* *school/church/college* or is going *to school/church/college*, where the nouns *school, church, college* are meant less as places than as institutions where some function is carried out (like learning/teaching or worshipping). In the English of the US and parts of Canada this distinction is not extended to hospitals. So while a patient (in BrE) is *in hospital* (i.e. benefiting from the function of a hospital) and while someone can visit him or her *in/at the hospital* (purely as a place), both are said to be *in/at the hospital* in AmE. Here no distinction is made between *hospital* as a function and *hospital* as a place.

Not all function words are used in such a similar way throughout the English-speaking world as is the article. One of the most complex areas of grammar and one in which a certain amount of regional difference can be found is that associated with a small set of verbs, the ***auxiliary verbs***, and especially with those used to indicate lack of certainty on the part of the speaker, namely the ***modal auxiliaries***.[11] To get a better grasp of the use theory of meaning we will look at how the auxiliary *have* and the modal auxiliary verbs *must, shall,* and *should* are used.

Case study 2.4: The auxiliary *Have*

Have is both a full verb ('to possess, participate in', etc. as in *have a book, have lunch*) and an auxiliary verb of the ***perfect***, e.g. *he has/had seen the movie*. There are also two forms of ***negation*** of *have*: directly (*haven't/hadn't*) or with the auxiliary *do* (***do-periphrasis***, *don't/didn't have*). In all varieties of English there is agreement that the perfect-auxiliary *have* should be negated directly (e.g. *he hasn't / hadn't seen the movie*). However, when *have* is used as a ***full*** or ***lexical verb*** (*I have a problem*), usage varies: Some people say *I haven't a problem*; others can only be heard saying *I don't have . . . .* Furthermore, some speakers vary in their usage, using now *do + not* and now *have + not*. While there is no hard-and-fast regularity in this, it is perhaps generally possible to say that North American speakers use *do*-periphrasis except with perfect *have*, while speakers of BrE are slightly more likely to use direct negation of lexical *have*. But here too there is variation, some people, for example, accepting present-tense *I haven't a thing to say* but avoiding past-tense *I hadn't a thing to say*. Whatever observations we might make on this, one thing is clear: in drawing the line between the two

---

> ### *Project 2.3: The negation of* **Have**
>
> Make a short informal investigation of the usage of *have* in the English spoken around you. Record a short sample of spontaneous spoken English if possible and make a count of how *have* is negated as (a) the perfect auxiliary; (b) a lexical verb meaning 'possess'; (c) a lexical verb meaning 'participate in' (e.g. *have a good time, have lunch, have a date*). If you do not have the opportunity to make such a recording, do the same with a short sample of written English. (If you are ambitious, do both and check for differences between spoken and written English.)

---

11 The main modal verbs are *must, shall/should, will/would, may/might,* and *can/could.*

negative forms of *have*, speakers are able to distinguish between the differing uses of this word, and that lends support to the use approach to meaning.

Case study 2.5: *Shall, Should,* and *Must.*

Among the modal auxiliary verbs two are particularly interesting: *shall* and *must* (see Example 2.1). The reason for this is, first, that both can share certain features of meaning, namely an expression of obligation on the part of the speaker, as in *You shall/must do as your mother says.* This means that the two modals stand in competition with each other, as it were. However, it seems that the burden of imposing obligations on others has led to a reluctance to use these modal auxiliaries in some varieties of English.

Shall seems to be largely restricted to the following three cases. First, almost everywhere in the English-speaking world *shall* is used to impose obligation in what are regarded as rather old-fashioned and formulaic-sounding legal texts (*The lessee shall pay X to the lessor . . .*).

Second, it is often used to express some notion of futurity, though only in the first person (*I/We shall be there at five*).[12] This future use, which might conceivably be regarded as self-obligation of the first person speaker (= promise), is not universal. It is often regarded as particular to southern England and as recessive elsewhere.

Finally, in many varieties, but not in Ireland, *shall* is used to ask what the addressee considers desirable (*Shall I get an aspirin for you?*). Here standard, familiar IrE could have (in addition to *should*, for example) *Will I get an aspirin for you?*

Example 2.1. Using modals in ENL varieties

Must for *shall*: In SAE there is a 'neutral' use of *must* as in *Must I seal the envelope?*, where other varieties of English have *shall* or *should*. 'Here SAfrE must does not signal "Am I compelled to?" and there is . . . an Afrikaans parallel in the "neutral" uses of modal *moet*.' (Branford 1994: 492)

Will for *shall*: 'Trudgill ... suggests that New Zealand English uses *will* rather than *shall* in a phrase like *Will I turn out the light?*, and that this might show Scottish influence.' (Bauer 1994: 400)

BrE: *Shall* for *will*: '*Shall you be at the embassy reception? – No, I'm afraid I shan't*. Both [the use of *shall* in second person questions and the use of the negative contraction *shan't*] are virtually unknown in AmE.' (McArthur 1996: 47)

AmE: *Mustn't* for *can't*: 'A negative inferential sentence like *If you got wet you mustn't have taken your umbrella* is AmE rather than standard BrE, which uses *can't* . . . .' (McArthur 1996: 48)

---

12 *The Oxford Companion to the English Language* also mentions 'a promise or a threat' and gives a 2nd person example (p. 601).

Must. In some types of StE *must* is also under considerable 'pressure': people avoid it and prefer to use the form *should*, which is the more usual **tentative** or **polite form**, or the paraphrase *have to*, which is used to report obligation rather than to impose it as when one 8-year-old reminds another, *You have to be home by six*, where *must* would be out of place.

Should is regularly used in subordinate clauses to report **imperatives** in **indirect speech**. Throughout the English-speaking world it is common to report a command like *Stop that!* by saying *She said you/he should stop that*. Among the various verb forms used to report imperatives there are two contrasting ones which occur after verbs of suggestion (e.g. *suggest, advocate, propose, recommend*) and after adjectives of desired future action (e.g. *be important, be mandatory, be essential*): *should* + verb or the **subjunctive form** of the verb:

She suggested he should stop that
It is mandatory that he should be there

She suggested he stop that
It is mandatory that he be there

The subjunctive seems to be recessive in BrE while it is healthy and well in AmE and AusE. Table 2.5 sets out the stylistic differences between AmE and BrE found in one study.

Table 2.5. *Should* vs. the subjunctive in BrE and AmE (Svejcer 1978)

Should after *suggest*, etc.: AmE: bookish BrE: neutral

Subjunctive after *suggest*, etc.: AmE: neutral BrE: formal

Project 2.4: Shall *and* Must

Against this background listen for any of the instances of *must, shall,* and *should* just discussed. How are they used in your spoken English-language environment? How are they used in local printed material? Try to restrict the material you use to the writing of a single region (either your own region or, if you live where English is not regularly used locally, a regional variety of your choice).

Which forms occur in the circumstances described? Have you found stylistic differences (e.g. formal/informal, familiar) or differences in medium (written/spoken)?

2.3 SUMMARY

In this chapter we looked first at the major historical sources of English vocabulary. We used material taken chiefly from the English of the British Isles to explore the lexical field of schools and universities. The main purpose of the chapter was to explore the fundamental question of meaning. Three approaches were chosen: reference (particularly in connection with names and toponyms), representation (eponyms, antonomasia, and the word field of education), and use (auxiliary verbs). It has not (I hope) been a case of *impenetrability*:

'Would you tell me please,' said Alice, 'what that means?'

'Now you talk like a reasonable child,' said Humpty-Dumpty, looking very pleased. 'I meant by "impenetrability" that we've had enough of that subject, and it would be just as well you'd mention what you mean to do next, as I suppose you don't mean to stop here all the rest of your life.'

'That's a great deal to make one word mean,' Alice said in a thoughtful tone.

'When I make a word do a lot of work like that,' said Humpty Dumpty, 'I always pay it extra.'

'Oh!' said Alice. She was too much puzzled to make any other remark. (Lewis Carroll, *Through the Looking-Glass*)

English in America: How to Compare Meaning and Vocabulary

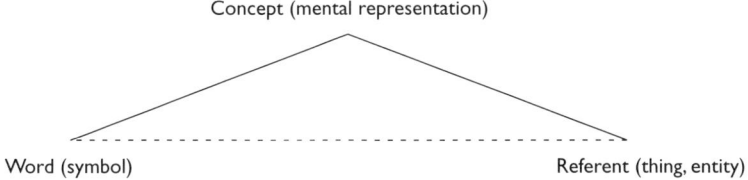

When I first went to England many years ago, I remember going to a restaurant in London and ordering roast beef and Yorkshire pudding. The meat was fine and so was the gravy-soaked bread that came along with it. But the waiter didn't bring the dessert. When I asked him when I would get the Yorkshire pudding – after all, it was part of the order – I was politely told, 'You et it.' It turned out to be the cornbread kind of thing soaked with gravy that I had eaten.

3.1 HOW TO COMPARE VOCABULARY

Up to now we have been making comparisons of the words of English in some of the countries in which the language is used but have not been explicit about how such a comparison might be undertaken or what complications might be involved. In order to get a grip on the various aspects that are involved when making a comparison we will start out with a model called the semiotic triangle (Ogden and Richards 1949) and later expand it in some interesting ways.

3.1.1 The semiotic triangle

In the *semiotic*[1] *triangle* presented in Fig. 3.1 (adapted from Ogden and Richards in Lipka 1992: 43) the three points where the sides are joined are related to each other in a way which reflects the distinctions developed in the previous chapter.

```
                    Concept (mental representation)


Word (symbol)                                    Referent (thing, entity)
```

Fig. 3.1. The semiotic triangle

---

1 *Semiotics* is the discipline that deals with signs and symbols as they are used to communicate. Language is perhaps the most important (certainly the most distinctly human) type of symbolic communication. But we also send symbolic messages in the way we dress, smile, move, use our eyes, etc. The triangle is also known as the 'triangle of signification' or 'referential triangle.' Cf. Eco (1979).

We saw that words are related to the 'things' (entities) which they designate by way of the ***mental representations*** we have of them. The dotted line between word and referent is intended to indicate that this relation is indirect.

In comparing vocabulary between varieties of English all three points offer a perspective[2] of their own, and we will explore each. Before beginning with this we will familiarize ourselves with semantic and lexical relations within English vocabulary which we need to know about when comparing varieties. These centre around the concepts of homonymy and polysemy (§3.1.1.1) and lexical fields (§3.1.1.2). After that we will return to the relations between words, things, and concepts in the form of a typology for comparison (§3.1.2).

3.1.1.1 Homonymy and polysemy

When word forms are identical but are associated with different and unrelated meanings, we are dealing with ***homonymy***. Homonyms are distinguished as distinct lexemes despite similarity in form – either identity in pronunciation (***homophones***) in spelling (***homographs***), or in both (***homonyms***) – and they are usually recognized as such for reasons of distinctly different historical origins and meanings, as with *lie*₁ 'to occupy a prone position' and *lie*₂ 'to make a statement contrary to the known truth'. When the two are confused within a given context, this is known as ***ambiguity***, as with the following homophone:

> Window washer working on a particularly difficult window:
> This window is a /peɪn/ (i.e. *pain* or *pane*)

The existence of various meanings of a single lexeme is referred to as ***polysemy*** and may be the result of semantic shift:

(a) He washed the dish after supper
(b) He cooked the dish for his guests
(c) He thinks she's a real dish

In (a) *dish* has a literal meaning like 'round, flat object made of metal, porcelain, wood, plastic, etc. from which food is eaten or on which it is served'. The variation in the material used is part of the ***vagueness*** associated with the concept. In contrast (b) is an example of ***metonymy***, in which the associated idea of the food is expressed by *dish*; and (c) denotes, via ***metaphor***, a woman who is compared to (good) food.

3.1.1.2 Lexical and semantic relations

The concept of ***word fields*** (a.k.a. ***lexical fields*** or configurations) is useful for showing the variety of semantic relations which may exist between lexemes. A

---

2 Cf. Algeo (1989) for a typology based on the referent and Benson *et al.* (1986) for one based on the word.

given lexical field encompasses words from particular real-world (i.e. non-linguistic) areas of activity or fields of knowledge, such as baking or education. Some of these fields are recognized in dictionaries, where field labels are used, e.g. *medicine, nautical, technical*. Above and beyond this, words in a given lexical field which belong to the same **word class** stand in a **paradigmatic**[3] relationship to each other, i.e. they can replace each other. For example, the lexical field 'bodies of moving water' includes *rivulet, stream, brook, creek* (AmE, AusE), *river*, etc. Each of these could occur in the blank in the following: *The leaves floated down the* _____. Members of a given word field share relatively more **semantic features** (cf. §§3.3.1 – 4) than do words in different fields or even other words within the same area. The examples above all share the features (conventionally given in square brackets and small caps) [BODY OF WATER] and [MOVING], but they clearly differ as to size.

Synonymy occurs when there is identity (or virtual identity) of meanings, but two different lexemes within a single language variety, e.g. *barbecue* and *grill*, as in *Let's grill/barbecue the tuna fish*. Theoretically, it should be possible to replace the one word with the other in any context. However, there are sure to be some differences. For example, in an interrogation the police can metaphorically *grill* a suspect, but they cannot *barbecue* him or her. As long as both words share the same **denotational meaning** (§2.2.2), the differences are often ignored as usage conditions and may be either metaphorical or **connotational**. Connotation includes (especially interesting in this chapter) regional or **dialectal variation**, as with BrE *tap* and Southern AmE *spigot*. But the differences may also lie in the stylistic level (neutral *girl* vs. slang *chick* or *bird*), the technical field (medical *contusion* vs. everyday *bruise*), or the degree of present-day currency (obsolete *eximious* vs. current *excellent*).

Difference of both form and meaning is essentially what vocabulary is all about, and some of the differences of form and meaning are of central interest to **lexicology**, namely those in which there is a relation between the meanings of the items involved. Here we are always dealing with lexemes within a given word field. Generally, two types of relationship are recognized: oppositional ones and hierarchial ones. **Opposites** can be of a variety of types, e.g.

- **complementary pairs**, which are either/or oppositions, e.g. *male/female*
- **antonyms**, which form the two extremes on a scale, e.g. *short/tall* with various degrees of middle height in between (a.k.a. **gradable antonyms**)
- **converses**, which are relationships seen from two contrasting perspectives, e.g. *give/take*
- **reverses**, which are movements or processes in two opposing directions, e.g. *bring/take, up/down, open/close*

---

3 **Syntagmatic** relations, i.e. relations between words in a sequence, will be dealt with especially in §§ 3.5, 6.3, 7.3, and 8.1.

Hierarchical relationships involve a superordinate term and subordinate ones which may be considered to be included under it:

- *hyponymy* (a.k.a. *inclusion*), a relationship between general and specific, e.g. *dog/poodle, retriever*, etc. The general term is the **superordinate** and the specific terms are the **(co-)hyponyms.**
- **incompatibility** (a.k.a. **heteronymy**), a relation which involves more than two members of a category without distinct end terms and which share one or more elements of meaning; these are *taxonomic sisters*, but are mutually exclusive: *days: Monday, Tuesday, Wednesday, . . .; colour: red, blue, green, ...*
- *meronymy,* a part–whole relationship, where the part is different from the (superordinate) whole, as with *house: basement, pantry, attic, living room.* Cf. also collective–member, as in *fleet of ships, pack of wolves, school of fish*; also part(itive)–mass, as in *grain of sand, bar of chocolate, sheet of paper.*

There are many other semantic relationships which will not, however, be considered here (cf. Saeed 1997: ch.3).

3.1.2 A typology for comparison

The idea of the typology is to

> show how subtle are the distinctions . . . how manifold the ramifications of minor cultural differences, how delicate the semantic lacework that edges the dialects of the English-speaking world. A typology of interdialectal differences can help us to be aware of the diversity that overlies the unity of English and to understand the ways in which English varies across cultures. (Algeo 1989: 241)

There are numerous ways in which the relationship between word, concept, and thing/entity (referent) can be distinguished. On a general level we can distinguish the types of match between them shown in Fig. 3.2. In this schematic presentation a, b, c can be referents, words, or concepts; x, y, z are then the words or concepts associated with each.

(i) *A one-to-one relationship between a referent and a name or between a concept and a word. The double-headed arrows indicate reversibility. Cf. Case study 3.1, Exercise 3.1, 3.3.1, Case study 3.4, 3.3.3 and Project 3.1.*

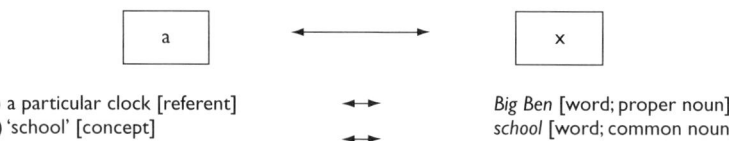

a) a particular clock [referent]   ↔   *Big Ben* [word; proper noun]
b) 'school' [concept]   ↔   *school* [word; common noun]

(ii) *A one-to-many relationship with various kinds of overlap. One type of analogous referent has various names. One word may be paired with similar concepts; one concept may be expressed by different words. Cf. Case study 3.2, Case study 3.3, Exercise 3.2, 3.3.3, Exercise 3.4, Project 3.2, 3.4.1, Exercise 3.5 and Exercise 3.6.*

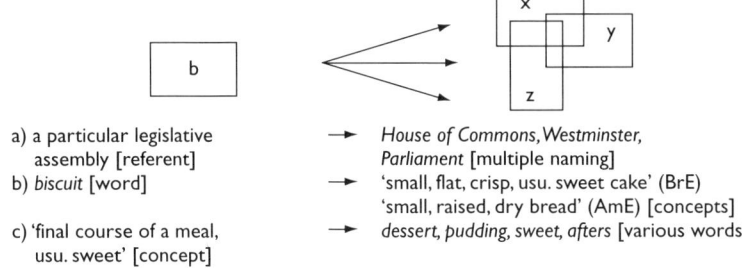

a) a particular legislative   →   House of Commons, Westminster,
    assembly [referent]   Parliament [multiple naming]
b) *biscuit* [word]   →   'small, flat, crisp, usu. sweet cake' (BrE)
                        'small, raised, dry bread' (AmE) [concepts]
c) 'final course of a meal,   →   *dessert, pudding, sweet, afters* [various words]
    usu. sweet' [concept]

(iii) *A one-to-many relationship without overlap. One word has distinctly different meanings; or one concept is expressed by different words; or (final example) one concept applies analogously to several referents. Cf. 3.2.1, Exercise 3.3, 3.3.4, Case study 3.5, Project 3.3, 3.4.2, 3.4.3 and Exercise 3.7.*

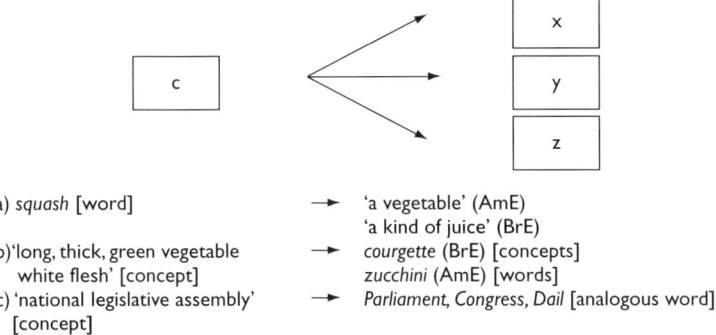

a) *squash* [word]   →   'a vegetable' (AmE)
                        'a kind of juice' (BrE)
b) 'long, thick, green vegetable →   *courgette* (BrE) [concepts]
    white flesh' [concept]   *zucchini* (AmE) [words]
c) 'national legislative assembly' →   *Parliament, Congress, Dáil* [analogous word]
    [concept]

Fig. 3.2. Types of match between referents, words, and concepts

Having introduced the most important terms used to characterize semantic and lexical relationships, we now move on to a comparison of vocabulary between geographical varieties. To do this we will orient ourselves according to the three points of the semiotic triangle, starting with referents (§3.2), then going on to words (§3.3), and finishing with concepts (§3.4). The final sections of the chapter also carry us further, this time concentrating first on lexical expressions and thus going beyond the scope of the single word: phrasal verbs (§3.5). In §3.6 we expand our view beyond open class words (nouns, verbs, adjectives) to one of the closed classes: prepositions. In §3.7, we return to the question of the sources of vocabulary and expand our view here, too, with a look at Caribbean English.

3.2 COMPARISON FROM THE POINT OF VIEW OF THE REFERENT

What speakers of one variety talk about can differ from what speakers of another talk about for the straightforward reason that the physical and cultural environment in which they communicate is not identical. Indeed, within a single language variety there may be innumerable sub-varieties that also do not share the same physical or cultural world. Sometimes there is something in a person's surroundings which he or she wants to talk about, but there is no (single) word available in the language to refer to that action, state, quality, thing, or whatever. One solution for bridging this *lexical gap* is to use some kind of descriptive expression (a circumlocution of sorts). For example, AmE has a single word (*braces*) for what in BrE are usually designated with a descriptive expression, i.e. adjective + noun: *curly brackets* (or *brace brackets*), viz. the pair { }. Another solution (besides descriptive expressions) to the problem of lexical gaps is to borrow or invent a suitable word. This kind of adaption or change in the language will be one of the major subjects of Chapter 4.

Case study 3.1: Identical referents: arithmetic

There are referents which are truly identical, even from society to society. As an example we will look at numbers and mathematics, which form a symbolic system independent of any given language or variety of a language.[4]

Identical words

The vocabulary used to refer to numbers and to arithmetic operations is almost completely identical wherever English is used. The numbers, for example, are called by the same names, whether simple digits:

1	one	4	four	7	seven	
2	two	5	five	8	eight	
3	three	6	six	9	nine	(for 0, see below)

or more complex integers and fractions, e.g.

23	twenty-three
112	a/one hundred (and) twelve
¼	a/one fourth, a/one quarter
.87	point eight(y-)seven

The simpler mathematical operations are everywhere the same, as Table 3.1 shows. However, 'everyday' school language differs somewhat. For example, in subtraction BrE usage allows *three from six is (three)*. Everywhere children learn *the multiplication tables*, but in BrE also simply *the tables*. In division there is a remainder when the division does not *go out exactly* (BrE) or *come out even* (AmE).

Similar words

There are a few cases where the form of a word differs slightly. *Mathematics* is universally recognized and used, but the shortened forms differ. What Americans

---

4 This does not mean that mathematics plays the same role in every society or in the lives of the various people living in a given society.

Table 3.1. Mathematical operation

Operation	Symbol	Formal expression	Informal expression	Result
Addition	+	six plus three equals	six and three is	the sum
				(6 + 3 = 9)
Subtraction	−	six minus three equals	six less three is;	the difference
			six take away three is	(6 − 3 = 3)
Multiplication	×	six multiplied by three equals	six times three is; six threes are	the product (6 × 3 = 18)
Division	÷	six divided by three equals	six through three is; three goes into six ... times	the quotient (6 ÷ 3 = 2)
Identity with	=	equals	is	

call *math* is *maths* in BrE.[5] A similar <-s> is attached when talking about the kinds of calculation undertaken in math(s): British and Irish children do their *sums* (AmE: *arithmetic*).

Different words

Because of the essential identity of designations for the numbers and for operations, the few differences which crop up can cause not only mutual amusement but perplexity and, on occasion, serious misunderstanding. This is most obvious with the one digit which was not listed above: 0. Perhaps the most neutral name for this number is *zero*, but the word *zero* is not used everywhere; rather, the numeral has a number of alternative names depending on the context. For example, in a match a score of zero (i.e. no points won) in tennis and similar racket games is universally called *love*.[6] The following list contains terms for 0:

> common to AmE and BrE: *love*, *nothing*, *null* (technical, mathematical), *oh*, *zero*
> AmE only: *cipher*, *nix*, *zilch*, *zip* (scores)
> BrE only: *duck* (cricket), *nil* (scores), *nought*

Exercise 3.1: Expressions for 'zero'

For each of the following fill in the blank with the appropriate expression for 'zero'. If more than one expression is possible, give the alternatives and indicate whether they are restricted according to variety, i.e. AmE vs. BrE.

---

5 The reverse also occurs, as in PE or Phys. Ed., where Americans practise *sports*, but Brits engage in *sport*. Another incidental number/name difference of this calibre: quintuplets are *quints* (AmE) or *quins* (BrE).

6 Assuming that *love* has not been chosen for *zero* because that's all the unsuccessful player gets out of the game, the following (mythical?) etymology is sometimes given for this meaning of *love*: *Love* comes from the French *l'œuf* ('the egg') because a zero is round like an egg. Cf. the American expression for zero in sports: *goose egg*.

1. They lost the football game six _____ .
2. My telephone number is 49590 (four-nine-five-nine-_____).
3. 8 − 8 = 0 (Eight minus eight equals _____.)
4. The inflation rate has fallen to 0.8%. (_____ point eight per cent)
5. Temperatures are expected to fall below _____ tonight.
6. He gave up the second set 6 _____.
7. What an idiot! He's an absolute _____.
8. Time and effort I invested. And what did I get out of it? _____!
9. Since nobody has ever risen from the dead, this is a case of a _____ set.
10. The first batsman was out for a _____.

Resource you might use: Brown and Henke (1983).

One further, well-known difference is the expression of numbers above the millions. While *million* everywhere consists of a number followed by 6 digits (e.g. twenty-three million is *23 + 000,000*, i.e. *23,000,000*), practice varies for numbers followed by 9 digits (e.g. *23,000,000,000*). In North America this is called *billion*; but in BrE *billion* can refer to a number followed by 12 digits as well as to one followed by 9. To avoid misunderstanding BrE texts often say *23 thousand million* for AmE *23 billion*. BrE usage seems to be moving in the direction of North America, which is also Australian practice, but confusion is possible where knowledge of the world is an unreliable guide. For example, when we read, 'Billions of radioactive particles were set free in the reactor accident', we cannot be sure what number is meant, but then all that is really important is that it was a lot, more informally, *zillions* or even more emphatically *godzillions*, or as BrE sometimes has it, *squillions*.

Case study 3.2: Identical dimensions, different words: units of measurement

Very often we find referents which are not identical but only similar. For example, where the metric system has been adopted we find standardized units of measure such as kilograms (weight), metres (length), hectares (surface), litres (volume, both liquid and dry), and degrees (temperature). Throughout the English-speaking world, however, there are diverse other standards of measurement. What remains constant is the concept of measuring weight, length, surface, volume, and temperature, whatever the unit may be.

Identical words
While the traditional English units are, for the most part, standardized uniformly wherever they are used, two ways in which differences turn up are worth mentioning. The first is that gallons and bushels are not of equal size everywhere. This means that a Continental (i.e. US) gallon (3.785 litres) is smaller: it is .8327 of an Imperial (UK, etc.) gallon (itself 4.546 litres). And of course fluid ounces, pints, and quarts are correspondingly different. Likewise, dry measure

differs, with a US bushel (35.238 dm³) being .9689 of a British bushel (36.369 dm³). Temperatures in Britain are now generally given in centigrade (Celsius) while American temperatures are usually given in Fahrenheit.[7] It goes without saying that monetary units like dollars (Australia, many Caribbean countries, Canada, New Zealand, Singapore, the USA, etc.), nairas (Nigeria), pounds (UK), punts (Ireland), rands (South Africa), rupees (India, Pakistan, Sri Lanka), shillings (Kenya, Tanzania, Uganda), and many more differ from each other in value though all are based on the hundred-system (one dollar has 100 cents, etc.).

Different words

The second major difference involves the default units used. A default unit is the one people tend to think in terms of – i.e. it is what is most likely to be at the centre of a prototype (§3.3). Americans buy gasoline by the *gallon* just as the British buy petrol by the *litre*; in other words they do not use the 'same' default unit. Americans buy milk by the *quart*, half-gallon, or gallon, while the British still tend to think of milk as coming by the *pint*; the Americans reserve *pints* and *half-pints* for cream or half and half (half cream and half milk). And, of course, you go for a *pint* at the local in Britain or Ireland while a (12-ounce) *can* is common in the US.

New words

The Internet gives us bits, a ***blend*** of ***binary digit***. But also *bytes, kilo-, mega-,* und *gigabytes*. More fancifully it adds the *bozon,* 'the quantum unit of stupidity. From *bozo* a clown, a loser. Adjective *bozotic*' (Flexner and Soukhanov 1997: 78).

Case study 3.3: Pakistani English terms

Just as Great Britain and the US have been slow or even unwilling to give up traditional units of measurement in favour of international metric ones, so too we can find other Anglophone countries in which the situation is similar. Pakistani English (PakE), 'an institutionalized variety of South Asian English' which is widely used in newspapers, periodicals, and pedagogical materials and is characterized by the 'frequent use of Urdu[8] lexis' (Baumgardner and Kennedy 1994: 173), is one such case.

In PakE three systems of measurement exist side by side: the metric, the traditional British, and the Sanskritic/Persian, as can be seen in present-day spoken and written PakE. Since 1967 the metric system has been the only official system, but Baumgardner and Kennedy remark: 'For many Pakistanis, especially those belonging to the older generation, the more familiar systems of measurement are in fact the indigenous and the British' (p. 183).

---

7 To convert Fahrenheit into Celsius subtract 32, divide by 9 and multipy by 5, e.g. 49°F − 32 = 27; 27 ÷ 9 = 3; 3 × 5 = 15°C.
8 Urdu is one of the major languages of Pakistan.

Like the inch (distance from end of thumb to first knuckle) or foot (12 inches), pace (one step by a walking man) or mile (1000 paces), so too Pakistani measurements may depend on parts of the body (p. 174). For example an *ungal* (< *ungali* 'finger') refers to the breadth of the finger.

Often such measures are restricted largely to one particular area of activity. Baumgardner and Kennedy mention a number of units for land surfaces including the series from the *marla* (25.29 m^2) to the *karam*, the *kanal*, the *bigha* (*wigah*; also *jareeb* < Arabic; also used for length), and the *murabba* (25 acres or 10.125 hectares) (1994: 176f.).

Another example is the *girah*, which equals three *ungal* or 5.715 cm or 1/16 yard, used to measure cloth, as is the *gaz* 'length from one shoulder to the tip of the finger of the opposite arm' (= 1 yard or .9144m; 32 inches, 16 *girah*). The *balisht*, the distance from the tip of thumb to the tip of little finger of a stretched hand, is used for kites, as is the *gitth* 'hand span' (< Punjabi). The *guth*, which is much longer (approx. 400 m), is used for kite string (Baumgardner and Kennedy 1994: 175f.).

Very small weights sometimes derive from the names for seeds. English has *grain* (a seed) as the smallest unit; PkE has *khashkhash* 'a poppy seed' and *chawal* 'grain of rice' (= 8 *khashkhash*). Urdu/Punjabi, which is a source of borrowing into PakE, uses leguminous units (beans). In PakE we find the *ruttee* (*ratti*) (a bean) traditionally used by goldsmiths, the *masha* (*masa*) (also 'bean'), which equals 8 *ruttee*), and the *tola* (= 12 *masha*) (Baumgardner and Kennedy 1994: 177f.). The tola is also used for spices and foods, as is the *chattank* (= 5 *tola*), the *pao* (4 *chattank*), the *seer* (= 4 *pao* or 933.12 grams), the *dhari* =5 *seer*, and the *maund* = 40 *seer* or 37.3242 kg).[9] The latter is used for drugs, flour, wheat, red chillies, cotton; and *maundage* is used to mean something like 'weight'.

In order to understand the following quotation it is necessary to know some of the above.

> He said that Gujrat police recovered five maunds of charas, one kg heroin, 131 bottles of liquor, two maunds of lehan [raw materials for making liquor] and raided four distilleries from where five drunkards were arrested. (*The News*, Lahore, 16 August 1991; cited in Baumgardner and Kennedy 1994: 184)

For the next quotation about the population of Pakistan, '65 millions, out of which 6 crores live in villages and the rest live in cities' (Baumgardner and Kennedy 1994: 185), it is useful to be acquainted with the PkE alternatives in the area of numbers (see Table 3.2). This mixture will remain, for, as Gumperz and Hernández-Chavey remark, 'words are more than just names for things. Words

---

9 These last three (*pao, seer, maund*) also show up as liquid measure (Baumgardner and Kennedy 1994: 180).

Table 3.2. Traditional numerals in PkE (Baumgardner and Kennedy 1994: 180)

lakh (*lac*)	100,000
crore	[see Exercise 3.2]
arab	1 billion
kharab	10,000 *crore*; 100 *arab*
nil(am)	100 *kharab*
padam	100 *nil(am)*

also carry a host of culturally specific associations, attitudes, and values' (1972: 99).

Just how relevant are words of this sort to the wider English-speaking community? Because of immigration some of them are in use in GB and the USA, and several of the terms discussed are found in British and American dictionaries (see Table 3.3).

Exercise 3.2: Units of measurement

The following units do not have universal currency in the English-speaking world. For each indicate what type of unit it is, e.g. liquid, dry measure, weight, money, length, time, number (if appropriate, tell what it is typically used to measure); and indicate at least one place where it is in common use.

Unit	Type of unit	Where used
1. buck		
2. bob		
3. cent		
4. crore		
5. dime		
6. dram		
7. fortnight		
8. gill		
9. perch		
10. quarter section		
11. quid		
12. stone		

Resource you might use: a good desk dictionary.

3.2.1 Analogues: national institutions

Comparison is generally difficult because it is seldom the case that the referent is really identical in different societies (and their sub-societies). The case study in Chapter 2, schools and education, is a good reminder of this. For although we will find educational systems everywhere, we cannot assume that they are structured in the same way. In the US the sometimes remarkable distinctions from state to state, to say nothing of the often enormous local disparities in the

Table 3.3. PkE units of measurement in AmE and BrE dictionaries

	Crore	*Lakh*	*Masha*	*Maund*	*Ruttee*	*Seer*	*Tola*
OED	+	+	+	+	+	+	+
CODCU	+	+		+		+	
OALD	+	+					
RHD	+	+		+		+	+
WNWD	+	+		+		+	+
W3	+	+		+	+	+	+

OED	*Oxford English Dictionary (1988)*
CODCU	*Concise Oxford Dictionary of Current English,* 8th edn (1990)
OALD	*Oxford Advanced Learner's Dictionary of Current English,* 4th and 6th edns (1989, 2000)
RHD	*Random House Dictionary of the English Language,* 2nd unabridged edn (1987)
WNWD	*Webster's New World Dictionary of American English,* 3rd college edn. (1988)
W3	*Webster's Third International Dictionary of the English Language* (1971)

schools, should serve to illustrate this point further: a ghetto school and a school in a rich suburb of one and the same city are worlds apart, and the meaning of the word *school* will be correspondingly different.

One practical strategy in cases where a particular referent is present in one speech community, but not in a second one which is being compared, is to look for what is structurally similar. From the area of food and eating, which we will be looking at extensively later in this chapter, we have (AmE) *granola* and (BrE) *muesli*, which are not identical, but analogous: grainy breakfast cereals including nuts and fruit. This also means that, although the UK does not have a senate, a vague analogy to the US Senate may be seen in the British upper house, the House of Lords. We may use the term ***analogue*** to compare the two. 'Analogs are things that differ from each other and have different names, but fill analogous positions in different systems' (Algeo 1989: 238).

Exercise 3.3: Analogues

American institutional terms are given below. Your task is to complete the table by supplying the analogues for the UK.

US institution / term   **UK analogue:**

For example: Congress   Parliament

1. President of the USA
2. Secretary of the Treasury
3. Attorney-General
4. Secretary of State
5. Supreme Court
6. US Constitution
7. Republican Party
8. AFL-CIO
9. CIA

10. Federal Reserve Bank
11. Medicare and Medicaid
12. Social Security

Resources you might use: encyclopedias; *Britain: An Official Handbook*.

3.3 COMPARISONS FROM THE PERSPECTIVE OF THE WORD

When making a comparison from the point of view of the word we find the same word in different varieties for the 'same thing' (§3.3.1, Case study 3.4), the same word for something similar (§3.3:2, Project 3.1, §3.3.3, Exercise 3.4, and Project 3.2), the same word for something different (§3.3.4, Case study 3.5 and Project 3.3), and, finally, the lack of a word in one variety despite the existence of a referent, a so-called lexical gap (§3.3.5).

3.3.1 Same word, 'same thing': prototypes and semantic features

In the rest of this chapter we adopt a slightly more abstract way of comparing vocabulary. We will concentrate on the relationship between concepts and words. For practical purposes, that is, we will assume that there is a close relationship between referents and concepts. But referents, as real-world things, actions, states, qualities, etc., are of course specific and include many individual differences. One university will not be the same as another; or – to use an example from the next lexical field we have chosen for this chapter, food and eating – one kind of bread will differ from another. At the centre of our understanding will be the word–concept relationship, which is abstract enough to encompass the individual differences between referents. But before we proceed to this subject, we will look again at the *prototype* (see also §2.2.3.2), which will, however, be expanded in the next section to include what are called *semantic features* or *meaning components*.

Case study 3.4: Bakery products

Prototypes are images we store in our minds as examples of concepts. Depending on individual experience and cultural environment there may be considerable variation.

Central to bakery products is bread. A typical instance of *bread*, whatever the concrete referent may be, may vary between Lagos, London, and Los Angeles, and in this sense the prototype invoked by the one or the other speaker may differ considerably. The usual, or default, referent will be light and relatively insubstantial in some cases and firm and chewy in others.

What holds these varying prototypes together is the concept of 'bread', which might be defined as baked food consisting of flour/meal, milk/water, and (usually) something which causes it to rise. The resulting product can be light or firm; it can consist of the flour of wheat, rye, sorghum, corn/maize, oats, etc.; it can be bland, sweet, salty, etc. The concept of 'bread' relies on a minimal necessary set of semantic features or meaning components, i.e. characteristics of the

concept which may be considered to be essential. A suitable prototype will mani-
fest this minimum set. If one of these essential features does not occur, then a
potential referent cannot be included in the class defined by the concept.

In our example 'bread' has been analysed into a set of semantic features or
meaning components in a process called ***componential analysis***. The features are
conventionally enclosed in square brackets and marked with a plus, which means
that the feature belongs to the concept, or possibly a minus, if missing, or ±, if
variable. The set of features as a whole is listed as a ***feature matrix***:

[+baked]	This excludes 'dough' or 'batter'.
[+flour/meal]	This excludes 'roast beef'.
[+milk/water]	This excludes 'meringue'.
[+leavening]	This excludes 'cracker' or 'cookie'.

Exceptionally, one of these features may be missing from something called *bread*.
There is, for example, *unleavened bread*, but it will be a marginal member and not
at the centre of the prototype. As we can see, the concept is more abstract than
either any given referent or any particular person's prototype.

3.3.2 Same word, same concept and food prototypes

In making comparisons we can try to find out whether a given word has the same
features in two different varieties of English. If the concept associated with a
word has an identical set of features, there is no difference. In the example above
we have supposed that 'bread' is an identical concept[10] wherever English is used.

We can assume that the vast majority of the words in the language are fitted
out with the same sets of features everywhere, for otherwise we would continually be confronted with ambiguity and misunderstanding. As far as food is concerned, we seem to manage all over the world with generic words like *cheese*,
meat, *fruit*, *vegetables*, and *milk*. The fact that different countries and different
cultures make different sorts of cheese, taboo different kinds of meat, grow different classes of fruit, consume different varieties of vegetables, and drink different types of milk is of no further importance, for we are able to learn and use,
with little difficulty, new words for the local distinctions.

If you have travelled, you will perhaps have observed that the jam or jelly you
are served at breakfast (or the type most widely found on supermarket shelves)
varies from place to place (inside and outside the English-speaking world).
Although I would hesitate to make a rule out of my observations, I am surprised at the frequency of grape jelly in the US, of raspberry in the UK, of

---

10 Of course, we are overlooking uses which are e.g. metaphorical (*Jesus said, 'I am the Bread of
Life.'*); idiomatic (*Gimme some bread* [= money, dough], *man!*); highly restricted (the wafers used
at Christian communion and referred to as *bread*); or connected with a particular connotation
(*Bread is the staff of life.*). This aspect will be treated in Ch. 4.

strawberry in Germany, and of apricot in France. Surely this will have an influence on the kind of prototypes of jelly/jam that people have. But it will not change the concepts:

jam		*jelly*	
	[+fruit]		[+fruit]
	[+crushed]		[+crushed]
	[+sugar]		[+sugar]
	[+boiled]		[+boiled]
	[+bits of fruit]		[−bits of fruit]

Note that the two agree in four features, but differ in one. This one difference is what makes the concept 'jam' *distinctive* from the concept 'jelly'.

Project 3.1: Prototypical meaning

See if you can confirm the statement made above by checking how similar the words given below are in their default or prototype meanings. Ask at least three people (you may include yourself) who each speak a more or less different variety of English what they think is typical of the following. This is not a question about their personal favourites, but about the type of English spoken.

Cheese
Meat
Fruit
Vegetable
Beverage

3.3.3 Same word, similar concept

We will now look at instances in which the same word is in use in different varieties of English, but is not used for the same concept. In doing so we leave behind the large area of substantial agreement in the vocabulary of food and eating and find, first, the same word for a similar concept. Here we are looking at words which overlap in meaning. An example is the word *bun*, which in AmE may be sweet or not, whereas in BrE it is consistently sweet. In terms of semantic features we can set up the following matrix of features:

bun	AmE	BrE
	[+bread]	[+bread]
	[+hand-sized]	[+hand-sized]
	[+soft]	[+soft]
	[+round]	[+round]
	[±sweet]	[+sweet]

This comparison shows the tremendous similarity of the word *bun* in AmE and BrE. Not only are four out of five features identical, but we must remember that behind [+bread] there are further 'inherited' features such as [+baked], [+flour/meal], [+milk/water], [+leavening] and, of course, even further back ones like [+edible] and [+manmade]. All of these further features are inherited from the single feature [+bread] because the meaning of bread entails such features as baking, the use of flour, edibility, etc. By choosing a feature like [+bread] there can be a significant reduction of the number of features required to make a distinctive matrix of meaning features. This exclusion of **redundant features** increases the **economy** of the definition.

A second example is *pie*. This is common enough to figure in idioms like *as easy as pie* ('a piece of cake; very easy'), *pie in the sky by and by* ('illusory future benefits'), *to put your finger in the pie* ('to interfere'), or to want *more of the pie* ('a larger share of something'). In America typical pies are apple (cf. the saying *As American as apple pie*), cherry, peach, blueberry, etc. A look at the index of *The Fannie Farmer Cookbook*, a typical American cookbook (BrE *cookery book*), reveals 55 main entries for *pie*, of which 45 are sweet (including two types of cake). Ten entries only are meat or fish pies. In Ireland and the UK pies are more typically savoury and contain meat, e.g. *shepherd's pie*, *steak and kidney pie*, *pork pie*, *cottage pie*. The American default pie is more likely to be sweet, usually with fruit (which the British prefer to call a *tart*); the BrE default pie, savoury.

Exercise 3.4: The semantic features of *pie*

Make a matrix of features like the one given above for *bun*, but this time for *pie*. The features should be selected to ensure distinctiveness while guaranteeing maximum economy (try to make do with a maximum of four features). The difference between the two varieties will be expressed as a difference in at least one feature, i.e. its presence [+], absence [−], or optionality [±].

The order of features is not especially important. And do not worry about including general features of the overall field of food [+edible] or those of the field of prepared foods [+manmade] or, even more specifically, ones prepared by applying heat [+cooked].

pie	AmE	BrE
Feature 1		
Feature 2		
Feature 3		
Feature 4		

Resource you might use: a good desk dictionary.

Projects 3.2(a–d): Breads and bread-like foods

Bakery products make up one of the most confusing word fields in English seen across its varieties. Occasions for misunderstanding are legion (such as the story recounted at the beginning of the chapter about what happened to the author).

Now I would like you to carry out some research of your own. I want you to look at four different types of item: more or less small separately prepared pieces of pastry eaten at or after a meal (or between meals) which are (a) sweet and (b) not necessarily sweet. In a further step investigate more substantial bread-like items – sometimes making up the whole of a meal – (c) with fruit in or on them and (d) with something else in or on them.

For each of the following items mark the ones which are common or typical for your regional variety of English with two x's and those which *may* occur with one x. Find out what the others refer to and name at least one region in which they are common or typical.

(a) More or less small separately prepared sweet pieces of pastry: [+small], [+sweet]

Item	Common (xx)	Possible (x)	Region where common
1. bagel			
2. biscuit			
3. bun			
4. cake			
5. cookie			
6. cracker			
7. Danish			
8. doughnut			
9. muffin			
10. pastry			
11. puff			
12. roll			
13. tart			
14. wafer			
Other:			

Do as above for
(b) more or less small separately prepared not necessarily sweet pieces of pastry: [+small], [±sweet]

Item	Common (xx)	Possible (x)	Region where common
1. bagel			
2. bannock			
3. battercake			
4. biscuit			
5. bun			
6. cracker			
7. crumpet			
8. dumpling			
9. flapjack			

10. pancake
11. muffin
12. pasty
13. patty
14. roll
15. scone
16. tasty
17. turn-over
Other:

Do as above for
(c) more substantial bread-like items with fruit in or on them:
[−small], [+fruit]

Item	Common (xx)	Possible (x)	Region where common
1. cake			
2. cobbler			
3. crisp			
4. crumple			
5. dumpling			
6. flan			
7. fruitcake			
8. pie			
9. popover			
10. scone			
11. tart			
12. turnover			
Other:			

Do as above for
(d) more substantial bread-like items with something other than fruit in or on them:
[−small], [−fruit]

Item	Common (xx)	Possible (x)	Region where common
1. enchilada			
2. falafel			
3. pita			
4. pizza			
5. sandwich			
6. toast			
Other:			

3.3.4 Same word, different concept (tautonyms)

More dramatic than the preceding is the case in which the same word in used in different varieties with distinctly different meanings. We will stay within the same general word field of food and eating, as is the case with the homonymy of *squash* for a vegetable in AmE (similar to the British *marrow* or *courgette*) but for juice in BrE.

In the narrower field of bakery products an American *cookie*, an American *biscuit*, an Anglo-Irish *biscuit,* and an Anglo-Irish *scone* are all comparable inasmuch as they are smallish. An American *biscuit*, however, is a dry type of baked dough which is not sweet ([+small], [−sweet]), and it resembles what the British and Irish call a *scone*, except that scones may be sweet ([+small], [±sweet]); neither are truly hard or crisp. A BrE *biscuit*, on the other hand, is often like what the Americans call a *cookie* ([+small], [+sweet]), though some BrE biscuits are more like crackers, crisp and not sweet ([+small], [±sweet], [+crisp]), while AmE *cookies* may also be soft and raised. Hence, there is only a partial overlap. *Cookie* is not an everyday term in BrE, nor is *scone* in AmE; and as Fig. 3.3 shows, the concept behind the words, including the identical words *biscuit*, are not the same.

AmE *cookie*	BrE *biscuit*	AmE *biscuit*	BrE *scone*
+small	+small	+small	+small
+sweet	±sweet	−sweet	±sweet
±crisp	+crisp	−crisp	−crisp

'Small' bakery items: AmE *biscuit* (solid line) vs. BrE *scone* (dotted line)

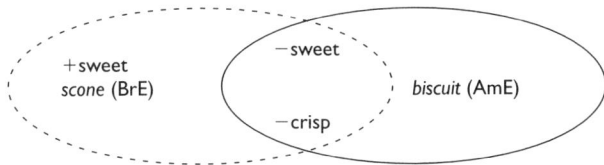

'Small' bakery items: AmE *cookie* (solid) vs. BrE *biscuit* (dotted)

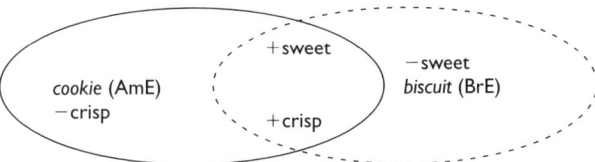

'Small' bakery items: AmE *biscuit* (solid) vs. BrE *biscuit* (dotted)

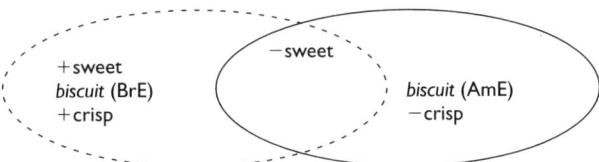

Fig. 3.3. Semantic features

Case study 3.5: The eating day

Most people structure their day by their eating routines (and, of course, by the demands of their work). There is usually a rhythm of major and minor eating occasions. The major occasions are widely respected (if sometimes in the breach), while the minor ones are subject to variation determined by institutional rules, schedules, and opportunities. Within a given culture class, age, occupation, gender, ethnicity, religion, and probably other factors as well may contribute to the relative time of the major eating events of the day, such as how early breakfast will be and whether Ramadan is being observed, or, perhaps, Lent. These same factors are also likely to have a great deal of influence on what people eat.

If we look at the eating day in America, we see that people start off with *breakfast* and continue with *lunch* (or combine the two on a sleepy day for a late-breakfast-cum-early-lunch called a *brunch*[11]). In the evening they end up with *supper*. But they often dignify the heavier cooked meal – be it at noon or in the evening – as *dinner*. Various *coffee breaks* can be interspersed as work or wish determine. The whole is perhaps garnished with *happy hours* and *TV* and/or *midnight snacks*.

What Americans eat is highly unpredictable, since ethnic, regional, and individual factors are so variable. There are, of course, certain stereotypes, a few of which we can mention in passing, especially since the words used may be of interest for the topic of Project 3.3.

- ■ Southern breakfasts may include *(hominy) grits*
- ■ New York lunches may include *pastrami subs*
- ■ Down-home (Southern) dinners may consist of *yams, collard greens* (with vinegar), and *country ham* with *red-eye gravy*
- ■ Western cuisine is more likely to use *salsa* than some other parts of the country

There is little purpose in pursuing this line further since there is a tremendous variety to the foods people eat, which has not, even today, been fully levelled by the franchised fast-food chains.

Projects 3.3 (a and b): The eating day

Project 3.3a: For non-Americans
If you are not American, outline, compare and contrast the major and minor culinary stations of your day with the scheme given above for America.

Do not include incidental eating adventures, but only those that are more or less institutionalized. One test of institutionalization is the existence of fixed lexical items, either single words like *breakfast* or highly fixed complex lexemes like (*school/morning recess*).

---

11 Extremely lazy fellows may resort to *brinner*. I have come across a British reference to *tunch* at 3.10 p.m.: too late for lunch, too early for tea (David L. Seymour, 'Tunch', *English Today* 38 (1994), pp. 61f.).

What factors influence the scheme? Think about institutional requirements (schools, hospitals, offices, factories, work shops, or home), but also social class differences (amount of leisure, money), or ethnic/regional traditions (especially the choice of what you eat at a meal or snack).

Project 3.3b: For Americans
Find out, compare and contrast how the words *dinner, supper,* and *lunch* are used in any three of the following areas: the South, the Northeast, the Far West, the Maritime Provinces, and Jamaica.
  Does your eating day look like the one given in the text? Are there fixed coffee breaks, recesses, or snacks? If so, what are the determining factors? Think about institutional requirements (schools, hospitals, offices, factories, work shops, or home), but also social class differences (amount of leisure, money), or ethnic/regional traditions (especially choice of what you eat at a meal or snack).

3.3.5 Lexical gaps

A further look at the eating day would reveal that the British and Irish are likely to include (afternoon) *tea* as one of its stations. Since tea in the British Isles is a more or less extensive snack (sometimes a full meal), surely any healthy American will have a corresponding concept (something to eat and drink between meals), yet to call it *tea* would be unusual, to call it *high tea* or *cream tea* would be impenetrable. This is a case of a ***lexical gap***: there is the idea of a mid-to-late-afternoon snack, but no fixed word for it.

3.4 THE PERSPECTIVE OF THE CONCEPT

We will not treat the case of same concept, same word (cf. §§3.3.1–2), but we will look at cases of same concept, same word plus an additional word (§3.4.1, Exercises 3.5 and 3.6). After that we will look at those fascinating cases where speakers of two varieties mean the same thing, but use different words to do so (§§3.4.2–3 and Exercise 3.7). Finally, we will look at conceptual gaps, i.e. cases where one community of speakers simply has no idea of what another variety means and, consequently, has no word for it (§3.4.4).

3.4.1 Same concept, same word plus different word

Where varieties share the same word for a concept, but at least one variety has a further word for the same thing which is not shared, we have what one linguist has called an opposition with ***unilateral local markedness***. If both varieties have a special local term in addition to the shared one, this is called ***bilateral local markedness*** (Svejcer 1978: 22f.). In the following scheme Varieties 1 and 2 can be national, regional, or local in nature or even a class, gender, or ethnic variety. *X* stands for any particular concept, as Table 3.4 (a and b) shows.

Table 3.4(a). Scheme for unilateral markedness (1)

Opposition with unilateral markedness	
Variety 1	Variety 2
lexical item$_1$ for x	lexical item$_1$ for x (only)
lexical items$_2$ (etc.) for x	

Table 3.4(b). Scheme for unilateral markedness (2)

Opposition with bilateral markedness	
Variety 1	Variety 2
lexical item$_1$ for x	lexical item$_1$ for x
lexical item$_2$ for x	lexical item$_3$ for x

Examples of unilateral markedness

First we will look at a shared term for which there are marked local AmE words (see Table 3.5(a)). The verb *broil*, for instance, is regularly used in AmE (cooking with direct heat, especially from above), but is much less common in BrE than is the shared verb *grill*. *Barbecuing* or *charcoaling* are even more specific ways of broiling, again chiefly used in AmE: the one indicates an open fire, often outside, the other a particular type of fuel. *Deep fat frying* (BrE *deep frying*) is used the same in both varieties, but to *french fry* is more specifically American, where it is usually reserved for long thin strips of potato fried in this manner (*french fries*; BrE *chips* – not to be confused with AmE *potato chips*, which are called *crisps* in BrE and in IndE *finger chips*).

In a second example (see Table 3.5(b)) a general, shared item has, this time, several unilaterally marked BrE alternatives. Elaborate, multi-course meals

Table 3.5(a). Opposition with unilateral markedness (1)

Variety 1 = AmE	Variety 2 = BrE
lexical item$_1$: *grill*	lexical item$_1$: *grill* (only)
lexical items$_{2-4}$ *broil, barbecue, charcoal*	
lexical item$_1$: *deep fat fry*	lexical item$_1$: *deep fry* (only)
lexical items$_2$ *french fry*	

Table 3.5(b). Opposition with unilateral markedness (2)

Variety 1 = AmE	Variety 2 = BrE
lexical item$_1$: *dessert* (only)	lexical item$_1$: *dessert*
	lexical items$_{2-4}$ *afters, sweet, pudding*

('from soup to nuts', as the expression has it) are composed largely of courses named for what they contain (*soup*, *fish*, *coffee*, etc.). However, there are a few generic terms for commonly occurring courses: the *starter(s)*/*appetizer*/*hors d'œuvres* precede the *main course* (itself more a descriptive phrase than a lexeme), and the whole is followed by the final sweet course, the *dessert*, which may include *cake*, *pudding* (AmE), *ice cream*, *sherbet* (AmE)/*sorbet* (BrE), *fruit*, or *nuts*. The concept 'dessert' is present in both varieties. This would be shared lexical item$_1$ in the chart above. In addition, however, BrE has the terms *afters*, *pudding*, and *sweet* (lexical items$_{2-4}$), all of which are missing in AmE.

Exercise 3.5: Who eats dessert?

The multiplicity of words in the example of grilling, broiling, barbecuing, and charcoaling above can be justified (to some extent at least) in the distinctions in meaning which they can be used to make. But what purpose does it serve that BrE has four words for 'dessert' while AmE manages with only one? The answer lies in the fact that there are sub-variety distinctions involved, in this case social class differences, for not everybody uses all four words.

When seemingly parallel terms show up, there is frequently a further sort of distinction which goes beyond denotation alone. For example, a *bulkhead* is a wall, a *head* is a toilet, a *galley* is a kitchen, a *brig* is a jail, but in each case the italicized term is the one used in the navy or aboard ships and, sometimes, planes instead of the more general one. Differences in who uses a word or when a particular word is likely to be used are frequently, but by no means consistently or uniformly, given in dictionaries as **usage (style, status, descriptive) labels**. They may involve social class (seldom given in dictionaries because perhaps too touchy or too subjective), sub-regional differences (Scottish, Canadian, Southern American, New England, etc.), field (animal husbandry, music, nautical, printing, etc.), stylistic levels (informal, non-standard, slang, vulgar, disparaging, offensive, facetious, baby talk, literary, etc.), or temporal distinctions (old-fashioned, archaic, obsolete).

Using at least two different British dictionaries, check on the usage labels attributed to each of the four words for "dessert". Do the two dictionaries agree? Are there any content differences?

		Usage label	Content differences
afters	Dictionary 1		
	Dictionary 2		
dessert	Dictionary 1		
	Dictionary 2		
pudding	Dictionary 1		
	Dictionary 2		
sweet	Dictionary 1		
	Dictionary 2		

Examples of bilateral markedness

Throughout the US it is possible to buy sandwiches which consist of a small loaf of bread sliced open and filled with various combinations of cold cuts (BrE cold meat), cheese, sausage, lettuce, tomatoes, etc. The generic and shared name for this is the *hero (sandwich)*; but the local names for such sandwiches are legion: see the following exercise.

Exercise 3.6: Heroes

For each of the following terms for hero sandwiches, find out where it is used. Check in at least two different American dictionaries for completeness of coverage and agreement or not.

A good (American) dictionary will list most of them. For a complete run-down see Flexner and Soukhanov (1997: 171).

	Term	Place		Term	Place
	bomber			*Cuban sandwich*	
Dict. 1				1	
Dict. 2				2	
	grinder			*hoagie*	
Dict. 1				1	
Dict. 2				2	
	po' boy			*spuckie*	
Dict. 1				1	
Dict. 2				2	
	sub(marine)			*torpedo*	
Dict. 1				1	
Dict. 2				2	
	wedge (wedgie)			*zep (< zeppelin?)*	
Dict. 1				1	
Dict. 2				2	

3.4.2 Same concept, different words (synonyms)

Up to now we have had opportunity to point out various partial overlaps and special local terms. The kind of variation we want to look at now is the type most often mentioned. It is so common that Algeo (1989: 219) says of such one-to-one correspondences that they make up 'a distinct art form, the parallel list'. Yet we should also bear in mind Algeo's warning:

> Simple equivalences between languages or dialects are more nearly the exception than the rule. . . . Dialects are actually related to each other by a complex interplay of partial, overlapping, mutually influencing, and occasionally even simple and direct equivalences. (p. 221)

In our chosen field of food and eating we have already mentioned that 'a thin slice of potato fried until crisp and usu. salted' is a *potato chip* (AmE) (*RHWCD*) or a *potato crisp* (BrE).

3.4.3 International variation in the area of food and cooking

The international variation in food terminology is especially evident in Table 3.6. Burridge and Mulder (1998: 278) give the following recipe with alternative terms to illustrate the difficulty of producing a recipe understandable for American, Australian, British, and New Zealand users:

> For an entree/main course, serve lamb with ears/cobs of corn and a Caesar salad made from 1 head romain/cos lettuce, 2 slices/rashers of broiled/grilled bacon, and 2 hard-cooked/hard-boiled eggs.[12]
> Wrap lamb cutlets/chops in parchment/baking-paper or (aluminum/aluminium/tin) foil with a little broth/stock to cut down on calories /kilojoules. Bake on an oven tray/baking sheet at 350°F/Gas Mark 4 for 30 minutes.

However, we should note that most readers recognize as synonyms *ears* and *cobs*, *slices* and *rashers*, *hard-cooked* and *hard-boiled*, *aluminum*, *aluminium*, and *tin*, *broth* and *stock*. In fact, the only real international problems might be (a) with *entree/main course* and *cutlet/chop*, which are current everywhere but may designate different things, (b) with *romain* and *cos lettuce*, which are regionally restricted names for the same thing, and (c) with *kilojoules* and *calories*, which are part of the metric/non-metric divide. (Americans would also be helpless with baking temperatures in *centigrade/Celsius*.)

Exercise 3.7: Cooking utensils

Our attention has been directed at AmE/BrE differences more than anything else. For this reason the following exercise is intended to expand this twosome into a threesome.

Table 3.6. Variation in food terminology

AmE	AusE	BrE
eggplant	eggplant	aubergine
snowpeas	snowpeas	mangetout
zucchini	zucchini	courgette
shallots	shallots	shallots
scallions/green, bunch, or spring onions	shallots/scallions	spring onions

---

12 In IndE *full-boiled eggs*, which contrast with *half-boiled* 'soft-boiled'; AmE, AusE, BrE, and NZE have no equivalent to IndE *quarter-boiled* and *three-quarter-boiled*, a conceptual gap.

Label each of the following as AmE (A), BrE (B), or common (C). Then find out what AusE usage is. Can you find a pattern, i.e. is AusE closer to AmE or BrE? To what extent can AusE be seen as an independent variety?

can opener	cooker
dish towel	draining board
faucet	fish slice
fridge	spatula
refrigerator	sink
stove	tap
tea towel	tin opener

Resources you might use: an illustrated learner's dictionary such as the *Longman Dictionary of Contemporary English* or *Longman Dictionary of English Language and Culture* or the *Macquarie Dictionary* (for AusE).

3.4.4 Conceptual gaps

An illustration of a conceptual[13] gap is (AmE) *pudding*, which is an everyday sort of dessert (see above) in America and is made traditionally of milk, sugar, flour, and flavouring, but is more commonly made (cooked or instant) from pudding powder that can be bought in a food store. What North Americans commonly call *pudding* would best be ordered as *blancmange* in the British Isles (better known in the US as *cornstarch pudding*, which is more a descriptive term than a single lexeme), but expectations should not be too high; expect a bland kind of (AmE) *custard*, without the eggs. And by its very name (*blanc* is French for 'white'), do not expect chocolate, strawberry, butterscotch, or caramel flavour. There not only is no word in BrE which means what *pudding* does in AmE, there is also no straightforward concept of (AmE) 'pudding'.

The other way around, the idea that *pudding* might be savoury is common in Britain and Ireland (cf. *steak and kidney pudding*, *blood/black pudding*, *Yorkshire pudding*). Most BrE puddings (savoury or sweet) are combinations of food held together in a bowl or cloth as containers and cooked by boiling or steaming:

[+boiled/steamed]
[+mixture of ingredients]
[+container]
[±sweet]

While not wholly unknown, such puddings are certainly not the default setting in North America. A combination of sweet and savoury boiled items is simply not a conceptual category in AmE.

---

13 Sometimes called *referential gaps*. 'Conceptual' seems more appropriate because we are concerned not with whether or not a particular referent is present or not, but with whether it is a recognizable concept in a given variety.

A second, more specific example of pudding is *spotted dick*, which, if offered an American for dessert, is likely to provoke a roar of a laughter or an embarrassed blush since *dick* (a.k.a. *peter*) is AmE for BrE *willy* (a.k.a. *John Thomas* or *John Willie*) – all colloquial terms for penis). In the reality of BrE *spotted dick* is a (BrE) pudding made with flour, suet, and raisins or currants, but many Americans have no idea what a currant is (a small, seedless raisin; but also a European fruit of the genus *Ribus*).

Exercise 3.8: Regional cuisine

Find out what the following mean and where they are used.
1. bannock
2. butty
3. cornbread
4. cruller
5. half-round
6. hushpuppies
7. johnny cake
8. soda bread

Resources you might use: a good desk dictionary of AmE.

3.5 COMPLEX LEXICAL COMBINATIONS: PHRASAL VERBS; COLLOCATIONS; IDIOMS

Up to now we have been looking at vocabulary, generally single words, under paradigmatic aspects (hyponyms, synonyms, and opposites). In this section we will look at word combinations, more or less fixed expressions. This adds a syntagmatic perspective to the study of vocabulary. While staying within the general field of food and eating, we will observe such complex or multi-word items as collocations (§3.5.1 and Exercise 3.9) and idioms (§3.5.2 and Exercise 3.10), particularly the kind of idiom known as phrasal verbs.

3.5.1 Collocations

Collocations are lexical[14] items consisting of lexical words from two different word classes which co-occur habitually. Different from idioms (see below), each word in a collocation contributes its own meaning to the whole in a distinguishable way. For this reason, collocations are ***transparent*** in meaning; that is, the meaning of the whole can be worked out from the meaning of each of the words in it (cf. Cruse 1986: 40f.). For example, *heavy drinker* can be understood as the combined meaning of the adjective and the noun 'someone who drinks a lot/too

---

14 These are sometimes called *lexical collocations* as opposed to **grammatical collocations**. The latter consist of a combination of a lexical and a grammatical item such as phrasal and prepositional verbs (see below) and other expressions involving prepositions, e.g. *at sight, on time, sick of* (cf. Gramley and Pätzold 1992: 61ff.).

much alcohol'. Both words can combine with others relatively freely in the meanings they express in this combination (*heavy smoker* or *serious drinker*), but *heavy drinker* is itself relatively fixed and hence a collocation. This is also the case with *white wine*. Such wine is hardly white in colour; it is probably somewhere between relatively clear-to-yellowish and amber. The collocational meaning of *white* is at least partially defined by its occurrence together with *wine*.

Some collocations do not allow so much freedom. When one (or sometimes both) of the words cannot be replaced, we speak of a *unique (fixed, frozen) collocation*. Only eggs (and metaphorically brains), for instance, can be addled. Both potatoes and onions have skins. So why do you peel a potato rather than skinning it while you can peel or skin an onion? The answer lies in how fixed the collocation is. Many combinations are fairly free without being unrestricted. For example, you can *reek* of any *alcoholic drink* such as *beer*, *wine*, or *whisky*.

Many, if not most, collocations, like *reek* + *(of) drink* are the same in most varieties. But there are quite a few differences as well. For example, if you drink too much you may have to *throw up* (shared), *upchuck* (AmE; mild), *puke* your *guts out* (AmE, strong), or *bring* everything *up* (BrE), all expression for 'to be sick (on/at your stomach)'.

Exercise 3.9: Drinking collocations

Determine which words collocate by putting the proper letter(s) in the blank provided. In some cases you may have to add grammatical words such as *to the* or *as a* to combine the two parts of the collocation. a–j belong in blanks 1–6; k–q, in 7–12. Some blanks take more than one answer.

1. _____ drinker	a. blind	f. stinko	7. drunk _____	k. beer	o. kite
2. _____ drunk	b. cold	g. stone	8. full _____	l. booze	p. scruppers
3. _____ liquor	c. dead	i. take	9. dead _____	m. deacon	q. tick
4. _____ sober	d. heavy	j. wet	10. high _____	n. fiddler's fart	
5. _____ swig	e. hold		11. sober _____		
6. _____ whistle			12. swill _____		

Resource you might use: *BBI Dictionary of English Word Combinations*, 2nd edn.

There are also interesting national differences in the slangy, colloquial vocabulary for being drunk. One informal survey (see Table 3.7) shows data for a set of 25 North Americans (USA 19: 11 m, 8 f; Canada 6: 2 m, 4 f; average age 30) and 14 English people (9 m, 5 f; average age 26). Of the 11 terms mentioned at least 4 times in one of the varieties, only 4 are shared and one of these was not elicited among the informants from the US.

3.5.2 Idioms

Idioms are made up, like collocations, of more than one word form, but they are not full sentences.[15] Idioms are **opaque** (rather than *transparent*), which

---

15 The proverb is a fixed expression on the sentence level; see §6.3.

Table 3.7. Expressions for drunkenness (from Falkenhagen and Hanke 1999)

Expression	North America	England
f-uped/fucked up	5 (4 m, 1 f)	–
hammered	9 (6 m, 3 f)	4 (4 m)
loaded	6 (2 m, 4 f)	–
pissed	3 (1 m, 2 f) (all Canadian)	13 (9 m, 4 f)
rat-assed/-arsed	–	8 (4 m, 4 f)
slaughtered	–	4 (2 m, 2 f)
sloshed	7 (3 m, 4 f)	2 (- m, 2 f)
smashed	8 (6 m, 2 f)	2 (2 m)
trashed	4 (2 m, 2 f)	–
wankered	–	4 (4 m)
wasted	9 (5 m, 4 f)	–

means you cannot derive their meaning from their individual components as you generally can with collocations. Within the framework of food and eating we can take a verb like *cook*, which is clear enough when used normally and non-idiomatically with an object like *dinner*. But if we take an object like *the books*, we have an idiom in which *cook* may be paraphrased as 'manipulate' and *the books* (always plural) must be specified as 'account books'. This idiom is shared throughout the English-speaking world. There are, however, quite a few idioms which are not used in all varieties.

Idioms can be of various sorts. **Metaphorical idioms** are ones like *piece of cake* 'easy' (< as easy as eating a piece of cake, i.e. very easy). If something is either surprising and good or (ironical) bad, *That takes the cake* ('wins the prize') may be used. A person who works gainfully to support a family (a 'breadwinner') may be said to *bring home the bacon* (BrE infml). If you *take the gilt off the gingerbread* (BrE) you spoil the effect of something good.

Pragmatic idioms (cf. §7.3.2) are ones which accompany and help to constitute various activities. For instance, it is not common in the English-speaking community to accompany the start of a meal with good wishes (*bon appétit, guten Appetit, buon appetito*, etc.) so that phrases like very informal (AmE) *chow down* are seen either as a joke or as stylistically inappropriate. On the other hand, drinking is accompanied by pragmatic idioms such as (AmE) *Down the hatch!*, *Bottoms up!*, *Mud in your eye!*, or (BrE, now widely shared) *Cheers!* – all with varying situational appropriateness.

Phrasal verbs are a third type of idiom, and they are fundamental to English all over the world, including combinations such as *look up* ('check up [in a reference book]'), *look out* ('be attentive', cf. also BrE *mind out*), and *look over* ('examine'). Native speakers continue to encounter and learn them throughout their lives, and unfamiliarity with the phrasal verbs in use outside one's own variety can lead to puzzling situations, such as that of the young American girl who was staying overnight with some English friends and was asked by her host when, the next morning, he should *knock her up* (BrE 'wake someone', AmE 'make pregnant').

Phrasal verbs consist of a verb and a particle: *look* + *up*. If they are transitive, they normally allow a noun direct object to come before or after the particle associated with the verb, e.g. *We picked out an appetizer* or . . . *picked an appetizer out*. (A pronoun object must come before the particle, cf. . . . *picked it out*, not: *. . . picked out it*.) Whether transitive or not, the particle is never fully unstressed. Most important, phrasal verbs are largely idiomatic, though to varying degrees. *To look something up* is not a transparent derivation from *look* + *up*. But often enough you can make a fair stab at the meaning: either it is literal, as in *throw up*, *spew up*, or *bring up* ('vomit') or it is semi-literal. *Up* is often a marker of intensity, so when you *eat something up* or *drink it up*, you eat or drink it completely. And BrE *to brew up* (some tea) consists of literal *brew* + *up*, which here lends the idea of quantity.

Exercise 3.10: Collocations and idioms

First identify as a collocation (C) or an idiom (I). For the collocations give a 'translation' which is literal and non-collocationally fixed. In the case of the idioms give a non-idiomatic translation. Mark as AmE (A), BrE (B), or shared in common (C).

	C/I	Translation	A/B/C
1. cheese it			
2. cheese off			
3. chew out			
4. chew up			
5. chug-a-lug			
6. cook out			
7. freshen a drink			
8. get one's teeth into something			
9. grab a bite			
10. greasy spoon			
11. hot up			
12. lay the table			
13. local pub			
14. pig out			
15. plump out			
16. slim down			
17. top up a drink			
18. tuck in (to food)			
19. wash up			
20. wipe up			

Resources you might use: good desk dictionaries of AmE and BrE; a dictionary of phrasal verbs.

3.6 PREPOSITIONS

We will close this chapter by looking at prepositions. Prepositions are surely one of the most difficult aspects of English for non-native speakers to learn. And, considering how functionally and lexically essential these words are for the structure and meaning of the language, it is surprising the amount of variation that even native-speaker communities show from group to group.

Variation in the field of prepositions is of two kinds. A number of prepositions function largely as grammatical markers. But most are lexical in nature. Prepositions which are grammatical in nature have little lexical content. That is, they express relationships more abstract than those of place and time, as with *in, on, at,* or subject matter, such as with *about, concerning,* and *in regard to.* Grammatical prepositions are ones which primarily express grammatical functions like 'subject of'. This is what *of* does in *the destruction of the hurricane* (= 'the hurricane destroyed [something]'), where *hurricane* may be seen as the subject of *destruction.*

3.6.1 Grammatical prepositions

There is little or no variety in the use of grammatical prepositions in GenE throughout the English-speaking world. Among the few which allow a certain degree of variation we will restrict ourselves to two: *to* and *for.*

3.6.1.1 Indirect objects

Indirect objects occur in sentences in which there is a so-called ***ditransitive verb***, i.e. a predicate which takes two objects (a direct and an indirect one). These include verbs of speaking, showing, or giving. There are two major ways of marking an indirect object in English: with *to* and with zero preposition:

> Mother gave a package to me
> Mother gave me a package

To is used to mark change of possession. In the idiomatic expression *to lend someone a hand* ('to help someone'), for example, there is no change of possession and therefore there is no *lend a hand to someone* ('to make a present of a hand to someone').

As a result it can be said that *to* is a highly grammatical, morpheme-like marker of the indirect object which has retained a bit of lexical content (change of possession). When *to* and zero alternate with each other (a phenomenon called ***dative alternation***), there is also a difference in word order. *To* with an indirect object regularly comes after the direct object. When the indirect object comes first (whether as a noun or a pronoun), no preposition occurs:

> The mayor gave the prize to the winner/her
> The mayor gave the winner/her the prize

Whether such alternation is possible depends not only on the meaning of change of possession but also on the provenance of the verb: Latinate verbs like *donate* resist forms without a preposition:

> The winner donated the prize to the city
> *The winner donated the city the prize

In general, this pattern is followed throughout the English-speaking world. However, where both the direct and the indirect object are pronouns, there are varying patterns. Most varieties put the latter in second place and introduce it with the preposition *to*. However, BrE also allows versions of the sentence without *to* (cf. Quirk *et al.* 1985: §18.38):

> The mayor gave it to her (General)
> The mayor gave her it (BrE)
> The mayor gave it her (BrE)

These BrE alternatives, while understandable, are strange to the ears of speakers of other varieties.

3.6.1.2 Grammatical words
In some of their uses both *to* and *for* have, in the course of the development of the English language, been ***grammaticalized*** to purely structural markers bleached of any lexical meaning they may once have had. These processes of grammaticalization have proceeded somewhat differently in various parts of the English-speaking world.

3.6.1.3 The infinitive marker to
The infinitive is often introduced by the particle *to*, e.g. after a verb like *want* or *hope* (cf. *I want/hope to see you soon*). Speakers of GenE everywhere share this structure. However, there are a few exceptions, usually ones involving non-standard forms, but also ones where there is variation in GenE as well.

A different marker: one non-standard variety uses *till* in this sense. Hence we find Northern Ireland expressions like the following

> She went *for till ask* them (Todd 1989: 347)

The combination *for to*, which is parallel to *for till* in the example, was once quite frequent, but is today found only in old-fashioned varieties, although it is familiar to many people from the song 'Oh! Susanna', which in this case represents Southern American usage in the nineteenth century:

> I'm goin' to Lou'siana my true love *for to see*. (S. Foster)

Other varieties, pidgins or creoles and therefore clearly not part of GenE, use *for* in the place of *to* as the marker of the infinitive, cf. East Cameroonian Pidgin English:

True Things Whe Every Man He Must Savi *For Go* For Haeven [*sic*]
(Dillard 1973: 141)
'True things which everyone must know to go to heaven'

In some varieties of (non-standard) English *for* even divides into two. In the following example of Jamaican Creole English both *faa* and *fi* come originally from
for. The first is used to mean 'because' (cf. the conjunction *for*) and the second is
used as the infinitive marker and for the preposition *for*:

faa mi no miin fi marid
for me not mean to married
'Because I didn't mean to get married'

yu waa marid now you go aks fi di gerl
you want married now you go ask for the girl
'If you wanted to marry now, you would ask for the girl' (Pollard 1989: 55)

3.6.1.4 No marker
In GenE there is some variation betweeen *to* and zero marker after certain verbs.
This chiefly affects the modal verbs *need*, *dare*, and *ought* as well as the verb *help*.
AmE and AusE speakers seem to prefer negated *need* with *to* (*They don't need to
see a lawyer* vs. *They needn't see . . .*) more than BrE speakers do. In several studies (Svartvik 1968; Greenbaum 1974; Collins 1989) it was found that AmE, AusE,
and BrE speakers rated *dare* + *to* as less acceptable than *dare* + zero, and in one
study AmE speakers used *ought* + zero about 40 per cent of the time
(Greenbaum 1974: 247), while AusE speakers preferred zero over *to* by about 4
to 3 (Collins 1989: 141f.). With *help* (as in *Will you help me (to) do it?*), we find
that the construction with *to* is more common in BrE and that with zero is more
frequent in AmE (Quirk *et al.* 1985: §16.52).

3.6.1.5 The complementizer for
For is regularly used to introduce certain infinitive constructions like GenE *It was
nice for him to come*; in such cases *for* is called a ***complementizer***. After verbs of
emotion such as *like*, *love*, *hate*, etc. this construction, as in *We would love for him
to come*, is fairly often found in AmE but virtually not at all in BrE, where we find
We would love him to come.

3.6.2 Lexical prepositions

The other side of the prepositional coin is the lexical side, and it allows considerably more choice. Some differences are noticeable but relatively trivial, such as
the greater preference for *whilst* or *amongst* in BrE where AmE is largely
restricted to *while* and *among*. Sometimes there are slightly different prepositions,
as when a British speaker says *in respect of* where an American would say *in
respect/regard to*. Other differences involve the use of forms in AmE which are
rare in or absent from BrE (or, occasionally, vice versa) (see Table 3.8).

Table 3.8. AmE and BrE differences in prepositions and expressions of time

BrE	AmE
apart from	apart from/aside from
behind	behind/(in) back of
different from/to	different from/to/than
on behalf of	on/in behalf of
on top of	on top of/atop
Expressions involving time:	
quarter to (five)	quarter to/till / of
twenty past (five)	twenty past/after
at/over the weekend	on/over the weekend[16]
it's past/gone eight	it's past eight
it's eight-thirty/half eight	it's eight-thirty
Monday to Friday	Monday to/through Friday
on Tuesdays	on Tuesdays/Tuesdays
We haven't seen him for two weeks	We haven't seen him in two weeks

Closely related to such differences are the uses of some conjunctions. AmE has the conjunctions *plus*, *like*, *on account of*, which are rare or non-standard in BrE. Thus an American might say *I got the flat fixed plus I got some gas.* BrE has *immediately* and *directly*, which are not current at all in AmE: *Immediately we have the puncture repaired and top up the petrol, we can leave.*

BrE may use zero in the following where AmE has *to be* or *like* (depending on the verb): *He looks (like) a decent sort (of guy)* or *She seems (to be) an intelligent student.*

Only a few differences are significant in the sense that they mark meaning distinctions. For example BrE makes a distinction which is missing in AmE, that between *round* and *around*. While both varieties use *around* as a preposition for scattered distribution in an area, AmE freely uses it for circular movements while BrE often takes *round* for the latter:

There's trash all around the room (scattered distribution, both AmE and BrE)
They walked round the hill (circular movement; only BrE)
They walked around the hill (both AmE and BrE)

Where more careful BrE has only *out of* (as in *to walk out of the room, door, house*, etc.) AmE (and less formal BrE and AusE) distinguish between *out of* for volume or container (*out of the house, the box, the freezer*), but uses *out* for two-dimensional ports of exit (*out the door, window, gate*).

---

16 Cf. NZE *in the week-end* as well as *on the week-end*.

Table 3.9. Postpositions in South African Indian English

(a) *side* for direction or approximate location, 'to, towards, around' as in *I am going farm-side* ('to the farm'); *If you're going Nandhoo's house-side* ('to Nandhoo's house'), *ask for some beans*

(b) *time*: 'in, at, on' as in *Afternoon-time* ('in the afternoon') *it gets too hot*; *They only come to visit eating-time* ('at meals')

(c) *part*: 'in' *morning-part* 'in the early morning'; *evening-part* 'in the late evening'; *late-part* 'late in the day, late at night' (Mesthrie 1987: 268f.)

Case study 3.6: Prepositions in some SAE varieties

Afrikaans-influenced SAE has prepositional usage different from both AmE and BrE. Here are some examples: *by* 'at, with' (*to work by a chemist*); *under* 'among' (*sickness under my flocks*); *otherside* 'on the other side of'; *on* 'at' (*on lunch*) (Branford 1994: 493). These examples as well as further cases may be explained as interference from Afrikaans (or **substratum** influence).

South African Indian English (spoken by South Africans of Indian origin) reveals some structures in which the object precedes the preposition which governs it. This is especially true in its extreme non-standard or **basilect** forms, which go back to Indian languages such as Gujarati and Urdu. Table 3.9 shows postpositions derived from English nouns.

3.7 THE SOURCES OF VOCABULARY IN CARIBBEAN ENGLISH

In the final section of this chapter we return to the question of the origins of vocabulary. Here our concentration is on the Anglophone Caribbean,[17] an area in the western hemisphere which has a very different social and linguistic history from that of the US and Canada. The interest of these countries for our purposes lies in the multiple external sources which have gone into the vocabulary of CarE. In this sense we are returning to the theme begun in §2.1, where we reviewed the historical sources of the vocabulary of English.

Most of the Anglophone Antillean countries have a higher percentage of native speakers of English than, for example, the US. However, since the majority of the inhabitants of these states are descendants of African slaves who were imported there on a massive scale during the seventeenth and eighteenth centuries, the way in which this population became speakers of English is dramatically different. The initial 'stages' in the process is one in which **pidgin** and then **creole** varieties of

---

17 The islands of the Bahamas, the Turks and Caicos Islands, the Cayman Islands, Jamaica, Puerto Rico, the American and the British Virgin Islands, Anguilla, St Kitts-Nevis, Antigua-Barbuda, Montserrat, Dominica, St Lucia, St Vincent, Barbados, Grenada, Trinidad-Tobago as well as Belize and Guyana on the mainland.

English developed. According to one theory[18] the slave population had no common language to resort to and so communicated using grammatical categories and structures retained from their native African (***substrate***) languages, which themselves showed a certain number of similarities (although it is uncertain just how great these similarities might be); however, they used words which were, for the most part, borrowed from English. In this sense English is, as ***superstrate languages*** usually are, the ***lexifer language*** and chief source of vocabulary of this new 'mixed' variety. Holm reports that creoles usually draw less than 10 per cent of their vocabulary from languages which are not the lexifer (1988: 71).

Pidgin Englishes grew up not only in the Caribbean Islands, Guyana, and Belize, but also in Suriname, parts of North America, along the coast of West Africa, in Hawaii, New Guinea, the Solomon Islands, Vanuatu, and Australia (especially Queensland and the Northern Territory).[19]

As a new generation of children adopted a pidgin as their one and only language, it became a creole, which by definition is a native language. Since creoles are used in all areas of communication, they necessarily expand their vocabularies massively. Here, of course, is where the question of sources comes in. Some of the sources (besides the main superstrate source, GenE) are summed up in the following list:

1. African (substrate) survivals
2. Retentions from English (Scottish, Irish) dialects
3. The colonial lag (e.g. through isolation)
4. Interplay with various European languages and the languages of recent indentured labourers
5. The present-day competition of BrE and AmE in the Caribbean
6. Pan-Caribbean tendencies
7. Local processes of word formation

The list is above all interesting because it emphasizes the importance of the various external political and demographic factors which can impinge on a language (or variety). Each of these points also plays a role in the language situation in other countries as well (North America, Australia, New Zealand, South Africa), but shows up perhaps somewhat more clearly when we look at a population which, in its majority, was originally non-English-speaking. Below are brief comments on and examples of these seven points:

---

18 See e.g. Baudet (1981); Holm (1988) gives a survey not just of English pidgins and creoles but also of ones based on other languages. A further important but different approach sees the development of pidgins and creoles as the result of universal principles of language acquisition. For a summary of theories of creolization see Muysken (1988).

19 Slavery was not universally involved, but the lack of a local language of communication under the conditions of trade in polyglot situations (especially West Africa) or of contract plantation labour (especially Australia) had the same overall effect. The further development of the pidgins to creoles and on to English has taken place in varying degrees from place to place, but nowhere so completely as in the Caribbean and North America.

1. African survivals are recessive (often used for obsolete cultural items): included is *unu*, the second person plural personal pronoun (only attested in Barbados and Jamaica) (see also Case study 6.5) or *chamba* 'to cut' from the name of a people of Nigeria and Cameroon who scar their faces (Cassidy 1967); but also *nyam* 'to eat', which is still frequently used.

2. Retentions from dialects are not always easy to establish, possible examples being *krabit* 'cruel' (Moskito Coast Creole) < Scottish *crabbed*, *crabbit* 'ill-tempered' (Holm 1988: 77); Craig (1983: 202ff.), lists Scotticisms in present-day Jamaican Creole and other Caribbean creoles, some of which 'have become parts of Standard Caribbean English' (p. 204).

3. The colonial lag is reflected in the overuse of elsewhere less frequently used composite adverbs and conjunctions such as *wheretofore*, *herein*, *hereunder*, but also flowery phrases and classical references, including, as in the following example from a sermon, bogus words intended to impress the listeners:

   It fills my heart with phil-long-losophy, entrong-losophy, joken and conomaltus, impro, imperium, pompry, comilatus, allus comigotus, which is to say I come here today without any study Dia Gratia, by the grace of God, I have tried my best. Time is tempus fugit. (Roger D. Abrahams quoted in Roberts 1988: 28)

   These tendencies, where the tradition of a curriculum of classical English literature and the Bible is often the source of vocabulary, are also reported for India and West Africa.

4. Influence comes from various other European languages (***adstrate languages***), e.g. *maugre* 'thin' or *sampata* 'rough sandal' ultimately from Portugese *magro* and *sapato* (Cassidy 1967); especially on the Windward Islands (Dominica, St Lucia St Vincent, Grenada, and including Trinidad) where French (Creole) was originally dominant; also Indic words especially in Guyana and Trinidad, e.g. Guyanese English *doghla* of mixed parentage (from Bhojpuri) (Holm 1989: 463).

5. Doubtless there is strong AmE and BrE influence, especially in advertising; BrE influence from 300 years of colonialism plus British influence on the educational system; AmE influence in the increase in tourism from North America and in disc jockey language (Roberts 1988: 5, 22, 26f.).

6. Pan-Caribbean influences include Rasta (Rastafarian) terms (Dread Talk) such as *downpress* instead of *oppress* ('up-press') (Roberts 1988: 36ff.)

7. More local processes of word formation include African ***calques*** (or ***loan translations***; see below §§4.3.1.2, 6.1.1, 6.1.3–4, 6.3.3, Case studies 8.6 and 8.7) such as *big-eye* 'greedy'; reduplication such as *big-big* 'very big' including onomatopoeic *pooka-pooka* 'sound of a kettle on the boil' (Holm 1988: 89); or a ***folk etymology*** (see §4.3.1.3) such as *bull-jowl* 'a hot dish' (from French *brûle-gueule*)

In general the vocabulary of CarE can be checked in the *Dictionary of Caribbean English Usage* (1996). In Chapter 4 we will pick up these seven points again to look at the development of the vocabulary of AusE, NZE, and SAE.

3.8 SUMMARY

In this chapter we have discussed how words and meanings differ from each other and how they may be compared, chiefly by using semantic features. In doing this we looked at the word field of numbers and at the vocabulary of food and drink. However, we did not restrict ourselves to simple words, but also looked, in the syntagmatic dimension, at complex or multi-word lexemes such as idioms, collocations, and phrasal verbs. A section on prepositions concentrated on variation in their use both as grammatical and as lexical words. The chapter closed with a study of CarE which illustrated variety in the origins of vocabulary.

English in the Southern Hemisphere: Vocabulary Change

Of making many words there is no end. (Ecclesiastes 12: 12 slightly modified for our purposes)

4.0 INTRODUCTION

In the previous chapters we have looked at what meaning is and how words and meanings can be compared across varieties, in other words, the what and the how of meaning. In this chapter we will look at some aspects of why change has taken place. That is, we will emphasize some of the possible reasons for the differences we find between the regional-national varieties. This is a matter of both changes in the lexicon (§§4.1–4) and of changes in and the stylistic assessment of the meanings of words (§§4.5 and 4.6).

In this chapter we will be looking particularly at the three major native speaker varieties of English that grew up in the process of British colonialism and the consequent settlement of Irish and British emigrants in the southern hemisphere from the eighteenth to the twentieth centuries: Australian English (AusE), New Zealand English (NZE), and South African English (SAE). In examining these varieties we will focus on the processes involved in lexical and semantic change.

4.1 VOCABULARY CHANGE IN SOUTHERN HEMISPHERE ENGLISH

When we apply the list given at the end of Chapter 3 to AusE, NZE, or SAE we find that (1) the native languages of the Australian Aborigines, the New Zealand Maoris, and the South African Afrikaaners, Sans, and Xhosas contributed to the respective regional varieties (examples in §4.3.1); but so did (2) the regional dialects of Britain and Ireland (§4.4), (3) the retention of older forms no longer current in standard BrE as well as the loss of words retained in BrE (§4.2), and (4) the languages of non-English-speaking immigrants (§4.3.1). Of course, (5) BrE has been the primary model for all three varieties, but the increasing influence of AmE especially on AusE has been the subject of much comment and various studies (see references in Collins and Blair 1989). Since the colonization of all three countries began within the same period of just over 50 years and drew on a similar source of immigrants, it is not surprising that (6) they share a number of features including vocabulary (see the example of *bush* in §4.3.2.1, Case study 4.1 and Exercise 4.3). Each variety also shows (7) some evidence of especially favoured local processes of word formation (§4.3.2).

As in the preceding chapters, we approach vocabulary from two sides. First we will be concerned with new words. This is hardly unexpected in dealing with new and different lands and societies. We will take the most obvious point to illustrate this: what might be called ***natural kinds***, i.e. things which exist in the natural world and demand names, esp. plants, animals, and the way the landscape looks.

The second approach will put more emphasis on changes in meanings, both with and without corresponding changes in the words used. In this case we will concentrate more on ***manmade artefacts***, including social phenomena. But before we proceed to new words, let us look at words lost.

4.2 LOSS OF VOCABULARY

When a language is transported to new regions, as English was, it comes to be used for aspects of the natural–physical and the social–institutional environment which differ in many ways from the original environment (in the British Isles). Many familiar aspects of British landscape are rare or do not exist:

> Such common English topographical terms as down, fen, bog, chase, dell and common disappeared, save as fossilized in a few localisms and proper names. (Mencken 1963: 127)

Mencken's words were directed at the situation in the United States *vis-à-vis* the British Isles, but they may be applied with more or less variation to all three major Southern Hemisphere native-speaker varieties focused on in this chapter. This does not mean, of course, that Australian, New Zealand, and South African users of English do not know what *down, fen, bog*, etc. are, but they will, as a rule, know them only indirectly – from books and possibly from video material of some sort (movies, TV, Internet). Of course, places like Australia, New Zealand, and South Africa will have new topographical features which will need to be named, but that is a topic for the next sections.

Words for plants and animals native to the British Isles but not to the overseas areas may go the same way as the fens and bogs; nonetheless, as we will see in the next section, many of these words often turn up, recirculated in a sometimes modified form in association with a new set of referents.

The vocabulary which refers to the institutional and social environment is only slightly different from that of the UK since many of the political structures and public institutions were transferred wholesale. However, with the passing of time there comes a drift which shows up here, too. So if one of the new English-speaking countries does not have a *Privy Council*, this does not mean that such a word, so historically important for the former colonies, is unknown. More parochial institutions such as *local authorities* will be correspondingly vaguer in meaning for most non-British speakers.

In addition to this there is also what has frequently been called the **colonial lag** (a.k.a. 'arrest of development'). New developments in the language of the old home country are picked up only later (Kytö 1991: 21; cf. also Trudgill 1999). On the other hand, a more fluid social situation engenders 'a certain richness of dialects and registers' and greater opportunity for change from above or below. In the new lands social mobility encouraged and quickened the rate of change, but it also showed respect for educated usage, which has nurtured prescriptivism (Kytö 1991: 24).

4.3 NEW VOCABULARY

The converse of the losses just mentioned is the much more significant addition of new words for new aspects of life. We will look first at borrowing (§4.3.1), then at word formation (§4.3.2).

Australia is not only a large country (7.7 million km²; 4000 km from east to west and 3700 from north to south) with an arid and semi-arid centre and west of the country different from anything to be found in the British Isles. It is also a continent, and it is geographically isolated from the more highly populated centres of Eurasia, America, and Africa, which among themselves had a significantly greater interchange of biological forms.[1] One consequence of geographical isolation over thousands of years was that species are to be found in Australia which are sometimes significantly different from those found elsewhere. All this richness in forms of life meant that naming problems were inevitable.

While North America was a challenge to the resources of the English language, the similarity of plant and animal forms allowed a fairly easy transfer of names even though they were sometimes pressed into service for species only superficially similar. In this way the American bison was called the buffalo; the red-breasted thrush (*Turdus migratorius*) was called a robin (the British robin is the *Erithacus rubecula* and the Australian flycatchers of the genus Petroica are robins as well). New and different North American species such as skunks, raccoons, and opossums borrowed their totally new names from American Indian names for these animals (viz. from Algonquian *segankw*, *aroughcun*, and *opassum* respectively). The following exercise gives you the opportunity to identify a number of distinct animals from various parts of the English-speaking world.

Exercise 4.1: Indigenous animals

Identify the country of origin and give the etymological source of the following.
1. armadillo
2. cockabully
3. gemsbok

---

1 The Americas were partially isolated from Eurasia by open seas or the arctic ice-fields; sub-Saharan Africa and Eurasia were largely separated by the Sahara Desert. Nonetheless, there were periodic interchanges of biological forms via migrations and trade.

4. ground hog
5. hedgehog
6. Illawarra shorthorn
7. kiwi
8. koala
9. Manx cat
10. meerkat
11. numbat
12. pipi
13. platypus
14. prairie dog
15. quagga
16. roedeer
17. taniwha
18. waterbuck
19. woodchuck
20. wild boar

Resources you might use: *Dictionary of South African English, Macquarie, Australian Concise Oxford Dictionary.*

4.3.1 Borrowing

One of the most important resources for dealing with the problem of how to refer to new phenomena is borrowing. This can take two chief forms, loan words and loan translations.

4.3.1.1 Loan words

When a word is taken directly from another language we speak of a ***borrowing*** or ***loan word***. Native plants and animals not known in the British Isles and North America are especially often named via borrowing from languages already in place before the arrival of English. They may be colonial languages like Afrikaans or indigenous ones like the Aboriginal languages of Australia. Hence we find *kangaroo* < *gaŋuru* in the Aboriginal language Guugu Yimidhirr. While Australian English has borrowed extensively from the various aborginal languages spoken there, New Zealand has drawn principally on Maori, the single Austronesian language of its original native inhabitants, and South Africa has borrowed particularly from Afrikaans, the other major European language spoken there, words like *wildebeest* or *gemsbok*. All three southern hemisphere varieties have also drawn on the languages of the many immigrants who have settled in both countries, and SAE has also taken over words from various African languages such as Zulu or Xhosa.

The names of foods and ways of and occasions for cooking and eating are especially easily borrowed, as we saw in Chapter 3. In connection with the regional emphasis of this chapter we can mention the widely practised *braai* (< Afr. < Dutch *braden* 'broil, grill, roast') for a barbecue or outdoor grilling in South Africa. In

Table 4.1. Maori words in NZE

kainga	village, home
pa	Maori village or settlement, originally fortified
marae	courtyard of a Maori meeting house, the centre of social life in a Maori community
whare	a Maori hut; any hut; a bach (< bachelor flat) or weekend house
rangatira	Maori chief; in general any boss or superior
wahine	girl or woman (usu. Maori)
tangi	traditional funeral wake
mana	prestige, standing
tapu	sacred

Australia small sausages are *cheerios*, esp. in Queensland (and also in New Zealand), but they are also called *frankfurts* (from German; cf. also AmE *frankfurters*), *savs* or *saveloys* (ultimately from Italian *cervellata*; also common in BrE).

There is an obvious motivation to use loan words when talking or writing about cultural phenomena which are not closely associated with the European roots of English. Hence when talking about traditional Maori village life the NZE of whites (*Pakehas*) and Maoris has a wide range of lexical items such as those shown in Table 4.1.

4.3.1.2 Loan translations

A second type of borrowing is the ***loan translation*** or ***calque***, a word translated element by element from another language. New Zealand, for example, is also known as *Aotearoa* (< Maori *ao tea roa*), which translates as 'Land of the Long White Cloud'. We also find, for instance, AusE *Dreamtime* < Aboriginal *alcheringa*, which is also used as a loan word in English, for the mythological time when the world was created. There are, despite these examples from New Zealand and Australia, relatively few loan translations from Maori and the various Aboriginal languages.

The situation is, however, different in South Africa, where a look at the *Dictionary of South African English* immediately provides numerous loan translations, esp. from Afrikaans. This may well be because of the similarity of images and morphological structure in two so closely related Germanic languages as English and Afrikaans (see Table 4.2). Here we see not only how new things and social phenomena have been enriched by the process of calquing, but also how dense the system of borrowed items may be: the definition of *after-ox* uses *span*; *to lead water* uses *sloots*, *furrows*, and *water erven*.

4.3.1.3 Modified borrowings, e.g. folk etymologies

Words easily change their shape when they are borrowed. Sometimes this is a matter of spelling conventions, as when the German word for a kind of fish

Table 4.2. Calques from Afrikaans in SAE

---

after-ox < Afr. *agteros* 'One of the hindmost pair in a *span* (q.v.) of draught oxen . . .'

antheap < Afr. *miershoop* 'anthill'

bad friends < Afr. *kwaaivriende* 'at enmity, not on speaking terms: . . . usu. temporarily'

to lead water < Afr. *water lei* 'To irrigate, usu. by means of *sloots* (q.v.) or *furrows* (q.v.) from a public supply in towns which have *water erven* (see *erf*) from farm dams or other irrigation schemes . . .'

lungsickness < Afr. *longsiekte* 'pleuro-pneumonia, a highly infectious disease of cattle, and horses'

---

commonly found in the waters around Australia, the *Schnapper* (*Chrysophys auratus*), is written with <s> and not <Sch>. This is an accommodation to both English spelling patterns (German common nouns are capitalized) and English phonology (the sound combination /ʃn-/ of <schn-> is not native.[2]

One of the more fascinating ways in which words are re-formed is when they take on not just a native spelling and/or pronunciation but a history as well, a so-called **folk etymology**. Australian *palberry* suggests from its form that it is a berry like the strawberry, raspberry, blueberry, etc.; yet the **morph** {berry} in *palberry* comes not from English but from one of the Aboriginal languages (Morris 1972), where the name is *palbri*, which just happens to match one of the common pronunciations of *-berry*.[3] A second example quoted by Taylor (1989: 216) is *yellow Monday*, *yellow Tuesday*, *green Monday* 'kinds of cicadas' < Yellow Monday Creek < Aboriginal proper name *Yel-lo-mun-dee* given to the creek. Here not only is a name which in fact had nothing to do with either yellow or Monday interpreted as if it did, but variants of the first type of insect named after the creek near which they presumably live are named with **taxonomic sisters** of either the colour name or the weekday name, or both.

Exercise 4.2: Loan words and loan translations

(a) For each item tell whether it is a loan word or a loan translation. In the case of loan words what changes have been made to anglicize the words?
(b) Say where each item came from (source language).
(c) Say whether the item is from AusE, NZE, or SAE.

1. aardwolf
2. bandicoot

---

2 However, a number of Yiddish words beginning in <s(c)hl->, <s(c)hm->, or <s(c)hn-> are found in AmE and consequently in other varieties as well: *s(c)hlep, s(c)hlock, s(c)hmo(e), s(c)hmuck, s(c)hmal(t)z, s(c)hnook, schnoz*.
3 Morris calls this a 'corruption' of *Palbri* via the law of Hobson-Jobson, which is a reference to Yule (on Indian English): 'Oriental words highly assimilated, perhaps by vulgar lips, to the English vernacular' (Yule 1969: p. ix).

3. camelthorn (tree)
4. dallgyte
5. elephant's food
6. kai
7. marae
8. yallera

Resources you might use: *Dictionary of South African English, Macquarie, Australian Concise Oxford Dictionary.*

4.3.2 Word formation

A further way besides borrowing in which the vocabulary of English has expanded to accommodate to the natural and social world in which it is used has been to employ means internal to the language itself for devising new words. This is the area of **word formation** (or **lexical morphology**), and it includes what is known as **composition/compounding** and **derivation**.

Among the more recent additions to English, derivations and compounds account for 54.9 per cent; conversions for 19.6 per cent, and shortenings for 18 per cent, while new meanings (14.4 per cent) and borrowing (7.5 per cent) are less prominent (cf. Cannon 1987: 279; summarized in Gramley and Pätzold 1992: 23). The specific regional contributions of Australia, New Zealand, and South Africa to English vocabulary seem to rely perhaps more on borrowing than is the case for English as a whole, but compounds are also very prominent (§4.3.1), as are semantic shifts (§4.5). Derivations (§4.3.2.2) and shortenings (§4.3.2.4) follow, while blends represent only a small source of additions (§4.3.2.5). These comments about southern hemisphere English are, we must warn, impressionistic; actual attempts at counts are not available to us.

4.3.2.1 Compounds

A **compound** is the result of the process of putting together two (or more) individual words to form a complex word. For instance, the word *bush*, which is the usual Australian word for woods or forest-like lands (common in South Africa and New Zealand as well), is combined with *tucker*, a common Australian word for both food and eating, to make the compound *bush tucker* 'plain food, as can be got from the woods'. Both elements in a compound can occur independently and are therefore called **free morphs**.

Compounding is perhaps the most common way of expanding the vocabulary of English. It allows users to combine two familiar words to form a new lexeme. Furthermore, such combinations are largely **transparent**, as we see in the example of *bush tucker*. This means that there is an obvious combination of the meanings of the individual words to make up the meaning of the new combined form. This is known as the principle of **compositionality**.

Very often compounds are written as two words, which means that they are accepted into dictionaries a little reluctantly. Certainly, dictionaries seem not to list compounds in anything like the numbers in which they are in use. This may be justified perhaps because compounds are frequently transparent and their meanings are relatively accessible without a dictionary. Furthermore, many of them do not become lexicalized,[4] but have a very transitory life.

Case study 4.1: The Australian bush

We will use the example of *bush* as the point of departure for further observations on compounding. *Bush* itself may have come, in its specifically Australian incarnation, ultimately from AmE (Ramson 1981: 41); but surely the South African usage, reinforced by the Dutch word *bosch* (Baker 1966: 75), also has been influential. It is used to refer to wooded lands and has largely displaced the British and American words *woods* and *forest*. As such it is a genuinely Australian word, and the compounds it appears in will therefore be equally Australian (or South African or New Zealand) in provenance.

Bush is a frequent compound element, more than a page and over 60 main entries in the *Macquarie Dictionary* (Delbridge 1981). Although some of the entries are derived from the meaning of *bush* in the sense of a shrub (e.g. the North American *bushtit*, a chickadee-like bird), most are (1) based on the meaning 'land covered with bushy vegetation or trees' (*Macquarie*). This is then (2) associated with an extended meaning 'the countryside in general, as opposed to the towns'. Then, in the manner of city people all over the world, who tend to consider city life urbane and sophisticated *vis-à-vis* rustic and unrefined country life (though the latter is often nostalgically regarded as quaint),[5] *bush* (3) takes on the meaning of 'uncivilised; rough; makeshift'. This means that Australian compounds including *bush* will modify the element they are combined with in one of these senses. So *bush bashing* makes use of meaning (1): 'clearing virgin bush' or 'making a path through virgin bush'. But a *bush ballad* has meaning (2), a ballad 'dealing with aspects of life in the Australian bush', while *bush breakfast* represents meaning (3) 'a rough, improvised breakfast partaken of while camping in the bush'.

Exercise 4.3: Compounds with bush

Find out whether the following are AusE, NZE, SAE, or AmE (or more than one of them) in provenance. For the AusE terms decide whether meaning (1), (2), or (3) as given above is the more prominent. Which of the terms may now be regarded as a part of GenE?

4 A compound which has been become lexicalized has attained a certain amount of institutionalization: it is recognized and used over a longer period of time and in a larger speech community. It is no longer a **nonce** from. Often **lexicalization** is connected with some non-transparent, or **opaque**, specialization of meaning, Cf. Bauer (1983: ch. 3).

5 Cf. *boor/boorish/boring* (cf. also Boer) or *villain*, all derived from words for 'farmer' or 'farm worker'; cf. §4.5.2 on pejoration.

	Regional provenance	Meaning	(if AusE) 1, 2, 3
1. bushbaby			
2. bush carpenter			
3. bushcraft			
4. bush cure			
5. bush-faller			
6. bush farm			
7. bushfire			
8. bush lawyer			
9. bush league			
10. bush-line			
11. bushman/Bushman			
12. bush-pilot			
13. bushrat			
14. bush week			
15. bushwhacker			

Resources you might use: *Dictionary of South African English, Macquarie, Australian Concise Oxford Dictionary, Random House Webster's College Dictionary.*

4.3.2.2 Derivation

Among the processes[6] involved in derivation, two of the most frequent have to do with whether some element is added to the original lexeme (or **base**) and/or whether an element of the original word is cut out of the word or not. A combination of these two factors gives us four different paradigmatic cases, as shown in Table 4.3.

Conversion or *zero derivation* is a type of *word class* change without the addition, removal, or change of any element in the word. In this process a noun may be used as a verb (e.g. *a radio > to radio*; *a telephone > to telephone*) or a verb can be used as a noun (*to jump > a jump*; *to read > a read*). Furthermore, a noun can be used attributively as an adjective, cf. *fun* (n.) as in *a fun thing*. Even prepositions/particles like *out, down, up*, etc. can become verbs (*to out (as a gay)*, *to down (a drink)*, *to up (the stakes)*, etc.). The most frequent type of conversion is from noun to verb, probably because there are so relatively few verbalizing affixes in English.

Table 4.3. Processes of word formation

Process	Combination	Deletion	Example
Conversion	−	−	out (prep.) → to out (v.)
Blend	+	+	br(eakfast) + (l)unch → brunch
Clipping (shortening)	−	+	kangaroo → roo
Affixation	+	−	milk + o → milko

---

6 Other processes not dealt with: internal change of vowel (*sing : song*), of consonant (*extend : extent*), or of stress (*éxport : expórt*)

The only derivative morphemes PE [Present-day English] has for denominal verbs are -*ate*, -*ize*, -*ify*. They have restricted range of derivative force: -*ate* is latinizing and learned, -*ify* is learned while -*ize* is chiefly technical. All three derive almost exclusively on a Latin morphologic basis. . . . English *be*- has never played a serious role in denominal derivation . . . . Nor has the type *em-bed* ever become productive to any larger extent. (Marchand 1960: 296)

The English of Australia, New Zealand, and South Africa is fully integrated in the process of conversion. Examples from AusE include the following: *ocker* (n.) 'the archetypal uncultivated Australian working man' (*Macquarie*) used attributively as in *ocker humour*; *boomerang* (n.) 'throwing stick that returns' and *to boomerang* (v.) 'to backfire'; or *kangaroo* (n.), the animal and *to kangaroo* (v.) '(of a car) to move forward in a jerky manner' (*Macquarie*).

4.3.2.3 Affixation
Affixation is a process in which a free morph is combined with a bound morph, a prefix, or a suffix. Modern English has a number of highly productive affixes. For example, the prefix {over-} can be added to verbs which express activities to indicate that too much has taken place, i.e. something has been *overdone*, cf. *overcook*, *overeat*, *overstay* (*a welcome*). Likewise, the suffix {-ness} can be added to an adjective to make a noun designating the quality expressed by the adjective, its *nouniness*, so to speak.

Once again the Englishes of Australia, New Zealand, and South Africa are not essentially different. A few elements may, however, be especially typical of the one or the other variety such as derivations in {-Y} and {-O} (see §4.3.2.4).

4.3.2.4 Clipping
Speakers of English have a great tendency to shorten words. Often it may even be hard to reconstruct the original unclipped source. Who besides the linguistically well informed know that *bus* comes from Latin *omnibus* 'for everyone' or that *pants* comes from *pantaloons*, ultimately named after an Italian buffoon who wore pants (close-fitting trousers). Many more clippings are simply alternatives of longer forms, e.g. *specs* < *spectacles* or *specifications*, *bra* < *brassiere*, *gas* < *gasoline*, *petrol* < *petroleum*.

Australians are no different from other speakers of English in this sense, contributing clippings such as *Abo* < *Aborigine*, *com* < *communist*, *kanga* (or *roo*) < *kangaroo*.

Clipping + {-Y}. The clipped form is often given a **diminutive suffix** as in SAE *trooper* > *troop* + *ie* 'lowest ranking soldier'; *tante* > *tann* + *ie* 'aunt' (from Afrikaans *tante*); *terrorist* > *terr* + *y*. The suffix serves to make the final word more familiar, sometimes endearing (*tannie*), but it can also be used disparagingly as in commie (< *communist*). The ending itself is spelled either as <-y> or as <-ie>, with no apparent reason why one or the other is used.

AusE seems, more than other varieties, to add a {-Y} to clipped forms (Dabke 1976: 40). For instance, *Australian* is clipped to *Aus and expanded to *Aussy*, or, more affectionately, *Ozzie*. Furthermore, the pronunciation of <-ss> in *Aussy* and of <-zz-> in *Ozzie* is voiced /z/. This seems to be a regular process in AusE and may be seen as emotive (cf. Dabke 1976: 43f.). Other examples are *Terry* >*Tezza, Karen* > *Kazza*, or *Sharon* > *Shazza*.

The suffix {-Y} (without clipping) is also frequently added to words in GenE (pure affixation). The effect of the {-Y} goes in same two directions. For one, it can produce a diminutive, esp. with proper names, e.g. *Bill* > *Billy*; *Ruth* > *Ruthy*; *Dad* > *Daddy*. For another, it can be disparaging, as in de-adjectival AusE *swiftie* ('deceitful trick').

However, the suffix {-Y} is also used in a third way to indicate an animate being that is, in some often unpredictable manner, involved in an activity revolving around the base lexeme. GenE examples are *booky* ('a bookmaker at a betting office') or *cabby* ('a taxi cab driver'). In AusE a *surfie* is 'a devotee of surfing, esp. of surf-board riding' (*Macquarie*). Going back, for example, to our item *bush*, a *bushie*[7] is 'a person, usu. unsophisticated and uncultivated, who lives in the bush. Cf. *townie*' (*Macquarie*). But note how variable and unpredictable the meaning can be: 'Among bus and truck drivers *bushy* . . . means "a stop in the middle of the bush" (Dabke 1976: 40).[8] Words involving this third use of {-Y} are not necessarily endearing or derogatory; they are merely informal and may 'evoke the especially tough world of the Australian male' (Dabke 1976: 41).

A fourth and final use of {-Y} is as a suffix to adjectives which become nouns and refer to something with the quality of the adjective. A *fastie* is, therefore, a deceitful practice (cf. *swiftie*, mentioned above, and at least one meaning of *quickie*), and a *littlie* is a 'small child'. As these examples indicate, it is unpredictable where and how the meaning of the adjective will apply. Furthermore, to judge from the list in Baker (1966: 369–73) there seem to be many examples of all four {-Y} types whose half-life is quite brief. For example, *falsy* is given by Dabke as 'faked registration form' (1976: 42), but *falsies* (plural only) show up in *ACOD* and the *Macquarie* only in the meaning of breast contour enhancers, which is the meaning found in other varieties as well. For a more recent list, see the *Australian Phrasebook* (Angelo *et al.* 1998: 34ff.).

---

7 Spelling of {-Y} varies unpredictably between <-y> and <-ie>. However, note that *Macquarie* distinguishes between a *surfie* (n.) and *surfy* (adj.) 'abounding with surf; forming or resembling surf'; cf. also *bushie* (n.) and *bushy* (adj.) '1. resembling a bush. 2. full of or overgrown with bushes'. Non-Australian dictionaries do not include these '-ie' meanings; ACOD has only the one spelling, *bushy*, but both meanings, and it only has the "Austrailian" meaning of *surfie*.

8 Some forms in {-Y} may be inanimate such as *wheely* for the action of making 'violent accelerating and skidding turn or start in motor vehicle' or 'travelling short distance with front wheel(s) off ground' (ACOD).

Exercise 4.4: The ending {-y, -ie}

All of the following words can take {-Y}. Your task is to mark with a (1) those which are clipped before suffixation (as diminutives); with a (2) those which add the suffix without clipping, but with a diminutive effect; with a (3) those where the suffix is associated with some animate being carrying out an activity associated with the base; and with a (4) those designating something with the quality of the adjective base. Give the meaning; double-check in an Australian source.

	1, 2, 3, 4	Meaning
1. bikkie		
2. bluey		
3. brassie		
4. Brizzie		
5. broomie		
6. cozzie		
7. darkie		
8. hottie		
9. kookie		
10. matey		
11. milky		
12. swaggy		
13. trucky		
14. weirdy		
15. wharfy		

Resources you might use: *Macquarie, Australian Concise Oxford Dictionary*, Baker (1966).

Clipping + {-O}. An Australian who suggests meeting *this arvo* (or *sarvo*) has used just a clipping in {-O}: *afternoon* has been shortened to *af* and then the *suffix* {-O} has been added. The letter <r> is only there to indicate that the <a> is pronounced as a broad /aː/, but is not itself pronounced. The /f/ of *afternoon* has been softened to a voiced /v/, possibly to add an emotive note (see comments above on *Ozzie*). The forms *afto* and *aftie* are alternative versions. {-O} like {-Y} turns up perhaps more often in Australia and New Zealand than elsewhere. {-O}, like {-Y}, is found in (1) diminutives, both endearing ones (*Billo*, more intimate than *Billy*, cf. Dabke 1976: 45f.) and derogatory ones (*commo* 'communist, commie'); (2) diminutives without clipping (*kiddo*); (3) someone associated with an activity (*milko* 'milkman', no different from *milky*) or an activity *smoko* ('break from work for a smoke or tea'); (4) something with the quality of the adjective base (*weirdo* 'weird, strange'). The parallelism between {Y} and {O} is quite obvious.

4.3.2.5 Blends, abbreviations, acronyms

Blends or *portmanteau words* are combinations of parts of two different words, one or both of which have been clipped before being put together.[9] A recent AmE creation is *bobo* (*bourgeois-bohemian*) used somewhat disparagingly of certain types of person. Frequently the end of the first word and the beginning of the second is missing. Table 4.4 shows some of the better-known examples of this.

Abbreviations and *acronyms* are shortenings which are treated as independent means of word formation. An abbreviation is an expression consisting of the initial letters of a phrase whose meaning it carries, each pronounced as a letter. An example is GenE *BO* /biːəʊ/ 'body odour'. More specially AusE is AAP /eɪeɪˈpiː/ for the Australian Associated Press, AAT /eɪeɪˈtiː/ for Australian Antarctic Territory, or ABC /eɪbiːˈsiː/ for the Australian Broadcasting Commission/ Corporation. The examples given are probably typical of abbreviations: they are commonly used instead of the full names of organizations. And inasmuch as national organizations are not always well known outside their own country, they belong to the distinct vocabulary of the given national variety.

Acronyms differ only inasmuch as the initials make up or can be construed to make up a pronounceable word. UPE /ˈjuːpiːˈiː/, an abbreviation for the South African University of Port Elizabeth, is attended by *Uppies*, an acronym for UPE students. And the University of South Africa is Unisa /juːˈniːsə/ or /juːˈnaɪsə/. Perhaps the best-known South African acronym is Soweto (< South West Township). Some of the most widely recognized ones from AusE and/or NZE are

Table 4.4. GenE and AusE blends

smoke	+ fog	=	smog
motor	+ hotel	=	motel
breakfast	+ lunch	=	brunch
slimy	+ lithe	=	slithy
sky	+ hijack	=	skyjack

Among the AusE contributions to this area we find

aboriginal	+ originality	=	aboriginality
jack	+ kangaroo	=	jackaroo (*also:* jackeroo)
jill	+ kangaroo	=	jillaroo
squatter	+ aristocracy	=	squattocracy

9 We can return to Alice in Wonderland, who, when she asked Humpty-Dumpty to explain the poem 'Jabberwocky', was told:
'Well, 'slithy' means 'lithe and slimy'. 'Lithe' is the same as 'active'. You see it's like a portmanteau - there are two meanings packed up into one word.' (*Through the Looking-Glass*)

ANZAC from the First World War (< Australian New Zealand Army Corps), ANZUS, the Pacific defence alliance (< Australia, New Zealand, US), COAG (< Council of Australian Governments), and *wowser*, said to come from '*We Only Want Social Evils Remedied*' ('puritanical, moralistic person').

4.4 STANDARD AND NON-STANDARD

In this section we will look at how some varieties which exist in English alongside GenE have left their imprint on English in Australia and New Zealand.

4.4.1 Words from other varieties of English as a resource

Aside from the introduction of new words for new things, which we observed in §4.3, language change is dependent on the presence of alternative words or structures to express what is essentially 'the same thing'. Two or more equivalent forms may exist for a long time side by side, sometimes with only small differences in meaning. That is, for example, the case with *begin* and *start*, two lexemes which are often, but not always, mutually replaceable (you can *start* a car, but you cannot *begin* one; you can be a *beginner* at university, but not a *starter*). However, in such pairs one lexeme may eventually displace the other, as was the case when *mote*, which existed side by side with *may* for hundreds of years, was totally replaced by it.

Often enough a word disappears from the standard language but continues to be used in a local dialect. When such a local form is carried overseas, as was often the case when North America, Australia, New Zealand, and South Africa were settled by emigrants from the British Isles, a formerly local word may show up in a broader spectrum of use and may become standard in the developing variety. AmE words like *fall* ('autumn'), a *deck* (BrE *pack*) of cards, or the past participle *gotten* (where BrE has *got*) are such cases.

In AusE and NZE there are a number of such cases. The following exercise gives you the opportunity to find out about a few of them.

Exercise 4.5: Dialect and standard

The left-hand list contains words common in AusE and NZE, though sometimes colloquial in style. The right-hand list contains AmE and BrE equivalents. Match the lists by letter.

1. billy	_____	a. bundle
2. bonzer	_____	b. genuine
3. cobber	_____	c. can or pail
4. crook	_____	d. idiot
5. dag	_____	e. mate
6. dinkum	_____	f. racket, scam
7. larrikin	_____	g. rowdy

8. lurk	_____	h. sick
9. nong	_____	i. stand a round of drinks
10. shout	_____	j. terrific
11. swag	_____	k. unkempt, untidy person

Resources you might use: *Macquarie, Australian Concise Oxford Dictionary*.

4.4.2 Aboriginal English

In parts of Queensland and Western Australia as well as in the Northern Territory, Aboriginals who once spoke mutually unintelligible mother tongues have frequently adopted a common language which varies between a creole such as (Roper) Kriol or Torres Strait Broken (Cape York Creole) and a non-standard form of English often called Aboriginal English. The latter, which is spoken especially in remote areas, is 'used generally to denote speech varieties between so-called St AusE and creoles' (Sandefur 1983: 55). Both the creoles and Aboriginal English are recognized as mother tongues in bilingual educational programmes.

> These Creoles are distinct languages. . . . They show an ingenious blend of English and Australian structural features, producing a language that seems quite appropriate to the bicultural milieu in which many Aboriginal Australians find themselves. (Dixon 1980: 73f.)

How this can work is demonstrated in the system of personal pronouns of Kriol (Case study 6.5).

4.5 MEANING CHANGE

4.5.1 Denotation: semantic broadening and narrowing

Change in vocabulary is not only morphological as dealt with so far, it also has to do with additions of meaning or *semantic broadening*, as when a word like *bush*, which in AmE and BrE has little association with wooded countryside, takes on this additional element of meaning. In such a case we can speak of the extension of meaning to a new class of referents. But note that broadening of meaning can also include an extension of the field of collocation, as when *buy into* (normally: *a business*) is extended to *buying into* an argument in AusE (*ACOD*), or the field of application expands, as with NZE *cadet*, which is applied not only to the military, but also to someone learning sheep-farming (*ACOD*). AusE *mob* is not restricted to people but includes animals (*a mob of cattle*) or even mass nouns (*mobs of booze*). Furthermore, it can be used as an intensifier (*it's mobs better*).

The converse of semantic broadening is *semantic narrowing*. This can involve the addition of semantic features, which has the effect of limiting what a word can refer to. A classical case of this is the word *corn*, which traditionally has the following features:

> [+grain, seed]
> [+edible]   = 'cereal'

In AusE (as in AmE) the meaning of *corn* has been narrowed by the addition of:

> [+Zea mays] = 'maize'

One of the grounds postulated for this semantic shift is that maize was the dominant type of grain grown in the early years of settlement. It became the default reading of *corn* just as the default reading in England is *wheat* and in Scotland and Ireland, *oats*.

Case study 4.2: Settling the land

It is often features of the land that lead to such shifts. The superabundance of trees in America in frontier times made them a bother, hence the use of the word *lumber* for timber, a usage typically North American. BrE *creek* 'a narrow inlet from the sea' has come to mean a small stream, tributary to a river in both North America and Australia, where many a (BrE) creek turned out upon further exploration to be an (AmE/AusE) creek.

A further consequence of settling a 'new' (for Europeans) land is naming places.[10] Australia, New Zealand, and South Africa have drawn on the same set of principles as other colonial lands heavily settled by European emigrants. One major source of names comprised the names already in use by the indigenous peoples. Other sources are European place names, the names of important or prominent persons, topographically oriented names, and, finally, wishful or whimsical ones:[11] see Table 4.5.

Besides naming the land, Europeans administered it by dividing it up in order to make private ownership possible. In this process Australia followed the lead of the US in making land available by dividing it up into areas one mile wide on all four sides, which is called a *section*. Exercise 4.6 works with a number of words used to describe the land or features of the way it was settled in Australia, but also aspects of urban settlement, all of which are typically Australian.

---

10 Cf. Ekwall (1970) for England; Stewart (1970) for the US, Orkin (1971) for Canada, Friel (1981) for Ireland.
11 Not agreeing on how to pronounce the name *Eurelia* one conductor was said to have walked through the train announcing *You're a liar* only to be followed by a second reinforcing the first with *You really are* (cf. Turner 1972: 198).

Table 4.5. Place names

	Australia	New Zealand	South Africa
Indigenous	Wagga Wagga	Kaitangata	Thabazimbi
	Katoomba	Wanganui	Umzinto
European place names	New South Wales	Richmond	East London
	Perth	New Plymouth	Aberdeen
Prominent persons	Tasmania	Wellington	Port Elizabeth
	Victoria	Queenstown	Prince Albert
Descriptive	Salt Lake	Bluff	Silver Streams
	Great Sandy Desert	Cloudy Bay	Oatlands
Wishful, whimsical	Mt Curious	Chaslands Mistake	Good Hope
	Disaster Beach	Hen and Chickens Islands	Hole in the Wall

Exercise 4.6: Semantic shift

The following words are either totally distinct to AusE or have a meaning in AusE different from AmE or BrE.
(a) Give a definition of the term and
(b) mark it as totally distinctive of the variety or,
(c) if different, mark it as a case of broadening or narrowing.

1. bachelor flats
2. black stump, beyond the
3. block
4. bush
5. duplex
6. flatettes
7. granny flat
8. home unit
9. homestead
10. never-never
11. outback
12. o.y.o. (own your own)
13. paddock
14. project houses
15. scrub
16. squatter
17. the suburbs
18. station
19. township
20. villa homes

Resources you might use: *Australian Phrasebook, Macquarie, Australian Concise Oxford Dictionary*.

Case study 4.3: AmE and BrE models for political institutions

The words used in Exercise 4.6 were chosen because they represent the further development of GenE words. We should note that AusE has relied on both BrE and AmE for some of the vocabulary[12] needed to describe the settlement of a new country.

Political institutions, while clearly Australian in character and content, have drawn on both AmE and BrE usage. American influence is reflected in the use of *section*, and also the division of Australia into states and territories, each with its own nickname, much like American states: *Apple Isle* (Tasmania), *Festival State* (South Australia), *Garden State* (Victoria), *Outback Australia* (Northern Territory), *Premier State* (New South Wales), *Sunshine State* (Queensland), and *State of Excitement* (Western Australia). Furthermore, each state is headed by a governor and has its own capital. There is a separate ACT (Australian Capital Territory) for the capital at Canberra – reminiscent of Washington, DC (District of Columbia, also a non-state, federal territory). The federal *parliament* (not AmE *Congress*), meeting at Parliament House, consists of two houses, a lower *House of Representatives* (not BrE *Commons*), and a higher *Senate* (not BrE *Lords*). For the time being, the head of state is the Queen, represented by her Governor-General and the head of the government (not AmE *administration*) is the prime minister (not the AmE *president*).

Case study 4.4: Means of transportation

Borrowing words for new experiences is not a recent process, nor one that has only come about as international travel and the new media have brought people from distant parts of the world into ever greater contact. Rather, it has been a part of the reality of English ever since the period of overseas expansion began. We have picked transportation as an area central to the spread of English, and we will use this area to see how AmE, AusE, and BrE are related.

Transportation made overseas expansion possible in the first place, and part and parcel of this has been a continuous progression of inventions. The earliest of these were in the area of sailing. So not unexpectedly, English vocabulary in this area is relatively unified, as English overseas expansion had not yet begun. However, the English-speaking world was divided by the time canal-building developed and, soon afterwards, the train came into use. Here the vocabularies of AmE and BrE vary. The car and air travel came in at the high point of

12 In this context the following remarks about NZE are especially interesting 'Given a pair such as *torch* and *flashlight*, the British version is the one most likely to be used in everyday speech, and the American one is likely to be used commercially, to make the product sound more appealing. Thus one would normally pull the *curtains*, but the shop might sell you *drapes*. Other pairs with a similar relationship are *lift/elevator*, *nappy/diaper*, and possibly (although there may be a semantic distinction here) *biscuit/cookie*'. (Bauer 1994: 419)

separation of AmE from BrE. Not surprisingly, the vocabulary differences are especially noticeable here. The question which will interest us here is, 'Where does the vocabulary of transportation in AusE come from?' Traditions vary considerably, as we see with even such low-tech vehicles as *baby carriages* (older: *baby buggy*) (AmE) or *prams* (older: *perambulator*) (BrE, AusE) for infants, and *strollers* (AmE) or *push chairs* (BrE) for young children, where AusE has *strollers*, *pushchairs*, and *pushers*. Older Australian kids *dink* (in South Australia they *donkey*) when they *double* (AmE) on a bike. These examples probably reflect the situation well. AusE usually follows the lead of BrE, sometimes adopts lexemes from AmE, and also sometimes offers its own word.

A further example of how terms differ and interlock – despite the growing global market – can be seen in Fig. 4.1.

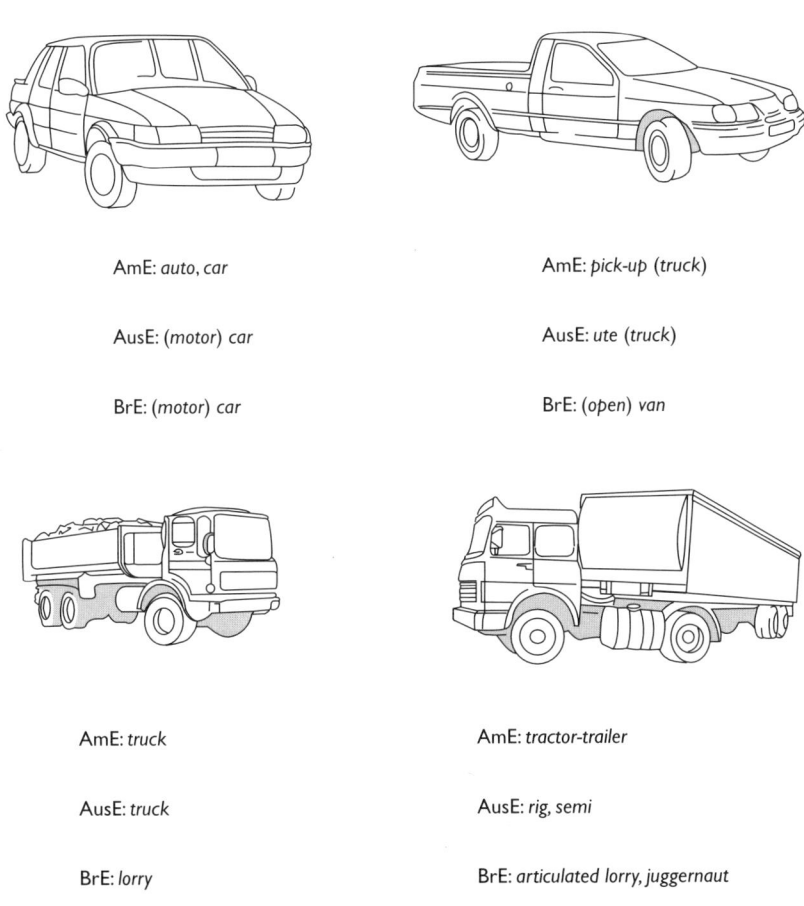

AmE: *auto, car*

AusE: *(motor) car*

BrE: *(motor) car*

AmE: *pick-up* (*truck*)

AusE: *ute* (*truck*)

BrE: *(open) van*

AmE: *truck*

AusE: *truck*

BrE: *lorry*

AmE: *tractor-trailer*

AusE: *rig, semi*

BrE: *articulated lorry, juggernaut*

Fig. 4.1. Vehicle names

Exercise 4.7: AmE, AusE, and BrE vocabulary in the field of transportation

In the following you will find two parallel lists of terms from the area of transportation which in most cases differ in BrE and AmE. You are to complete the third column, which has been provided for AusE. This can give us an insight into the relative influence of AmE and BrE on AusE, as well as some idea of the degree of its independence.

AmE	BrE	AusE
Automobiles		
1. fender	mudguard	
2. hood	bonnet	
3. trunk	boot	
4. carburetor	carburettor	
5. bumper	bumper	
6. (house) trailer	caravan	
7. gas(oline)	petrol	
Streets and roads		
1. interstate, freeway, expressway, superhighway, throughway	motorway	
2. asphalt, macadam, blacktop road	asphalt, bitumen, tarmac road	
3. speed bump	speed bump, sleeping policeman	
4. parking space	parking place	
5. sidewalk	pavement	
6. shoulder, verge	verge	
Trains		
1. (train) engineer	engine-driver	
2. conductor	guard	
3. cow catcher	–	
4. bumper	buffer	
Planes		
1. airplane	aeroplane	
2. runway	tarmac/runway	

Resources you might use: *Macquarie, Australian Concise Oxford Dictionary*.

4.5.2 Connotation: amelioration and pejoration

The two phenomena of broadening and narrowing are not enough to cover semantic change adequately. There are also changes in which the associations, or *connotations*, of a word take on a new character. When a word is upgraded it adopts a more positive meaning, and we speak of **amelioration**. The converse of this, **pejoration**, is the case when a word takes on a more negative or derogatory meaning. The word *witch*, for example, is traditionally connected with evil and magic, and witches are generally conceived of as old and ugly women. Evidence for this lies in the appearance of and the role attributed to witches in fairy tales. The matrix of semantic features for *witch* might look as follows:

[+woman]
[+practitioner of black magic]

These two features cover the first meaning under the entry for *witch*[1] (n.) in *Macquarie* adequately.

> 1. a person, now esp. a woman, who professes or is supposed to practise magic, esp. black magic or the black art; a sorceress.

This, of course, disregards the older usage according to which a witch might be a man. However, this is probably well justified in light of the fact that nowadays a man who is a witch would be designated as a *male witch*. The definition does not exclude, but also does not explicitly include, those who practise white magic (positive, force for good), *white witches*. These are somewhat ideological, certainly controversial points which lie beyond the present discussion. But what about meanings 2 and 3 in the *Macquarie*?

> 2. an ugly or malignant old woman; a hag
> 3. a fascinatingly attractive woman

What has happened here is that features merely associated with the *witch* of definition 1 have attained the status of independent meanings: definition 2 picks up the negative connotation of *witch* and is, in this sense, an example of pejoration. Definition 3 has done just the opposite and stressed only the practice of magic, the enchanting or charming activities of an enchantress. Here we have amelioration.

4.6 TABOO WORDS AND EUPHEMISMS

This section continues the theme of amelioration and pejoration by examining the extreme case of pejoration. This is when a word grows so negative, chiefly because of its associations with a taboo[13] area, that it cannot be uttered at all, or can be used only under certain extenuating circumstances. Of course, just what areas are subject to taboos may vary from one English-speaking society to another. So it was that an American friend of mine who had first fallen on her behind and then skinned her knee ice skating could not understand the puzzled looks she got when she remarked at a church reception in England that she had 'fallen on her fanny and then bummed up her knee', which explained why she had a bloody knee (*fanny* AmE 'rear end, bottom', BrE 'female genitals'; *bum up* AmE 'hurt', BrE *bum* 'buttocks'; *bloody* AmE literally 'having bled', BrE mild expletive).

---

13 The word *taboo* has been borrowed into English from the Fijian (a Melanesian language) word *tabu* or the Tongan (a Polynesian language) word *tapu*. It has also been borrowed once again into English from Maori, another Polynesian language, as *tapu*, a word which describes the sacred or something which can only be dealt with in an often highly prescribed way. Cf. §4.3.1.1.

In this section we have chosen some of the more conventional areas of sensitivity and taboo in European-based culture: certain religious terms, ethnic group membership, elimination of bodily wastes, and sexual organs and sexual acts.

Not every word used to refer to these subjects is itself taboo. The very fact that they could be inoffensively named above is demonstration enough. This draws our attention to the different levels of vocabulary and the stylistic function often associated with them.

One of the many ways in which the vocabulary of English may be divided up is according to its etymological sources. Numerous **learned words** (a.k.a. **hard words**, cf. §2.1.4.1) have entered the English language from Latin or Greek; and because they are of less than everyday currency, they are felt to be immune from **vulgar** use. The vocabulary of the elimination of bodily wastes includes *defecation* (the release of feces) and *urination* (ditto of urine). While the subject itself is too delicate to be appropriate for casual conversation, there is no questioning the fact that the corresponding **taboo words**[14] of Germanic (*shit*) or Vulgar Latin (*piss*) origin are simply too drastic for 'polite' company. This leads then to the dilemma of a choice between the effete and the rude, not a welcome situation.

The most widespread way people deal with taboos without resorting to hard words is to devise new expressions which have an everyday colloquial quality to them without being offensive. Such words or expressions are called **euphemisms**. They may be used to stand in for a **four-letter word,** as when the mildly offensive word *hell* is rendered as the phonetically similar *heck*. Sometimes, indeed, the offending word is in fact quite innocent, as is the case with *hoar frost*, where *hoar* refers to the grey-white colour frost has. However, since *hoar* and *whore* are pronounced identically, the latter is tabooed by some speakers of English. So it is that we may find instead the expression *Jack Frost*, which is felt to be more appropriate to use when talking to children. Hence the 'cute' stories in children's books about an elfin figure (Jack Frost) coming to paint leaves and the like with his white frost.

Exercise 4.8: Euphemisms

Complete the following columns by supplying now the phonetically similar euphemism and now the taboo word. The tabooed terms stem ultimately from the areas of religion (= profanity), bodily excrements (= dirty words), or sex (= obscenities). Label the words accordingly.

---

14 Sometimes also called (Anglo-Saxon) **four-letter words** even though they need not be Anglo-Saxon (=Germanic) in origin (cf. *piss*), nor need they consist of only four letter (cf. *bitch*). The characterization fits the majority of them, nevertheless.

Taboo	Euphemism	Area
1. bloody	_____	_____
2. damn	_____	_____
3. _____	doggone	_____
4. _____	gosh	_____
5. _____	fudge	_____
6. _____	jeez	_____
7. shit		
8. _____	son of a biscuit eater	_____

Resources you might use: *The Slang Thesaurus.*

So long as an area of reference is itself the subject of contempt, disgust, or other negative attitudes, the result is a cycle of unending **semantic derogation**. This is particularly perfidious because the attitudes which lie below the surface of whatever words are used will contaminate one new term after the other. Stanley (1977) collected as many words as she could for both females and males as 'sexually available', for example, *honey pot* or *hustler*. She found (a) that there are far more such terms for women (220) than for men (she collected only 22) and (b) that all but four of the female terms (*lady of the night, entertainer, concubine, mistress*) are derogatory, i.e. demeaning and shameful (*leasepiece, loose woman*); they often involve allusion to cost (*put out, giftbox*) and frequently relie on **metonymy**, in which a part of the body stands for the whole (*ass, tail*), or on **metaphor**, especially animal metaphors (*bitch, bird*).

> Again and again in the history of the language, one finds that a perfectly innocent term designating a girl or woman may begin with totally neutral or even positive connotations, but that gradually it acquires negative implications, at first perhaps only slightly disparaging, but after a period of time becoming abusive and ending as a sexual slur. (Schulz 1975: 65)

The association with sex seems to contaminate the terms; consequently, there is a constant need to look for new euphemisms as one established term after the other undergoes semantic pejoration.

Case study 4.5: Ethnic designations and slurs

In the atmosphere of heightened sensitivity to ethnic group membership, Americans have abandoned the (public) use of offensive names for ethnic groups in favour of more neutral and acceptable terms. Sometimes this results in the successive replacement of one term by another seemingly *ad infinitum*. In the case shown in Fig. 4.2 the parent term for dark-skinned Americans of African origin is *negro* (today only acceptable in AmE when spelled with a capital <N>), which was borrowed from the Spanish word for 'black'. Only the last two in Fig. 4.2, which draw on ethnicity and origin, are independent of colour (= race); hence the dotted line.

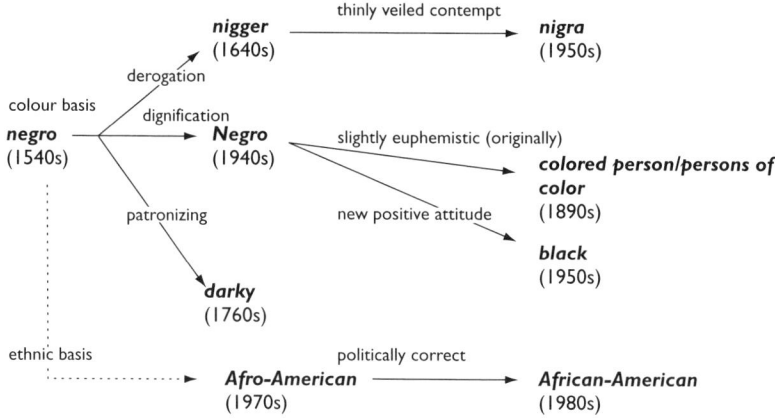

Fig. 4.2. Expressions for African-Americans in AmE

negro: disrespectful when not capitalized
Negro: acceptable, but dated
nigger: extremely offensive, a racial slur
darky/darkie: old-fashioned and patronizing
colored person: dated, sometimes offensive
nigra: short-lived thinly veiled white racist concession to civility ('*I won't say nigger, but I won't say Negro either*')
black: acceptable; probably most widely used
Afro-American: precursor of *African American*
African American: currently most politically correct

Exercise 4.9: Southern hemisphere terms for non-whites

Label the following often highly offensive ethnic-racial designations in terms of connotation. Indicate if a term is specifically AusE, NZE, or SAE.

1. Abo
2. blackbird
3. boong
4. coloured
5. darkie
6. hori
7. Indigenous Australian
8. Kaffir
9. Koori
10. nigger

Resources you might use: *Dictionary of South African English, Macquarie, Australian Concise Oxford Dictionary.*

Exercise 4.10: Generic names as euphemisms

Among the more common and better-known euphemisms, generic personal names play a prominent role. The example of *Jack Frost* was, for instance, quoted at the end of §4.6. The following exercise extends this area.

The names below are used generically and therefore not necessarily capitalized. They all serve as common nouns with colloquial meanings. Find at least two different uses of each; in most cases one is a euphemism. Are the individual uses regionally restricted? If so, to what region?

1. *dick*   use 1:
                         use 2:

2. *fanny*   use 1:
                         use 2:

3. *jack*   use 1:
                         use 2:

4. *jock*   use 1:
                         use 2:

5. *peter*   use 1:
                         use 2:

6. *willy*   use 1:
                         use 2:

Resources you might use: good desk dictionaries of different varieties (see Table 1.1).

Exercise 4.11: Tabooed animal names

Animal names are sometimes used as insults, often with sexual implications (*pig, swine, dog, vixen, cat, cow, stud*, etc.), but only a few have become tabooed and been replaced by euphemisms.

The items below are examples of animal names which are so strongly associated with taboos that they have been replaced by new, euphemistic designations for the animal concerned.

(a) For each give the euphemistic term which has replaced it.
(b) What has motivated the substitution in each case?
(c) Comment on regional restrictions if appropriate.

        ass →
        bitch →
        cock →
        coney →
        pussy →

Resources you might use: desk dictionaries (see Table 1.1), dictionaries of slang (see Table 1.6).

Project 4.1: Euphemisms and taboos for body parts and bodily functions

An investigation conducted by the author has shown that there seems to be a great deal of agreement between Australia, the British Isles, New Zealand, North America, and South Africa in regard to what is tabooed and what is considered an acceptable euphemism for the taboo expression. Some of the clearer divisions found are presented in the comments on the projects at the end of the book. However, before you look at them you should try to carry out your own survey.

The following is part of the questionnaire used to find out more about taboo language.

Try to get answers from some of the English-speakers in the area where you live and then compare them to the results found here. To what extent does the variety of English you have investigated fit the results from AmE, AusE, BrE, NZE, or SAE?

Project: The vocabulary of World English

Dear 'Informant,'
In connection with a project whose aim is to study similarities, but especially differences in the vocabulary of English in various areas of the English-speaking world, we would like to collect some information about your use of English. Although we are interested in a great many areas, we have limited our questions to only a few – ones in which there seems to be a great deal of local variation in use.
But first we would like you to note down a few (anonymous) points about yourself:

Where do you live (city or metropolitan area) or where have you lived for the most significant period of time as far as the way you talk English is concerned?

_____

How long have you lived there?
Sex:
Age:
Race/ethnicity (e.g. white, black, Irish, Jewish):
Class (e.g. working class, middle class):
Level of education (years of school, higher education/degrees):

Finally, do you assess yourself as a native speaker of English, as a speaker of a regional variety or other noticeable dialect, or as a second-language user of English?

TABOO WORDS AND EUPHEMISMS:
These questions may be embarrassing, so please regard them strictly as the subject of an investigation. You yourself may not talk about some of these things or use the terms we are interested in finding out about, but you may be aware of what other people of your sex, ethnicity, region, and general level of education use.

1. In the following list a neutral or technical word has been used. We are interested in what the tabooed (impolite, 'dirty') words for each of the following are. Can you also indicate what the everyday euphemistic (acceptable, informal, possibly used with children) expressions are?

Neutral	Taboo	Euphemistic
Example:		
buttocks	ass/arse	bottom
faeces		
urine		
intestinal gas		
penis		
vagina		
female breasts		

2. What expressions are used to make exclamations of disgust, despair, etc.? Please answer in the senses indicated.

Taboo	Euphemistic (acceptable substitute)
Example:	
Oh shit	shoot, shucks

Project 4.2: Follow-up project

Our investigation showed a remarkable degree of, but not complete, 'globalization' in the use of taboo and euphemistic terms. Does your own local usage fit into this? If you find distinct local forms, name them and try to find out something about their currency. For example, who uses them? Are they older forms or newer ones? If so, can you confirm the usage as correlating with the age of the speaker? Are there noticeable differences in use between males and females?

4.7 SUMMARY

This chapter was concerned with questions of both vocabulary change and meaning change. In the area of vocabulary we looked at borrowing, both loan words and loan translations, but also at folk etymologies. We saw that borrowing shows up in words used for both the natural and the social world, as revealed by examples of expressions from Maori and Afrikaans as well as ones from Australian Aboriginal languages and Native American languages. The major types of word formation were also introduced: compounding, conversion, affixation, clipping, and also blends, abbreviations, and acronyms. This was followed by a brief look at non-standard varieties of English and at AmE and BrE as sources for AusE vocabulary.

The second half of the chapter dealt with meaning change. First, narrowing and broadening of meaning were exemplified in the fields of settlement of the land, of the terminology of political institutions (territorial units, political bodies), and of transportation. Then this review of vocabulary change was rounded out with an exploration of amelioration and pejoration as well as a closer look at taboo words and euphemisms, especially as regards ethnicity and bodily functions.

5 Whose English? English as a Second, Foreign, or International Language

There's a word for everything. (saying)

5.0 INTRODUCTION

This chapter is intended as a kind of introduction to Chapters 6–8. The emphasis will be on words in their social context. This means that our attention will turn from concentration on more strictly language-internal questions (*lexical semantics* and *word formation*) to a more external linguistic observation of vocabulary. We look, especially in Chapter 6, at vocabulary change in what are frequently called the *New Englishes* (the title of one of the increasingly many books about English in countries formerly in British or American colonial possession; cf. Pride 1982). We also examine, especially in Chapter 7, some of the communicative norms of *ENL* (English as a Native Language) as well those that ESL (English as a Second Language) has been adopting and continues to adopt in societies with cultures that do not derive from the traditional British homeland of the language. In Chapter 8 our attention turns to include aspects of the use of English, be it ENL, *ESL*, or *EFL* (English as a Foreign Language).

The present chapter provides some necessary background on: *language contact* (§5.1), especially in connection with ESL in Africa and Asia (§5.2); language features according to user characteristics, *dialects*, and variation according to the situation of use, *diatypes* (§5.3).

5.1 LANGUAGES IN CONTACT

In looking at languages in contact we will be dealing with several major geographical areas: West, East, and parts of Southern Africa as well as South and Southeast Asia. In each of these regions there are a number of anglophone countries which have a colonial past in common, but which often have very different language histories and language policies. As a result, even immediately neighbouring countries such as *Uganda*, *Kenya*, and *Tanzania* have not gone through equivalent developments. Consequently, the kinds of English used in each country are noticeably different from each other. The most obvious innovations in the New Englishes which distinguish them from ENL varieties as well as from other ESL varieties are lexical items.

What are the lexical fields, the lexical aspects of grammar, and the social and pragmatic practices which will best enable us to see the contributions of these countries to the English language? The lexical fields in which we can perhaps observe the most innovation are some of the same ones that we looked at in Chapter 4: fauna and flora. In order not to be too tedious, we will look at these areas only briefly, though long enough to get some idea of the special nature of English in these areas (§6.1).

What promises to be more fascinating is how English has been partially assimilated to non-English languages and non-European cultures, cases in which English linguistic elements are used differently because of the differing underlying linguistic categorization (§6.4), a different use of lexical expressions (§6.3.3), different modes of address (§7.2), lexical variation in pragmatic idioms (§7.3), but also variation in style and register (§8.1). We will look at some of these aspects in connection with social structures and practices, such as family structures and religious traditions, the class system, and the relations and attitudes between the generations and between the sexes. We will try to indicate some of the ways in which these factors have had or are having an impact on the language in both ESL and ENL countries. Above all, this will include a look at how people address each other and how they refer to others – especially via kinship terms and modes of address, both of which offer perhaps the best examples of *English across Cultures, Cultures across English*, to quote the title of yet another book (García and Otheguy 1989).

When speech communities centred around different languages come into contact with each other, and especially when the contact is protracted, they have a mutual influence on each other, especially through the process of borrowing. This can be in the area of pronunciation (phonetics and phonology), grammar (syntax and morphology), or, of course, vocabulary (semantics and lexicon).

5.1.1 Language status

When English is used by non-native speakers in countries where English is a *second language*, the type of English varies over a wide *continuum*. At one end there are extremely fluent anglophones who may have English as their *primary language*, if not *native language*, those who perhaps only seldom have any need or opportunity to use their original *native* or *first language*. At the other extreme is the very imperfectly learnt English of the 'unlicensed and self-appointed tourist guides, small shopkeepers, hotel-bearers, street vendors, narcotics dealers, porters, beggars, boatmen, rickshaw pullers, taxi-drivers, and commercial agents' (Mehrotra 1982: 156).

The terms just introduced plus *foreign language* (see esp. §8.3) can best be distinguished according to two criteria, how the language is used (its status) and how it is acquired (see Table 5.1). Note, however, that *first* and *foreign language* refer to two different things depending on whether they are defined by how they were learnt or how they are used; hence the subscript numbers in the following.

Table 5.1. Languages as native, first, second, foreign, and primary

Language	Mode of learning	Use
Native	'Natural', i.e. not learnt in the framework of formal instruction	May be used in situations in which it is a $first_2$, a second, a $foreign_2$, or a primary language
$First_1 \neq first_2$	$First_1$: first learned = native	$First_2$: official; main one used (default)
Second	Often learned in school	Government use; official status
$Foreign_1 \neq Foreign_2$	$Foreign_1$: often learned in school	$Foreign_2$: no official use/status; often taught in school
Primary	May be $first_1$/native, second, or $foreign_1$	Most frequently used

A $first_1$ language defined by mode of learning is the first one a person acquires, his or her native language. A $first_2$ language defined by use is one which has the status of an official language. A $foreign_1$ language according a mode of learning is a language someone learns after their native language. According to use, a $foreign_2$ language is one which has no official status in a given country.

A native language is one learnt naturally; it is usually the $first_1$ language someone learns. So from the point of view of learning, a native and a first language are identical. A second language, like a $foreign_1$ language, stands in contrast to a native or $first_1$ language because it has to be learnt, whereby the circumstances of learning may be relatively natural (through exposure to it in situations where it is used) or artificial (by means of formal teaching).

A primary language cannot be characterized by how it is learnt, for a $first_1$ or native language, a second language, and a $foreign_1$ language may all serve as a person's primary language, i.e. the language used most frequently. Many immigrants to English-speaking countries use English widely, or even exclusively. For them English is their primary language, but it can never become their native language. A native language, in contrast, cannot be characterized by how it is used, for it can be used in all sorts of framework, including ones where it is an official or $first_2$ language, a second language, or a $foreign_2$ language. When the immigrants just mentioned use their native language, say German, in an English-speaking country like Australia, it is a $foreign_2$ language from the point of view of its status.

5.1.2 English as a second language

In the case of English, second-language status is quite common. Not only are bilingual Canada (French–English) and Ireland (Irish–English) and multilingual South Africa (Afrikaans, Zulu, and other African languages plus English) cases where English is, for some people, a second language; in addition, English is a second language in numerous countries in Asia and West and East Africa, i.e. an official or semi-official language. This status is sometimes shared with one or more other languages. In these states English is typically not the native language of more than a (relative) handful of people.

Estimates of the number of second-language users of English are hard to substantiate and controversial.[1] Whatever the exact figure may be, 'English is the major language of wider communication and the primary natural language candidate for an international language in the world today' (Conrad and Fishman 1977: 7).

5.1.2.1 Domains (or areas of use)

One of the most obvious ways in which languages in contact affect each other involves the speakers' choice of language in multilingual communities. Which language do they use in the more intimate circle of the family, which at the market, the workplace, the place of worship, in public administration, the courts, the military, the national legislative body, etc.? This is the question of *domains* (Fig. 5.1).

English, an outside or *exogenous* language, has attained its prominent position as a second language in so many countries of Africa and Asia because of its importance in national unification as well as in education, technology, communication, and commerce, as the following list shows:

- the usefulness of English in science and technology as opposed to the less well elaborated vocabularies of the *vernaculars*;
- the availability of suitable schoolbooks in English;
- the status of English as an international language of wider communication, useful in trade and diplomacy;
- the lack of a single indigenous language that is widely accepted by the respective populations; here English is neutral *vis-à-vis* mutually competing native languages and hence helps to promote national unity. (cf. Gramley and Pätzold 1992: 420).

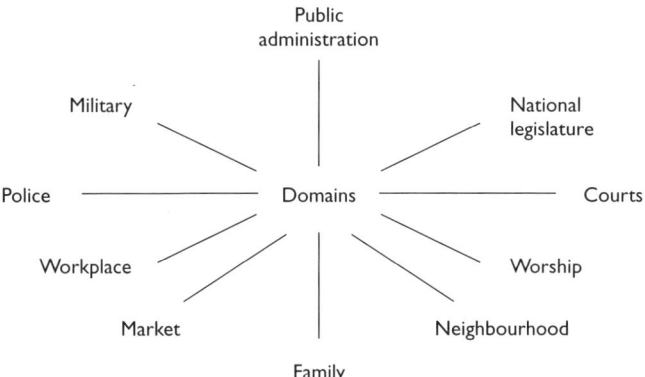

Fig. 5.1. Examples of domains (areas of use)

1 Cf. Crystal (1997), who opts for unrealistically high numbers: 450 million ENL users; an estimate of overall users (EFL, ESL, EFL) of 1.2–1.5 billion.

The first two reasons have to do with the fact that many of the native languages often do not have the terminologies and teaching materials at their disposal which English as a widely used international language does have. The development of vocabularies suitable for use in many fields of discourse, especially those of science and technology, demands precious resources in terms of both time and money. When there is a tradition of education in English (often a legacy of the colonial past), it is more economical to adopt English in these domains.

As the third point indicates, this is especially convenient in countries in which several regional native languages compete with each other. This is the case with *Hindi*, Telugu, Bengali, Tamil, etc. in India. Rather than recognize the priority of one of these (above all Hindi), many speakers in the south of India, where Hindi is not native, favour English as a 'neutral' outside language. In East Africa, in contrast, Kiswahili has been developed for use in more and more domains and is becoming the national language of Kenya and Tanzania. The same is true of Pilipino, a further 'national' development of *Tagalog* in the Philippines.

5.1.2.2 Diglossia

The kind of a situation in which the vernaculars and English are not usually in competition but, rather, are complementary often leads to what is known as *diglossia*:[2] English functions as a *High language*, i.e. it is used in formal and public situations and as the written language, while the local languages are the *Low languages*, whose domains are characterized by informal, private, vernacular, oral communication. In fact, it is possible to speak of *triglossia* in some countries: the low languages are the *autochthonous* languages; the intermediate languages are the various regional languages of wider communication; and at the top we find superimposed on the whole the outside or *exogenous language*, English (Brann 1988: 1416) (see Fig. 5.2).

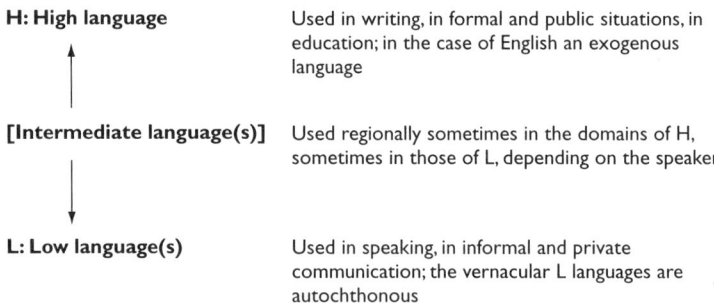

H: High language   Used in writing, in formal and public situations, in education; in the case of English an exogenous language

[Intermediate language(s)]   Used regionally sometimes in the domains of H, sometimes in those of L, depending on the speaker

L: Low language(s)   Used in speaking, in informal and private communication; the vernacular L languages are autochthonous

Fig. 5.2. The diglossic (triglossic) model

2 This concept stems originally from Ferguson (1964).

The relative prestige of the High language derives from its association with education, religion, business, or some other area of activity which is associated with power as opposed to a language which is more peripheral to the centre of power, the Low language.

English frequently remains an instrumental language and is less likely to be chosen in domains where emotions and feelings are important, areas such as family, neighbourhood, and worship. But even in societies which are highly multilingual and where there is a fair amount of language mixture (cf. 'mixed' marriages, multilingual West African residential compounds), as in parts of Nigeria, English may be used even in more intimate domains.

5.1.2.3 The language continuum

One form of English which is widely used throughout West Africa in the more informal domains is **Pidgin English.** It is especially important as a market language, and for some people who are fluent in StE it may be their stylistically more informal variety and in this sense may stand in **complementary distribution** with the StE. However, what interests us here is the fact that in those West African countries in which StE is the H language (or one of them) and where Pidgin English is also widely used, we find a kind of **continuum** which runs from British StE (in Liberia the orientation is toward AmE), through a local educated second-language variety, and a local vernacular, to West African Pidgin or a creolized variety of it. What is meant by 'continuum' is that there is a series of minimally different language varieties from a non-prestigious Low language or **basilect** via a series of increasingly more highly esteemed intermediate varieties or **mesolects** to StE, the High language or **acrolect**, the language of the establishment. This is what we find where English coexists with English-oriented **pidgins** or **creoles** (§§6.1.1+4 and Exercise 6.1); see Fig. 5.3.

This diversity of levels is one of the results of the history of European–African contact on the west coast of Africa. European imperialism from 1450 onwards led initially to trade contacts which gradually expanded as a part of the West Indian–American plantation and slave system, in which West Africa was the major source of slaves. Throughout the period of the

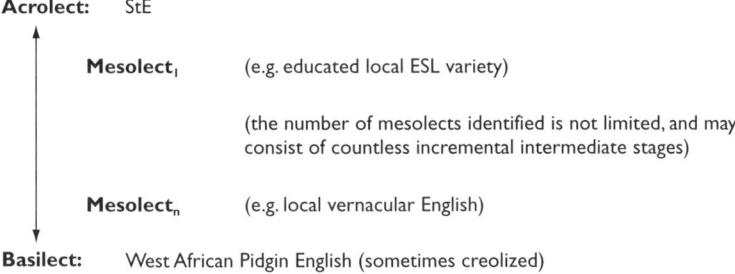

Fig. 5.3. The continuum model with a StE acrolect and a Pidgin English basilect

international slave trade (outlawed by Britain in 1807 and the US in 1808) Europeans and Africans did business using contact languages called *pidgins* (see §3.7).

Pidgin English, though not always in mutually intelligible forms, continues to be used today all along the West African coast from Gambia to Gabon. It is a diglossically Low language and as such may be considered to be an indigenous vernacular. Perhaps it is so easily learnt not only because it is simplified but also because it is structurally so close to the indigenous languages. Its range of domains is described, for Cameroon, as including use in connection with (manual) labour, church, market, playgrounds, pubs, prison, the armed forces, the police, and even courts (Todd 1982: 137).

Furthermore, *creolized* (mother tongue) forms of it are, as remarked above, in wide use in Sierra Leone. Creolized forms of Pidgin English continue to develop among the children of linguistically mixed marriages in urban centres, especially in Cameroon and Nigeria (see Shnukal and Marchese 1983; Agheyisi 1988).

5.1.2.4 EFL standards

English is unlikely to replace the vernaculars, although cases of exogenous languages replacing autochthonous ones are not unknown, as we can see in the historical cases of Latin and Arabic, where the following conditions applied:

(1) military conquest

(2) a long period of language imposition

(3) a polyglot subject group

(4) material benefits in the adoption of the conquerors' language (cf. Brosnahan 1963: 15–17)

Further factors are playing a role in Africa and Asia today:

(5) urbanization

(6) industrialization/economic development

(7) educational development

(8) religious orientation

(9) political affiliation (Fishman *et al.* 1977: 77–82)

In most of the countries where English is a second language the period of colonial contact was too short and the emotional rejection of English as a colonial language is too strong for replacement to be a serious probability. Yet the educated élite often take as much pride in their command of the language as they feel resentment at its intrusion. And it is they who are the speakers around whom possible 'local' standards, either a regional one such as Standard West African English or a national one such as Standard Nigerian English, are centred.

From the point of view of what the language is, the concept of second language is only gradually different from that of foreign language. For it is less the quality of a speaker's command than the status of the language within a given community that determines whether it is a second or a foreign language. In an unambiguous case a foreign language is, for example, a language learnt in school and employed for communicating with people from another country. A second language, in contrast, may well be one learnt in school too, but one used within the learner's country for offical purposes, i.e. 'by the government for its own internal operating and promoted through the power of the state' (Conrad and Fishman 1977: 8).

'So long as English continues to have the status of a second language (and not a foreign language) in India, it will create its own local standard' (Verma 1982: 176). This statement is perhaps not unreasonable; however, the idea of a local standard is not universally accepted. Kachru (1986a: 22) quotes a study in which two-thirds of the Indians questioned reported a preference for BrE and only just over a quarter accepted Indian English as their preferred model. Some scholars realize that IndE is not and cannot be identical with its one-time model, BrE, yet they have fears of a chaotic future in which 'English in India . . . will be found disintegrating into quite incomprehensible dialects' (Das 1982: 148). IndE has its own independent language tradition. Yet the English which most *educated* Indians produce is a part of international StE; there are, of course, differences in pronunciation, some in grammar, and a noticeable number in vocabulary and usage.

In Singapore the English language is probably undergoing indigenization into what might be called 'a semi-native variety' (Platt and Weber 1980: 48), as its range of domains (see §6.1) expands and it is used among friends and even in families (Platt 1991: 376).

Some scholars have emphasized the negative aspects of such 'nativization' or 'indigenization', which is said to tend towards a fall in (international) intelligibility (Prator 1968: 466, 473) and, in Africa for example, to 'preclude the development of African languages' (Bokamba 1983: 95). A neglect of the vernaculars includes the danger of producing 'thousands of linguistically, and hence culturally "displaced persons"'(Spencer 1963: 3). On the other hand, English may be spreading 'apparently accompanied by relatively little affect – whether positive or negative' (Fishman 1977: 126). 'In its Indianized variety, it has become a pan-Indian elite language' (Kachru 1988: 1283). Indeed, some would go so far as to maintain that, 'The use of a standard or informal variety of Singaporean, Nigerian, or Filipino English is . . . a part of what it means to *be* a Singaporean, a Nigerian, or a Filipino' (Richards 1982: 235).

5.1.2.5 The substratum

Another type of contact is more subtle and difficult to spot, and among the experts it is also the object of much controversy. When a language is introduced in an area where it is not native and when underlying linguistic and social categories of users' mother tongues shape the way they use English, some scholars speak of a ***substrate influence***. What this means is that non-English grammatical categories and non-English lexical-semantic conceptualizations change the face of the English used. Fig. 5.4 shows this, together with the familiar process of borrowing given here as typical of adstrate influence. It may, for example, be substrate influence which affects the use of grammatical *aspect* (the progressive or continuous form) so that it is possible to hear sentences such as *I am having a cold*, which in ENL varieties would very likely be in the simple form (*I have a cold*). Among the points that are frequently mentioned are the following:

(1) the use of ***non-count nouns*** as ***count nouns***: SingE (like IndE), for instance, can have *chalks, luggages, fruits, mails, informations, vocabularies*, etc.; or *a furniture, an applause* (see Tongue 1974: 49f.); in Kenyan English Zuengler (1983) lists *fruits, ammunitions, hardwares* (all usually non-count in ENL), and *trouser* (usually an invariant plural in ENL);
(2) the use of the ***article***: Tay, for example, mentions a tendency to have fewer indefinite articles in SingE: *You got to have proper system here* (1982: 64);
(3) a functionally different use of *yes* and *no* (*Isn't he home? Yes [he isn't]*);
(4) a generalized *tag question* (*It doesn't matter, isn't it?*); see also Angogo and Hancock (1980); Bamgbose (1983); Tingley (1981); Todd (1984a).

Since these points show up in various African and Asian Englishes, they may simply be due to the intrinsic difficulty of such phenomena in English.

One study of prepositional use in Nigerian English suggests that a local norm is developing which is influenced by both mother tongue interference and what are termed 'stable Nigerianisms'. A meaningful sociolinguistic division of Nigerian English is one which, in accord with the educational structure of the country, recognizes 'two or three broad categories (corresponding to the masses/sub-élite/élite classification)' (Jibril 1991: 536).

Within West African English (WAE) there is, in other words, a great deal of variation: the higher the education of the user, the closer his or her usage will be to StE. In this sense standard WAE is perhaps less a fixed standard than a more or, indeed, less well learnt second language. A good deal of the difference between ENL and the ESL of educated West Africans is due to first-language

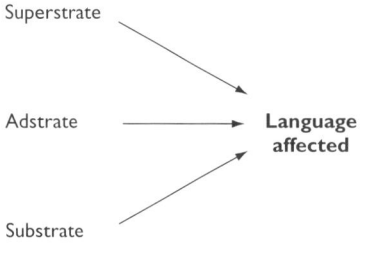

Superstrate	Influence exercised by a prestigious language (H, acrolect) on a language, e.g. Norman French on Old English; English on English-oriented pidgins and creoles
Adstrate → **Language affected**	Borrowing between languages in contact with each other, e.g. French words borrowed into English, English ones borrowed into German
Substrate	An exogenous language adopts 'non-native' grammatical categories and lexical-semantic conceptualizations retained by its speakers from their original language

Fig. 5.4. Non-native influences on languages

interference. There are, nevertheless, features of educated WAE which form a standard in the sense that (a) they are widely used and no longer likely to change through further learning and (b) they represent the linguistic norms of the WAE speech community; that is, they are not recognized as 'errors' even by the relatively most highly educated anglophone West Africans.

In the final account it is difficult to assess such differences in usage. Are they the result of imperfectly learnt Anglo-American StE, whose origins may lie in native-language interference (learners' English)? Or are they instead independent developments within the one or the other New English which are due to the influence of the native substratum? Do they perhaps lie within the spread in variation that ENL itself allows? Think how often English is full of surprises for all of us. The plural form *Englishes*, for instance, is a relatively recent possibility. We will return to this question when we look at the system of **personal pronouns** in two English-oriented creoles, as well as various differences in the use of tag questions and of negation in §6.4.2 and Exercise 6.5.

5.2 ESL IN AFRICA AND ASIA

In the ESL countries we are focusing on English is a minority and institutional language. It is sometimes the 'default' language, i.e. the language used when no other common language is available. The choice[3] would normally be, first of all, the local language, then the regional language (such as Hausa, Yoruba, or Ibgo in Nigeria or Hindi, Bangali, Tamil, etc. in India), then Pidgin (where present, as in West Africa), then English. This makes English a language which is relatively infrequent in use. This is most likely to be true in private and familial situations. In education, public administration, the press, radio, and TV, English is often much more prominent. In Gambia and Liberia, for example, it is the exclusive language of education. In Singapore, English is omnipresent in education. What this tells us is that the choice of language may depend on user characteristics (region, gender, age, level of education, even religion; see §5.3.1) or on features of use (administration, education, media, military, international trade, family, friends, etc.; see §5.3.2).

5.2.1 Africa

We will look first at Africa and concentrate on the use of English in those countries which do not have significant English native-speaking populations. This means that we will not be considering South Africa. However, it should be pointed out that English there is a non-native language for the vast majority of the population (cf. §4.1). For this reason the question of domains is important

---

3 However, the choice is not always a free one. Certain languages are mandated for official use in many countries. In South Africa, for example, English is the expected and *de facto* 'thread language' of the armed forces despite an overall policy of language parity among the country's 11 official languages (cf. De Klerk and Barkhuizen 1998).

there, too, as is implicit in the remark in fn. 3 above about the use of English as a 'thread language' in the South African defence force.

5.2.1.1 West Africa

In the West African countries of Nigeria, Ghana, Cameroon, Liberia, Gambia, and Sierra Leone it is said: 'Polyglossia, rather than diglossia, is the norm and *code-switching* and *code-mixing* are typical phenomena in the daily speech of [English-Speaking West African] inhabitants' (Bokamba 1991: 499). Yet English is well established. In Sierra Leone, for example, it has been a native language since the recolonization projects of the British at the end of the eighteenth century in which African slaves were 'repatriated' (even if they came originally from somewhere far distant from Sierra Leone). Many of them spoke English or an English pidgin. Liberia, as a state, traces its history to emancipated English-speaking slaves resettled there from the United States.

Despite the continued presence of native speakers of English, above all in Sierra Leone and Liberia, English counts as a second language throughout West Africa. This is chiefly because only a few people use it as a home language. A much larger number of Sierra Leoneans speak the English-derived creole Krio than English itself. According to Ehret (1997: 171) probably everyone in and around the capital of Freetown (2.5 million) has a passive command of Krio and maybe half of them use it as their primary means of expression. As a result of the multilingual situation, English in Sierra Leone has borrowed numerous words from the *autochthonous languages* such as Mende (the largest group, spoken by approximately one-third of the population) or Temne, or from Krio. Thus we find *bonga* for a kind of fish and *black tumbla* for a kind of wild fruit (Pemagbi 1989). Indeed, 'What actually distinguishes WAVE [West African Vernacular English] from other non-native varieties of English is its lexicon, including the occurrence of certain types of *code-mixing* and regionally-bound idiomatic expressions' (Bokamba 1991: 503).

Liberia has the highest percentage of speakers of English, 40 per cent, of all the African countries except, perhaps, South Africa. Elsewhere the estimate lies between 10 per cent and 20 per cent. The low numbers have, at least in part, to do with the low overall rate of literacy in many of these countries. However, the number of *native* speakers of English (Liberia, 5 per cent) or of an English creole (Krio in Sierra Leone, also 5 per cent: see Brann 1988: 1421) is much lower.[4] In other words, English is chiefly a second language among West Africans; yet it is sometimes rightfully seen as a primary language in the sense of familiarity and daily use. Indeed, there are numerous fluent, educated speakers of WAVE who 'have grown up hearing and using English daily, and who speak it as well as, or

---

4 Ehret (1997: 171f.) emphasizes that the notion of native language is hardly appropriate to the Sierra Leone situation, where children grown up multilingual, as numerous languages are used in the residential compounds.

maybe even better than, their ancestral language' (Angogo and Hancock 1980: 72). It is very likely that the number of English-users is going to increase; that, at least, is what extrapolation from the number of Africans who are learning it in school tells us.

Case study 5.1: West African Pidgin English

Although Pidgin English has little prestige, it does signal a good deal of group solidarity. The passage from a novel by Chinua Achebe shown in Text 5.1 gives us a good example of the complex linguistic situation in Nigeria. Joseph and his interlocuters use enough StE to show their educational level and enough Pidgin English to indicate their solidarity with each other.

Text 5.1. Pidgin English: StE code-mixing

'Good! See you later.' Joseph always put on an impressive manner when speaking on the telephone. He never spoke Ibo or pidgin English at such moments. When he hung up he told his colleagues:
  'That na[1] my brother. Just return from overseas. B.A. (Honours) Classics.' ...
  'What department he de[2] work?'
  'Secretary to the Scholarship Board.'
  'E go[3] make plenty money there. Every student who wan' go England go[3] de[2] see am[4] for[5] house.'
  'E no be[6] like dat,' said Joseph. 'Him na[1] gentleman. No fit[7] take bribe.'
  (Chinua Achebe, No Longer at Ease)

Notes
[1]na 'be' (marker for a following predicate complement)
[2]de + infinitive (progressive, cf. StE be + Ving)
[3]go 'will' (future, cf. going to)
[4]am 'him, her, it, etc.' (pronoun without gender)
[5]for 'to, at, etc.' (generalized preposition of place)
[6]be 'be' (copular verb, uninflected)
[7]fit 'be able to' (modal verb)

For those people who have a command of both StE and Pidgin English, the latter may well represent a further register, a stylistically more informal option. This would also explain why vocabulary can easily 'leak' from the pidgin/creole into StE, as will be exemplified below.

5.2.1.2 East Africa

The main 'anglophone' countries of East Africa are Tanzania, Kenya, and Uganda.[5] All three have one thing in common: the presence of Kiswahili as a widely used lingua franca. Structurally Kiswahili is therefore somewhat parallel to Pidgin English as used in West Africa. However, while Pidgin English is almost totally without prestige, this is not true of Kiswahili, which, like English, is used

---

5 Besides the three named: Zimbabwe, the Seychelles, Zambia, Malawi.

widely in education. Kiswahili is the preferred national language in Tanzania; it is probably gradually displacing the autochthonous mother tongues, and it is leading to a situation in which English is less a second and more a foreign language. Nevertheless, English is used for work, in education, and in reading. In one somewhat older study Christians favoured English and were more literate on average than Muslims (54.5 as against 25.2 per cent). Overall, however, whoever was literate in English was also literate in Kiswahili (Barton 1980: 191).

Case study 5.2: Kiswahili and English domains

Each language implies a different type of social reality. English and Kiswahili are each associated with different behavioural roles (as is Pidgin English in West Africa, for instance, where it is stereotyped as a joking, funny language):

> Certain social-psychological situations seem to influence language mainte-nance among the bilinguals. One of the respondents [among a group of fif-teen informants] said that whenever he argued with his bilingual wife he would maintain Kiswahili as much as possible while she would maintain English. A possible explanation is that Kiswahili norms and values assign different roles to husband and wife (socially more clear cut?) from the English norms and values (socially less clear cut, or more converging?). Maintaining one language or the other could then be a device for asserting one's desired role. (Abdulaziz 1972: 209)

In Kenya, where Kiswahili is also the official language, English has a contin-ued presence as second (official) language and is the language of the civil serv-ice, the police, the legal system, and the military. It is widely used in commerce and industry and in the media. Attitudes toward English are relatively positive, especially since it is associated with high-status jobs; it is even the primary home language in some (exclusive) Nairobi suburbs; and many middle- and upper-class children seem to be switching little by little to English (Abdulaziz 1991: 393, 397f.). However, probably only about 5 per cent of the population is com-petent in English as compared with 60 per cent in Kiswahili (Sure 1991).

The situation in Uganda is different inasmuch as there is some resentment of Kiswahili in some groups. This has given English a stronger footing. Furthermore, here English remains the medium of education from upper primary school (year four) on, if not earlier (cf. Abdulaziz 1988: 1348-51).

In all three countries English is a diglossically High language in comparison to Kiswahili; but Kiswahili itself is High in regard to the various local languages. The (local) mother tongues provide ethnic identity and solidarity in Tanzania and in Kenya; Kiswahili helps to establish a feeling of national identity (in Tanzania and Kenya); and English serves to signal modernity and good educa-tion in all three (Abdulaziz 1991: 392, 400).

Domains, or fields of use, are the parameter which defines the role of English in East Africa. They include:

■ high court, parliament, civil service
■ education
■ the media (radio, newspapers, films, local novels, plays, records)
■ traffic signs, advertisements
■ business and private correspondence
■ (some restricted) home use (Schmied 1985b: 241)

5.2.2 Asia

English plays an especially important role in India, Singapore, and the Philippines. In none of them is English a native language; it is, rather, a legacy of colonial times. In other former colonial possessions in Asia in which English once had a similar status, such as Sri Lanka, Malaysia, or Pakistan, its role has gradually been reduced to that of an important foreign language.

5.2.2.1 India

English has been present in India for hundreds of years, but it has been an outsider's language throughout. The British colonial administration used it, and colonial educational policy encouraged its wider use for the creation of a local élite. Certainly, English is well established as one of the most important diglossically High languages of India. It is a 'link language' in the Indian Administrative Service (civil service); it is a medium of modernization and Westernization; it is an important language of higher education, science, and technology. It has the constitutional status of an 'associate official language' next to Hindi, the official language and the language of over one-third of the population.

The role of English may be attributed not only to the British colonial past but also to the general spread and use of English throughout the world, especially in science, technology, and commerce. Its position is strengthened by continuing resistance to Hindi in the south of India, where non-Hindi speakers feel that the privileged status of Hindi puts them at a disadvantage. English, a non-native language for everyone, puts everyone on equal linguistic footing.

Since the late 1950s the 'three-language formula,' has been practised in secondary education. According to it everyone is educated in their regional language, in Hindi, and in English. (If the regional language is Hindi, then another language, such as Telugu, Tamil, Kannada, or Malayalam, is learned.) Just how successful this policy has been is the subject of debate; however, as far as English is concerned, it has led to a situation in which the number of users lies at 3–5 per cent of a population of 1 billion.

Within this general framework English has played an especially noticeable role in the area of publishing (newspapers, magazines, a large number of books, and both scientific and non-scientific journals). This, of course, explains one of the most important motivations for learning English: people feel that it improves their chances of getting a good job such as bank manager, university or college teacher, high-level civil servant, or lawyer. 'English is felt to be the language of power, a language of prestige' (Sridhar 1983: 149). It has been pointed out that English is the language of the 'classes', not the 'masses'.

Where English is used it not only signals a certain level of education, but also serves to cover over differences of region and caste. Through a judicious use of code-switching and code-mixing, various speaker identities can be revealed. English, for example, is used not only for certain domains and to fill in lexical gaps in the vernacular, but also to signal education, authority, and a cosmopolitan, Western attitude (Kachru 1978: 110–14).

One study reveals that English, much as in West Africa, is used less in intimate areas of communication such as with family or neighbours and more in the domains of business, politics, technology, communication with strangers, or pan-Indian communication (Sridhar 1983: 148f.).

5.2.2.2 Singapore

The city-state of Singapore maintains a policy of four official languages, Chinese, Malay, Tamil, and English. Malay remains the 'national language', and is widely used as a lingua franca; yet it is English which is on the increase, so much so, in fact, that it has been referred to as 'a language for the expression of national identity' (Tay 1982: 52). In contrast, Malay is associated with the ethnic Malays, just as Mandarin and the Chinese vernaculars are associated with the ethnic Chinese, and Tamil with the ethnic Indians. In contrast, English, an outside language, is viewed as an inter-ethnic lingua franca (Platt 1988: 1385), 'a unifying working language at the national level' (Kuo 1980: 59), which has 'a key role in increasing levels of modernization and development in Singapore' (Gopinathan 1980: 184).

The pre-eminent position of English is most evident in education. The language of teaching is to be one of the four official languages; if this is not English, English is the second school language. Today virtually 100 per cent of the students in Singapore are in English-medium schools (Platt 1988: 1384; 1991: 377). What this means is that about 60 per cent of teaching time is in English. Nonetheless, with 40 per cent of the time devoted to Mandarin, Malay, or Tamil, literacy in these languages is being maintained.

English is also prominent in the media. Parliament conducts its work chiefly in English, and it is the sole language of the courts. Naturally, it is predominant in international trade. Nevertheless, English is not in universal use. It is a diglossically High language, reserved for more formal situations. And even though there is a local Low (L) vernacular variety of SingE that is found in a wider range of more informal situations including both inter-ethnic and intra-ethnic communication, English is seldom a home language (Platt 1988: 1385f.).

5.2.2.3 The Philippines

In the Philippines the revised bilingual educational policy of 1987 helps to maintain English as highly important for science and technology and for international relations such as trade and worker migration into and out of the country. Although Pilipino, the 'national' variety of Tagalog, is spreading throughout the Philippines, English remains predominant in government administration, legislation, the law and the judiciary, higher education and the professions, business and commerce, science and industry (Sibayan 1988: 92).

English may be heard in banks and book stores. The fact that it is used for numbers and counting reflects the influence of schooling. Books and the so-called serious newspapers and magazines are in English; technical reports are in English; communication upwards – with a department head or boss – tends to be in English. In other words, the more formal the occasion is and the higher the level of education, the more likely it is that English will be used (Gonzalez and Bautista 1985: ch. 2). Despite the increasing spread of Pilipino, English continues to dominate in the 'controlling domains of language' (Sibayan 1988: 92).

In contrast, at markets, in the popular press, and on radio and TV, Pilipino and the other vernaculars predominate – except for the news, which is generally in English. Once again, as in Africa, India, and Singapore, the vernacular is the language of emotion, used, for instance, for swearing and for dreaming. Yet the Philippine population is obviously quite aware of the advantages of English, and parents want their children to learn it because of the advantages it offers, namely social mobility, higher-paying jobs, power, and prestige (Pascasio 1988: 117).

Project 5.1: Users and domains

After this rather wide-ranging review of English in various parts of Africa and Asia, we would like to suggest that you undertake a survey of what languages are used in the area you live in and what domains they are most likely to occur in.

- Who uses them (rural, urban folk, older, younger people, professional groups, etc.)?
- In what social circumstances (home, pub, school, business, public administration, etc.)?
- With what relative prestige (high or low public esteem)?
- Under what conditions of use (e.g. informal, letter writing, laws, contracts, television (type of programme?), school or university reading, etc.?

Remember that many languages are difficult to observe because their domains are restricted to the home or are seldom used in public because of their lack of public prestige. Think of ancient indigenous languages and markedly 'different' dialects of the standard language of your region, but also immigrant languages, and the languages of important foreign groups (investors, educators, foreign workers). Some of you may be surprised at the variety you discover.

5.3 USER AND USE

There are two relatively distinct ways in which we can approach variation within a given regional or national variety of English. These approaches can be grasped using what is known as the register model of language (cf. Gregory and Carroll 1978). *Register*[6] encompasses two different approaches. One, *dialects*, is concerned with features of language users which are less susceptible to voluntary behaviour (§5.3.1). The other, *diatypes* (register in its narrower sense), describes how language is used in concrete situations (§5.3.2).

5.3.1 Dialects

How people use English depends very much on what they are. And what people are is itself a complex phenomenon. Each of us has multiple identities: we have a certain gender identity (usually male or female, though there are also more complex cases), a regional, national, ethnic identity, an age group, an occupational one, an identity dictated by our leisure activities and educational level, a religious and political one. In many of these facets of our 'self' we identify with the group concerned by taking on features it has – including language features. Indeed, many studies have shown similarities among members of the same group. Some of these identities are relatively permanent (gender, ethnicity); others may vary over time. Age surely does; region, nationality, occupation, hobbies, sports, politics, even religion and education may do so as well. Yet all of these, and possibly further factors, seldom change in a rapid back-and-forth, flip-flop fashion. Linguistics therefore regards them as relatively permanent features of the user. In Fig. 5.5 the arrows show the influence from the group directed toward the individual speaker-user, but of course each individual also contributes to the collective speech behaviour of each of the groups he or she belongs to.

In the case of ESL the language will remain largely non-native in many of the countries of Africa and Asia which we are looking at. Furthermore, it is important

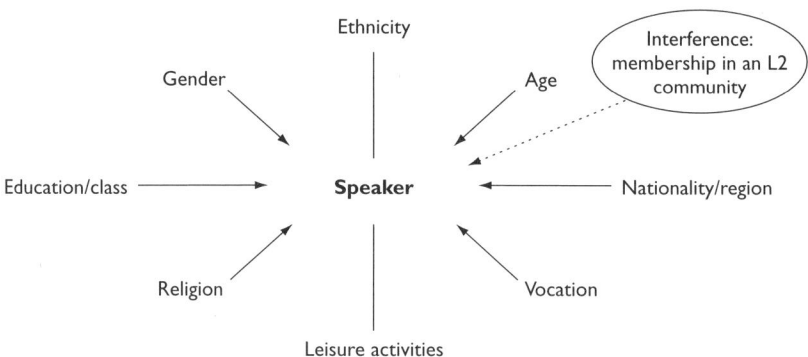

Fig. 5.5. Identities which influence user speech

6 *Register* is sometimes also used to refer to *field of discourse*.

to recognize that the use of English there is largely an urban and an élite phenomenon. This means that the full range of possible influences illustrated in Fig. 5.5 may be restricted to the factors of education/class, region (= urban), and vocation. Some of the variation which ENL users have may not be (as) relevant for ESL (as for ENL), e.g. religion, ethnicity, leisure activities. Consequently, these varieties may show less variation than there is among ENL users. However, they may gain in variety through native language interference, as indicated by the broken-shafted arrow in Fig. 5.5. (see also §5.1.2).

5.3.1.1 The linguistic study of lects

The social features of language users are all examples of dialectal variation. And, indeed, for some of them linguists use terms with the morpheme {-lect} to designate the corresponding type of variation: the word *dialect* itself is probably most often associated with regional dialect. Social dialects are frequently called **sociolects** and centre around class and education. **Genderlect** and **ethnolect** (a.k.a. **ethnic dialect**) speak for themselves. Usage patterns related to age and religion have no established designations.

Project 5.2: Dictionary usage labels

Dictionaries often given regional labels (e.g. *Brit.*, *US*, *Aust*, etc. or *CanE*, *CarE*, *NZE*), often with a limitation like *chiefly Brit* or *esp. US*. Designations of vocabulary as typical of one particular gender, age group, social class, ethnic community, or religious persuasion are not given.[7] Vocation plays a role only inasmuch as some field labels are common.

Compare the usage labels in two different monolingual English desk dictionaries, e.g. in the *Random House Webster's College Dictionary* and in the *Longman Dictionary of Contemporary English*. Try to categorize the labels according to whether they give information about

- region (as indicated above)
- style (see §5.3.2.3)
- field (see §5.3.2.4)
- currency (e.g. *out of date*)
- other (see §5.3.2.3)

5.3.2 Diatypes

Diatypes are determined by features of the situation of use. Common ways of characterizing contexts of use include whether language is spoken or written (the medium of communication), what its purpose is (functional tenor), how the nature of the relationship between the participants can be described (style, personal tenor), and the field of discourse. The traditional model presented in Fig. 5.6 touches on medium, style, and field while neglecting purpose.

---

7 However, a given usage may be labelled *sexist*, *offensive*, etc.

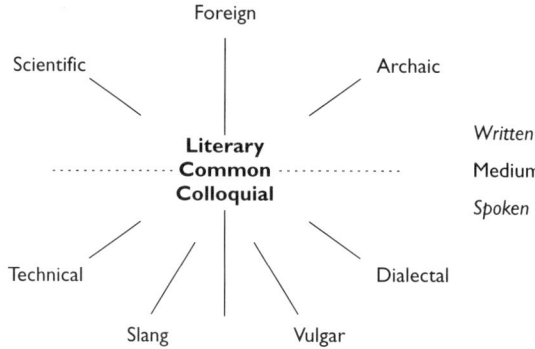

Fig. 5.6. The OED model of English vocabulary

5.3.2.1 Medium

Medium is most basically a matter of whether the language is spoken or written. It will play an explicit role when we look at English on the Internet (§8.4.1). But it is obviously of importance when we look at some speech acts which are typically dialogic and spoken (§7.3.1) and at some types of formulaic text which only occur in writing (§8.1.2–3).

5.3.2.2 Purpose (functional tenor)

In the register approach *functional tenor* is the term often used to designate the communicative purpose which a text is used for. This aspect of an utterance is also referred to as the *speech act* (see Schiffrin 1994), and it is central to the branch of linguistics known as *pragmatics*. Speech acts are commonly defined by the purposes they fulfil,[8] which are classified very generally as asserting, directing, committing, expressing, and declaring or more specifically as subtypes like promising, threatening, or offering, as in Table 5.2.

Table 5.2. Illocutionary acts

Type	Subtypes	Examples
Representatives / assertives	Statements and assertions	*(I maintain that) he was there!*
Directives	Requests and questions	*(I request you to) please leave me alone*
Commissives	Promises, threats, and offers	*I'll be on time (I promise I will)*
Expressives	Thanking, apologizing, congratulating	*Gee, thanks!* *I'm sorry, I apologize*
Declaratives (a.k.a. performatives)	The marriage, baptism, sentencing formulas	*By the authority vested in me I declare you husband and wife*

8 This aspect of the speech act is called the *illocutionary act*; see §7.3.1.

The speech act may be explicit, meaning that it contains words which explicitly designate the act being carried out, for example in the table *(1) maintain, request, promise, apologize, declare,* etc. More often, however, illocutionary acts are implicit: *He was there* rather than *I maintain that he was there; Are you coming?* rather than *I ask whether you are coming?* Greetings, thank you's, apologies, and the like belong among the speech acts, but are treated separately under the heading of **pragmatic idioms** (§7.3.2).

5.3.2.3 Style (personal tenor)

The nature of our relation to others as expressed by 'those features which are restricted to a certain social context' (Crystal and Davy 1969: 10), sometimes termed **personal tenor**, is expressed in the **style** of our communication. This comes out in the choice of words, but also in the type of text we select. A wedding invitation is frequently very fixed in its wording, and this is quite appropriate to the formality of the occasion (§8.1.3).

Style involves a number of factors and can be divided into a number of different levels. One of the most widely accepted criteria of style is surely that of formality, with a basic dichotomy between *formal* and *informal*. That this is not fine enough can be seen in the various suggestions for further distinctions. Quirk *et al.* (1985) avoid the rather ambiguous term 'style' and replace it with 'attitude'. This has the advantage of allowing us to include attitudinal aspects like 'derogatory' or 'humorous', even though it makes personal tenor a polyvalent field. The preference of Quirk *et al.* for the label 'attitude' rather than 'style' lies in their wish to emphasize the fact that the **personal tenor** between people communicating involves a great deal more than the degree of formality, as suggested by their scale (§1.3.3) (see Fig. 5.7).

Other factors that may play into our estimation of style are distance (including politeness as more distant and slang as a sign of in-group closeness) and, of course, attitude (including ironic, angry, negative-derogatory, humorous, and much more). Style depends in part on purpose, on dimensions of medium such as colloquial (i.e. informal spoken), and on field (e.g. technical language).

Joos's study of style (1961) also takes a variety of factors into account including social relationship, vocabulary, and grammar. He recognizes five types: frozen, formal, consultative, casual, and intimate, as elaborated in Table 5.3:

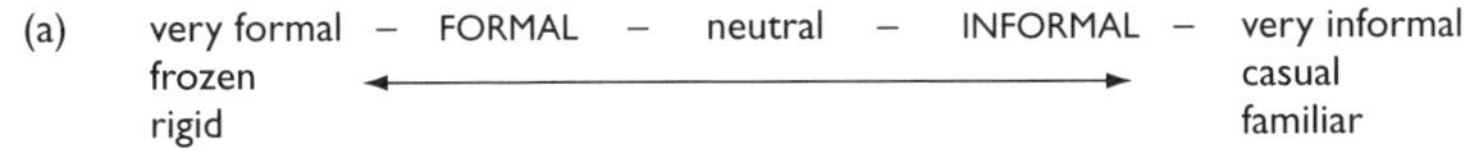

(a) very formal – FORMAL – neutral – INFORMAL – very informal
     frozen   ◄───────────────────────────────►   casual
     rigid   familiar

The use of small caps for FORMAL and INFORMAL is intended to indicate that these are the terms chiefly employed.

Fig. 5.7. Attitude (style) (Quirk *et al.* 1985)

Table 5.3. Five styles and selected characteristics (Joos 1961)

	Social	Linguistic
Frozen	Individual	Rereadable
		Allusive, literary vocabulary
Formal	One-way participation	Detachment
	No interruption	Cohesion (planning)
		No ellipsis (grammar)
		Fussy semantics
		Technical vocabulary (**jargon**)
Consultative	Two-way participation	Background information
	Coming to terms with strangers	Backchannel behaviour
		Complete grammar
		Unmarked vocabulary
Casual	In-group friends, acquaintances	Ellipsis
		Slang (vocabulary)
Intimate	Not public	No grammar; either no words or no intonation
		Private vocabulary

Frozen: for print and declamation; people remain social strangers: no two-way participation. Vocabulary contains archaisms and extremely formal words.

Formal: 'Thus conversations between strangers begin in formal style; among urbane strangers in English-speaking cultures, the formal span is only the ceremony of introduction, whose function is to insure that no real business shall be impeded by formality; it then lasts for one consultative speech-span, appproximately six seconds' (p. 35). Emphasis is put on exact vocabulary ('fussy semantics').

Consultative: 'The two defining features of consultative style are: (1) The speaker supplies background information – he does not assume that he will be understood without it. (2) The addressee participates continuously.[9] Because of these two features, consultative style is our norm for coming to

9 **Backchannel behaviour:** the participant's use of *yes, yeah, unhunh, that's right, oh, I see, yes I know,* etc. to indicate active listening.

terms with strangers' (p. 23). Vocabulary includes all-purpose words like *thing* for more specific or exact ones like *item, plan, problem,* and *event*.

Casual style is for friends, acquaintances, insiders: 'there is absence of background information and no reliance on listeners' participation. This is not rudeness; it pays the addressee the compliment of supposing that he will understand without those aids . . . we have two devices which do the same job directly: (1) ellipsis, and (2) slang, the two defining features of casual style' (p. 23). Vocabulary: slang.

Intimate: no public information: The message meaning is in the intonation, not the wording or grammar (which are minimal). Or it is in the word, without grammar or intonation. This brevity is not rudeness, but the highest compliment (p. 31). Vocabulary includes private language, which 'is not ephemeral, but part of the permanent code of this group – it has to be, for intimacy does not tolerate the slang imputation that the addressee needs to be told that she is an insider' (p. 32).

The two approaches reviewed offer a differentiated understanding of style. In most dictionaries the labels *formal* and *informal* predominate and can be associated with the same in Quirk *et al.* or with formal and casual in Joos. Unlabelled entries are presumably neutral/consultative. Entries marked as *archaic, obsolete, old-fashioned, poetic,* or *pompous* (often abbreviated) are all presumably examples of very formal/frozen. Labels like *colloquial, derogatory, slang, taboo, vulgar* are less clear and spread over the areas covered by both informal/casual and very informal/intimate. Labels such as *appreciative, euphemistic,* and *humorous* indicate attitude, and remain hard to place on the linear formal–informal scale of style.

5.3.2.4 Field of discourse

What type of language we choose also depends on what we are talking about. Sports, politics, religious beliefs, cooking, education, fashion, etc. all have their own vocabulary, as we have seen repeatedly in the preceding chapters and will continue to see (Case study 8.4 and §8.4.3). ***Fields of discourse*** involve subject matter. However, there is an overlap with domains of communication, which are social areas of activity, as when a Nigerian speaks Igbo at home, Pidgin English at a market, and StE in the office. Field labels are common in dictionaries and include *Computers, Football, Maths, Music,* and *Psychoanal.*

5.4 SUMMARY

This chapter introduced and discussed some of the central concepts that will be employed in Chapters 6–8. Language contact is concerned with the relative status of ESL (diglossia, continuum, ESL standards), what domains the language is used in, and the (putative) effects on vocabulary of substrate influences.

The middle section of the chapter offered a review of the use and status of ESL in West Africa, East Africa, and Asia (South Asia, Singapore, the Philippines). In the final part user categories (dialect, sociolect, ethnolect, etc.) and use categories (medium, style, function, and field) were introduced.

The New Englishes: Linguistic Dimensions of Vocabulary Difference

Fine words! I wonder where you stole 'em.   (Swift, Verses occasioned by
Whitshed's Motto on his Coach)

And torture one poor word ten thousand ways.
(Dryden, *Britannia Rediviva*)

6.0 INTRODUCTION

In this chapter we will be looking at cultural and natural environments different
from those of Australia, the British Isles, North America, New Zealand, and
South Africa,[1] and will, in connection with new words for new things, return to
word formation (§6.1). Differences in the associations we have with words is
something investigated in §6.2, where we look at some of the different connotations people associate with colours and colour words. In §6.3 we turn to the different linguistic and cultural environments of countries where English is either a
first or a second language, and explore some of the effects which the immediate
presence of non-English native or first languages may have on English. In §6.4
we take a second look at the pronoun system (cf. also §2.1.3) and at some of the
differences that show up in the use of *yes* and *no*, negation, and tag questions.

6.1 EXPANDING THE VOCABULARY OF ENGLISH

A prominent scholar in the area of world Englishes has remarked, 'There are
three major ways of expanding the vocabulary: borrowing from other languages,
coining new words and expressions, and extending the meaning of existing
words' (Görlach 1989b: 281). In the earlier chapters we have seen numerous
examples of this. When we look at some of the ESL countries of Asia and Africa,
there are many more. We will restrict ourselves for reasons of space to an exemplary look at West Africa, India, and Singapore, and look specifically at borrowing, word formation, and semantic shift.

---

1 Although Australia and the US contain subtropical and tropical areas, most of their territory, like
that of the British Isles, southern Canada, New Zealand, and South Africa, lies in the temperate
zone. West Africa and South and Southeast Asia, in contrast, are more tropical and subtropical
and therefore have sometimes very distinct flora and fauna.

6.1.1 West Africa

The vocabulary of West African English, like that of any area, has special words and expressions for the local flora, fauna, and social practices. Some of these words may be known and used more widely, e.g. *calabash*, *kola*, *palm wine*. Furthermore, the need to talk about West African culture and institutions has ensured the adoption of numerous other, less widely known items among local English speakers. This, more than grammar, is said to give WAE 'its distinctive "flavour"', because it reflects the sociolinguistic milieux in which English is spoken' (Bokamba 1991: 502). The words themselves may be borrrowings, or occur through word formation or semantic shift.

6.1.1.1 Borrowings

(a) from autochthonous languages

■ *loan words* from a native language, e.g. *awujor* 'ceremony giving the ancestors food', *krain-krain* 'a leafy vegetable', *akara balls* 'beancakes'

■ *calques/loan translations*, e.g. *next tomorrow* 'day after tomorrow' from Yoruba *otunla* 'new tomorrow'; *We'll wash it* 'celebrate something with a party and drinks'

(b) from pidgins or creoles: *tai fes* 'frown', *chop* 'food'

(c) from other languages: *palaver* (Portugese) 'argument, trouble', *piccin* (Portugese) 'child'

(d) from older stages of the language; although not borrowing in the strict sense, this includes words like the now somewhat outdated *deliver* 'have a baby', *station* 'town or city in which a person works'

6.1.1.2 Word formation

(a) using processes of *affixation*, e.g. *co-wives* 'wives of the same husband', *rent-age* '(house)rent'

(b) *reduplication*, e.g. *slow slow* 'slowly'

(c) *compounding*, e.g. *bush-meat* 'game', *check rice* 'rice prepared with krain-krain' (see above: borrowing); *head tie* 'woman's headdress'

6.1.1.3 Semantic shift

■ English words with an *extension of meaning*, e.g. *chap* 'any person, man or woman', *corner* 'bend in the road', *arrangement* 'special arrangement, preferential treatment, mutual arrangement' (*By arrangement you can go to heaven*)

■ *narrowing of meaning*, e.g. *cane* 'bamboo', *globe* 'light bulb'

■ *pejoration*, e.g. *smallboy* 'low servant'

For these and further examples , see especially Pemagbi (1989), Bokamba (1991), but also Jibril (1982), Bamgbose (1983), and Willmott (1978/9).

6.1.2 South Asia

The occurrence of Indian words in English discourse is probably more common in 'more informal, more personal, more relaxed, and sometimes more culture-sensitive' situations (Mehrotra 1982: 160–2); nevertheless, there may be opportunity or need to use Indian terms in formal texts as well, cf.:

> Urad and moong fell sharply in the grain market here today on stockists offerings. Rice, jowar and arhar also followed suit, but barley forged ahead. (Kachru 1984: 362; cf. also Case study 3.3 on PkE terms)

The vocabulary of IndE is universally recognized as containing numerous characteristic items. For convenience they can be classified in the same way as in the preceding section:

- Borrowing of Indian words, which often 'come more naturally and appear more forceful in a given context than their English equivalents. *Sister-in-law* is no match for *sali*, and *idle talk* is a poor substitute for *buk-buk*' (Mehrotra 1982: 160–2)
- Word formation, e.g. *black money* 'illegal gains', *change-room* 'dressing room', and including hybrid formations, e.g. *lathi charge* 'police attack with sticks', *coolidom* 'state of being a coolie'
- Semantic shift such as English words used differently, e.g. *four-twenty* 'a cheat, swindler' (Mehrotra 1982: 160–2)

For a collection of IndE vocabulary items, see Hawkins (1986) or Nihalani *et al.* (1979).

6.1.3 Borrowing

It is possible to borrow both the word form and its meaning (***loan word***) or only its meaning with a simultaneous translation of the original elements (***loan translation*** or ***calque***); alternatively, both sound and meaning are borrowed. Occasionally the sound is 'translated' into a more familiar English form without there necessarily being a change in meaning; this may be a case of ***folk etymology*** (see §4.3.1.3). Singapore English is spoken by a population whose native languages are Malay and Chinese and Indian languages. Thus it is not surprising to find borrowings from these languages in SingE (see Table 6.1).

6.1.4 Coining new words and expressions

Word formation is a very productive way of expanding the vocabulary. It includes analogy, calquing, neologism, and euphemism. Although the words created may be unfamiliar to English users outside a particular area, the processes used are not essentially different from those employed throughout the English-speaking world.

Table 6.1. Borrowings in SingE (see Tongue 1974: 69; Platt and Weber 1980: 83–7)

Malay	*jaga* 'guard, sentinel'
	padang 'field, open area'
	kachang 'peanut'
	kampong 'village'
	makan 'food'
Chinese	*towkay* (Hokkien) 'employer, business person'
	la (Hokkien) a speech discourse element, see Case study 7.3
Indian languages	*chop* (Hindi) 'stamp, seal'
	tamby (Tamil) 'office boy, errand boy'
	dhobi (Hindi) 'washerman'
	syce (from Arabic via Hindi) 'driver'
Other	*peon* (Portuguese) 'orderly, office assistant'
	amah (Portuguese) 'nurse'

Concrete examples include the making of new words by various means of derivation including **prefixation** (*enstool* 'to crown'), **suffixation** (*enstoolment* 'coronation'), **reduplication** (*quick quick* 'very quick') (examples from Bokamba 1991). Reduplications often have an intensifying effect, as with Krio *day-day* [= *die-die*] 'weak, flimsy'.[2] Furthermore, there is **conversion**, which can be exemplified by *day* 'die, be dead, dead, death' and **compounding** involving the same item, which gives us *dayman* 'corpse, ghost' (Görlach 1989b: 296). Some compounding may involve **pleonasms**, such as Jamaican Creole *hed skol* 'skull' (which may go back to an Africanism where the base item (*skull*) had a wider meaning (word for *skull* = calabash) (Holm 1994: 362).

Other patterns of word formation which the New Englishes use just as the 'old' ones do include clipping (as when *agriculture* becomes *ag*, to which the diminutive {-ie} is added, giving us IndE *aggie*. Likewise, abbreviations are common, for example IndE *BOR* ('British [soldier of] Other Rank [than officer]', as are blends such as IndE *jonga* (< *jeep* + *tonga* 'two-wheeled horse-drawn vehicle') (examples from Görlach 1989b).

---

2 In ENL varieties exact reduplication is infrequent, be it strict reduplication (*bye-bye*, *go go*) or reduplication with intruding words (*all in all*, *by and by*). Exceptions are found in children's language (*jam-jams* 'pajamas', *bang bang*) and onomatopoeic usage (*knock knock*, *wuff wuff*, *hush hush*). What is more frequent in ENL is rhyming reduplication (*helter-skelter*, *bow wow*, *wham bam*) as well as reduplication with vowel change (*riff raff*, *zig zag*).

Exercise 6.1: Word formation

In the following exercise you have two tasks to solve. First, try to find out what each of the words means. To help you, the source variety and references have been given.

Then give a characterization of the type of word formation process involved and illustrate it with another example (from whatever variety you wish).

Item	Meaning	Word formation process	Further example
big big CarCE[3]			
boy-chil' CarCE			
cow-itch IndE			
destool WAVE			
die man Sierra Leonean English			
goondaism IndE			
han elbo CarCE			
to safe CarCE			
shoe-bite IndE			
Tanzingereza Tanzanian English			

Resources you might use: Bokamba (1991), Görlach (1989b), Holm (1994), Pemagbi (1989), Schmied (1985a).

Case study 6.1: Word formation in PakE

There has been a certain amount of conjecture about whether the processes of word formation in the New Englishes are perhaps different from the same in ENL varieties. For the most part the conclusions have been negative. However, there is perhaps some evidence of more 'rule-bending' in the New Englishes. One study has reported on seven different processes of word formation in Pakistani English (see Table 6.2).

While none of the processes described here runs counter to the processes of English word formation, there are two ways in which they stand in contrast to ENL word formation. What is most immediately noticeable is the fact that a number of items involve the use of non-English words, cf. *challan ticket*, *hired assassin-cum-*

---

3 Caribbean Creole English.

Table 6.2. Word formation in PakE (Baumgardner 1998)

1. COMPOUNDING

Noun + noun compounds

      camel kid 'young boy sent to the Middle East for use as jockey in camel races'

      chocolate hero 'a boyishly attractive film hero'

      pen-down strike, tool-down strike, wheel-jam strike

      driver-cum-salesman, hired assassin-cum-dacoit

Compound verbs

      to airdash 'depart quickly by air'

      to head-carry 'carry on head'

Pleonastic compounds

      challan ticket < *challan* 'ticket'

      fruit mandi market < *mandi* 'market'

Compounds due to *rank reduction* (from the things contained to the container)

      matchbox 'box of matches'

      perfume bottle 'bottle of perfume'

2. AFFIXATION

Suffixation

{-ee}	*abscondee, affectee, afflictee, convictee, remandee*
{-(r)ess}	*teachress* a.k.a. '*lady teacher*'
{-y}	*maliky* 'like a malik or chief'
{-like}	*goonda-like* 'thuggish' < *goonda* 'thug')

Prefixation

{anti-}	*anti-awami* 'anti-people', *anti-mullah, anti-Shariat*
{counter-}	*counter-fatwa*
{super-}	*super-chamcha* 'sycophant' < *chamcha* 'spoon'
{de-}	*de-recognize*

3. CONVERSION

Adjective → noun

      faithfuls, abnormals, affluents, anti-socials, blinds, deads

Noun → verb

      to aircraft, to airline, to arson, to charge sheet

4. BACK-FORMATION[4]

      to scrute < *scrutiny, to renunciate* < *renunciation*

---

4 **Back-formation** is the creation of a new word by deleting what is assumed to be a suffix as when *enthuse* is formed from *enthusiasm*.

5. CLIPPING

>   *supple* 'supplementary examination' (institutionalized usage)

6. ABBREVIATION

>   *CCI* 'Chamber of Commerce and Industry'
>
>   *s/o* 'son of', *f/o* 'father of', *m/o* 'mother of'

7. BLENDS

With back clipping + front clipping

>   *bushirt* 'bush + shirt'
>
>   *Lollywood* 'Lahore + Hollywood'

With back clipping + second word

>   *telemoot* 'television + *moot* "meeting"'

Sandwich word (one word is inserted into another with some overlap)

>   Islumabad < '*Islamabad + slum*'

---

dacoit, maliky, goonda-like, mohalla-wise, anti-awami, anti-mullah, anti-Shariat, counter-fatwa, super-chamcha, and *telemoot,* something which only happens when the non-English language plays a serious role in the country it is used in.

The second point is that some of the processes illustrated in Table 6.2 may go beyond the normal bounds of ENL use. For example, *convictee* is formed despite the existence of *convict*, which is identical in meaning; the rank reduction of *box of matches* to *matchbox* goes against native usage; formations in {-ee} exceed the usual bounds, where, for example, adjective stems, as with *adhocee*, are unusual. Other processes are perhaps overused, e.g. Germanic stem + latinate suffix {-ism}, as in *brotherism*; pleonastic formations like *challan ticket*; and a relatively high number of compounds with *-cum-*. Furthermore, adjective-to-noun conversion with plural endings is more frequent in PakE (StE has colour terms like *the reds* and *the greens* and a few more, e.g. *broads, funnies, hopefuls, heavies,* but this is not a productive process).

Exercise 6.2: Identifying cases of PakE word formation

In the following sentences circle the PakE word forms and identify the word formation process involved.

1. In another incident a young girl Rabia Bibi d/o Karim jumped into Lower Jhelum Canal.
2. Then the self-righteous dictator Gen. Ziaul Haq was the perpetrator of the biggest rigging in the referendum, popularly called 'refraudum'.
3. Political and social sectors have demanded the Government provide shelter to poors.
4. Sindh inspector general of police has deconfirmed 23 inspectors who were promoted out of turn.
5. Speaking on the occasion, Mr Shahid Aziz, commissioner in Karachi, said that all the affectees would be paid compensation.
6. The district police launched a vigorous drive against cattle-lifting and recovered stolen cattle heads worth about Rs 2.5 lakh . . .

7. A youth, who was taunted repeatedly by his kins for having love-married his girl-friend, shot and injured his aunt, . . .
8. To character assassinate, demean and belittle the other seems to be a necessity for our politicians.
9. A large number of parents also visited the college but left . . .without collecting admit cards . . . for the coming examination.

Resource you might use: Baumgardner (1998).

6.1.5 Semantic shift

This third category is difficult to define, for it is not always clear when there has been extension of meaning. 'For instance, does the transfer to a new referent considered to have similar characteristics, such as the extension of a European tree name to an Indian or Australian species, qualify? Does the changed connotation of a word count, and how much change of connotation must there be?' (Görlach 1989b: 281).

Semantic shift is so prevalent that it almost always escapes our attention. It includes broadening and narrowing, pejoration and amelioration, as we saw in §4.5. and will again in §6.2. It may be based on analogy, as when a word with a European referent is used to refer to a similar but different non-European entity. For example, some African languages use a single lexeme for 'tree, wood, stick', e.g. Twi *dùá*. That is, the underlying semantic range is different from English, and this difference may be transferred to English or an English creole. So it is that *stick* means 'stick, wood, tree' in Bahamian CE. Twi *dùá* also means 'penis', as does Jamaican Creole *wood* (Holm 1994: 358).

One question that arises in connection with second-language users is whether some of their usages are not perhaps the kind of interference from their first languages which all learners experience. Bamgbose (1983: 103), for example, sees this possibility, but feels that 'the vast majority, at least in Educated Nigerian English, arise from the normal process of language development involving a narrowing or extension of meaning or the creation of new idioms . . . For example, when "travel" is used in the sense "to be away", as in My father has travelled (= "My father is away"), it is not a transfer of a first-language expression into English, but a modification of the meaning of the verb "to travel"'.

Further examples of semantic shift, whatever their ultimate cause, are given in Table 6.3.

Table 6.3. Semantic shift in Sierra Leonean English (Pemagbi 1989)

find	'look for'	*halt*	'switch off (lights)'
meet	'find'	*stranger*	'guest'
street	'any road'	*take-in*	'become pregnant'
unless	'except'		

Examples of this sort could be extended without end. We will, however, leave this field and move to the challenging topic of how distinctly non-English and non-European-oriented cultures map onto the English language.

6.2 CULTURAL DIFFERENCES IN CONNOTATION

While much of what we have looked at in the preceding sections of this book has been more or less self-evident, in this section we will consider some dimensions which are frequently overlooked because they are so much a part of the assumptions we make when using language that we do not expect them to be different. One of these[5] involves the different associations people have with particular words. If someone or something is *as black as sin*, we are likely to generalize from this and associate the colour black with sinfulness or with evil. This is called **connotation**, the term used to refer to the meaning a word suggests and which goes beyond denotation, strictly speaking.

Connotative meaning extends to evaluation, as when the association of black with evil may lend this word a ***pejorative*** connotation (*the black arts*, *blackguard*, *black magic*, *black mail*, *Black Mass*, or *black sheep*). Note that the word *black* is not used to refer to the colour black in any of these words and expressions. Rather, it is connected metaphorically with ideas of darkness, secretiveness, evil, or criminality. However, since *black* also has numerous positive connotations, its pejoration is counterbalanced by ***ameliorating*** associations (*to be in the black*, *black is beautiful*, *black gold*, *black tie*). Consequently, there is hardly any likelihood that the word *black* will undergo general or permanent pejoration. The same is true of *white*: it suggests both something positive (*white knight*, *white lie*) as well as having negative associations (*white elephant*, *white-livered*) (cf. the interesting study by Bennett (1988)).

Part of what is included in connotation is what usage labels designate. This may be a regional association, e.g. Australian (*bluey* 'swag'); a stylistic level, e.g. slang (*pinko* 'a political left-winger'); a technical field such as literary (*green* 'fresh, strong, full of life'); or currency of use as with old-fashioned *white slavery* 'abduction into forced prostitution'.

When a connotation is widely accepted, it may become part of the denotation of the word. Indeed, in a number of the examples given above it is difficult to distinguish between connotation and denotation. A well-known example is the association of red with Catholic cardinals because of the colour of their vestments. This colour association is so strong that the name *cardinal* was given to the red-feathered North American (male) songbird *Cardinalis cardinalis*. In much the same way the environmental movement has taken the association of the colour green with nature and raised it to one of their symbols, as we see in the environmental organization *Greenpeace* or the *Green* (political) *Party*.

---

5 Another involves the everyday metaphors we use; see §6.3.3.

What do you think about when you hear or see the word *green*? What about *black*, *white*, *red*, *yellow*, or *blue*? Some of our associations are surely based on individual experience or personal psychology, but some are doubtless the product of a shared cultural background. One of the questions we can ask within the framework of World English is to what extent connotative associations are shared in all varieties and to what extent they are culturally specific. To explore this we will examine some of the connotations associated with the colours blue and yellow.

Case study 6.2: The colour blue

In a questionnaire introduced in Project 4.1 we asked our informants about the associations they had with the colours black, white, red, yellow, green, and blue. In order to get a usable set of results we added to each a choice of possible associations. For *blue* the question looked as in Questionnaire 6.1.

Questionnaire 6.1. Associations of *blue*

> **Colour terms**
> People associate different ideas with each of the 'major' colours: yellow, red, green, blue, black, and white. The following is a partial collection of such associations. Please circle the letters of those you or people like you might possibly use. Don't circle ones you merely know about but never hear. Add any other associations you feel are current.
>
> Blue
> a. anaemia, weakness   b. bleakness   c. cold   d. distance
> e. fight   f. impracticality g. improper   h. nobility
> i. non-limitation   j. puritanicalism k. sadness   l. solidity   Other:

The results of 112 questionnaires from 35 North Americans, 35 South Africans, 26 Australians, and 16 Irish turned up the following results (see also Table 6.4).

■   *Blue* is almost universally associated with 'cold'; 86.6 per cent of the informants circled 'c. cold'. Furthermore, the distribution was relatively uniform: between 80 per cent and 93.7 per cent in all four varieties.

Table 6.4. Connotative associations of *blue*

Association	AmE		AusE		IrE		SAE		Total		Rank
	No.	%	No.	%	No.	%	No.	%	No.	%	
Bleakness	7	20.0	3	11.5	1	6.2	7	20.0	18	16.0	3
Cold	31	88.5	23	88.4	15	93.7	28	80.0	97	86.6	1
Nobility	3	8.5	5	19.5	2	12.5	7	20.0	17	15.1	4
Sadness	24	68.5	11	42.3	5	31.2	13	37.1	53	47.3	2

- The association with 'sadness' came in second, at an overall rate of almost half (47.3 per cent); however, here the distribution was somewhat skewed. Two-thirds of the North Americans (68.5 per cent) marked this, while less than a third of the Irish did (31.2 per cent).
- Virtually tied for a poor third place came 'bleakness' (16.0 per cent) and 'nobility' (15.1 per cent). Here the internal split ran from a high for 'bleakness' of 20 per cent (AmE and SAE) to a low of 6.2 per cent (IrE). For 'nobility' the cut ran differently: highs of 19.2 per cent and 20 per cent for AusE and SAE and lows of 8.5 per cent and 12.5 per cent for AmE and IrE.
- All the other results tended toward insignificance. (There were no hits for 'f. impracticality' and 'g. improper'.) However, 'other', which requires a certain amount of initiative, got seven instances of 'wet/sea' and five of 'relaxing/soothing'. Clearly, the list supplied in the questionnaire should be amended by dropping the current f and g and adding the two most frequently named 'other' associations.

What these results tell us is that there is a fairly great amount of agreement about the colour connotations of *blue* among ENL speakers, but that there is also a certain degree of regional–national difference – for whatever reasons, and what the reasons might be in the case of *blue* we can only guess.

Case study 6.3: The colour *yellow*

The suggestions for yellow in the questionnaire are given in the box:

Questionnaire 6.2. Associations of *yellow*

a. anger	b. Asian(ness)	c. caution	d. cheapness
e. cowardliness	f. mulatto	g. sensationalism	h. military solidarity
i. unhealthiness	Other:		

In the case of *yellow* there is no such uniformity in connotative meaning as we had with *blue* and 'cold'. The top-ranking association was with 'cowardliness', marked by just under one half of the informants. However, there was a noticeable split between the North Americans (62.8 per cent) and the rest (40–43.7 per cent). There is a similar split in the case of no. 3, 'caution': IrE had remarkably low results. The opposite is the case with the No. 2 association, 'unhealthiness', which was marked by a quarter of the AmE users and an average of almost half of the others. There is also a slight tendency toward this type of split in fourth-ranking 'Asian(ness)'. The entries 'happiness' and 'sun, brightness' added under 'Other' turned out to be astonishingly strong (see Table 6.5).

How should we treat these results?

- First of all, we can register a fair amount of agreement about connotations, but it is by no means uniform.
- We cannot make more than vague guesses at the reasons for the differences.

■ The numbers of informants here used are far too small to allow us to treat these results as anything more significant than tendencies.

Table 6.5. Connotative associations of *yellow*

Association	AmE No.	%	AusE No.	%	IrE No.	%	SAE No.	%	Total No.	%	Rank
Asian(ness)	9	25.7	10	38.4	5	31.2	11	31.4	35	31.2	4
Caution	20	57.1	6	23.0	1	6.2	9	25.7	36	32.1	3
Cowardliness	22	62.8	11	42.3	7	43.7	14	40.0	54	48.2	1
Unhealthiness	9	25.7	15	57.6	8	50.0	13	37.1	45	40.1	2
Happiness	3	8.5	3	11.5	–	0.0	3	8.5	9	8.0	6
Sun, brightness	3	8.5	3	11.5	1	6.2	4	11.4	11	9.8	5

Project 6.1: Colour and connotations

Conduct your own survey using the format introduced in Case studies 6.2 and 6.3. Consider modifying it to include the write-in associations presented above. You may instead want to try this with other colours. Here are suggestions for *red*, *green*, *white*, and *black* (see the instructions in Case study 6.2).

Red
a. anger   b. beauty   c. blood   d. danger
e. embarrassment   f. fire   g. heat   h. importance
i. indebtedness   j. Indian(ness)   k. limitation/stop   l. passion
m. radical/left wing   Other:

Green
a. environmentalism   b. envy   c. fear   d. freshness
e. gullibility   f. hope   g. immaturity   h. jealousy
i. life, energy   j. money   k. permission   l. recreation, sport
m. sickness   Other:

White
a. achievement   b. anger   c. auspiciousness   d. Caucasian(ness)
e. conservativeness   f. correctness   g. defeat   h. extreme heat
i. fear   j. harmlessness   k. passion   l. positiveness
m. professionality   n. purity, innocence   o. unhealthiness   Other:

Black
a. African(ness)   b. anger, hostility   c. beauty   d. dirt
e. devilishness   f. disaster   g. disgrace   h. evil, harm
i. failure   j. faintness, weakness   k. financial soundness   l. gloom, pessimism
m. ignorance   n. illegality   o. inferiority   p. mournfulness
q. mysteriousness   r. sarcasm   s. secretness   t. stiffness, formality
u. suppression   v. threat   w. unconventionality   Other:

6.3 FIXED EXPRESSIONS: PROVERBS AND IDIOMS

Among the numerous types of lexically complex expressions it is the metaphorical idioms and the proverbs that we want to devote our attention to. Since idioms were the subject of Case study 2.1 and 3.5, we will return to them here only briefly and will have more to say about the proverb. The point is to see both of them as expressions of the cultures and societies they stem from, for I believe that we tend to choose our more colourful language from the areas that are of more central concern to us. These areas vary, of course, from one English-speaking society to another and between subcultures within any one society in addition.

6.3.1 Proverbs

The collection of proverbs put together in *Poor Richard's Almanack* by Benjamin Franklin in eighteenth-century colonial America is a reflection of the individualistic work ethic so important to the Puritan attitudes of early America (see Table 6.6).

There are dozens more, most in the same tenor. The question is how many proverbs are shared throughout the English-speaking world and what determines which ones are current in a given society. English people are more likely to use the ethnocentric *An Englishman's word is his bond* while elsewhere it may be *A man's word . . .* (if this is not itself too sexist).

Case study 6.4: Ulster proverbs

Todd has suggested that even within one region, Ulster, there are two traditions, Catholic and Protestant, that are so distinct that they have different proverbs. The Catholic ones are said to show the influence of the Gaelic language background and the Protestant ones that of Scots, the language of Scotland and the Scottish settlers in Ulster from the sixteenth and seventeenth centuries on. Some of her examples are shown in Table 6.7.

The mention of a priest in one of the Catholic items and of a Highlander in one of the Protestant ones suggests there is at least some superficial truth to the hypothesis. Just how much underlying cultural difference there may be is surely harder to determine. Both sets clearly rely on experience. There is a touch more

Table 6.6. Early American proverbs

Early to bed, early to rise, makes a man healthy, wealthy, and wise.

There's time enough to rest in the grave.

Time is money.

God helps them that help themselves.

Little strokes fell great oaks.

If time be of all things the most precious, wasting time must be the greatest prodigality.

Then plough deep while sluggards sleep, and you shall have corn to sell and to keep.

Table 6.7. Ulster proverbs (Todd 1989: 352)

Catholic

A black hen lays white eggs.

The first taste o' the soup is the warmest.

The oul' dog for the hard road an' the pup for the pad.

There's always as much dhryin' [*sic*] on a Satruday [*sic*] as
   will do the priest's shirt.

There's more ways o' killin' a dog than by givin' it butter.

Time an' patience will get a snail to Van Diemen's Land.

What's bred in the bone comes out in the flesh.

Protestant

Eaten bread is soon forgotten

If you lie down wi' dogs, you'll get up with fleas

That'll be when Nelson gets his eye back.

Where's the snow that fell last year?

You can't take britches off a Highlander.

You can't whistle an' ate your breakfast.

Better to go to bed supperless than rise in debt.

fatalism in the Catholic set (*A black hen* . . . ; *What's bred* . . .) and maybe more emphasis on individual responsibility and provision for the future through postponement of pleasure in the Protestant ones (*Eaten bread* . . . ; *Better to go to bed supperless* . . . , and in several of the others, but in the 'Catholic' *Time and patience* . . . as well). For one thing, just how representative is this collection? Another point used to call Todd's theses into question is that members of both groups are familiar with items from both sets (Odlin 1991).

Yet Todd's basic thesis seems to hold true on a different level, one perhaps not intended by her. Non-Irish speakers of English may, indeed, be familiar with only some of those quoted above. I myself knew *If you lie down with dogs* . . . and *What's bred in the bone* . . .; the others were unfamiliar, some of them (e.g. *There's always as much dhryin* . . . ; *There's more ways o' killin'* . . .; *That'll be when Nelson* . . .) to the point of being uninterpretable, at least without any further context. Americans (such as myself) know proverbs that may be unfamiliar elsewhere like *Don't take any wooden nickels* ('Watch out') or cliché-like proverbs such as *That's the way the cookie crumbles* ('That's life') simply because nickels and cookies are so particularly American. Ones like *Don't change horses in midstream* may be more current in this American form (coined as it was by Abraham Lincoln to justify his re-election during the American Civil War) than in the fairly current English formulation *It is best not to swap horses while crossing streams.*

6.3.2 What proverbs are used, by whom, and why

Many people when asked will probably say they do not really use proverbs very much, or, indeed, at all. This seems to be especially the case among younger people. Can we say, therefore, that proverbs are on the way out? In one study based on a massive corpus search of some 330 million words,[6] proverbs were indeed rarely found in their canonic or citation form (i.e. the form listed in Simpson 1992). For example, the proverb *First come, first served* occurs most frequently of all, 179 times. All told, only 73 proverbs occurred 10 or more times, few indeed as compared with the over 1000 proverbs listed in Simpson.

However, when *variations* on these proverbs are considered, the corpus is found to contain 110 different base proverbs and considerably more tokens (instances of use). Variation refers to proverbs which

- are contracted (*He is refusing to give an inch* < *Give him an inch and he'll take a mile*)
- include substitution (*The proof of the cake is in the eating* < *The proof of the pudding . . .*)
- show up as an antonym (*All that glitters is gold* < *All that glitters is not gold*) or
- are expanded (*Casting synthetic pearls before real swine* < *Do not throw pearls before swine*).

Charteris-Black (1999) found that almost two-thirds of the variations of proverbs involved contraction, and one quarter substitution. One-eighth are accounted for by antonyms or expansion together (in equal proportions). Furthermore, this study showed that the shorter a proverb, the more likely it is to be used. Ones consisting of two words (e.g. *Time flies*) averaged over 50 tokens in the corpus; those of three words (e.g. *Time is money*), just under 50; those of four (e.g. *Better late than never*) approximately 35; those with five words (e.g. *All's well that ends well*), 23, and so on.

It seems, according to these findings, that proverbs are by no means dying out. However, their use is changing, itself a fine sign of vitality. Because of the strong tendency toward contraction and the other types of variation, these results also show that a mature,[7] fluent speaker of English must have an extensive degree of cultural literacy in order to recognize and process truncated proverbs. Much of the variation in proverbs is to be found in advertising and journalistic language, and is presumably favoured because of the humour and innovation it involves.

---

6 The Bank of English corpus (University of Birmingham, UK, and COBUILD), which consists of 80 per cent of written and 20 per cent of spoken English and is taken from British (70 per cent), American (20 per cent) and Australian (10 per cent) sources. See Charteris-Black (1999) for the details reported here.

7 Charteris-Black (1999) suggests that college students may not (yet) be fully culturally literate in this sense.

The very fact that such variation is so relatively frequent is a strong indication that cultural literacy in the field of proverbs is widely presupposed.

Exercise 6.3: Characterizing proverbs

Proverbs (complete ones!) are not always easy to identify; so for your help note the following points:

(a) they consist of whole sentences, unless contracted (metaphorical idioms do not, cf. 6.3.1: for proverbs see examples above)

(b) they may have an archaic syntactic structure, i.e. one which is not productive (e.g. *Easy come, easy go*)

(c) they may use rhyme, repetition, or alliteration and are often divided into two parts (*Easy come, easy go; Early to bed, . . .*)

(d) they are generic in reference (not *this* eaten bread, but eaten bread *in general*)

(e) they tend to make use of homely words (*hen, soup, dog, shirt, bread*)

(f) they are often metaphorical (*eaten bread* = something enjoyed or used in the present)

(g) they express some sort of 'wisdom' or (commonplace) truth, a precept for life (*Eaten bread . . . = 'Think about the future'*)

Which of the characteristics listed above do the following examples of proverbs demonstrate?

1. Pretty is as pretty does.
2. You can take the boy out of the country, but you can't take the country out of the boy.
3. Idle hands lead to mischief.
4. If you can't beat them, join them.
5. If it ain't broke, don't fix it!
6. Garbage in, garbage out.
7. The more, the merrier.

Project 6.2: Testing for shared proverbs

Pick five proverbs which are familiar to you and which you consider to be of general currency. Make email inquiries using contacts you may have (or can establish!) in three different English-speaking countries to see if these proverbs are shared. Be sure to get a gloss of each from your informants. You may find that the meaning given elsewhere differs from your own.

Often enough the 'same' proverb will show up in different varieties of English, but will reveal small differences. In IndE we find *Talk of the devil and you hear his footsteps* while the elsewhere more current *Talk of the devil and he will appear* is generally unknown there (Nihalani *et al.* 1979). Some people know *Too many cooks spoil the broth*; for others it is *the soup* that is spoiled. Some say *Nothing venture, nothing gain*; others have *Nothing ventured, nothing gained*.

6.3.3 Idioms

Idioms are shorter than a sentence, often consisting of a verb plus a second element as with phrasal verbs (e.g. *to goof off*) or metaphorical ones (e.g. *to beat around the bush*). They are syntactically and lexically relatively fixed: there is no *goof on*, no *to beat around the bushes*, nor any *to beat around the shrub*. Furthermore, their meaning is different from the sum of the meanings of the individual words that occur in them (cf. §3.5.2).

As to their variation throughout the English-speaking world, much the same thing is true of them as is true of proverbs. They may vary from country to country (or from group to group within a single country) due to:

- a different underlying foreign language pattern, e.g. SingE *to sleep late*, which is formed on the Chinese pattern, means *to go to bed late* and therefore means to be tired rather than to sleep longer and therefore possibly to be refreshed (Tongue 1974: 78). SingE also has the loan translation of Malay *goyang kaki*, literally *shake legs*, which means 'take it easy', rather than ENL *shake a leg* 'hurry' (Tay 1982: 68).

- a slightly different syntax, as when IndE has a plural instead of the more general singular in *to pull someone's legs* or *to laugh in one's sleeves*.

- a different choice of words, as when BrE has *too big for one's boots* ('conceited') where AmE has *too big for one's breeches*.

- new phrasal verb combinations as evidence, according to one linguist, of ESL insecurity:[8] *discuss about, voice out*, where the particles are redundant; or the opposite: leaving off the particle in *pick (up), apply (for)*; or choosing a different one from ENL varieties, e.g. *result into, deprive from* (Görlach 1988: 18).

- a different cultural-historical background, e.g. *put your John Hancock [under something]* 'sign [something]' is probably only meaningful and usable by an American, who will presumably know that John Hancock was the first to sign the American Declaration of Independence and that he signed it with a large and very noticeable signature so that 'John Bull [caricature of England/an English person] can read it without his spectacles'.

- a newly coined expression, as when NigE uses *as at now* for GenE *as of now* or *off-head* 'from memory' like *offhand* (Bamgbose 1983); or the useful IndE idiomatic expression *one by two* (*May we have coffee please, one by two?*) when one drink is ordered but two cups/glasses are required (Nihalani *et al.* 1979: 131).

- metaphors which may be specific to a particular cultural or linguistic background. While for ENL varieties emotions are considered to come from the

---

8 This should be treated with scepticism. After all, ENL varieties also vary in the same way. There is redundant *refer back* for *refer* (both GenE) and *approximate to (the truth)* (BrE) for (AmE) *approximate (the truth)*.

heart, the stomach is often the seat of emotions in non-ENL communities. In Africa *belly words* are the ones that come 'straight from the heart' (Angogo and Hancock 1980: 79). In Philippine English we find *close/open the light* 'turn the light off/on' (Llamzon 1969: 47), where the open/close metaphor is obviously based on one different from the more usual on/off expression.[9]

Exercise 6.4: Fixed expressions: binomials and trinomials

A particular type of fixed expression is the ***binomial*** and ***trinomial***, which may be illustrated by expressions like *spick and span* and *town and gown* (binomials) or *lock, stock, and barrel* (a trinomial). Here once again we have to do with constructions below the sentence level. They are both lexically fixed (no *lock, stock, and trigger*) and syntactically irreversible (no *span and spick*). Like idioms their meaning is not always literal: *town and gown*, for instance, refers by metonymy to 'normal' people (*town*) and university people (*gown*) and has connotations of conflict between the two. In contrast to the idioms introduced in §6.3.3, binomials (and trinomials) consist of two (or three) lexical items of the same word class, which despite the word element {-nomial} may be noun, adjective, verb, or other: *fish and chips, fat and happy, aid and abet, by and large, for better and for worse*.

> Bi- and trinomials are made up of irreversible combinations dictated by rhyme (*town and gown*), alliteration (*spick and span*), word field (food: *fish and chips*), repetition of meaning (*aid and abet*), adversative meaning (*for better and for worse*), or meronymy (parts of the whole: *lock, stock, and barrel*).
>   Your task is to
>
> (1) complete the following bi- and trinomials,
> (2) identify the principle (rhyme, alliteration, etc.) governing the combination,
> (3) give a gloss of their meaning, and
> (4) name the word class involved.
>
> | Bi-, trinomial example: | Principle | Gloss | Class |
> | --- | --- | --- | --- |
> | hale and hearty | alliteration | healthy | adjective |
> | 1. kith and _____ | | | |
> | 2. assault and _____ | | | |
> | 3. _____, line, and sinker | | | |
> | 4. left, right, and _____ | | | |
> | 5. huff and _____ | | | |
> | 6. from fruit to _____ | | | |
> | 7. _____ or break | | | |
> | 8. forgive and _____ | | | |
> | 9. _____ over heels | | | |

---

9 For more on everyday metaphors see Lakoff and Johnson (1980).

10. hire and _____
11. from _____ to riches
12. _____ and dry
13. _____ and fancy-free

Resources you might use: a learner's dictionary or a combinatory dictionary (*BBI Dictionary of English Word Combinations*), Seidl and McMordie (1988).

6.4 ENGLISH AGAINST A DIFFERING LINGUISTIC BACKGROUND

The grammatical system of any given language will not change nearly as quickly as its vocabulary. And, indeed, modern StE is remarkably unitary worldwide in its grammar while its vocabulary is, as we continue to see, highly varied. Yet when we go beyond the boundaries of the present-day standard language to look at grammatical differences in English, we find quite a few, including some which show up as word differences. In §2.1.3 we looked at the system of English personal pronouns and discovered change over time (temporal variation) as we moved from Old to Middle to Modern English. Even within the modern language there are remarkable differences between StE and some of the English creoles. Behind all this diversity lie differences in the underlying grammatical categories, differences which reflect the influence of non-English substrate languages (§6.4.1). Besides differences in underlying categories, there are also differences in the way constructions are used. In §6.4.2 we look at some of these: the use of the pro-forms *yes* and *no*, negation, and tag questions.

6.4.1 Grammatical differences: the system of personal pronouns

In the non-native, ESL varieties grammatical categories are sometimes realized differently than in ENL, as was pointed out in §5.1.2.5. Here we introduce somewhat more extensively the personal pronouns in two English-related creoles as well as in modern StE. The system of English personal pronouns serves as an example of the grammatical side of vocabulary. As elsewhere in grammar there is little variation in this area, and change is slow. Yet the cumulative changes have been large. And these changes may be said to indicate, in some cases at least, changes in social values. Most of them involve grammatical case, number, and gender.

Case study 6.5: Personal pronouns in Kriol and in Jamaican Creole

In the Other Englishes (not the 'New Englishes,' but the Pidgin and Creole Englishes) the pronoun system often reflects the person and number categories of the local (or substrate) languages. Kriol, the Kimberley/Northern area creole of Austrialia, has a pronoun system which distinguishes both a dual and a plural as well as exclusive and inclusive 1st person forms (see Table 6.8).

Burridge and Mulder emphasize the importance of the existence of this and other creoles for its speakers: 'As languages in their own right, as distinct from

Table 6.8. The Kriol personal pronoun system (partial) (Burridge and Mulder 1998: 288)

	Inclusion	Pronoun	Reference
FIRST PERSON			
Dual	Inclusive	*minyu*	me and you
	Exclusive	*mintupala*	two of us, excluding you
Plural	Inclusive	*wilat*	several of us including you
	Exclusive	*mifella/mela*	several of us excluding you
SECOND PERSON			
dual	–	*yuntupala*	you two
plural	–	*yupala*	you (more than two)

English, creoles such as these have become an important means of signalling their speakers' cultural and social identity. In this way, Kriol is now an important part of these speakers' Aboriginality' (p. 289). They also point out the following about Maori English in New Zealand: 'Maori-speakers often transfer terms and rules from the Maori address system to their English – for example, a three-way distinction in second-person pronouns *you* (singular), *youse* (dual), and *youse fullas* (plural)' (p. 12).

In early Jamaican Creole the distinctions of case were not made, but those of number (2nd person singular and plural) were (see Table 6.9).

In the meantime the presence of StE in Jamaica has exerted continuous pressure toward the standard. For example, case distinctions (*ai* 'I' and *mi* 'me') are now frequently made. Today *unu* is a strictly **basilect** (= low dialect) form, i.e. a form used in the type of Jamaican Creole most distant from the **acrolect** (= high dialect), which is StE. In **mesolect** forms (bridging the gap between the basilect and the acrolect) a 2nd person plural pronoun closer to StE has been adopted (*you all*).

6.4.1.1 Modern English personal pronouns
Personal pronouns have shown a clear tendency to appear in their strong (or **disjunctive**[10]) forms (*That's me* (*I); *Me and him, we went to the movies last night*; *Who's there? Me!*). In Early Modern English (1500–1700) the 2nd person subject-form pronouns *thou* and *ye* began losing out to *thee* and *you*, the object forms. We are, of course, aware of the loss of *ye* (and know it today only from the King James/Authorized Version of the Bible and older works of literature, such as Shakespeare's earlier plays). The parallel loss of *thou* is less evident because of

---

10 **Disjunctive** refers to the appearance of a pronoun *disjoined* from the subject, i.e. either in apposition, in conjunction, or in a position after the verb. See examples in the text.

Table 6.9. The early Jamaican Creole personal pronoun system (Holm 1988: 201ff.)

	Singular	Plural
1st	*mi* (I, me, my)	*wi* (we, us, our)
2nd	*yu* (you, your)	*unu* (you, your)
3rd	*im* (he, him, his, she, her, it, its)	*dem* (they, them, their)

Unu has the variants *wuna* in Barbados, *yina* in the Bahamas, etc. Cf. Ibo *unu*, Yoruba *nyin*, Wolof *yena*, Kongo *yeno*, Mbundu *yenu*, and Common Bantu **nu*.

the general loss of *thou/thee* in English.[11] In IndE we may find the reflexive *myself* instead of the disjunctive *me*, as in A: *Who wrote this?* B: *Myself*. In addition, the reflexive *itself* has been extended to emphasize an expression of time or place in IndE despite the lack of an antecedent as in or *Shall we have the meeting here itself?* or *Can I come and see you today itself?* (cf. Nihalani *et al.* 1979: 105, 126).

At the same time notional number has grown increasingly common. As a result indefinite pronouns such as *everyone, no one, someone, anyone*, etc. have come to be understood not as referring to *one*, which appears as an element in each, but to the plurality of *everyone* = 'all people'; *no one* = 'no people'; *someone, anyone* 'any people'. So we say, *If anyone* (grammatically singular, notionally plural) *wants* (singular) *to, they* (plural) *can pick up their* (plural) *project assignments next Monday*. That a plural personal pronoun (*they/their*) is used to pick up the reference to a 'singular' indefinite pronoun is also convenient because it helps us to avoid using a sexually exclusive pronoun like *he/his* or *she/her* or the more circumstantial *he or she* or *his or her* or the awkward *s/he*.

Exercise 6.5: Explicit 2nd person plural pronouns

Except for a few dialects and some retention in religious language and among Quakers (see fn. 11), the older 2nd person singular forms are no longer current, as mentioned above. Yet the need to distinguish singular *you* from plural *you* is often felt. How do we solve this problem? Depending on the variety (including the colloquial and creoles), we find the following alternatives used to distinguish plural reference explicitly: *una, y'all, you guys, youse, yiz, you'uns*.

Using dictionaries (and the random remarks made in this book up to now) try to find out where each of the alternatives listed above are used.

Pronoun	Where used	Level of usage
1. all you (aa-yu)		
2. una/unu		
3. y'all		

11 Examples would be uses like the following:
'And so thee still thinks of going to Canada, Eliza?' she said,. . . .
'Yes, ma'am,' said Eliza, firmly. . . .
'And what'll thee do, when thee gets there? Thee must think about that, my daughter.' (Harriet Beecher Stowe, *Uncle Tom's Cabin*, 'The Quaker Settlement' [1851f.]).

Pronoun	Where used	Level of usage
4. yiz		
5. you guys		
6. youse ones		
7. youse		
8. you'uns		

6.4.1.2 Generic reference

Generic reference is a problem which is directly related to the question of the choice of 3rd person singular pronouns, the *he or she, s/he* problem referred to above. More generally, of course, generic reference (in this context) has to do with the use of any sorts of term for people which do not specify their gender. The word *man* is said to designate any human being. The difficulty is that *man* calls up the image of men rather than both men and women, which explains the (unintended) humour of a biology textbook which speaks of 'pregnancy in man'.

As far as pronouns are concerned, the traditional interpretation of the grammatical category of gender is that the pronoun *she* is used for referents that are female while *he* is employed for males, for both, or for indeterminate referents. Many people argue, quite rightly, that generic *he* excludes females. In one study Graham (1975: 58) counted 940 uses of *he* in a sample of 100 000 words. Of these 744 referred to male humans, 128 to male animals, and 36 to persons presumed to be male, such as sailors or farmers. This left only 32 as indeterminate and hence generic. Clearly the well-meant theory of generic reference is different in practice. And so it is no wonder that people (probably men most of all) unconsciously interpret *he*, generic or not, as masculine. As for women, another study shows how important creating identity can be when it reports that women get better results on maths problems which are female-oriented (Martyna 1980: 71ff.). Clearly, a widely acceptable solution to this problem remains to be found.

Project 6.3: Pronouns and stereotypes

An especially interesting investigation in this area reveals how personification is used in children's literature. MacKay and Konishi looked at children's stories to see where *he*, *she*, and *it* occurred. Animals were cross-referenced with *he* in 76 per cent of the cases; *she* was used for the other 24 per cent. In addition, *he* was typically used for large mammals such as lions, gorillas, and wolves; *she* for small ones such as small birds or insects (bees, ladybirds). Yet MacKay and Konishi do not advocate moving to a neutral form like *it* because this pronoun would have the disadvantage of lessening the emotional and personal involvement of the children (1980: 152ff.).

Try to replicate the findings of MacKay and Konishi. Choose three or four children's stories, preferably by different authors in order to gain greater representativity. On the basis of your corpus determine:

(a) What is the overall ratio of masculine to feminine pronouns?

(b) Is there a tendency similar to that outlined above, according to which the masculine pronoun is associated with large mammals and the feminine one with small non-mammals?

(c) Draw up a 'profile' of the connotations of *he* vs. *she* on the basis of your corpus.

Exercise 6.6: Personal pronouns and grammatical categories

In the case of numerous antecedents the use of the pronoun *he* (or *she*) may be justified because the typical referent of the word is male (or female). Even today most medical doctors in the United States are male; therefore, the use of generic *he*, some would argue, is not unduly misleading. For nurses, generic *she* is not fully unrealistic since most nurses are, in fact, female. But what about antecedents like *student* or *writer*? Both are equally likely to be men or women, so isn't generic *he* inappropriate?

One remedy suggested is to adopt a new sex-neutral 3rd person singular personal pronoun. The suggestions have included at least the following (each of which have been argued for with a variety of reasons[12]): *tey, hesh, e* or *E, co, thon, hir, po, re, xe, jhe, per*. The difficulty with any of these suggestions is that none of them is natural and any given one would require broad acceptance and have to be learnt. Since pronouns belong to the grammatical words of the language, changes come only very rarely (as we saw in §2.1.3). Over the last 1000 years the system of English personal pronouns has changed, but not often or quickly, and there is no reason to think change might be more likely or speedy today. However, the way the present-day personal pronouns are used is not all that straightforward, but allows for a great amount of flexibility, as the following exercise demonstrates.

When you compare the two charts in Fig. 6.1, which display two views of the personal pronoun system of modern English, you will find that the traditional normative pronoun system shows a strict distribution of pronouns in grammatical categories. For instance, *we* is 1st person plural. The actual descriptive system includes 'violations' of grammatical category, where, for example, *we* may be 1st or 2nd person and singular or plural.

Explain each of the violations and give an example of each case of non-normative use. The 'violations' are the following:

(a) Number: singular *we* and *they*
(b) Person: *we* as 2nd person; *you* as 3rd person
(c) Gender: neuter *she*; feminine *he*; masculine and feminine singular *they*

---

12 For example, *tey* (singular) is an modification of *they* (plural); *hesh* is a blend of *he* + *she*; *e/E* represents the vowel common to both *he* and *she*; *hir* has the vowel of *he* and the /r/ of *her* (in rhotic accents); *co* is Latin for 'together'.

	Singular			Plural
	Neuter	Feminine	Masculine	
1st person		I		we
2nd person		you		
3rd person	it	she	he	they

The traditional normative pronoun system

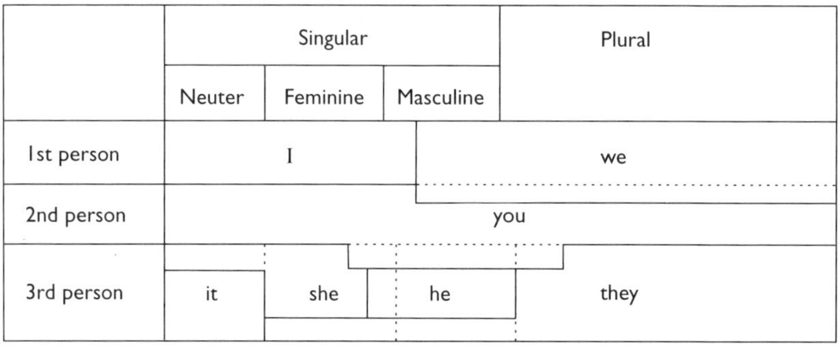

	Singular			Plural
	Neuter	Feminine	Masculine	
1st person		I		we
2nd person		you		
3rd person	it	she	he	they

The actual descriptive pronoun system

Fig. 6.1. The personal pronouns of ModE

6.4.2 The use of *yes* and *no*, and tag questions

6.4.2.1 *Yes, no,* and negation

Just how the seemingly simple words *yes* and *no* are used in English is more complex than we might at first anticipate. In the immediately preceding section we saw that even the standard and straighforward grammatical subsystem of the personal pronouns contains enormous variation in regard to how the basic categories of the system are actually applied. So it is with these two simple words as well. We might begin by asking what kinds of word they are. Since they can be used to replace a whole sentence, the first answer[13] is that they must be pro-forms, e.g.:

> A: Did you ask?
> B: Yes. (= I asked)

Frequently, of course, the answer given by B is supported by a short form of the sentence replaced, viz. *Yes, I did*. Usually usage is identical wherever English is spoken, but not always. The following is not necessarily clear, where A may, for example, have asked whether he or she might borrow B's pencil for a moment:

---

13 *Yes* and *no* have further uses as discourse markers (see §7.3.1).

A: You don't mind?
B: Yes.

Most Anglo-American speakers would take this to mean that the B does mind; yet this dialogue, quoted from Platt and Weber (1980: 79), represents an interchange in SingE in which B's *yes* means 'Yes, I don't mind.'

What has happened here? In the usual Anglo-American version *yes* is a proform which represents the exact proposition of the initial question, which contains a negation. The word *no* cancels the negation (*No, I don't*) while a *yes* confirms it (*Yes, I do*). In other words, it affirms or negates the content; the SingE affirms or negates the assumption of the original speaker. In the SingE version *yes* and *no* function on the level of the speech act (the pragmatic level) and are equivalent to saying *Yes, it is correct that I don't mind* or, in the negative, *No, it is not correct that I don't mind*. Where the original query is framed positively there is, of course, no difference between the two because the proposition and the assumption are equivalent, cf.:

A: Do you mind?
B: Yes (Anglo-American: 'I do mind'; SingE: 'It is correct that I mind').

Since the SingE use of *yes* and *no* is found in IndE (Kachru 1984: 374) and in WAVE (Angogo and Hancock 1980: 77f.), and the 'Anglo-American' type is usual in native-speaker English, it may be presumed that the difference in use is due to substrate language usage. Nevertheless, we should not overlook the fact that such 'other-Englishness' is sometimes at home in native varieties as well, as the IrE dialogue in Text 6.1 reveals. Young Paddy Clarke (under 10) is being punished for something which he was involved in but is technically innocent of (since he was not the direct perpetrator):

Paddy is, strictly speaking, telling the truth, but he is also flouting the pragmatic rules of ENL varieties since normally, if you didn't do something, you say *No* (= 'I didn't'). *Yes* is ambiguous between 'Yes, that's correct' and 'Yes, I did something'. This is a neat stratagem for getting out of a difficult situation without lying, and it is commonly known as prevarication, against which the court oath 'to tell the truth, the whole truth, and nothing but the truth' is directed.

Case study 6.6: Negation

Negation and negative words like *not*, *none*, *no one*, and *neither* sometime work in ways not expected in GenE. SingE, for example, often uses *all . . . not* for 'none', as in *All the locks don't work*, or *both . . . not* for 'neither', cf. *Both didn't go abroad* (Tongue 1974: 41).[14] And IndE has *no more* where other varieties might

---

14 The same is said about young Australians (cf. Angelo *et al.* 1998: 17).

have *not any more* (e.g. *He's no more working here*) (Nihalani *et al.* 1979: 127). What we have here are examples in which familiar rules of ENL sentence negation are not applied. What are these rules?

Text 6.1. Yes, I didn't (in IrE) (Roddy Doyle. *Paddy Clarke Ha Ha Ha*)

> – . . . it wasn't me.
> – What wasn't you? [. . .]
> – I don't know. I didn't do anything, I swear, Dad. Dad. Cross my heart and hope to die. Look.
> I crossed my heart. I did it all the time; nothing ever happened and I was usually lying.
> I wasn't lying this time, though. I hadn't done anything. It was Kevin who broke her window. [. . .]
> – She prob'ly thinks I did something, I said.
> – But you didn't.
> – Yeah.
> – You say.
> – Yeah.
> – Say Yes.
> – Yes.

Negation in StE is signalled by attaching *not* to the auxiliary (modal verbs, *do*, *have*, *be*), as in *The guests didn't come*. And this is what the SingE examples above have done. However, in StE, when the subject contains a quantifier like *all*, *some*, *one*, or *both*, the negation is attached to them rather than to the verb, which gives us *None/No one (came)* or *Neither (came)*.

A further rule of StE allows the negation to be attached to an object containing a word like *all*, *some*, *one*, or *both* instead of to the verb. This gives us the somewhat more formal-sounding *I saw no one* instead of the colloquial *I didn't see anyone*. This is what the IndE example above has done.

The rules of StE allow only one negation in each sentence. Theoretically, if someone uses two, they cancel each other, as in *Well, I didn't exactly see no one. Jean was there and we talked*. Here the speaker is using the second negative contrastively to say that he or she actually did see someone. Such cases are, however, relatively rare. What we are more likely to hear are non-standard but fully normal GenE cases of multiple negation such as *I didn't see no one (nowhere)* ('I didn't see anyone (anywhere)'), in which the effect of the further cases of negation is to heighten or emphasize the basic negation.

One variety of American English known as **Black American English (BAE)** uses multiple negation even more productively than GenE. Here we can have, in one and the same sentence, a negated subject, verb, object, and adverbials as in *Nobody didn't see nothing nowhere nohow*. Although this is a relatively extreme combination, it does not do anything more than to strengthen the negation, as is the case in the GenE example given above.

Some of the varieties of BAE which are more distant from StE go even further. Here negation can be added to a dependent clause (underlined), e.g. *I didn't see nobody doing nothing <u>I didn't like</u> nowhere* ('I didn't see anybody doing anything <u>I liked</u> anywhere'). For speakers unfamiliar with BAE this sentence might be interpreted differently: 'I didn't see anybody doing anything <u>I didn't like</u> anywhere.' This misunderstanding comes about because GenE does not allow the further transfer of emphatic negation into a dependent clause. If the dependent clause is negative, it carries an independent negative meaning.

Exercise 6.7: Multiple negation

Each of the following sentences contains instances of multiple negation, some of which are StE; some, GenE (but not StE); others come from BAE, spoken by many, but not all African Americans. Label each as an instance of one of these. Paraphrase each in StE.

1. He don't hardly know what to do.
   BAE/GenE/StE
   paraphrase:
2. It is not unlikely that they will come.
   BAE/GenE/StE
   paraphrase:
3. Ain't nobody at home.
   BAE/GenE/StE
   paraphrase:
4. You definitely cannot not go to her party.
   BAE/GenE/StE
   paraphrase:
5. Nobody didn't do nothing.
   BAE/GenE/StE
   paraphrase:
6. The teacher didn't go nowhere.
   BAE/GenE/StE
   paraphrase:
7. She don't believe there's nothing she can't do.
   BAE/GenE/StE
   paraphrase:
8. We don't think they won't come.
   BAE/GenE/StE
   paraphrase:

Resource you might use: Burling (1973).

6.4.2.2 Tag questions

Tags are elements added onto sentences to emphasize or to question what they say. They may show solidarity between speaker and hearer, or they may call something into doubt. Which effect they have depends on such things as whether the intonation they are spoken with is falling (emphasis) or rising (questioning), as in the following:

It's time to go, right ↑ ('Do you agree?')
It's time to go, right ↓ ('Come on!')

Tags can take all kinds of forms. They can be invariant (*right?*, *okay?*, *eh?*, *what?*, *yes?*, *am I right?*, *don't you think?*, *isn't that so?*, *wouldn't you say?*, etc.). IndE also has *not so?*; Pueblo English (American Southwest) has *no?* due to Spanish influence (Algeo 1988: 175).

Tag questions can vary grammatically according to the subject and the auxiliary of the clause they are attached to; furthermore, if the main verb is positive the tag is most often (but not necessarily) negative and vice versa, e.g.

It's time to go, isn't it?
He's ready to go, isn't he?
They can't find her, can they?

It is this second type which has been the subject of some observation. 'Varieties of English that have been heavily influenced by other languages use invariant question tags that superficially resemble the echo tag of mainstream English. An invariant *isn't it?* or *is it?* has been reported for Welsh, Chinese, West African, Indic, and Papua New Guinean English in constructions like "You're going home now, isn't it?" (Algeo 1988:174f.[15]). Cf.:

You went there yesterday, isn't it? (IndE; Verma 1982)
The Director is busy now, is it? (SingE; Tay 1982: 64)
Das waz a swiit stuori, duonit? 'That was a nice story, wasn't it?' (Miskito Coast CE; Holm 1994: 380)

In the following WelshE examples the tag is used, rather typically, with directives while seeking the approval of the person addressed:

Make a big castle, i'n' it?
Fill the boxes up, is it?
Let's finish this off, isn't it?
Let's take 'em all out, is it?   (Jones 1990: 179)

In SAE, for example, although not a tag strictly speaking, it has been suggested that *Is it?* has been adopted in this invariable form parallel to standard

---

15 Algeo (1988) gives a comprehensive presentation of tag questions, form and function.

Afrikaans *Is dit?*, regardless of the subject and the auxiliary that would be required by the initiating sentence in ENL varieties (Branford 1994: 492):

A: They got married on Friday.
B: Is it?

Tag questions have frequently been examined under the aspect of gender-specific use. Lakoff has suggested that women use more of the sort which seek confirmation of a personal opinion (e.g. *The way prices are rising is horrendous, isn't it?*) (1976: 16). Such tag questions show uncertainty typical of women as power-less members of society. Attempts to study this problem empirically have led to diverse results, including findings that men actually use more, which are, 'far from signalling lack of confidence, . . . intended to forestall opposition' (Dubois and Crouch 1975: 292). Another study found that girls produce twice as many tags as boys (Sachs 1987: 184).

It is not clear whether there are differences in the frequency of employ-ment of tag questions according to gender, nor is it clear what the important factors in their use are. In the studies quoted, too little is said about aspects of *register* such as the setting (formal, informal), the purpose (sustaining con-versation, forestalling opposition), or the relationship of the people interacting (power, solidarity). Furthermore, the type of intonation (rising, falling) is seldom mentioned.

Exercise 6.8: Tag questions

Test your mastery of the English grammatical tag questions by supplying the appropriate tag for each of the following sentences. The rules you are to observe are listed for you:

(1) Use the personal pronoun appropriate for the subject of the clause (gender, number), e.g. <u>Brenda</u> went, didn't <u>she</u>?.
(2) Use the same auxiliary or the verb *be* (or if neither occurs, use the auxiliary *do*, as in 1), e.g. We <u>shouldn't</u> arrive before eight, <u>should</u> we?
(3) Reverse the polarity: a positive main verb gets a negative tag (as in 1); a negative main verb gets a positive tag (as in 2).
(4) Warning: Some of the items cannot be handled well with the rules given above! (See solutions.)

  1. My mother hasn't arrived yet, . . .
  2. The drill sergeant can help us, . . .
  3. John's dog bit him, . . .
  4. Neither Jack nor Jill fetched the water, . . .
  5. My aunt may come, . . .
  6. Nobody told him, . . .
  7. Leave us alone, . . .
  8. Let's go early, . . .
  9. Did you see that, . . .
  10. I'm supposed to give a little talk, . . .

6.5 SUMMARY

In this chapter we looked at the domains in which English is used in ESL varieties in Africa and Asia and at examples of how the vocabulary of English has been extended in some of them. We then moved on to an observation of connotative associations using the example of colour words, and followed this up by examining some fixed expressions. Here the proverb was used as an example of how the shared knowledge and values of a social group can influence the items used. We also looked at metaphorical idioms and bi- and trinomials as further examples of fixed expressions.

The final part of the chapter focused on underlying grammatical categories, often due to substratum influences. The personal pronoun system was at the centre of attention, revealing variation at the periphery (English creoles) and between the normative grammatical pronoun system and actual usage. The final sections extended this perspective by looking at the use of negation and of tag questions both in the New Englishes and in ENL varieties.

English in Action: Social Dimensions of Vocabulary Differences

Suit the action to the word, the word to the action; with this special observance, that you o'erstep not the modesty of nature.

(Shakespeare, *Hamlet*, iii. 2)

'Have some wine,' the March Hare said in an encouraging tone.
Alice looked all round the table, but there was nothing on it but tea. 'I don't see any wine,' she remarked.
    'There isn't any,' said the March Hare.
    'Then it wasn't very civil of you to offer it,' said Alice angrily.

(Lewis Carroll, *Alice in Wonderland*)

7.0 INTRODUCTION

As the epigraphs indicate, words and deeds belong together. To offer someone something that's not available is to make fun of them in an insulting way. The match between words and action is, in other words, extremely important. What dictates how this may happen is a combination of who we are (our social features, such as gender, age, status, and where we come from) and the situation in which we are communicating. The linguistic area of *sociolinguistics* covers the first and *pragmatics* the second.

In this chapter I want to explore this theme by looking at what it means to be polite and at some of the varying ways in which this is realized linguistically in different (parts of the) societies in which English is used as a first or a second language. Our vehicles for doing this, after taking a look at politeness (§7.1), will be vocatives and modes of address, including kinship terms (§7.2), and communicative strategies, including speech acts and pragmatic idioms (§7.3).

7.1 POLITENESS

Politeness is highly conventionalized, and its conventions vary from society to society. Nevertheless, certain underlying principles seem to be shared throughout the world. The basic idea behind politeness is that of *face*. This has nothing to do with slugging someone in the eye or not; rather, *face* in this sense is the same as in the expression *to save (your, someone's) face*. There are two kinds: negative face and positive face. To respect *negative face* means not to impose on another; *positive face* means to enhance another's self-esteem. The one corresponds to the notion of not interfering with someone's desired actions; the other has to do with the need we all have of approval: 'notions of face naturally link up to some of the most fundamental cultural ideas about the nature of social persona, honour and virtue, shame and redemption and thus to religious concepts' (Brown and Levinson 1987: 13).

Beyond the fact that all human beings have face needs, there is the extremely complex question of what counts as imposition, i.e. as a **face-threatening act** (or **FTA**), and what enhances self-esteem in a given society. This is the field of ethnographers, who, among other things, seek to describe 'how confrontations or shamings are managed, how people gossip . . . how they clear their name from disparagement, and how face regard (and sanctions for face disregard) are incorporated in religious and political systems' (Brown and Levinson 1987: 14). Politeness is strongly related, on the one hand, to questions of (public) status and, on the other, to everyday notions of personal tact and sensitivity to others.

One of the important ways of respecting negative face is to maintain distance. The polite forms of English are linguistic reflections of this. Too much directness does not allow the addressee any path of retreat and is therefore an imposition on her or his territory and potentially face-threatening. Let us compare some of the ways in which we can impose our will on another by supposing that we want another person not to smoke in the room we're in, moving from least to most polite/indirect:

(1) Imperative   *Don't smoke in here (please)*.
(2) Interrogative   *Do you have to smoke in here?*
(3) Past modal   *You might stop smoking in here.*
(2) + (3)   *Could/Would you stop smoking in here?*

Since imperatives are so extremely direct, they cannot be used as polite forms (though the intonation may mitigate them, as when a final rising melody makes them less imposing). The use of an interrogative amounts to querying the necessity for someone to act in a particular way, or their ability or willingness to comply with the speaker's wishes. That is, it is not the proposition ('you smoke in here') which is being focused on, but the **preparatory conditions**. In this way the **speech act** 'request' is not only implicit (cf. §5.3.2.2) but also **indirect,** because we do not ask about the smoking, only about the personal conditions involved in smoking. The request that the other person should not smoke is not formulated directly, but is instead carried out by implication. The past tense, too, is indirect because it is a signal of distance from the situation. This distance is, however, not in the dimension of time, but is, rather, remoteness in reality, which together with a modal auxiliary is the conditional form.

Politeness may also be expressed via titles or honorifics in some varieties of English, for instance *Shut the window, Sir*, to which may be added *please* or *kindly* (Adetugbo 1979a:158, 160). The fact that past modals mark distance and therefore politeness lead, as Tongue (1974: 42) remarks, to the overuse of *would* for *will* in SingE: 'The writer's suggestion would be looked into'. In the SingE expression *Thank you-ah*, the *ah* is necessary for politeness: 'It is almost universal in telephonic conversation and is probably the most frequent interjection in the [SingE] dialect of English' (p. 85).

Another way of indicating politeness is to lengthen an expression from its shortest and most perfunctory form, as in the Ulster invitation to come in, mentioned in Case study 2.1 and repeated here:

Come in.	(very cool reception)
Come on in.	(warmer)
Och, come on on in.	(very warm) (Todd 1984b: 173)

We get greater length in the combination of indirect speech (a reported question) plus past modality (4), which becomes even more indirect when the main verb is in the past progressive form (5):

(4) indirect + (2) + (3)	*I wonder if you could stop smoking in here.*
(5) indirect + past proressive + (2) + (3)	*I was wondering if you could stop smoking in here.*

Wherever language is used, it reflects in one way or the other the underlying social system and values of its speakers. When a language is used within one single society only, it is sometimes difficult to spot the values – despite all the differences we can imagine there are: regional, social, ethnic, gender-related, religious, or whatever. However, in the case of English, which is spoken and written in many different countries, it is relatively easy to find a variety in which matches between society and language are different from what we are familiar with. One of the main goals of this chapter is to explore some of these differences.

7.2 VOCATIVES AND MODES OF ADDRESS

We will begin by reviewing some of the rules of address in ENL varieties. Modes of address turn out to be one of the most revealing ways to see relations between people. Put in other words: 'Personal address is a sociolinguistic subject par excellence' (Philipsen and Huspek 1985: 94).

7.2.1 Motivation for using vocatives

One of the first questions we should ask is why people use vocatives at all. One reason is, of course, to pick out one or more persons from within a larger group. Teachers regularly do this when they call on students. A parent may single out an individual child. A policeman may try to get one person's attention. And so on. However, vocatives are also used when this distinguishing function is not absolutely necessary. They are used to control people's behaviour, be they children at play or adults among one another (Emihovich 1981: 198). In literary works vocatives are said to be frequently aggressive, a point which is emphasized by their use with an exclamation point or a question mark (Kramer 1975: 200f., 207).

Project 7.1: Vocatives in fictional literature

Try to confirm Kramer's findings about the use of vocatives in fictional literature. Look at novelistic or short story fiction which contains a relatively large proportion of dialogue and determine whether it is indeed used aggressively or in order to control others.

If you are particularly ambitious, you might choose fiction from two or three different English-speaking countries. Try, however, to choose samples written at approximately the same time, say, within 10 to 15 years of each other.

7.2.1.1 What address consists of

A follow-up question concerns what is meant by 'address'. First of all this does not include the way we refer to people (although reference is sometimes very close to address). To address people we use a special class of words called **vocatives**. Only a few items are used exclusively as vocatives; these include the terms of respect (honorifics) *ma'am/madam, miss, sir*. They can consist of pronouns such as *you, you all, you guys*, etc. (cf. Exercise 6.5). But they can also extend to a name – first name (FN), last name (LN), nickname and diminutive (DN) – to a kinship term (KT) like *Dad* or *Auntie*, to a title (T) such as *Captain* or *Doctor*, or to a **descriptor** (D) like *Fatso* or *Room Service*. Furthermore, vocatives can be oriented towards gender (*ma'am, miss, buddy*), age (*granny, son*), status (*sir, ma'am*), education (*professor, stupid*), regional or national background (*Yank, Paddy*), race/ethnicity (*boy, Ikey*), religion (*Your Holiness, Brother*), job (*stewardess, operator, waiter*), and much more. In addition, vocatives can show respect (*ma'am, sir*) or can be derogatory (*asshole, cipher, wog*) or patronizing (*sonny*).

Criteria for choosing vocatives Central to this is what motivates the choice. There is fairly wide agreement that above all two dimensions are involved: (1) **power** and (2) **solidarity**. (The classical study is Brown and Gilman 1972.) These dimensions are especially useful because they can be applied to all the varieties of English we are looking at, despite individual differences between items.

Power, solidarity, and reciprocity When someone addresses another as *sir* (a respect form), the other is both distant and powerful. The converse is addressing someone, for example a servant, as *boy* (a term of disparagement), which indicates that the other is powerless and distant. A mother who calls one of her children by his or her first name (FN, e.g. *Philip, Vanessa*) is speaking from a position of relative power, but on a level of intimacy. The child will most likely use a kinship term (KT) like *Mom*, *Mama*, or the like to his or her mother, again, a signal of solidarity, but relative powerlessness. The dimension of power can most easily be distinguished by its non-reciprocal nature (see Fig. 7.1).

A word of caution: not every power relation is marked by non-reciprocity. For example, many firms have a general FN ↔ FN policy, but, of course, without distributing power equally. And some modern parents also use FN ↔ FN with their children.

The dimension of solidarity is less clearly marked than power since it may be practised both under conditions of an imbalance of power (e.g. parent ↔ child) or conditions of equality of power, as when two colleagues in different departments of a large firm, Miss Lee and Mr Singh, exchange title and last name (TLN ↔ TLN). Solidarity in the latter case is, however, rather weak. Indeed, the mode of address would be identical between two total strangers (no solidarity) who have just been introduced to each other. On the other hand, workers in the same firm, Fred and Mary, may well exchange first names (FN ↔ FN) as a matter of course without this being any indication of further familiarity (see Fig. 7.2).

Table 7.1 summarizes the relations given above in regard to the dimensions of power, where there may be a power differential (+) or where there is relative equality (−). Solidarity is (−) where there is distance and (+) where there is familiarity.

Applying the criteria of power and solidarity In order to recognize distance and familiarity it is necessary to assess the forms used in the social context of their use. That is, we have to know which items are respectful, which are insults, and which are familiar. When is it appropriate to address someone by vocation/function? When by TLN? FN? When by KT alone or with FN or LN? What makes it all the harder to answer these questions is the fact that appropriateness depends

(a) *sir* ◄──► *boy*

(b) *Mom* ◄──► *Vanessa*

(The more powerful is given *sir/Mom*; the less powerful is given *boy/Vanessa*; (a) is a distance, (b) is an intimacy relationship.)

Fig. 7.1. Non-reciprocal power relations

(c) *Miss Lee* ◄──► *Mr Singh*

(d) *Fred* ◄──► *Mary*

(Greater distance is indicated by the use of T; familiarity, by FN.)

Fig. 7.2. Reciprocal solidarity relations

Table 7.1. Power and Solidarity Relations

	Honorific (*sir*) ↔ Disparagement (*boy*)	FN (*Vanessa*) ↔ KT (*Mom*)
Power	+	+
Solidarity	−	+
	TLN (*Miss Lee* ↔ Mr Singh)	FN (*Fred* ↔ *Mary*)
Power	−	−
Solidarity	−	+

on the characteristics of both the speaker and the addressee as well as the nature of the situation in which they interact, such as the field of discourse; the level of formality, including degree and nature of emotion involved; the medium (speaking or writing); and the purpose pursued. In the remainder of this section we will explore some of these questions. We will begin by looking at some of the differences in the expression of kinship (§7.2.2). This will be followed by national differences in address, with special attention paid to names and titles (§7.2.3). Then we will proceed in §7.2.4 to distinctions based on such social features as age and rank, education and vocation, region, gender, race and ethnicity, religion and ideology.

7.2.2 Kinship terms

In most of the Western world the extended family, comprising several generations and a shared dwelling and working place, has been displaced by the kernel family embracing two generations (parents and younger children) at most. This is, of course, an understandable reaction to changes in economic subsistence patterns. Just as work patterns have grown more specialized and distinct, so too have family patterns. Mobility is expected; women are economically more independent; urbanization is common, as is the straitjacket of carefully orchestrated work schedules. Yet pockets of the older extended family continue to exist, along with their more or less modified division of roles between the sexes and the generations. We find them more often in rural areas and small towns and less often in industrial and post-industrial societies. The kinship terms of English have, all the same, remained relatively stable as illustrated Fig. 7.3.

This is the basic system,[1] in use throughout the English-speaking world. For our purposes there are two ways in which the vocabulary involved varies. For one there is lexical variation, as when the terms used vary from place to place and

---

1 It can be extended to include mothers-in-law, fathers-in-law, brothers-in-law, etc.; there can be a stepfather as well as a stepmother. Great-grandchildren follow the generation of the grandchildren, etc. In India the husband of your wife's sister (the wife's brother-in-law) is also known as a *co-brother* (Nihalani *et al.* 1979).

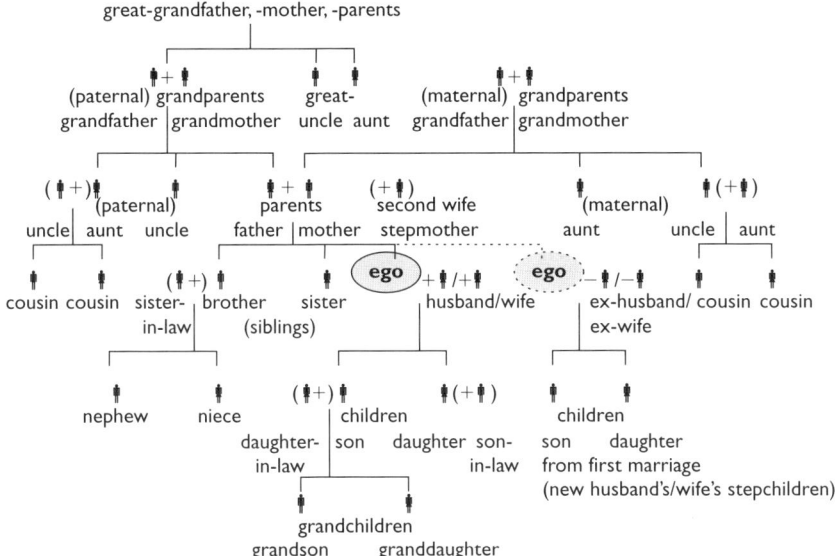

Figure 7.3: The basic kinship system

from speaker to speaker. The second point is that the system itself varies in some societies.

7.2.2.1 Diversity in kinship terms

It is part of the systematic use of the kinship system that FNs are used later-ally and downwardly while KTs are used upwardly. People do not regularly call a brother *brother* or a sister *sister*, nor a son *son* or a daughter *daughter*. They do this only in very marked situations (humorously, mock-seriously, or to mark a situation as extremely formal). In contrast, a grandfather or a grand-mother, a mother or father are not called by FN, but with a KT as a vocative. Upward and lateral relations (aunts and uncles) call for a combination of the two: KT + FN. The lists of terms in Table 7.2 are arranged in descending order of frequency (based on a survey of 25 speakers of AmE and 25 of AusE).

7.2.2.2 Motivation for change in the system of kinship terms

Many people feel a definite need for KTs which distinguish relationships more carefully than the basic system and its terms allow. Two types of upward kinship cause people feelings of unease because of the lack of suitable terms. Maternal grandparents cannot be distinguished from paternal ones, so grandchildren have to resort to varying strategies to deal with this problem; plus they have to avoid the use of FNs. Some strategies that are familiar to this author are the use of *Big Gramma* vs. *Little Gramma*; *Gramma* + LN_1 vs. *Gramma* + LN_2; *Gramma* vs. *Nanny*.

Table 7.2. Kinship vocatives (selection)

Kinship	Vocative	Kinship	Vocative
Grandfather	*Grandpa*	Grandmother	*Grandma* [*Gramma*]
	Granddad		*Nan(n)a*
	Gramps		*O(u)ma*
	Opa		*Granny*
	Grandfather		*Grandmother*
Father	*Dad(dy)*	Mother	*Mom(my)* [*Mum(my)*]
	Pa(pa)		*Ma*
	Father		*Mother*
Uncle	*Uncle* + FN	Aunt	*Aunt* + FN
			Auntie + FN

The second sensitive point has to do with parents-in-law. Many people feel that for a mother-in-law *Mother* is too intimate; *Mrs* LN is too formal; FN is too disrespectful. This leads to 'no end of social awkwardness' (Poynton 1989: 12) and, of course, to that ubiquitous solution: avoidance of all forms of address.

There is a tendency in the opposite direction as well: the basic terms are regularly used for relationships which go beyond the basic familial ones given in Fig. 7.3. *Father*, *Mother*, *Brother*, and *Sister* are widely used in a Christian religious context. Not only is God addressed as *Our Father*, the Pope is addressed as *Holy Father* (should you run into him). On a more everyday level, men who have taken religious orders are addressed as *Brother* + FN; women in orders, as *Sister* + FN. Their superiors are called *Father* or *Mother Superior*. Members of some Protestant churches call fellow members *Brother/Sister* + LN. In the US African Americans can call one of their soul brothers or sisters *Bro'* or *Sister*. And a prissy, effeminate, or cowardly boy is sometimes teased as a *sissy*. In BrE and British-influenced varieties such as AusE a senior nurse in a hospital is addressed as *Sister*.

Case study 7.1: KTs in some ESL societies

In some English-speaking countries, such as those in West Africa, where polygyny is practised, the *mother* of Fig. 7.3 may be extended to all the father's wives, his *co-wives*, by all the children of the various wives. Furthermore, the vocatives *Father/Daddy* and *Mother/Mommy* are sometimes addressed to more distant older relatives. Indeed, even older people who are unrelated may be addressed in this way in order to show respect toward them. 'Immediate bosses in their places of work get addressed as either *Daddy* or *Mommy* by subordinate young officers' (Akere 1982: 96). The bounds within which *Father* and *Mother* are valid is, in other words, wider than the conjugal family and may even be applied to someone from the same town or ethnic group (Akere 1982: 91; Adetugbo 1979b: 174). The NigE list shown in Table 7.3 is revealing.

Table 7.3. Kinship terms in NigE (Adetugbo 1979b: 174ff.)

father	father, older male cousins, uncles, father's friends (of same peer group)
mother	mother and mother's sister (aunt)
sister	only for an older sister
brother	brother and cousin (older only)
senior brother	older brother
junior brother	younger brother
brother	also 'any male from one's village or clan'
cousin	anyone from one's clan

Asked how many fathers he had, one village high school student replied that he had 23 – he had counted all the people he would address as *father* in his native language (Adetugbo 1979b: 176). *Cousin, niece, nephew* are also age-constrained. If the addressee is relatively older, the terms are *uncle, aunt*. In addition, kinship terms are widely employed by people from the same town or ethnic group when they are abroad.

Other culturally determined ways of expression may be found in East Africa, where a mother may address her son as *my young husband*, and a husband, his wife as *daughter*. A brother-in-law is a *second husband*, and an illegitimate child is a *brat* (Zuengler 1983: 116).

In India *mother-in-law*, *mother, sister, brother*, and *father* have distinct connotations. IndE has '*mother* as a term of respect, *sister*, of regard, and *father-in-law*, in the sense of abuse. *Bhai* ("brother") is used for any male of equal age; *father*, for all elder persons; and an uncle may be referred to as *father*.' Hence we see: 'A term restricted to the kinship system of a [particular] language may be used with extended meaning in another culture and transferred to an L2' (Kachru 1966: 273f., 272).

Of course the use of *uncle* and *aunt(ie)* for familiar but unrelated older friends of the family is well known in other parts of the English-speaking world. It is, for example, common in the British Isles, in North America, and in India, about which one scholar writes, 'These terms are not only used by middle-class children to address the parents of their friends . . . but are used by domestic servants to address their employers and by the children of the employers to address the domestics!' (D'souza 1997: 103). As for New Zealand: 'Maori-speakers often transfer . . . address forms such as *cuz, sis, bro, aunty*, and *uncle*, which reflect Maori kinship relationships' (Burridge and Mulder 1998: 12).

In South Africa we come across KTs borrowed from Afrikaans: *boet* 'brother' and *boetie* (diminutive) both for a relative and for a friend, signalling affection or friendship (sometimes reproof: *There's a lot of things you don't know, bootie*). There is also the form *bra* (sometimes *bla*) as in *Bra Victor, my bra*. The same is true of *nef* 'nephew', *oom* 'uncle', *tante* 'aunt', *ouma* 'granny', *oupa* 'grandpa', (including the diminutives *oomie, oopie*) for both affection and disrespect. For instance *oom* is used for an uncle, as a quasi-honorific (*Oom Schalk Lourens*) or in respectful 3rd person address (*What did Oom do in the Boer War?*), but also for a national figure (*Oom Paul* = Paul Kruger), as a common noun (*the ooms and oupas of the platteland*, cf. also: *Everyone is oom or neef to his neighbour*). But there is also *Ma*, an African honorific (*Ma-Hadebe* 'daughter of the Hadebe clan') or 'mother of' as in *Ma-Robert* (Branford 1994: 461ff.).

Project 7.2: Local KTs as modes of address

The lists of vocatives supplied in Table 7.2 are relatively restricted, but only for reasons of space. In actual fact there are multitudes of further vocatives in use. It is your task to canvass some of the English-speaking people around you to see what variations you can find.

Dear Informant,
[See the introductory text in Project 4.1]
Modes of address
How would you address the following in spoken conversation? For example, do you use kinship terms + name (*Aunt Elizabeth*), kinship terms without a name (*Granny*), first names (*Elizabeth*), familiar forms (*Bess(y)*), other forms? If you don't have one of the types of kin, please supply the kind of form you hear around about you.

If you use special terms for distinctions not listed (e.g. father's brother or mother's sister), please add them.

your mother	your father
your grandmother	your grandfather
your aunt	your uncle
your mother-in-law	your father-in-law

7.2.3 Names and titles

Pronouns play hardly any role in the English system of address. For one thing, English does not have distinct familiar and polite personal pronouns as do many other languages.[2] Of course, distinctions *can* be made: cf.

You! Come here. (rude, impolite)
Hey you! Come here. (mitigatedly impolite)

Yet in South Africa we see the influence of a further language on English, this time of Malay. While 3rd person address is found elsewhere,[3] it is probably more common in SAE:

---

2 e.g. the *tu/vous* of French, *tu/Usted* of Spanish, *tu/Lei* of Italian, *ty/vy* of Russian, or *du/Sie* of German.
3 Take this AmE example from Philip Caputo, *A Rumor of War*: 'PFC [Private First Class] Chriswell, the platoon's seventeen-year-old radioman, a reedy, sandy-haired kid who should have been shooting baskets in some small-town gym . . . had the irritating and unbreakable habit of addressing officers in the archaic third person: "Would the lieutenant like me to clean his pistol?"' (p. 26).

... the respectful third-person form of address, ...: 'When does Tannie (Auntie) want me to bring it?' In this, third-person *does* is in concord with *Tannie*. This practice has parallels in Malay, once the language of substantial numbers of slaves and others at the Cape, which avoids second-person pronouns in respectful speech. (Branford 1994: 490)

The great status/politeness differentiator, however, is names and titles. We can call someone by FN, DN, LN, TLN, or just T. However, we are not free in our choices.

America. If you are an American, you will find FN natural, but not up against certain age barriers. As was pointed out above, upward kin get KT (with or without FN). Non-family gets an M-form (*M, Mrs, Ms, Miss*) + LN if the age difference is anywhere from 15 years up unless you have been specifically allowed to dispense with these forms (and dispensation comes from the more powerful, i.e. usually the older). This is the rule for teachers, who get TLN, but give their (school, sometimes college) students FN. Work relations vary enormously, allowing (for boss ↔ employee): TLN ↔ TLN, TLN ↔ FN, and FN ↔ FN. And an organization as hierarchical as the military gives us examples like Text 7.1, where Ron Kovic, a sergeant and the author, is wounded and lying paralysed in the hospital:

Text 7.1. Address in the military (1) (Ron Kovic, *Born on the Fourth of July* (1976), p. 21)

> 'Can I call you by your first name?' I say to the nurse.
> 'No. My name is Lieutenant Wiecker.'
> 'Please, can I . . .'
> 'No,' she says. 'It's against regulations.'

or from Philip Caputo (Text 7.2):

Text 7.2. Address in the military (2) (*A Rumor of War* (1996), p. 8)

> We were shouted at, kicked, humiliated and harassed constantly. We were no longer known by our names, but called 'shitbird', 'scumbag', or 'numbuts' by the DIs [drill instructors].

The American system is essentially one with two major alternatives: FN and TLN. People of approximately the same age and status easily and virtually immediately exchange FN (FN ↔ FN) (cf. Brown and Ford 1964). For your orientation note the following general guidelines:

One may readily use FN with everyone except: with an adult (if one is an unrelated child); with an older adult (if one is markedly younger); with a teacher (if one is a student); with a clergyman or religious (particularly Roman Catholic and Orthodox); with a physician. (Hook 1984: 186)

Despite what non-Americans may think, FN is not necessarily a sign of intimacy or even familiarity; it is simply a feature of American society. To refuse to accept FN is quickly interpreted as unfriendly or snobby. 'First names are required among people who work closely together, even though they may not like each other at all' (Wardhaugh 1986: 260). Of course, such a refusal may be used for protection; compare Text 7.3, an explicit though fictional account of one woman introducing herself to a circle of other women.

Text 7.3. FN address to a woman (Sara Paretsky, *Indemnity Only* (1991), p. 183)

> When they got to me, I said, 'I'm V.I. Warshawski. Most people call me Vic.'
> When they'd finished, one said curiously, 'Do you go by your initials or is Vic your real name?'
> 'It's a nickname,' I said. 'I usually use my initials. I started out my working life as a lawyer, and I found it was harder for male colleagues and opponents to patronize me if they didn't know my first name.'

For intimacy, Americans use either nicknames or multiple naming (alternating between various forms of address such as FN, nickname, diminutive, etc.).

But what about status differences? In service jobs it has increasingly become the custom for service providers to identify themselves (often with a name tag) by FN alone. This is a remarkably retrograde development in a country which prides itself on its supposed equality, for the customer enjoys a status advantage and is given TLN or *sir/ma'am* (unless both sides are relatively young).

Britain and Ireland. While the same basic vocative system is practised in Britain and Ireland as in America, there are some perceptible differences. People switch just a bit more slowly from TLN to FN.

Universities. In British universities there is an alternative three-option system: T (*Dr, Prof.*) + LN is most deferential; the M-forms (*Mr,* etc. LN) are an intermediate stage; only then does FN come. Men, in addition, may indulge in mutual last-naming (without a title or M-form, i.e. LN ↔ LN (Ervin-Tripp 1974: 274f.).

In America a member of the teaching staff (the faculty) is seldom addressed by FN by a student. Yet if he or she gets FN, the move to FN does not come, as suggested above, from the more powerful, but most often from the student, albeit a graduate student. Age plays an important role here, however. Older male graduate students are most likely to initiate FN, and to do so more easily with professors under 40 (McIntire 1972: 289).[4]

For Nigeria, Akere (1982: 93) reports:

> In university communities, academic titles like doctor (Ph.D.) or professor are attached to greetings by students, and by colleagues who are not quite intimate. Junior administrative and technical workers in the university would use the abbreviated forms of these titles in greeting. Forms such as 'Good morning Doc', or 'Good afternoon Prof' are often heard. Their users employ them with an assumed air of familiarity with their addressee.

Australia. The AusE system is basically the same as that of AmE or BrE. As in the US, FN is widely used without necessarily implying equality or solidarity:

> Sellers of cars and real estate assume the social utility of addressing potential buyers by personal name [i.e. FN], while the would-be Don Juan who uses diminutive forms to newly-met potential bedfellows can be seen as preparing the ground for physical intimacy by decreasing social distance linguistically. (Poynton 1989: 57)

Nigeria. In NigE TLN is often reduced to simple T; the M-forms, including the Muslim title *Malam*, can be used for direct address without the LN, while ENL varieties do not make a practice of using *Mr* or *Mrs* without LN as a vocative. Furthermore, multiple titles are also used in NigE, e.g. *Chief Doctor Mrs* + LN (Akere 1982: 96). 'Apart from the fact that learners of English in Nigeria are exposed mainly to the literary style, a gerontocratic culture like ours makes it a little awkward not to address an elder person as *Sir*. . . . Parents may be addressed (in multilingual homes where English is favoured) as follows: "Good morning Sir" or "Good morning ma" [= ma'am?]"' (Adetugbo 1979a: 155).

India. In India we find forms of address which come from the non-native use of English in the context of Indian culture. Special terms express social relations such as master–servant and age–youth. The titles/vocatives shown in Table 7.4 are specific to IndE.

Singapore. Differences in forms of address transferred from an underlying native language to English may be exemplified by the polite forms in SingE. Polite

---

4 Another study shows the role of gender quite clearly: students, especially female ones, gave young female professors (aged 26–33) FN more often than they did their male teachers (Rubin 1981: 966). Male students preferred the M-form or *Dr* + LN, while women students preferred to give the more prestigeous *Prof.* + LN to male professors. Women students used M-forms and *Dr* + LN for female professors most often, while male students used M-forms + LN or FN. 'Thus, female students seem to be affording more status to their male professors' (p. 970).

Table 7.4. Vocatives in IndE (Kachru 1966: 272)

Caste	*Pandit, Thakur, Jamadar*
Profession	*Havaldar, Inspector* (*Sahib*)
	Note: *babu* or *baboo,* 'A term of respect used frequently in the north of India. In the south of India it is used for *sir, your honour*' (p. 286)
Religion	*Khwaja, Pandit, Sardar*
Superiority	*Cherisher of the poor, King of pearls, Huzoor, Ma-bap* ('mother-father'), *Friend of the poor*
Neutral	*Babu-sahib, Bhai, Master, Dada* (male), *Didi* (female), *Sab*[5]

reference (not vocatives) is via T + FN + LN (*Mr Arthur Orton*), but if the addressee is well known T + FN (*Mr Arthur*). A woman who is unmarried is *Miss Tan Mei Ling* [*Tan* = LN]. If she marries Mr Lim Keng Choon [*Lim* = LN], she has three options: She may be called *Mrs Lim Keng Choon* (rarely) or *Mrs Lim Mei Ling,* or *Madam Tan Mei Ling.* Obviously, 'the conventions governing naming and forms of address in Malay, Chinese and Indian languages are quite different from those in English' (Tongue 1974: 104). In Singapore–Malaysian English (also IndE),

> . . . *missus* is often considered more polite than the word *wife.* Thus, *your missus coming down?* was a polite inquiry by the manager of a large hotel. This is possibly an influence from Chinese, where the same word may be used for *wife* and the title *Mrs* (e.g., Mandarin *taitai*). (Platt 1984: 397)

Of course, the order of the names, LN, then FN, has been retained from the underlying languages. This is also true of South African IndE, where titles, etc. have a greater tendency to follow proper names (*Sanjeev boy*) (Mesthrie 1987: 268f.).

Project 7.3: University vocatives

Deepen your perspective on how vocatives are employed by finding out how members of the teaching staff address each other and how students do this among themselves. What forms of address are used between the teachers and students?

Be sure to note down the gender and approximate ages of the people you observe. Also check to see whether there are particular departmental styles, i.e. do sociologists behave differently from people from law, literature, or the sciences? How do support staff (secretarial, custodial, janitorial, administrative) fit in?

5 'In colloquial language *sab* is used as the weak form of *sahib.* It is equivalent to *master* and may be used without religious or status restrictions when one wants to show respect. Originally it was used for Europeans in India' (Kachru 1966: 286).

Exercise 7.1: Generic names

While in §6.4.1.2 and Exercise 6.6 we saw the upside of generic reference, a look at generic names shows that they are frequently derogatory. Identify the following by telling (1) what groups they are applied to and (2) what variety of English they are used in.

	Group applied to	Variety of English
1. *Paddy*		
2. *Sandy*		
3. *Pedro*		
4. *Sambo*		
5. *Bruce*		
6. *Sheila*		
7. *Jim Crow*		
8. *Mac*		
9. *Ikey*		
10. *Jim*		

Resources you might use: a good desk dictionary, Branford (1994), Partridge (1984).

7.2.4 Differences according to social features

Up to now we have concentrated mostly on the effects of power and solidarity on modes of address and have mentioned age, status, gender, and kinship as contributing factors. I would now like to explore some of these, and a few more of the multitudinous ways in which social attributes may directly affect both terms of reference for others and vocatives. What distinguishes the following examples more obviously from what we have looked at above is the disparaging nature of many of the forms.

7.2.4.1 Age and rank

Age. Girls are politely and deferentially called *Miss*; disparaging terms tend to be sexually derogatory (see 7.2.4.2). Young boys are rather patronizingly addressed by older people as *Son* or *Sonny*. In return older people are disrespectfully termed (sometimes even addressed as) *old fogey*, *old fart*, *pop(s)*, *gramps*, or *granny*.

Rank. Attitudes toward titles are problematic. It is frequently a *faux pas* to ignore then, especially in more traditional societies, while in some countries, such as Australia or America, insisting on a title is seen as snobby or conceited. Turner on AusE speaks of 'an egalitarian mateyness,[6] aided by immediate use of first names'. Furthermore, first names are 'abbreviated or given the Australian diminutive in -*o* (*Stevo* from *Stephen*) or the distinctive Australian change of /r/ to /z/ in *Bazza* for *Barry* or *Tez* for *Terence* . . . . Another change converts *Maurice* to *Mocker* or *Oscar* to *Ocker*' (Turner 1994: 322).

---

6 The use of *mate*, as a designation or a vocative among men, is widespread for a friend or companion. *Maat* 'good buddy, mate' (as in *ou maat* 'old friend') is also used in SAE, but not as frequently as AusE *mate* (Branford 1994: 462).

This egalitarian attitude explains the reaction of one American to his neighbour, who pretentiously put up the following sign on the turn-in to his rather luxurious house:

> **Private Drive**
> General Nichols

His response was to post his own rather more modest driveway with his own sign:

> **General Entrance**
> Private Brown

A plethora of special titles go with special offices or positions. Judges, bishops, ambassadors, presidents, governors, mayors, military officers, royalty, and more have not only their titles but also vocatives prescribed by protocol and formal etiquette. That explains the humour of the following passage:

Text 7.4. Inappropriate address

> 'May I present Monsignor Ryan,' Mrs. McGraw grasped at an ecclesiastical straw.
> Molly pumped the prelate's hand enthusiastically. 'Hello there, Monsignor!' she said. 'Glad to make your acquaintance.'
>
> (Al Hine. *The Unsinkable Molly Brown* (1964), p. 83)

To greet a monsignor with a *Hello there* is incongruent in the situation, just as the vocative *Your Excellency* might well have been more dignified than just plain *Monsignor*. Under the entry for *faux pas* the *LDOCE* gives the following example sentence: *He committed a terrible faux pas when he called the Queen 'My dear'*.

Exercise 7.2: Appropriate vocatives

The list below contains ranks/offices. Your task is to find the corresponding vocatives. There is not always an informal alternative.

Rank/office	Formal address	Informal alternative
Example:		
Prince	*Your Highness*	*Prince*
1. Judge		
2. Bishop		
3. General		
4. Professor		
5. Pope		
6. Ambassador		
7. Governor		

8. King
9. Mayor
10. Medical doctor
11. Abbess

Resource you might use: Brown and Levinson (1987).

Note (in case you're writing) that a letter to Prince X would be addressed to *His Royal Highness X, Prince of Y*. A bishop, who is addressed formally as *Your Excellency*, becomes *The Right Reverend X* in the address at the head of a letter. That is, a 2nd person vocative becomes a 3rd person form of reference.

Education and vocation. These features play a role inasmuch as education plays a decisive role in determining relative status and vocation. In Exercise 7.2 we had a number of examples of ranks or offices whose incumbents may be addressed in a special way. To a judge, professor, and (medical) doctor we can also add less prestigious vocations, many of which have job names which also serve as vocatives, e.g. waiter (*Waiter!*), milkman (*Dear Mr Milkman . . .*). A professor, doctor, nurse, usher, and many others can be addressed in this way (*Excuse me, Professor/Doctor/Nurse/Usher, can you . . .*).

It is not clear what distinguishes jobs which allow vocatives identical to their designations from ones where the designation does not serve simultaneously as a vocative. For example, we have the designation *policeman/woman*, but the vocative *Officer, Constable*; a hotel service person may be addressed as *Room Service*. A teacher is not usually addressed as *Teacher*, but with TLN or an honorific (*sir, ma'am*, and esp. in BrE *Miss* for a young female teacher). Indeed, many jobs are filled by occupants who are addressed not by their job name but by an honorific (*sir, ma'am* [older], *miss* [under 30]): salesperson, filling station attendant, truck driver, lawyer, photographer, actor, etc..

Exercise 7.3: Region

Regional background and nationality have their own vocatives, both slurs (*hick, hillbilly, city slicker, boonie*) and more neutral nickname-like designations such as *Hoosier* (for someone for Indiana), *Frenchie* (French person), *Tex* (Texan), *Ozzie* (Australian).

Identify the following regional or national designations and label them as slurs or neutral. Indicate where they are used.

Term	Evaluation	Used for
1. *Tassie*		
2. *Groper*		

3. *Tar Heel*
4. *Paki*
5. *Rooi Nek*
6. *Brit*
7. *Kiwi*
8. *Reb*
9. *Pakeha*
10. *Sooner*

Resources you might use: Partridge (1984), Wentworth and Flexner (1960), a good desk dictionary.

7.2.4.2 Gender, race/ethnicity, and religion/ideology

In §§4.5.2 and Exercise 4.8 I pointed out the semantic derogation of women, and in Case study 4.5 and Exercise 4.9 we looked at ethnic slurs. Hence I will only mention in passing that the number of terms used perhaps to address a female and most certainly to refer to a female are to a very large extent derogatory, be they merely demeaning, as with *toots, babe*, or *chick*, or directly sexually disparaging, as with *broad, piece*, or *cunt*. The words available for reference to people by race or ethnicity are divided into the class of neutral terms (*Italian, Spanish, Black, Jew, American*) and more informal disparaging terms (*Wop/Dago, Spic, Nigger, Yid/Ikey, Yank/Gringo*).

Ideology has contributed all sorts of terms of reference and their connotations vary according to the speaker's own political-ideological standpoint: *red* (communist), *pinko/fellow traveller* (communist sympathizer), *green* (ecologically oriented), *middle-of-the-roader* (non-radical), *libber* (advocate of women's liberation), *pro-lifer* (anti-abortionist), *abolitionist* (historical: anti-slavery), etc. One of the few political-ideological vocatives in English is *Comrade* (to a communist fellow believer or a fellow struggler for an end to apartheid in South Africa).

Religion has been exemplified frequently, but nowhere have any of the more or less disparaging terms been mentioned. People considered overly religious are *Bible beaters/bashers/thumpers* (Christian fundamentalists), *Jesus freaks* (ditto), *God squadders* (moralizing, puritanical), *holy rollers* (Pentecostal), *mackerel eaters* (Catholics), *Prods* (Northern Irish Protestants), or *tea towels* (Islamic women).

Project 7.4: Disparaging vocatives according to religion

Dear Informant,
[See the introductory text in Project 4.1]
Modes of address/reference
Many insulting names are in use and pick up some characteristic of the person or group they are applied to. For example: *damn Yankee* is geographical; *dumb boob* refers to (lack of) intelligence; *bimbo*, to lax sexual morals or to lack of intelligence.
What insulting names or jeers do you know that refer to a person's religion?

Christian:
- Protestant:
- Catholic:
- Pentecostal:
- Fundamentalist:

Islamic:
Jewish:
Other (Hindu, Buddhist, Sikh, . . .):

Project 7.5: Modes of address

Dear Informant,
[See the introductory text in Project 4.1]
Vocatives
What insulting names are used for the following?

- Geographical origin
- Ethnicity
- Sexual orientation
- Age
- (Lack of) intelligence

Exercise 7.4: Choosing appropriate forms of address

Which of the following is appropriate as a form of address?
1. For a customer in a department store: *What can I do for you today, _____?*
   - (a) *fellow*   (b) *honey*   (c) *jock*   (d) *sir*

2. For a general in the army:
   - (a) *May I have the General's indulgence for a few minutes?*
   - (b) *May I have your indulgence for a few minutes, colleague?*
   - (c) *May I have your indulgence for a few minutes, sir?*
   - (d) *May I have your indulgence for a few minutes, my general?*

3. For your mother, whose name is Mary Smith:
   - (a) *Mary*   (b) *Mom/Mum*   (c) *Mrs Smith*   (d) *Sweetheart*

4. For your boyfriend (assuming you are female), whose name is Stephen:
   - (a) *Stephen*   (b) *Steve*   (c) *Stevio*   (d) all of above

5. For your greying teacher, whose name is Stephen:
   - (a) *Stephen*   (b) *Steve*   (c) *Stevio*   (d) none of above

6. For your colleague, a professor of English named James Sutherland:
   - (a) *James*   (b) *Jamey*   (c) *Prof. Sutherland*   (d) *Sutherland*

7. For the taxi cab driver who has just driven you to JFK (Kennedy Airport) in the nick of time:
   - (a) *Ta, guv*   (b) *Thank you, mack*   (c) *Thank you, mister*   (d) *Thank you, sir*

8. For your grandmother:
    (a) *Grandma*   (b) *Granny*   (c) *Nanna*   (d) *Ouma*

9. For someone female dear to you (assuming you are male):
    (a) *bitch*   (b) *cow*   (c) *kitten*   (d) *minx*

10. For someone male dear to you (assuming you are female):
    (a) *bear*   (b) *dog*   (c) *jackass*   (d) *swine*

Resource you might use: Brown and Levinson (1987).

Exercise 7.5: Choosing appropriate addressees

Who would you use the following vocatives for?

1. *Brother*
    (a) a male pal   (b) a male sibling
    (c) a member of a (Catholic) order   (d) a member of your (Protestant)
                                          church

2. *Miss*
    (a) any female school teacher   (b) a young female
    (c) a spinster   (d) the winner of a beauty contest

3. *Doc*
    (a) an egghead   (b) an M.D.
    (c) a PhD   (d) any man

4. *Mate*
    (a) an associate   (b) an officer on a ship
    (c) a skilled worker   (d) a spouse

5. *Operator*
    (a) a devious, possibly dishonest person
    (b) a person who runs a machine
    (c) a person who runs a telephone switchboard
    (d) a surgeon

6. *Yank*(ee)
    (a) an American   (b) a New Englander
    (c) a North American   (d) a northerner

Resource you might use: Brown and Levinson (1987).

Exercise 7.6: Interpreting power and solidarity

In this exercise we will try to pull together some of the things we have been discussing by asking you to interpret encounters in terms of power and solidarity.
To help coordinate these two dimensions try to visualize the relations between the
two as the axes on a coordinate system (see Fig. 7.4).

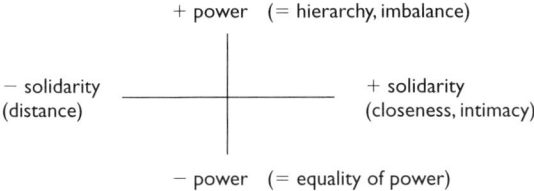

Fig. 7.4. The power and solidarity axes

Using these two dimensions, imagine a situation in which a large Californian farmer employs migrant Mexican labourers to bring in his harvest. How might he address an individual worker with whom he is not acquainted? One possibility is the following:

Farmer: *Pedro!*
Migrant labourer: *Sir?*

In terms of solidarity we are dealing here with a situation of extreme distance (−solidarity). As for power, there is an obvious imbalance (+power). This dictates non-reciprocal use of vocatives in which the more powerful, the farmer, flaunts his greater power by using a patronizing generic term of address. The worker is, in contrast, constrained to using an honorific. Since the farmer's address demands some kind of reaction, the worker probably does not even have the option of using no vocative at all. This puts this relationship in quadrant I of Fig. 7.5.

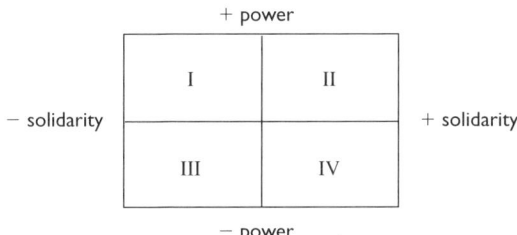

Fig. 7.5. The power and solidarity quadrants

For the following six constellations:

1. Give possible vocatives that might be used between:
   (a) mother ↔ child
   (b) teacher ↔ student (approximately grade 8)
   (c) boss ↔ employee (large office)
   (d) colleague ↔ colleague (different university departments)
   (e) sports club member ↔ sports club member
   (f) waitress ↔ customer

2. Characterize the nature of the relationship in terms of power, solidarity, and reciprocity and decide which quadrant is appropriate for it.

3. Comment on the further factors which may have helped to determine the choice of vocatives (e.g. region, gender, age, family relationship, ethnicity, hierarchical status).

Case study 7.2: Ritual insults and camaraderie forms

Solidarity usually demands certain vocative forms over others, ones that show closeness, such as FN, nickname, diminutive, or multiple naming. We have, however, seen that the standards which apply to interpreting a relationship as one of solidarity (or not) vary from country to country and from one communicative situation to another. There is an additional way in which solidarity can be expressed, using *semantic inversion*. This is the 'non-canonical' use of derogatory and taboo terms. One of these, the use of *ritual insult*, is illustrated in the following passage. Trampas is the villain of this western novel; he is playing poker with the hero, the Virginian.

Text 7.5: (Ritual) insult (Owen Wister, *The Virginian*, 1902)

> There had been silence over in the corner; but now the man Trampas spoke again.
> '*And* ten,' said he, sliding out some chips from before him. Very strange it was to hear him, how he contrived to make those words a personal taunt. The Virginian was looking at his cards. He might have been deaf.
> '*And* twenty,' said the next player easily.
> The next threw his cards down.
> It was now the Virginian's turn to bet, or leave the game, and he did not speak at once.
> Therefore Trampas spoke. 'Your bet, you son-of-a____.'
> The Virginian's pistol came out, and his hand lay on the table, holding it unaimed. And with a voice as gentle as ever, the voice that sounded almost like a caress, but drawling a very little more than usual, so that there was almost a space between each word, he issued his orders to the man Trampas:-
> 'When you call me that, *smile*!' And he looked at Trampas across the table.
> Yes, the voice was gentle. But in my ears it seemed as if somewhere the bell of death was ringing; and silence, like a stroke, fell on the large room.

In this text the order to smile indicates that calling someone a *son of a bitch* is either a deadly insult (note the pistol) or a masculine ritual of solidarity which demands the appropriate non-verbal behaviour, such as smiling.

Who practises this semantic inversion depends, at least, on factors like class and gender. It is usually men, and usually those with less power, who may address each other in this way or with what are called *camaraderie forms* such as *mate* or *buddy*. Women's camaraderie forms and use of ritual insults seem to be rare. It is more customary for females to express endearments directly, something many men have difficulties with (cf. Poynton 1989: 65f.; see also Exercise 8.2 and Case study 8.4).

Exercise 7.7: Fun naming

What, however, both women and men may practise is *fun naming*. This is the use of a designation which has nothing to do with the addressee and whose only motivation is that the name rhymes with some *fixed expression* or *routine formula*. Perhaps the best known and most widely used of these are *See ya later, alligator!*, to which the fun naming response is *In a while, crocodile!*

See how many of the following you can complete:

1. I'll be back, _____.
2. Alright, _____.
3. No way, _____
4. That's the truth, _____.
5. Here's the money, _____.
6. Like your tail, _____.

7.3 COMMUNICATIVE STRATEGIES

7.3.1 Speech acts

When we speak we *do* something (i.e. we act) at various levels. For one, we *utter* something (an *utterance act*). This involves producing certain sounds, syllables, words, sentences. This act of speaking is not what is meant by a speech act. What is meant is that in, for example, saying *It snowed yesterday*, we are performing the act of making a statement or assertion. According to one approach there are five different types of *illocutionary* speech acts, as these acts are called (cf. §5.3.2.2):

Representatives/Assertives	e.g. statements and assertions
Directives	e.g. requests and questions
Commissives	e.g. promises, threats, and offers
Expressives	e.g. thanking, apologizing, congratulating
Declaratives (a.k.a. **Performatives**)	e.g. pronouncing a couple husband and wife, sentencing someone to prison or baptising a person in the name of the Father, Son, and Holy Ghost (cf. Searle 1976: 10–16)

An unidentified number of individual types make up these categories. We will look at just a few, in particular those that are most conventionalized, such as *pragmatic idioms*, which consist of highly formulaic speech in well-defined situations of use, including greetings (§ 7.3.2.1), apologies (§7.3.2.2), compliments (§§7.3.2.3–4), and thanks (§7.3.2.5). These are especially interesting because each of them is also part of what is called an *adjacency pair*.

Adjacency pairs are speech acts which occur in pairs such as question and answer. It is considered highly impolite not to answer a question. This is so deeply imbedded in language behaviour that its violation is only tolerated when it comes from very young children and psychologically disturbed people, including people under the influence of alcohol or drugs. Because the mechanism is so strong this is a favoured stategy for maintaining a conversation. It is said that many women employ it to get their husbands to talk. Other adjacency pairs are perhaps somewhat less compelling. But it is also impolite not to return a greeting and not to acknowledge an apology, a compliment, or someone's thanks.

All of this is part of **conversation**, which consists, on an elementary level, of an **opening**, characterized by greetings and other **phatic elements** (small talk), negotiation of possible topics, **central phases**, where one or more topics or 'pieces of business' are connected by various transitional phases, and finally **closings/ endings**, which include:

- signals of willingness to end the encounter (verbal or non-verbal, such as a remark on the time or a look at your watch, but not too eager)
- confirmation of the 'business' transacted
- reference to possible future meetings
- goodbyes

Topics may be fixed, as at business meetings, or they may be quite free, as in relaxed conversation among social equals. Nevertheless, there can be problems in such matters as who gets to determine the topic and who may hold the floor and how long.

Turn-taking is necessary since conversation is dialoguic. This may be accomplished when the current speaker selects another or when the next speaker self-selects. Speaker change may be signalled verbally or non-verbally. The current speaker can, for example, trail off, establish eye contact with a potential next speaker, or even address someone by name. The hearer who wants to get the floor can make preparatory sounds such as clearing her/his throat or taking on a more rigid posture. In some cases this may involve interruption.

Interruption is the case when a hearer takes the floor before the previous speaker has finished or reached a transition-relevant place. This should be distinguished from overlap. **Overlap** is an extremely fine switch in speaker–hearer roles in which the final word of the previous speaker and the first word of the new speaker co-occur. Interruption may be a sign of dominance behaviour. This may explain why men probably interrupt women more than vice versa. However, interruption can also serve as a sign of empathy and enthusiasm. In any case, there are many factors which play a role in interruption behaviour (e.g. power/gender/age, group size, occasion, participant role).

Neither interruption nor overlap are to be confused with **back channel behaviour**, which is a sign of active listening. This includes minimal responses such as the sounds *mhm, uhuh* and murmured *yeah, okay*, etc. But it also includes non-verbal behavior such as head-nodding and longer utterances such as *Did he really?*

These themes (interruption, overlap, back channel behaviour) all contribute to the structuring and smooth flow of conversation. Another way to do this is to use **discourse markers**, which are words whose meaning consists largely of the function they have within speech, functions which may be:

- organizational (turn taking) (e.g. *well*)
- topic structuring (e.g. *now* to sum up or to introduce a new topic or *okay* to end an old one before moving on)
- informational (e.g. *you know*)

Well is also an example of a marker which introduces the second member of a question–answer adjacency pair, e.g.:

A: *Do you have a minute for me?*
B: *Well, sure, if it doesn't take too long.*

Among the many sentence initiators we also find the words *yes* and *no*, which are not just pro-forms for sentences as pointed out in §6.4.2.1: cf. A: *They say the play was terrible.* B: *Yes/Yeah, I was there and I can tell you it was abysmal.* Other such initiators include SAE non-negative *no*, *ag*, *aikona* (emphatic, negative, e.g. *Aikona-closed! Aikona tomatoes* 'no tomatoes' < Nguni *hayi khona* 'not here'), *shame*, and *yes–no* (Branford 1994: 489).

Now, as in *Now, what this means is. . .*, is used to structure a topic, here, for example, preliminary to some kind of summary. However, *now* can also be used by a speaker to keep the floor as he or she moves on to a new topic (*Now, what I want you all to do is. . .*). *You know* is a marker of shared knowledge (or an appeal to accept something as general knowledge), e.g. *He's a real sorehead, you know.* A less widely known informational discourse marker is *la* (see Case study 7.3).

Exercise 7.8: Opening and closing formulas[7]

Our choice of words depends not only on what kind of a person we are (gender, age, occupation, religion, education, etc.) and on where we come from (country, region, rural or urban), but also on the type of text we are performing. In English there are formulas used to introduce a text and they vary according to genre. The classical riddle begins with a formula like *What goes/holds/is/has. . . .* Some examples are shown in Table 7.5 (test yourself).

The fairy tale not only has a formulaic beginning (see the following exercise), but also regularly ends with the words *. . .and they lived happily ever after.* Prayers end with *Amen*, traditional West Indian folk tales with *Jack man dory, me story done* or *I step on a piece of lead and the lead bend, and my story end*; formal speeches, with *Thank you for your attention*. Formal (parliamentary) sessions close with *The meeting is adjourned*, and telephone calls, with *(good-)bye*.

---

7 See also §8.1.2 on formulaic language.

Table 7.5. Riddles

What is black and white and /red/ all over?

What goes into the water red and comes out black?

What goes into the water black and comes out red?

What goes into the water yellow and comes out white?

What has four legs and flies?

What has four wheels and flies?

What has six eyes and can't see?[8]

In the following exercise your job is to match the genre and its typical opening formula. Put the appropriate letter in the box following the name of the genre.

1. Business letter	☐	a. *A funny thing happened to me on the way to . . .*
2. Fairy tale	☐	b. *Cric . . . crac*
3. Formal speech	☐	c. *Dear Madam, Dear Sir*
4. Funny story	☐	d. *Have you heard the one about . . .*
5. Joke	☐	e. *Hello!*
6. Prayer	☐	f. *The meeting is called to order.*
7. Parliamentary session	☐	g. *Ladies and Gentlemen!*
8. Telephone call	☐	h. *Oh Lord, . . .*
9. West Indian folk tale	☐	i. *Once upon a time*

Case Study 7.3: The discourse marker *La*[9] in SingE

'Perhaps the most striking and distinctive feature of L [= diglossically Low] English is the use of a particle *la* . . .' (Richards and Tay 1977: 143).

> *Yes we go lah. All sorts of things will come out lah.*
> *Can 'ah?*   'Can it be done?'
> *Why 'ah?*   'Why is it so?' (Augustin 1982:256f)

Its origins are not fully clear. This element may have come from Hokkien Chinese. Possibly it was borrowed by both SingE and Malay, but it may have made its way to English from the Malay question marker *kah*. Even its functions are differently understood. While one source says it functions to signal the nature of the relationship between the people talking: 'there is a positive rapport between speakers and an element of solidarity', and points out that *la* is not used if there is lack of intimacy or disagreement (Richards and Tay 1977: 145f.), another states:

---

8 Answers: a newspaper (/red/ = *read*) or an embarrassed zebra (/red/ = *red*); a red-hot poker; a lobster; a baby's nappie/diaper; two birds; a garbage truck; three blind mice (cf. Opie and Opie 1959: 74 for some of these).

9 Also *lah*, *'ah*. Other elements include *Ai* (or *Aa*) = a general filler and *man*, an intimate one (Tongue 1974: 86).

The range of meanings it possesses is prodigious; depending upon the way it is pronounced, it can function as an intensifying particle, as a marker of informal style, as a signal of intimacy, for persuading, deriding, wheedling, rejecting and a host of other purposes. With many [L SingE] speakers, no utterance, esp. a response utterance seems complete without at least one -*lah*. (Tongue 1974: 114)

Whichever interpretation lies closer to the facts of usage, both agree inasmuch as they fit in with the understanding of *la* as a discourse marker of the informational type, one that appeals to shared knowledge.

7.3.2 Pragmatic idioms

7.3.2.1 Greetings and leave-takings

It is usual polite behaviour for people who know each other to say hello when they meet for the first time on any given day. This is normal phatic behaviour, i.e. keeping the channels of communication and goodwill open.[10] Above and beyond this, the type of greeting selected is an indication of the nature of the social relationship. Among the Yoruba there are many different greetings with a wide spread of social significance. 'In the indigenous cultures, there are greetings for almost every sphere of activity' (empathy, sympathy, joy, sorrow . . .). 'The terms *Hi*, *Hello*, and *How are you?* can be used by older or senior persons to younger or junior ones, but not vice versa. Such verbal behaviour coming from a younger person would be regarded as offhand. Informal forms like *Morning*, *Afternoon*, *Hi*, or *Hello* are most frequently used among equals' (Akere 1982: 91f.).

In ENL varieties a simple *Hi!* (but especially combined with FN) signals an informal relationship between more or less equals. This is also used downward from the older/more powerful to the younger/less powerful, who in turn are more likely to give the older a more formal *Good morning (afternoon)*, M + LN.

Frequently, people add an inquiry about the wellbeing of the other, as in *Hi, how are ya?* This is as unlikely to be meant literally as is the *Have you eaten?* in SingE (which has borrowed the notion of this polite question from Chinese). Indeed, in the case of *How do you do?*, which is seemingly a question about someone's wellbeing, the appropriate reaction is to reply with the same words *How do you do?*, for in reality this is a pragmatic idiom used only when people are introduced to each other in a relatively formal situation.

Exercise 7.9: Greetings and leave-taking formulas

Characterize the following greetings according to who might use them and how formal or informal the situation is. Do the same for the second list of inquiries about wellbeing as well as for the list of leave-taking formulas and those for getting rid of someone.

10 For a review of both the concept of phatic communion and specifically of greetings see Coupland *et al.* (1992).

1. *Good morning!*
2. *Morning!*
3. *Hello!*
4. *Hello, X.*
5. *Hi!*
6. *Hi there!*
7. *Howdy!*
8. *Kia ora.*

Inquiry about wellbeing

1. *How's it going?*
2. *Are you rightly/bravely?*
3. *How's tricks?*
4. *How are ya?*
5. *What's up?*
6. *Is it well with you?*

Leave-taking

1. *See you/ya (later).*
2. *Bye.*
3. *Goodbye.*
4. *Cheerio.*
5. *So long.*
6. *Hooray!*
7. *I will go ahead of you.*

Getting rid of someone

1. *Beat it.*
2. *Can you please go away.*
3. *Fuck off.*
4. *Get lost.*
5. *Get the hell outa here.*
6. *Git.*
7. *Hamba.*
8. *Piss off.*
9. *Scram.*
10. *Vamoose.*
11. *Voetsak.*

Project 7.6: Greeting and leave-taking

It was pointed out in §7.2.1.1 that power and solidarity are not distinguished in English by using differing 2nd person pronouns, but by things like the choice of names. The choice of greetings and leave-taking formulas may well differentiate status as well.

Your project is to observe either how people of clearly differing status greet each other in English or how they say goodbye. (Choose one only.) Who greets/says goodbye first? Are names and titles used? What greeting/departure formulas are used? Are other acts involved such as shaking hands, nodding the head, bowing, waving a hand?

Try to draw up a profile of the criteria for exchanging greetings/goodbyes between people of different status. Can you add any remarks on the effect of gender or age?

7.3.2.2 Apologies

When one person has injured another in some interpersonal social rather than serious physical fashion, the matter is best dealt with by making an apology. That is, we are talking about cases where the injury has damaged the other's face. Like the other pragmatic idioms we have been looking at, the act of excusing oneself also consists of an adjacency pair, the actual apology, and the acceptance of it. Common formulas for the apology itself include the following:

Perfunctory	Emphatically polite
Excuse me	*Please excuse the bother.*
(Oh,) I'm sorry	*I'm sorry for your trouble!*
No offence meant	*I regret that I should have said something so risqué in your presence*
Forgive me	*Would you please forgive my boldness?*

As in so many cases, the perfunctory note is avoided and politeness is achieved by lengthening the formulas and perhaps including polite signal words such as *please* or using distancing forms such as the conditional or interrogative.

An expressions like *Sorry* is not used just for an apology. In NigE, for example, it may be extended to 'an expression of sympathy or pity for a person involved in an accident,. . . In a classroom situation, for example, if a lecturer accidentally drops his lecture notes or a piece of chalk, his students would say "Sorry Sir"' (Akere 1982: 92). In Tanzania we might hear not only *Sorry*, but also *Pole*, an expression of regret and sympathy (Schmied 1985a: 222). These are, of course, expressions of sympathy with someone's lack of success. In an ENL variety when a friend fails to get a scholarship he or she was applying for, we might express our regret by saying *Rotten luck! That's tough! (That's) too bad! Better luck next time! What a pity! That's a shame!* or *(I'm) sorry (to hear) about that!*

The acknowledgement of an apology is usually a short disclaimer of any offensive such as *Oh, that's okay, It's not so bad, It doesn't matter*, or a non-verbal response such as a nod and a smile.

7.3.2.3 Compliments

Compliments are most frequently directed toward personal appearance, possessions, results of skills and effort, for example, *Your new hair-do is fantastic!*; *That's a great jacket you're wearing*; or *I really liked your report in class today*. They belong to the area of positive face because they serve primarily to make the addressee feel good, but they also help to establish or maintain solidarity. Compliment behaviour varies according to a number of the social dimensions of the participants. In this section we will emphasize gender differences especially, but will also report on some differences between countries (the US and South Africa).

7.3.2.4 Paying compliments

There are differences in the way people frame compliments. In one study among New York students females clearly preferred a personal 1st or 2nd person focus

(*I liked your report*; *Your report was great*) while males went more for the impersonal minimal *Great report.* vs. the more expanded female *What a great report!*
(Herbert 1990: 203). It is also suggested that males produce fewer compliments,
i.e. it is harder to find examples of them to collect. Compliments on ability will
more likely come from someone with higher status. Females receive more compliments about their appearance (Wolfson 1984: 241ff.). Furthermore, compliments may be used more by women to signal solidarity while males may see one
as face-threatening, esp. possession compliments (*Nice sweater!*), which may be
interpreted as meaning 'I want it' (Wolfson 1984: 219).

Project 7.7: Paying compliments

In his study of Binghamton University (New York) students Herbert (1990: 205–7) found

■ approximately 60 per cent of compliments by males are impersonal in form (especially from a male to a male) vs. only 20 per cent of those by females
■ 2nd person ones are most common between two females, about equal in mixed dyads (groups of two), and infrequent between males
■ 1st person forms predominate among females, but are rare among males. Furthermore, 90 per cent of the 1st person compliments were of the form *I love/like x*, but no males used *love* vs. *like*

Your project is to observe compliments to see if you can replicate these findings. Try to collect 10 examples of compliments from men and 10 from women (which is it easier to observe?). Note whether the person being complimented is female or male. Are the verbs *love* or *like* used? If so, what is the distribution between the genders?

Case study 7.4: Compliment acknowledgement in SAE

Compliments occur in adjacency pairs, which sometimes causes trouble for the
person whose job it is to supply the second member of the pair. Paying a compliment is relatively unproblematic. Some people, as we know, have a hard time
saying anything positive about anyone or anything, but then it's their choice
whether they become active or not. In the case of compliments, however, once
one has been produced, the recipient of the compliment is not so free. There is a
strong expectation of a response.

The simplest and perhaps standard way of responding is simply to say *Thank
you*. However, there are some cultural traps involved because this not only
involves the socially desired behaviour of acknowledging the compliment but
also means accepting the compliment as true, which violates the precept of modesty (avoid self-praise). Herbert (1990: 209–11) concludes that the function of
compliments among Americans is not always strictly complimentary, but also
serves to establish or confirm solidarity (which non-Americans may not per-
ceive). Hence when someone does not accept a compliment they may have recognized this function and this may be like saying: 'I recognize that your
compliment was intended to make me feel good. I choose to avoid self-praise and
thus assert that we are equal' (p. 211).

Herbert found that male compliments were acknowledged far more by females than the converse: 'Compliments from females will most likely not be accepted, whereas compliments from males will, especially by female recipients' (p. 217). In other words, compliment acknowledgement is possibly a part of the negotiation of a relationship between unequals. On the other hand, women use the compliment adjacency pair less for praise and more for solidarity or conversation advancement. For example, female-generated compliments elicit a lot of history-type responses, such as someone explaining where or how she got the item praised, which gives the compliment-acknowledgement pair a conversation-advancing aspect (p. 221).

South Africans accept compliments at the rate of 76.26 per cent vs. 36.35 per cent for Americans.[11] But Americans use more compliments, and this can be compared to greater use of FN. That is, compliments – like FNs – are used to indicate solidarity (Herbert 1990: 220). In SAE compliments are different: 'Negotiating social relations is simply not the issue here [in SAE]' (p. 221). The pattern of compliment-making in SAE is similar to the way males handle compliments in AmE: there are fewer of them, and there is less to negotiate in social relations. In SAE, as for males in AmE, compliments are accepted more frequently. For American females compliments serve more for solidarity or as tokens of goodwill (see Table 7.6).

Table 7.6. Comparative use of compliments (Herbert 1990: 222)

	SAE, AmE males	AmE females
Function:	offer praise	offer solidarity
Frequency:	infrequent	frequent
Response:	acceptance	non-acceptance

Project 7.8: Acknowledging compliments

In the Binghamton corpus there were 12 types of response:

1. Appreciation token — *Thanks*, a nod
2. Comment acceptance — *Yeah, it's my favourite, too*
3. Praise upgrade — *Really brings out the blue in my eyes, doesn't it?*
4. Comment history — How/where/why acquired, etc.
5. Reassignment of the force of the compliment — *It's my brother's; it's easy to do*
6. Return — *So's yours*
7. Scale down — *It's really quite old*
8. Question — Sincerity: *Do you really think so?*
9. Disagreement — *I hate it*
10. Qualification — *It's alright, but Len's is nicer*
11. No acknowledgement — Topic shift, no response
12. Request interpretation — *You wanna borrow this one, too?*

---

11 In Herbert's findings at the University of Witwatersrand. Cf. the different results of Chick's replication of this study at the University of Natal (Chick 1996).

Your project consists of observing compliment acknowledgments to see which of the responses listed you can find. Again try to collect 10 examples of compliments from men and 10 from women (and again, which is it easier to observe?). Note whether the person responding is female or male.

7.3.2.5 Thanks

Thanks and acknowledgement are also an adjacency pair. The number of ways of saying thank you is immense. The range of thanks includes those shown in Table 7.7.

Table 7.7. Expressions of thanks

Expression of thanks	Description
Ta	Informal, perfunctory, BrE
Thanks	Informal, perfunctory
I thank you	Mock formal
I thank you very much	Unidiomatic, foreign
Thanks a lot	Neutral
Let me express my heartfelt gratitude	Formal
How nice of you! Thank you.	Very sincere

The ways of acknowledging a thank you are more restricted. Standard formulas are *You're welcome*; *Not at all*; *It's nothing really*; *That's okay*; and *Don't mention it*. This last expression is obviously not completely transparent to non-native speakers, as seen by the reaction of two French girls hitch-hiking in Scotland. When they thanked the lorry driver who let them off at their goal, he responded, *Don't mention it*, which prompted them to reassure him: *Oh no, we won't say a word to anyone*.

Exercise 7.10: Cultural misunderstanding

The following interchange is quoted by Todd (1989: 335f.). At two places Jim (BrE) mis-understands what Mbunwe (CamE) is saying and vice versa. What are the misunderstandings and how might they be explained?

Jim:	*Would you like a cup of coffee?*
Mbunwe:	*Thank you.* (meaning 'No' but interpreted as 'Yes')
Jim:	*How do you like it?*
Mbunwe:	*Like what?*
Jim:	*How do you like your coffee?*
Mbunwe:	*Very well indeed.*

7.4 SUMMARY

Chapter 7 dealt with a variety of social dimensions of the vocabulary of English. The first step was a look at what politeness is, defining it in terms of positive and negative face and defining social relations in terms of power and solidarity. We then looked at how the choice of vocabulary in the area of vocatives reflects these central dimensions. As has been the case throughout this book, this review included numerous examples of how the expression of politeness and of power and solidarity vary in the English-speaking world in terms of region, age, status, kinship, gender, ethnicity, and several other social criteria. The second half of the chapter explored the pragmatic idioms involved in greetings, leave-takings, apologies, compliments, and thanks.

8 International English: How Native and Non-Native Speakers Use Words

After the Second World War an American officer who had served with and gotten to know a number of English officers during the war was invited to spend a few days at the country house of one of them, where he would be able to take part in a fox hunt. Everything went very well and the American was warmly welcomed and made to feel at home – until returning from the hunt, when a number of the company took a noticeably chillier attitude toward him. After a while he took his host aside and asked him what was wrong. It took a bit of prodding on the American's part until the host finally explained, 'In England when one sights the fox it is customary to call "Tally-ho!" and not to yell "There goes the son of a bitch!"'

> Proper Words in proper Places, makes the true Definition of a Stile.
> (Swift, *Letter to a Young Gentleman Lately entered into Holy Orders*)

8.0 INTRODUCTION

In this chapter the focus will be on the use of English, in particular on the diatypical features of register as introduced in §5.3.2. Style, formulaic language and texts, and slang (§§8.1 and 8.2) and field (Internet, youth language, academia, Special Englishes, terminologies: §8.4) dominate, but these areas also offer ample opportunity to examine medium, since examples of both spoken and written English play an important role. In addition, the international aspect of English will be expanded to include a look at borrowing between English and other languages (Dutch, German, French, Spanish: §8.3).

8.1 STYLE

One of the perennial difficulties in comparing *style* across varieties is knowing how to decide what counts as formal and what as informal style (see §5.3.2.3 for criteria). There is always an underlying choice involved in which the speaker/writer follows the dictates of the situation to make his or her stylistic choice. Although the field and the medium of discourse as well as dialectal features (age, region, gender, etc.) play a significant role in this choice, formality is the most obvious criterion for style. Clearly it is inappropriate to compare informal AmE with formal BrE as in the epigraphic text. Assessment of formality is not completely arbitrary, but it can be very controversial.

8.1.1 **Style in regional varieties of English**

For SAE Chick points out the results of mismatches in 'culturally-preferred interactional styles' (1991: 459). Afrikaans speakers of English came over wrong with their English-speaking partners in role-playing because of their different, more direct style. English speakers are more aloof, cold, unreliable, inconsistent in the eyes of Afrikaans speakers; the latter more conservative, authoritarian, dogmatic and inflexible in the view of English speakers (Chick 1991: 459f.).

Another example of style differences across cultures involves the evaluation often made of IndE, which is said to have a bookish and old-fashioned flavour – at least from a Eurocentric point of view. This is sometimes attributed to the reading models in Indian schools, which may draw on older English authors (cf. Mehrotra 1982; Das 1982), as in Table 8.1.

Yet the outsider should beware of jumping to conclusions, for it is difficult to grasp many of the subtleties of the use of IndE, for example, the perception of a subtle change in perspective via an active–passive switch:

> A subordinate addressing his boss in an office in India writes, 'I request you to look into the case,' while the boss writing to a subordinate will normally use the passive, 'you are requested to look into the case.' If the latter form is used by a subordinate, it may mean a downright insult. (Mehrotra 1982: 166)

The standards of style are different in IndE compared to ENL: there is a 'tendency towards verbosity, preciosity, and the use of learned literary words', a 'preference for exaggerated and hyperbolic forms' (Mehrotra 1982: 164); 'stylistic embellishment is highly valued' (Kachru 1984: 364), a kind of *style calque* in which the stylistic expectations of the background Indian languages are carried over into English. Profuse expressions of thanks are valued as 'culturally appropriate and contextually proper in Indian situations' (Kachru 1986b: 33):

> I consider it to be my primordial obligation to humbly offer my deepest sense of gratitude to my most revered Guruji and untiring and illustrious guide Professor . . . for the magnitude of his benevolence and eternal guidance. (Mehrotra 1982: 165)

Table 8.1. Stylistic choices in IndE (Das 1982: 148)

IndE	ENL	IndE	ENL	IndE	ENL
ancient	old	comely	pretty	places of residence	homes
be domiciled	live	consume	eat	proceed	go
be in possession of	have	demise	death	resplendent	dazzling
blithe	happy	make application for	ask	retain	keep
bosom	chest	mournful	sad		

That this is not true only of IndE is demonstrated by the following example from African English of an apology for having to break a date: 'a vaguely anticipated prior engagement now threatens to materialize, desolated to have to postpone our tête-à-tête' (Angogo and Hancock 1980: 78).

Furthermore, speakers of IndE may mix metaphors and levels of style in a manner amusing or strange to speakers of ENL. One clerk in asking for several days leave to go to his mother's funeral explained that 'the hand that rocked the cradle has kicked the bucket' (Mehrotra 1982: 162). Likewise the following wish: 'I am in very good health and hope you are in the same boat' (Das 1982: 144).

Style is notoriously difficult to assess. Perhaps the most difficult aspect of such an evaluation is the lack of a usable standard of measurement. Who is the arbiter of style? This is a question which cannot be resolved among ENL users, and even less so in ESL varieties in which local traditions are involved which may either go back to traditions in an underlying language and/or culture or may result from a restricted input from ENL, as suggested by the teaching models in Indian schools.

8.1.2 Formulaic language

One possible approach to studying stylistic differences is to look at texts which are relatively fixed in the choice of forms available. Letters are one such text type (§8.1.2.1 and Project 8.1). Another is the kind of text we find in very specific circumstances such as in the classified ads in the matrimonial columns of newspapers (Case study 8.1 and Project 8.2).

8.1.2.1 Salutations and closings in letters

Conventional style dictates that a business letter be opened with a fairly standardized salutation. Virtually all begin with the word *Dear*, which has lost all meaning of dearness or belovedness and which is followed by *Madam* or *Sir*. Many ESL users treat this convention differently. NigE extends *Dear Sir* to personal letters in cases where it is impolite to use the name of the addressee if he or she is older (Bamgbose 1983:107). Among younger ENL users, in contrast, there seems to be an increasing movement to informality, as marked by the move to a simple *Hi!* (or *Hi* + FN!) at least for informal letters.

Closings vary more widely. Especially conservative BrE closings to business letters have either *Yours faithfully* or *Yours sincerely,* the former conventionally employed when the addressee is personally unknown to the writer and is therefore addressed as *Dear Sir* or *Dear Madam*. If the addressee is known and addressed by name, BrE ends with *Yours sincerely* or *Yours truly*. AmE uses *Sincerely yours, Yours sincerely*, or *Yours truly* with little differentiation. This gives us the variations shown in Table 8.2 (note the colon after *Sir* or *Madam* and the periods after *Mr.*, *Mrs.*, and *Ms.* in AmE). Both varieties use more informal closings such as *With best/friendly wishes.* Even more informal and friendly is *With warm/best/friendly regards.* Also possible is simply a perfunctory *Regards* for a good acquaintance or associate.

Table 8.2. Salutations and closings in BrE and AmE business letters

BrE	Salutation:	*Dear Sir,*	Salutation:	*Dear Mr/Mrs/Miss/Ms X,*
		or: *Dear Madam,*	Closing:	*Yours sincerely,*
	Closing:	*Yours faithfully,*		or: *Yours truly,*
AmE	Salutation:	*Dear Sir:/Dear Mr. X,*		
		or: *Dear Madam:/Dear*		
		Mrs./Miss/Ms. X,		
	Closing:	*Sincerely yours,*		
		or: *Yours sincerely,*		
		or: *Yours truly,*		

A series of examples from a guide to letter-writing published in India makes the suggestions shown in Table 8.3.[1]

Project 8.1: Salutations and closings in letters

Find out what formulaic salutations and closings are used in business and in informal letters in English in the area where you live. Do they conform to the types given above? If not, what reasons might be given to explain the deviation? (For example, divergent underlying non-English patterns; youthful entrepreneurs and buddy-buddy style; organizational guidelines mandating the use of zero formulaic expressions or of particular ones; etc.)

8.1.3 Formulaic texts

A large number of texts are relatively fixed in the type and order of their content as well as the phrasing used within them. A wedding invitation, for example, is traditionally engraved and printed on a heavy, elegant, and expensive type of

Table 8.3. Salutations and closings in IndE (Görlach 1989a)

Type: to a pen friend (writer: female)		Type: to a girl friend	
Salutation:	*My dear Manohar,*	Salutation:	*Dear Rummi,*
Closing:	*Yours ever loving*	Closing:	*With love,*
Type: to one's wife (first such letter)		Type: business letter (answering a classified ad)	
Salutation:	*Dear Rummi,*	Salutation:	*Dear Mr. . . .*
Closing:	*With profound love and kisses,* or: *Your own,*	Closing:	*Yours in expectation,*

---

1 The style in the body of the sample letters runs from cases of effusive thanks (. . . *and Oh, you beat me. I mean you have overwhelmed me with your charm, manners and gallantry of heart*) to business-letter formulas (*Your letters of the 15th*).

paper. The parents of the bride invite the addressee to the ceremony and/or reception and give the time and place written out in full. Because such a text is so extremely formal and special, Americans (as in the example given in Fig. 8.1) even resort to British spelling, as seen in the word *honour*.

> *Mr. and Mrs. Richard Berger*
> *request the honour of your presence*
> *at the marriage of their daughter*
> *Sally Elizabeth*
> *to*
> *Samuel Housten Vance*
> *Saturday, the sixth of May*
> *two thousand and one*
> *at eleven o'clock*
> *St. Mary's Church*
> *Idlewild*
> *Georgia*

Figure 8.1. Formulaic text: wedding invitation

In the following section we explore a further type of formulaic text, matrimonial ads, to which we return in §8.4.1.1, where we will see how matrimonials look on the Internet.

Case study 8.1: Matrimonial advertisements

Classified advertisements in newspapers are a good example of register: they are universally written (medium); they clearly involve the goal of finding a partner (function); they are composed in an abbreviated type of language (style) using a code that includes conventionalized abbreviations and vocabulary from the area of personal relationships (field).

Text 8.1. Matrimonial advertisements (newspapers)

> RAVISHING WOMAN BUSINESS EXECUTIVE (49), sensual, merry, creative and optimistic, fond of horse riding, tennis, nature, art, with a passion for writing and wide horizons, would like to meet 45/60 yr old man combining humour and happiness here or at the other end of the world.
> (*International Herald Tribune*, Apr. 2000)

> CURVY LONDON LADY. Vivacious, curvaceous, attractive, privately educated brunette, mid-20s, GSOH, N/S thrives on cocktails, laughter, twilight, good cuisine, seeks successful, good-looking, stylish, witty, professional white male, late 20s–early 30s, N/S. London. (*Independent*, Apr. 2000)

Alliance invited from parents for Sindhi only fair tall son September 75/177/10,000B.Com/DVES well established business non smoker, non drinker, vegetarian from Sindhi tall good looking professionally educated girl. Preferably Doctor/Engineer/Lawyer/CA response with photograph horoscope compulsory.

(*Times of India,* quoted in Divakaruni 2000: 24)

As the examples in Text 8.1 illustrate, classifieds typically use a more or less telegraphic style which serves both to shorten the text (which is paid for by the word/line) and to add a note of urgency. The use of the article is reduced (*ravishing . . . executive* not *a ravishing . . . executive*) as is the frequency of relative pronouns (*. . .brunette . . . [who] . . . thrives on . . . seeks male [who is in his] late 20s–early 30s*). The copula *be* and auxiliaries may be elided (*alliance [is] sought from. . .*), and multiple attribution (*vivacious, curvaceous, attractive, privately educated brunette*) is the rule. Nevertheless, there are differences which are worth mentioning.

The same matrimonial ads differ from each other not only in the details about the person for whom a partner is being sought but also because they represent different sets of values. The first two, both centred in Western views of partnership, share a great deal and stand in contrast to the ad from the *Times of India*. A comparison shows that the texts have the following elements in common:

■ attributes of the person who is looking for a partner
■ attributes wished for in the potential respondent
■ statement of desired action (*would like to meet, seeks, Alliance invited*)

Yet despite the similiarities there are a number of contrasts: see Table 8.4.

While both stress the importance of physical appearance, the Indian ad emphasizes economic solidity and a healthy lifestyle and makes the role of the family obvious: it is the parents who have placed the ad and who act as intermediaries. Although the first woman in the Western ad is too old for family to speak for her, the other shows that younger Western men and women act on their own. The Western perspective is much more individually oriented and emphasizes personal lifestyle features and emotional goals (e.g. happiness). The language of the two also differs, though not dramatically. While both texts contain abbreviations (*yr = years*; *CA = Certified Accountant*), the Indian text includes abbreviations not generally familiar to non-Indians: *B.Com/DVES*. Furthermore, the sequence *September 75* (= birth date), *177* (= height in cm), and *10,000* (= income) is conventionalized enough not to cause misunderstandings. In a similar way *GSOH* and *N/S* are standard enough to appear in this way, as is *TLC*, which also commonly crops up.[2]

---

2 *GSOH* = good sense of humour; *N/S* = non-smoker; *TLC* = tender loving care.

Table 8.4. Comparison of matrimonial ads

Type of feature	Western	Indian
Personal traits of person looking	Appearance (figure, hair colour)	Appearance (height, skin colour)
	Personality	Ethnicity
	Age	Age
	Sexual interests	Education
Lifestyle of same	Profession	Economic solidity
	Healthy habits	Healthy habits
	Leisure activities (sports, nature, art, food, drink)	
	Intellectual life	
	Sense of humour	
Other points	Marriage not mentioned	Marriage intended
		Family
		Horoscope
Partner attributes	Age	Age (implicit: *girl*)
	Looks	Looks and size
	Profession/success	Education
	Race	Ethnic group
	Personality	

Project 8.2: Comparing matrimonial advertisements

Look at the matrimonial columns of at least three newspapers from different cultural areas in the English-speaking world. Can you substantiate the similarities and differences noted in Case study 8.1? If your findings are different, what can you attribute this to?

8.1.4 Class and style

Class lies at the foundation of sociolinguistics, and many a study reveals linguistic differences which correlate with social class differences. Yet it seems that relatively little can be said about class within the framework of a book like this one. Why is this? For one, class studies concentrate on middle-class and working-class speakers, often with further distinctions such as 'upper-middle-class', 'middle-middle-class', and 'lower-middle-class', but the truly marginal, the underclasses and the especially the upper class, are less often studied. This may well lie in the difficulty of access to the two groups.

Secondly, even within sociolinguistic studies, the most revealing findings seem to be in the area of pronunciation, especially finer distinctions in vowel quality. This is understandable inasmuch as most speakers are less aware of and therefore have less control over their pronunciation. Lexical distinctions are cited from time to time, but are clearly less prominent when it comes to conclusive findings.

What claims we have are often controversial and often perhaps only anecdotal. How many Americans are aware of the social class associations that items are said to have in BrE, for instance that *lounge* 'is definitely non-U; *drawing room* definitely U' [U = upper-class] (Benson *et al.* 1986a: 36)? British speakers might be interested to know that in the US 'Proles say *tux*, middles *tuxedo*, but both are considered low by uppers, who say *dinner jacket* or (higher) *black tie*' (Fussell 1984: 152). Few Americans and few writers would agree on this, and no dictionaries give help with the category of class.

Finally, despite language scholars' awareness of variation, it seems that it is StE which is and is likely to remain the default mode. But StE is by definition class-marked: it is the sign of education and power. So while StE is not the same as upper-class English, it is the kind of English which is marked off from non-prestigious slang (*humongous*), non-standard words (*nohow*), vulgar usage (*crapper*), baby talk (*beddy-bye*), and other somehow 'divergent' types. That they are indeed 'divergent' is revealed by the fact that dictionaries provide labels for them.

Case study 8.2: U and non-U

Dictionaries do not offer labels to indicate class differences in usage such as UC, MC, or WC. For this we must turn to speculations such as those offered in connection with U and non-U English.[3] Table 8.5 shows a recent comparative list. The adjective *appalling* is supposedly U, as are *absolutely* and *brill*. *Rod's* may be used for *Harrod's*. Prep and public school slang like *thicko, wee, twit, nit* 'idiot' are also possibly part of sub-varieties of U English.

Table 8.5. U and Non-U vocabulary (Wales 1994: 7)

U	Non-U	U	Non-U
America	The States	cake	pastry
helping	portion	ice	ice-cream
lavatory	toilet	looking glass	mirror
pudding	sweet, dessert	relatives	relations
rich	wealthy	Royalties	Royals
scent	perfume	scurf	dandruff
sick	ill	sofa	settee
spectacles	glasses	table napkin	serviette
wireless	radio	writing paper	notepaper

3 The terms stem from Ross (1959); see also Buckle (1978).

Exercise 8.1: Stylistic evaluation

The following words have been 'classed' differently over time. To get some idea of historical change in stylistic evaluation a look at Samuel Johnson's *Dictionary of the English Language* (1755) in comparison with the *Collins COBUILD English Language Dictionary* (1987) should be revealing. Johnson's dictionary was largely a one-man enterprise based on wide reading and was surely much more subjective than modern corpus-based dictionaries like *COBUILD*.

For the following items compare the stylistic evaluations given in the two dictionaries. If no rating is given the word may be considered to be neutral.

	Johnson	COBUILD
doughty		
expropriate		
far-fetched		
hussy		
lingo		
piss		
stout (n.)		
tiny		
topping (adj.)		
width		

8.1.5 Jargon

Resistance to **bureaucratese** (or **gobbledygook** or **jargon**), in America now sometimes called 'inside the Beltway' (i.e. inside the superhighway which encircles Washington, DC), is sometimes great. It includes a rejection of the overuse of hard words (see §2.1.4.1), especially when coupled with obscurity in thinking and wordiness. This also includes **euphemisms** such as *police action* instead of *war*. Sometimes cynical euphemisms are cited as when *human remains pouches* were used instead of body bags to transport dead soldiers back to America in the Persian Gulf War. A frequent euphemistic devise is to quote the first letter only of the objectionable word, e.g. *l-word* (*liberal*) or the *r-word* for *recession* (in *Fedspeak*, the language of the American Federal Reserve Bank, also euphemistically known as a *down period*).

Traditional legal language (**legalese**) has been one of the chief butts of criticism, as in the following (not particularly extreme) example (from an American insurance policy):

> If the Policy does not contain the provisions relating to Owner and Beneficiary as specified on the reverse hereof, the Company is hereby directed to modify the Policy by including such provisions therein, superseding any existing Policy provisions relating to the same subject and in conflict therewith, such modification to be effective as of the date this is signed upon its recordation at the Home Office of the Company.

Burridge and Mulder (1998: 240–2) list the following attributes of bureau-cratic writing (including some of their examples):

- a high proportion of lexical to grammatical words
- long complex compounds (*prototype crisis shelter development plans*)
- doublespeak (*reality augmentation* for *lies*)
- long strings of more or less synonymous words, e.g.

> *No person shall prune, cut, carry away, pull up, dig, fell, bore, chop, saw, chip, pick, move, sever, climb, molest, take, break, deface, destroy, set fire to, burn, scorch, carve, paint, mark, or in any manner interfere with, tamper, mutilate, misuse, disturb or damage any tree, shrub, plant, grass, flower, or part thereof, . . .*

- nominal style (*in the event of default in the payment of* 'if you don't pay what you owe')
- lengthy sentences (average legal English: 55 words; the insurance policy example has 69)
- complex sentences (multiple embedding) (see American insurance policy above)
- a high relative number of passive sentences (making it unclear who is responsible for something)
- affirmatives as negatives of their opposite (*a not insignificant amount* 'quite a bit')

This has been instrumental in creating and sustaining the movement for Plain English, a movement directed chiefly against the impenetrable use of language. Next to abbreviations and acronyms this includes indirection and trite expressions rather than straight speech. The movement enjoys support in all the major native-English-speaking countries.

8.2 GROUP LANGUAGE AND SLANG

The type of language referred to as **slang** is more than a level of formality. That is, slang cannot be understood simply as informal, colloquial, careless, sloppy language even though these notions are indelibly connected with the idea of slang in many people's minds. Slang is, rather, first and foremost, group language. This restriction – at least in its origins – is the key feature of slang. That is, slang has an extremely important social function with regard to the groups that create it: it helps to establish solidarity and is associated with group identity. An elderly white American woman who talks about *dissing* ('to show *dis*respect toward someone') may be using (relatively) recent slang, but she is violating numerous restrictions on its use, chief among which is that this is typical of young black males. While slang usage such as this may drift upward into the language of the more powerful and outward into that of out-group users, this is far from automatic; and by the time this happens, the original group will probably have long since turned to a different expression.

The fact that slang is typically connected with the subcultures of youth is perhaps what leads many people to see it as informal, colloquial, careless, or sloppy, for that is how many people evaluate young people's language, the language of the (as yet) weak, the (as yet) outsiders. Some would maintain that the powerful, too, have their slang, be it the slang of politicians, the police, the military, or professional athletes. The appendix to the venerable *Dictionary of Slang and Unconventional English* by Eric Partridge[4] is illustrative of this, as we see from looking at some of the categories which it supplies, for instance 'Bird-watchers' slang', 'Clergymen's diction in the Church of England', or 'Eton, Westminster, Winchester'.[5] This is clearly a very wide interpretation of slang. For this reason, it is more useful to separate out specialist languages such as that of bird-watchers, perhaps clergymen's diction as well, and refer to it as *jargon*. Nor should be confused with the **Special Englishes** (see §8.4.3).

Slang is also a style, a way of talking. The user of slang will value its rhetorical effect, which may well be based on some sort of discrepancy such as incongruity or **semantic inversion** (*bad* 'good'), irreverence (*God-squadder* 'pious, fundamentalistic person'), or exaggeration (*gut-bucket* 'low dive, i.e. bar'). Slang, as these examples show, manifests an attitude of disrespect for authority as it tries to be witty or humorous and as it exploits the solidarity of the shared code. Indeed, despite mention of slang among the powerful, what is central to the idea of slang is that it is the in-group language of outsiders.

In this connection it is good to remind ourselves of the similarities between slang and taboo words: 'These words [taboo words] are seen by various researchers in a number of ways, such as inhibited use, as ways of breaking the rules, and as symbols of protest and reaction against certain figures in authority' (Hughes 1992: 291). In much the same way, the use of slang may be seen as the linguistic protest of the subordinated against those in charge. Distancing oneself from the vocabulary norms of GenE is also a rejection of middle-class norms by marginalized groups, be the group defined by race and ethnicity (Case studies 8.3 and 8.4 and Exercise 8.2), by rank in a hierarchy (cf §7.2.4.1), by age (Case study 8.5), or by their illegal behaviour (itself of diverse motivation; see §8.4.2).

Case study 8.3: Slang in the Harlem renaissance

In the 1920s the vast migration of African Americans from the rural American South to the cities of the North created a kind of cultural critical mass that led to enormous creativity, among other things in the areas of literature, art, clothing, and music. Part of the group identity of these new urban blacks found its

---

4 Much the same can be said of Wentworth and Flexner (1960); cf. Flexner (1960: vii, 596).
5 Clearly a mixture of youth (i.e. schools) and associations of power (high costs and exclusivity).

Table 8.6. Terms for skin colour in Harlem English (Watson 1995: 88)

Light-skinned	*high yaller, yaller, pink, pink-toes, mustard seed, punkin* [sic] *seed, honey, lemon-colored, copper-hued, olive*
Middle ranges of skin colour	*high brown, cocoa brown, chestnut, coffee-colored, nut brown, maroon, vaseline brown, seal brown, sealskin, low brown*
Dark-skinned	*blue, charcoal, ebony black, eight-rock, eight-ball, inky dink, dark black, low black, lam black, damn black*

expression in in-group language.[6] To illustrate this we will look at some of the areas involved.

Appearance. Colour was (and still is) a sensitive point. While many blacks feel racial pride and emphasize that black is beautiful, many others aspire(d) to appear as 'white' as possible. This put(s) a premium on light skin and straight hair. The terms given in Table 8.6 surely represent a mixture of attitudes. *High yaller*, for example, is largely negative in connotation, while *honey* or *olive* have more positive connotations.

Hair could be straight and Caucasian-like, which made it *good hair, righteous moss, righteous grass, near my God to thee, kind hair*. Or it was *nappy hair: bad hair, naps, tight head, mailman hair* ('Each knot's got its own route'), *every postman on his beat*. A *jar-head* was a black male whose hair had not been straightened.

Exercise 8.2: Metaphor and metonymy

People (types). Then as now, there was a wide variety of words available to designate blacks. In the 1920s they included such standard terms as *Negro, black, coloured, Afro-Americans, Aframericans, Libyans* (rare), *Ethiopians*. However, there were also more slangy words. Many of these words, such as *nigger*, had an in-group use by men which emphasized solidarity, as we saw when we looked at **ritual insults** (Case study 7.2). Used by an outsider, the word *nigger* was and remains an insulting slur.

What is interesting to note about slang is the way it is created. While slang is the product of all the processes of word formation which we have reviewed (§§4.3 and 5.2), it is especially the use of **metaphor** and **metonymy** which are central to it. As an example of metaphor let us take one of the Harlem expressions for a black person who conformed to white expectations of subservience (loyalty, cheerfulness, etc.): an *Uncle Tom*. This is a name taken from Stowe's novel *Uncle Tom's Cabin*, in which the eponymous hero had just these characteristics. Other expressions for such a person are *pancake* and *handkerchief head*, which in all

---

6 Many of the terms listed in the following were taken from Watson (1995).

likelihood came from the cheerful-looking mammy-like figure of a kerchief-wearing Aunt Jemima, which was used to sell a popular brand of American pancake mix. This association of an attribute of one thing with another is the essence of metonymy.

One final morphological process which affects slang should also be mentioned, the use of **secret language** expressions. By their very nature secret languages conform to the central criterion of slang: restriction to a marginal group. One such language is **Pig Latin** (a.k.a. **Hog Latin**, **Dog Latin**), in which the first consonant (or consonant cluster) is moved to the end of the word and the syllable <-ay> is added, as when *speak* becomes *eakspay*.[7]

In the following you will find a selection from among the many slang-like words used by Harlem blacks in the 1920s to designate black people. Your task is to explain the motivation (metaphor, metonymy, secret language).

booger, boogie
charcoal
cloud
crow
Old Cuffee
ink
jig, jigaboo, zigaboo
Russian
suede
shine
spade
spagingy-spagade

Do the same for black words for white people:

fay, ofay
fagingy-fagade
Mister Charlie
pink, pinktail

Case study 8.4: AmE hype slang

In the following section an example chosen from innumerable possibilities shows one of the strongest stylistic tendencies in present-day ENL varieties: the move toward informal language filled with slang and **four-letter words**. In this case (Text 8.2) we have an American soldier in Vietnam who has gone wild under the pressure.

---

7 Cf. **back slang**, in which a word is spelled backward and pronounced accordings: *boy* becomes *yob*, and *police* becomes *ecilop*, which is often shortened to *slop* as in *The slops are coming!*

Text 8.2. AmE hype slang (Philip Caputo, *A Rumor of War* (1977), p. 258)

'We'll wipe their ass. Can you dig it? Old fuckin' Luke the Gook's gonna die.' . . . 'Can you dig it? With my brand-new, nylon, camouflaged super fuckin' Special Forces jungle hammock, I'm ready for anything.'

'The only thing you're ready for is the goddamned psycho ward,' said Hudson.

'Oh, man, *man*. I'm cool and outfitted for the boonies. With this jungle hammock and my platoon of badasses, *I am the greatest jungle-fighter in the world*. Look at me, look, I'm the world's greatest jungle-fighter.' He crept around grinning maniacally.

'You're the world's greatest asshole, Mac,' Hudson said.

McKenna whirled and sprayed the artillery officer with imaginary bullets. 'Ta,da. Ta,da. Tatatatata. You're zapped, you cannon-cockin' Texas shit-kicker, zapped by the world's greatest jungle-fighter. I'm a killer, man, a fuckin' killer.

'Can you dig it? I'm a killer and I've got a platoon full of the baddest badasses in the Nam. We're bad, baaaad fuckin' killers.'

Case study 8.5: School language

In a questionnaire returned from just over 100 British school students (n = 104; largely 14 to 15-year-olds; a few older; none over 18) from England, Scotland, and Wales, information was gathered among other things about the slang terms they use to refer to their teachers, to school itself, and to skipping school, to things and people they like/do not like, to boys/girls, to fashionable/unfashionable clothing, and to the state of being happy (McClure 2000).

Teachers, for instance, are referred to in their absence by TLN or LN alone in half the cases and by nicknames or invectives, many of them directed at teachers as a whole (e.g. *slave drivers*), by the other half. Well over half of the students referred to school using a negative, informal expression, the favourites being *shit hole* (21), *prison* (13)/*jail* (9), *hell-hole* (13), and *dump* (13). Skipping school is, in one of the most unanimous answers, *skiving* (80), but also *mitching* (33, Wales only, out of 34 Welsh students), and *bunking off* (23).

Words for something positive are (currently, it seems): *cool* (36), *smart* (32), *lush* (21, but only reported from Wales), *wicked* (15), and *ace* (14), while what is disliked is *crap* (35, favoured in Scotland), *shit* (22), *grosse* (13, only in Wales), and *minging* (13, Scotland and Wales). *Wicked* is a case of semantic inversion, i.e. where something means the opposite of what it does in GenE. *Cool* (60) and *smart* (42) occur once again to designate fashionable clothing, while unstylish clothing was mostly *sad* (37). *Cool* returns again as one of the few more widely used expressions for being happy.

Good friends are *mates* for almost everyone (75). People disliked were less unanimously *wankers* (23), *slappers* (19), *dick(head)s* (17), *bitches* (16), *twats* (15), *tossers* (15), *mong(ol)s* (15), *pricks* (13), and *bastards* (12). This helps to confirm the suspicion that there are more slang/taboo words for what is negative than for what is positive.

Boys are chiefly *lads* (56), often *blokes* (23), and sometimes *guys* (13). Girls are *birds* (24), *lass(i)es* (21), *chicks* (16), but also *slappers* (11) and *bitches* (11). Most but not all of the students who answered with *lad* (66.7 per cent) or *lassie* (80 per cent) were Scottish.

In some cases an unbelievable number of words was suggested. This was most evident for terms for people disliked, where 104 students suggested 133 different words, which besides those mentioned above included such less frequently mentioned items as *airhead*, *arse(hole)*, *bint*, *bogbreath*, *cow*, *cunt*, *dog*, *dweeb*, *elf*, *fag*, *freakaziod* [sic], *geek*, *git*, *hoot*, *knob(-head)*, *mutt*, *nerd*, *oi*, *pleb*, *sad(do)*, *scaff*, *scrote*, *scruff*, *slag*, *tart*, *twerp*, *wazzock*, *wierdo* [sic], and *wally*. The most poetic is surely *roo de poo candy assed jabronies*. Nevertheless, school slang, as presented by McClure, seems to cluster around a small number of relatively widely used terms. Although many of the terms are international, it is interesting and reassuring to note that there is room for local language cultures: *gross*, *lad*, *lassie*, *lush*, *mitching*, *minging*. In a slightly wider framework, although not demonstrated in the study just quoted, *bloke*, *bunking off*, *mate*, *mong(ol)*, *tosser*, *skiving*, and *wanker* seem to belong to BrE (and related varieties like AusE), i.e. at least not to AmE.

Project 8.3: Expressions of approval and disapproval

Slang is one useful way to express your attitudes toward other people. While there is nothing wrong with saying that someone is 'very nice' or 'dislikable', saying it with the in-group vocabulary of slang is a major step toward securing your addressee's approval, because you will not only be assessing the person referred to but also soliciting the solidarity of the person you are talking to.

In a questionnaire survey reported by Falkenhagen and Hanke (1999) there were clear differences between the slangy expressions used by North American informants and those used by English ones. A summary of the results (only items with a response rate of at least four are included) is given in Table 8.7.

Despite the relatively low numbers, the responses do indicate that there are significant national/regional differences in the slang expressions used. This is partial evidence for the in-group nature of slang. Nevertheless, a word of warning is also due. McClure (2000), in asking about people liked and disliked in a younger age group in England, Wales, and Scotland, turned up only one of the terms in the table, dog, used by four of her 104 respondees.

Table 8.7. Slang terms of approval and disapproval in AmE and BrE

Referent	Expression	N. America (N = 25)	England (N = 14)
An attractive person of the opposite sex	*babe*	9	–
	a bit of alright	–	4
	crumpet	–	5
	cute/cutie	7	–
	fit	–	4
	hot/hottie	12	–
	sexy	3	3
An unattractive person of the opposite sex	*biffa*	–	4
	dog	13	3
	shank	–	4

Project 8.3 will give you the opportunity to collect your own results in regard to slang expressions used to show approval or disapproval – or, if you prefer, attractive vs. unattractive persons of the opposite sex as in Falkenhagen and Hanke.

Dear Informant,
[See the introductory text in Project 4.1]

What colloquial or slang expression(s) might you use to indicate that you find something to be:

(a) very good (e.g. *Super! Groovy!*)?
(b) very bad (e.g. *That's the pits*)?

Exercise 8.3: Euphemisms for 'toilet' or 'toilet room'

Style plays a decisive role whenever we have to talk about subjects which are publicly tabooed, such as death, sexual acts, and body functions (cf. §4.6). Among these 'delicate' topics we find not only the area of the elimination of body wastes, but also the places where this occurs, which is the subject of this exercise.

How do you ask your host, a salesperson in a store, or a waiter/waitress in a restaurant where the toilet is? Many people, especially Americans, find the word *toilet*, itself originally a (French) euphemism meaning 'small cloth, doily, dressing table', too crude to use. The following terms are a selection from among the many words available in English to designate a toilet (room). Since many of these terms were taken from a *thesaurus*, they are missing any further definition in terms of such connotational features as style level or regional provenance. Your task is to differentiate them by telling what regional-national variety they are used in and how they might be assessed stylistically. The first two items are given as an example of how your answer might look.

	Variety used in	Stylistic level
bathroom	AmE	euphemistic-polite
bogs	BrE	slang, unrefined < *bog house* (*bog* 'defecate')

1. *can*
2. *cloakroom*
3. *comfort station*
4. *convenience*
5. *gents*
6. *the geography*
7. *head*
8. *jerry*
9. *john*
10. *ladies' (room)*
11. *latrine*
12. *lavatory*
13. *loo*
14. *powder room*
15. *restroom*
16. *thunderbox*
17. *washroom*
18. *WC*

Sources you might use: any good desk dictionary.

Exercise 8.4: Rhyming slang

Rhyming slang is a special case of slang in which a word is replaced by a phrase which rhymes with it. One of the perhaps best-known examples is the phrase *to get down to brass tacks* 'to get down to business'. Here the phrase *brass tacks* is used in place of *the facts*, which rhymes with it (the final /t/ is not pronounced). Rhyming slang is widely associated with **Cockney English**, a variety traditionally spoken in London's East End (cf. Barltrop and Wolveridge 1980; Franklyn 1960; Wright 1981); however, it is also found in AusE and NZE.

While rhyming slang has something of the nature of a secret language (cf. Exercise 8.2), it seems to be less an in-group code than another example of playful language (cf. Exercise 7.7). And it is perhaps at its best when there is some kind of link or association between the word meant and the words used, as in the following examples, which also show that the items used are by no means fixed. For example, we find all of the following as slang for a man's better half:

trouble/storm and strife	wife
fork and knife	wife
cheese/love and kisses	missus (wife)

Some examples of rhyming slang are difficult to recognize since they can be shortened, and in this way lose the rhyme as in *loaf* < *loaf of bread* (= 'head'). This mechanism can be used to mask vulgar or tabooed language. Sometimes users may not have any sense of the original vulgarity. In this sense saying someone is *Brahms* or that another is *a berk* or that someone gave you the *raspberry* may be inappropriate if you realize the following:

Brahms	< *Brahms 'n' Liszt*	pissed ('drunk')
berk	< *Berkshire/Berkeley hunt*	cunt ('stupid')
raspberry	< *raspberry tart*	fart ('loud, vibrating or spluttering noice made with lips and tongue to express contempt')

In the following exercise try to find out what each of the terms designates. These particular items have been chosen because they all refer to people.

Rhyming slang	Gloss
1. babbling brook	
2. blood blister	
3. bottle and stopper	
4. ducks and geese	
5. holy friar	
6. John Hops	
7. mutton shanks	
8. pot and pan	
9. septic tanks	
10. twist and twirl	

Sources you might use: Partridge (1984) or Wentworth and Flexner (1960).

8.3 NON-NATIVE SPEAKER VARIETIES

English is at the moment *the* global language, due most of all to the economic, political, cultural, and military power and size of the United States. As a result of the present pre-eminence of English, Anglo-American ideas, institutions, ways of dressing, eating, playing, singing, writing books, making movies, etc. are more and more widely visible. One indication of this influence is the way in which English words have been borrowed into various languages. This section will introduce us, on the international level, to attitudes towards and motivations for the adoption of English words (Dutch in §8.3.1), to ways of incorporating the borrowings into the linguistic system of the host language (German in Case study 8.6), to some of the areas and the extent of borrowing (French – and German – in Project 8.4), and to intra-national borrowing in Spanish–English relations in the United States (§8.3.2 and 8.3.3).

8.3.1 English in Dutch

Dutch/Flemish counts as a small language even though it has some 25 million speakers in the Netherlands and Belgium. Certainly, it behaves like a small language: native speakers expect their own fellow speakers to be multilingual and are surprised when non-Dutch speakers learn the language. Its openness to other languages is especially evident in the case of English. Eighty-three per cent of Dutch school students take English as one of their foreign languages. The Dutch media reveal an extreme amount of English. Movies titles are overwhelmingly English: Ridder quoted a figure of 100 per cent for 'so-called "art films"' in 1982 (1995: 44). A similar though somewhat weaker tendency can be observed in the titles of television programmes, including mixed Dutch–English titles such as *Muziekshow* 'music show' (see Case study 8.6 on the linguistic nature of borrowing). Advertising, especially in the areas of tobacco, alcohol, and cosmetics, is riddled with English; indeed, they are often entirely in English. Likewise, the language of sports, information technology, and business reveal large numbers of borrowings from English.

In the academic world English has attained a certain pre-eminence, especially in areas such as economics and medicine (less so in literature). The arguments given are ones we are now familiar with from Chapter 6: English is a language of wider communication, especially in the areas of science and commerce; and English gives Dutch graduates better opportunities in the international job market. The dangers cited are also familiar: deteriorating standards of education due to the use of bad English and the classes–masses dilemma of a widening gap between the educated élite and the rest of the population.

One of the questions Ridder addresses is why there is so much English in Dutch. Although the answers remain conjectural, the ones offered are probably quite reasonable:

- there is no equivalent Dutch word (e.g. a job title like *marketing representative*);
- English disguises the prosaic: 'translation of an English title would reveal precious little'
- the use of English confers status
- English sounds more interesting (and may be used more by show-offs and swindlers)
- English offers a vague way of expressing feelings
- English is fashionable, especially in the areas of popular culture (film, TV, pop music) (Ridder 1995: 48)

A second question Ridder asks is what this massive invasion of English means for the future of Dutch. Although many people think Dutch might someday be displaced, she more realistically points out that the language has already withstood invasions of Latin, Spanish, French, and German – and has, we might add, been enriched for all that. Furthermore, a large number of borrowings are later loan-translated into Dutch or replaced by Dutch words.

Case study 8.6: English in German advertising

Although German is a major language, the situation of English is only slightly different in the German-speaking countries from that in the Dutch-speaking ones – except that considerably fewer movies are shown in the English original in the German-language area. Rather than repeat what was said in §8.3.1, therefore, we will look at one area of borrowing more closely, that of English loan words in German fashion catalogues (Horstmann 2000).

Since we are looking at the field of advertising, it should be clear that aspects such as international communication, science, or technology disappear as motivation for borrowing. Instead, we are reduced to such points (listed in §8.3.1) as status conferral, interesting-soundingness, and fashionableness.

Four fashion catalogues, one including two different sections, were selected to reflect differing customer ages and budgets. Horstmann found percentages of English terms running from a high of over 50 per cent English words in a catalogue catering to young people (Quelle 'Young Fashion', spring/summer 1999) and one purveying sports clothing (Sport Scheck, summer 1999). A middle ground of around 25 per cent English words was found in a section directed toward 'Lady's fashion' (Quelle, spring/summer 1999) and in the German catalogue of the American firm Land's End (autumn 1999). The lowest results (18 per cent English) were found for another American company in *Conley's Katalog* (autumn/winter 1999), which is addressed to a middle-aged, fairly well-to-do clientele.

The surprisingly high percentage of English words must be seen in perspective. These catalogues do not represent running prose. Rather, they are the names of items presented together with pictures of the products. The total number of words on a page averaged at a high of 5.5 ('Young Fashion') and a low of 3.6 word per page (Conley's). More significant yet is that this means that of the 474 English words Horstmann counted, not a single one was a verb, and only very few (33) were adjectives.

The way in which words are borrowed is also of interest.[8] Because of the nature of the study no attempt was made to look for calques such as *vorgefertigt* ('prefabricated'). Yet even so, relatively few of the loan words are borrowed as pure English. Instead they tend to be integrated into German in spelling, morphology, or semantics. This includes capitalization (the rule for German nouns); only adjectives like *sophisticated, classic navy, tipptopp, denim-meliert* ('sprinkled denim') or *dunkel newport* ('dark Newport') remain uncapitalized. In addition, the respelling of *tip-top* in German orthography, the combination of *denim* with a German word, and the failure to capitalize *Newport* are further signs of integration into the German spelling system.

---

8 Ridder (1995) mentions many of the things Horstmann finds (see following) such as changed morphology, changed meaning, shortening plus change of meaning, loan blends, fantasy English (phenomenon creation), and adoptions with a meaning different from the English meaning.

The most noticeable aspect of the morphology of borrowed English words is the extremely strong tendency to compound them with German words, as in *Blusen-Top* ('blouse top'), *Jeans-Hemd* ('jean shirt'), *Mode-Hit* ('fashion hit'), or *Stretch-Hose* ('stretch pants'). These are sometimes called **loan blends** or **hybrids**. Non-English compounds (probably often **nonce words**) are also frequent: *City-Outfits, Colour-Blocking-Pullover, Top-Trend, Workout-Details*, etc. A further concession toward German morphology is to make invariable plurals like *pants* or *tights* singular, as in *Army Pant, Capri-Cargo-Pant*, or *Capri-Tight*. But consistency is not a virtue, since the same catalogue (Sport Scheck) which has these also has plural *Hot-Pants* as well as *Baggy-Jeans, Cargo-Shorts*, and *Cargo-Bermudas*. Occasionally a German ending shows up as in *Zippern* with the dative plural case inflection {-n}. Furthermore, we find the well-established clipping of the English word *pullover* to *pull* plus the diminutive {-i}, which gives us *Pulli* ('pullover').

Perhaps the most fascinating English 'borrowings' are those which are not English at all, but German creations which look English, a process sometimes called **phenomenon creation**. These include items such as *dressman* ('male model'; not in this investigation) and *twen* ('20-plus-year-old', on the model of *teen*). This study includes *Gesmokter* (probably from *Smoking*, the English-derived phenomenon creation for 'tuxedo, dinner jacket') and *Pullunder* 'tank top'. A variant of this is the borrowing of an English word with a non-English meaning. The word *Slip* does not mean 'a kind of underskirt or petticoat' but 'men's or women's underpants'.

The final question is that of semantic integration. The semantics of many of these items is hardly English, but hardly German either. Some are impossible to interpret without a picture, for example *Jeep-TV-Boom box* or *Action Sampler Set*. Whatever their denotational meaning, they will certainly have lost their English connotations, and if they have any German connotations, then these will be of the vaguest sort. Indeed, many of the words in the study seem to be intended to be function as mere stimuli, connoting fashion, in-ness, and style.

Lexical integration varies from well-established borrowings such as venerable *Pulli* (and *Pullover*), *Blazer, Jeans*, or *Dufflecoat* to more recent ones like *Top*, *Shirt, Stretch*, or *cool*. It is also interesting to note that one very frequent item, *Zip* or *Zipper*, appears in a subsequent season catalogue as *RV*, an abbreviation of the German word for *zipper* (*Reisverschluss*).

Project 8.4: English in French

In this section we suggest going beyond domains and motivation for borrowing English words, as well as beyond the degree and the kinds of integration of English words into another language. Here you might try to make your own observations on English borrowings into a particular domain of another language. The following project refers to French, but you should feel free to explore a different domain and/or a different language.

Look at the job advertisements in a French newspaper and find out how widely English is used.

■ Where is English used? In the job titles? In the descriptive text?
■ How much repetition is there?
■ Are particular areas of employment more likely to use English words?
■ Is there a French word available?

8.3.2 English in Spanish

Spanish as it is spoken in the US respresents yet another case of how English vocabulary is borrowed into a different language. Although there are places where the presence of Spanish is very obvious, and despite the fears many Anglos have about English losing out to Spanish in America, English is sure to remain the one major language of the US. Yet it would be wrong to deny the mutual influence of the two languages on each other. Words like *macho* have become as much a part of English as *yanqui* has become a Spanish word.

Borrowing is often concentrated in a particular field. Spanish–English contact in what is now the American Southwest led, in the nineteenth century, to numerous words being adopted into the vocabulary of English, especially words for features of the landscape and ones associated with cattle-raising and cattle-driving (see Exercise 8.5). Today Mexican cuisine is not only well known in the Southwest but has been popularized along with its Spanish-language terms. *Tacos, burritos, dorados, enchiladas, frijoles, tortillas, naches,* and *salsa* are, as a result, well known throughout the US though not always so familiar in other parts of the English-speaking world, nor indeed in every case in Spain, whose culinary culture is often very different from Mexico's (for instance, a Spanish *tortilla* is not the same as a Mexican one).

Exercise 8.5: Spanish words in English

Spanish-language terms were widely borrowed in the American Southwest. Some of these loan words have retained their Spanish spelling (*adobe, arroyo, bonanza, burro, mesa, patio, poncho, pueblo*) while others have been partly anglicized (*canyon* 'gorge' < Sp. *cañón* 'long hollow tube') or wholly (*vamoose* 'to leave hurriedly' < Sp. *vamos* 'let's go').

Terms from ranching and the cowboy culture
Your task is to give a brief gloss of the meaning of each and find out what the original Spanish word and its meaning were.

Term	Gloss	Source	Spanish meaning
1. bronco			
2. buckaroo			
3. calaboose			

4. chaps
5. cinch
6. corral
7. hoosegow
8. lariat
9. lasso
10. mustang
11. palomino
12. pinto
13. ranch
14. rodeo
15. sombrero
16. stampede
17. ten-gallon hat
18. wrangler

Sources you might use: a good desk dictionary of AmE, e.g. *Random House Webster's College Dictionary*, *American Heritage College Dictionary*.

Case study 8.7: English words in Puerto Rican Spanish

Although English continues to borrow words from Spanish, it is Spanish, especially as spoken within the borders of the US, where the pressure from English is strong and which is drawing noticeably on English. Under the influence of English *máquina* 'car' has become *carro* and *blumes* 'panties, knickers' have become *pantis*. We can hear *Ay te wacho* (< *watch*), or *Se esta liqueando el rufo* ('The roof is leaking'), where the use of Spanish endings shows that the language is alive and well and busy integrating the new, borrowed items. Sometimes the words are for new or different cultural phenomena; sometimes for lexical gaps, e.g. *weldear* 'weld' has been integrated next to *solder* 'solder or weld' (Valdés 1988). García and Ortheguy (1988: 181f.) quote the italicized examples shown in Table 8.8.

There is some indication of Spanish influence on the English of second-generation users who may use *rob* for 'to draw a card' under the influence of

Table 8.8. English in Spanish

Loan words	Necesito hacer un *part-time* para ganar dinero
Calques	El martes me *registré* en la universidad (phonological similarity leads to an extension of the Spanish meaning)
	Creo que *corrió* para alcalde de Hialeah. (Spanish word with English meaning of *run* 'go')
	Preguntale si *sabe como hacerlo* (phrasal calque 'know how to do it')
Code-switching	Sí, sí, él habla mucho, pero cuando llegó la hora no se atrivió a *bring it up at the meeting* (Yes, sure, he talks a lot, but when the time came he didn't have the guts to bring . . .)

Spanish *robar*, or *bad grass* 'weeds' on the model of *yerba mala*. This can even lead to the use of *become in* for 'become' because of Spanish *convertirse en*.

Borrowing also frequently reflects the new cultural context of New York, in which things are present which may well not have played any significant role in Puerto Rico. This is probably the case with *la boila*, *la factoría*, *el elevador*, *la carpeta*,[9] *lonchar*, *el super*, *el londri*, *el bloque*. Many of these things would have been absent from Puerto Rico: boilers, apartment house superintendents, city blocks; or they would have been less salient: factories, elevators, carpets, laundries. And *having lunch* is simply a different cultural act in New York from *almuerzar* is in Puerto Rico (cf. Zentella 1981).

8.3.3 Code-switching and code-mixing

Often there is a switch between languages without a change in either of the languages and with no adaptation toward the other system in form or pronunciation. The speaker simply begins a sentence in one language and ends it in the other: This is **code-switching**. Or the speaker fluently interweaves English words in a Spanish sentence, which is **code-mixing**:

> Dijo mi mamá que I have to study.
> Tengo la waist twenty-nine, tengo que reduce.

Many Spanish-speakers in the United States practise code-switching, and this may be reinforced by insecurity about the use of Spanish in formal situations as well as by feelings that Spanish is 'hicky' or 'uncool'. However, code-switchers are generally very proficient in both languages. One language is usually the base language, but the speaker(s) profit from the strengths of both languages, using their total speech repertoire.

Code-switching follows implicit rules and can be used to show solidarity and intimacy as well as for emphasis. It is true that shift may be motivated by the lack of a word or by anticipated difficulty with a construction, but it is also used to express a meaning more effectively, to employ the language of a particular domain, or to evoke cultural associations. The switching or mixing of codes helps the speaker to establish identity, to embellish a point, to reflect confidentiality or privateness. It is, in other words, not a sign of lack of fluency; rather 'code-switching is part of the full linguistic repertoire of fluent bilinguals and is predominantly directed at ingroup members only' (Zentella 1981: 233).

The rules for switching – which language in which situation – are learned early (5–6 years). Language shift may mean a shift of roles, e.g. English at work (hierarchical) and Spanish at lunch (equality, solidarity). In story-telling the narrative language may be Spanish with the quotes in English. Its rules include, for example,

---

9 Semantic reassignment because of similarity to an English word: *carpeta* 'folder' becomes 'carpet'.

knowing who to use what language(s) with, and this includes assessment of competence and stylistic appropriacy. Females are said to be more adept because of their sensitivity for such things. Overt norms may discourage code-switching, but covert ones probably exist as it is a firm part of proficient bilingualism, for it is widely practised in informal speech.

Case study 8.8: Spanish–English code-mixing

Text 8.3 is a literary example of Black English–Spanish–Chinese contact from the book *China Boy* by Gus Lee. Hector Pueblo speaks BAE with considerable admixtures of Spanish. The 1st person narrator is a young Chinese-American boy of perhaps 7 or 8 who is trying to learn to fight in order to survive on the streets.

Text 8.3. Spanish–English code-mixing (Gus Lee, *China Boy* (1994), 180ff.)

I told Tío Hector Pueblo what I was doing . . . Hector had said that he was going to teach me 'street,' . . .

'I ready, Tío,' I said. I flexed my right arm, showing him my new, developing bicep.

'Say, *soy listo*. Dat mean, 'I ready'' he said. 'Dat's a mighty fine muscle, my fren',' he added, nodding his head and pursing his lips in stern approval.

'*Soy listo, Tío*,' I said. 'Teach me secret kick?'

Instead, he taught me how to walk.

'*Joven*,' he said, 'you *walkando como un armadillo* dat go from four leg to two leg. . . .

'*Joven*, you gotta show some *prestigio*. You gotta roll yo' shoulder *back*. Now, put up yo' head, *tu cabeza*. Lif up high. Keep yo' back mo' straight. Don forget yo' shoulder. . . . Jesus Cristo, wha's wrong wif yo' body, chico? . . .

'Cho' *anger*, niño! *Enojado*! You pissed! All dese kids pound you, you *angry!* Even if yo' li'l body all shrivel' up an bent, no matta! Mean mug, dat's good. Now, you practice yo' *anger* face. . . .'

'I wan learn secret kick,' I said, . . .

'*Niño*, firs' you need a face. *Tu cara bonita*, it look so empty. Dat piss kids off, dey tink dey got no effec' on you.

'Yo' *cara*, she start more fight den no secret kick can finish, you get my meaning,' he said.

I thought he was talking about cars in his shop [Tío Hector runs a car repair shop].

'*Cara bonita*. Han'some face. Yo' han'some face, *niño*. *Hombre!* You so much work! I gotta teach walkando, yo' face, gotta teach yo' *secret kick*, gotta teach you *Español, también!*

'*Escucheme, joven*. You get big, someday, you 'member Hector Pueblo, hokay?' He smiled and rubbed my hair.

When I started taking formal Spanish language classes in junior high, I persisted in the belief that *walkando* was the correct idiomatic gerund for the infinitive *andar*, to walk.

'Señor Losada,' I said. '*Yo aprendí Español cuando era un joven, y la palabra correcta es "walkando."*'

Exercise 8.6: English words in Spanish

Mixtures of Spanish and English, sometimes called Spanglish (a term some reject), a.k.a. Tex-Mex, Texican, is characterized by borrowing. Give the English for the following examples and explain the processes involved (borrowing, semantic extension, semantic shift, shortening).

1. la ley
2. lechuga
3. jonrón
4. fullar
5. daime
6. bombo
7. shopear
8. mopear
9. embarrassar
10. croseando la calle

Sources you might use: a (bilingual) dictionary of Spanish, or Hendrickson (1987).

8.4 INTERNATIONAL ENGLISH

There is a great deal of consensus about the growing role of English as a language of international communication. It is by no means unusual for businesspeople, none of whom have English as their native language, to use it in their dealings, a default language, as it were. English also seems to be the preferred language of tourism when the target group is unspecified. International trade, international travel, satellite broadcasting, the Internet, the world press, world stock markets, multinational corporations, science, air traffic control, and many more areas rely to a remarkable extent on English. This is leading 'to a kind of "World" or "International English", one stripped of its local identifiers, with a core of common vocabulary, grammar, and spelling' (Burridge and Mulder 1998: 277). In this section we will look at some of these aspects, specifically the Internet (§8.4.1), youth culture (§8.4.2), and international terminologies and special languages (§8.4.3).

8.4.1 Internet English

The Internet seems to be introducing a revolution in communications. It is lowering the barriers to international communcication and, increasingly, commerce. Speculations about the consequences of this for the type of language used have been mooted from various sides. And, indeed, a few changes in conventions seem to have entered the scene. We will see this when we look into matrimonial advertisements in the Internet (§8.4.1.1). Because much of Internet communication is (still) by keyboard, the importance of literacy, often in English, has been enhanced, but some of the disadvantages of writing have also led to changes. In Exercises 8.7 and 8.8 we look at one of them, the increased use of abbreviations and in Exercise 8.9 at another, the use of emoticons.

8.4.1.1 Matrimonials

In this section we want to explore some of the changes in communication strategies that are due to the Internet. We do this by coming back to the topic of matrimonial advertisements, which we looked at initially in Case study 8.1. The results given here are based on a study by Tzankow (2000) in which she chose 50 matrimonial ads[10] from the Internet site: *http://personals.predawnia.org/peopleplanet.html.* Peopleplanet's Romance Center is said to provide 250 000 ads from 238 countries, mostly in English. As such it offers excellent source material for comparison, which is what Tzankow took advantage of by choosing 50 examples from the category of women looking for men and dividing them up into a random choice of ten items each from the USA (California), the UK (England and Scotland), India, West Africa (Nigeria, Ghana, and Cameroon), and East Africa (Kenya, Tanzania, and Uganda). While the study sought to look at a variety of areas, both social-cultural and linguistic, it is chiefly the degree of formularity of the texts (see Texts 8.4–6) which will interest us here.

Text 8.4. Internet matrimonial: England (*Peopleplanet:* downloaded 26 May 2000)

```
Hi im Kerry and I am looking for a genuine
down to earth man

Well I enjoy looking after children , pubbing and
clubbing and staying in and wathching television.      Age: 20
I dislike football and most kind of tv sports . Well
I am 20 years old and I am called kerry I live in      Heritage: Caucasian
Grimsby in Lincolnshire I have long blonde hair I      (white)
am 5'7 tall and I am medium build consider
myself attractive and I have a 1 year old son          Height: Taller than
called David I an looking for a kind considerate       average
male who is into cosy nights in and the
occasional night on the town. My ideal man             Build: Average
would be in the agerange 18-35 and must have a         I smoke and I have
good sense of humour. I am looking for a long          children
term relationship.                                     Occupation: Single
                                                       Parent
```

---

10 Nair remarks: (1992: 240f.): 'The use of the cover term "Matrimonial" itself reveals an ideology reifying marriage, apparently common to both cultures [India and the West], but it is a theme literally interpreted in India while the western advertisements allow a greater latitude for non-conventional readings of the dominant ideology.'

Text 8.5. Internet matrimonial: India (*Peopleplanet*: downloaded 26 May 2000)

```
I am a dentist.and just had complited my studies,
intensions for going out side india of merry a          Age: 22
docor in India.
pleas email me on                                        Heritage: Asian
if u r interested
My interest in                                           Height: Average
-music
-movies                                                  Build: Average
-sports
I like to travel also and i had seen all most all of    I do not smoke and I do
india.                                                   not have children
-my expectations are
-a doctor                                                Occupation: doctor
- a eng.
-or equal study [higher studies]
my nature is good and mixing.
```

Text 8.6. Internet matrimonial: West Africa (*Peopleplanet*: downloaded 26 May 2000)

```
Looking for a God fearing partner

Iam aveage in size, slim with chocolate color,
Iam 5ft.
I don't smoke, and don't drink, I do not have           Age: 28
children, but would love to have some day when I
have found the right partner.                            Heritage: Black

I am looking for a God fearing partner will love         Height: Average
me for who I am
from a good background. I don't care where he is         Build: Slim
from, he should be between the age of 35 -45             I do not smoke and I do
and so not smoke or drink                                not have children

                                                         Occupation: Computer
                                                         Operator
```

The overall structure of the Internet texts varies somewhat in sequence, but by their very nature they contain the same basic elements: a description of self by the seeker a description of the type of person sought, and a statement, often implicit, of desired action (*I'm looking for. . .*; *Want to find out more? Get writing babes!!!*; *Would like to have response from. . .*; *Please . . . e-mail me*, etc.). In this sense these texts are similar to their newspaper cousins treated in Case study 8.1.

Differences from newspaper ads are not, however, hard to find. The telegraphic style and the abbreviations of the newspaper matrimonial columns is not wholly missing (cf. Text 8.5), but they are far less prominent. Thirty of the 50 ads in

Tzankow's study used complete sentences only, and there were considerably fewer abbreviations. The length of the ads was generally between 70 and 100 words, and many of them employed paragraphing. The lack of strict limitations on length also meant that politeness phenomena could be employed (especially *please*). Yet there is also a great deal of directness as well, e.g. *The man for me is one that doesn't. carry around a whole lot of emotional baggage from his past relationships. . .; I'm not interested in playing games or destroying a family so no married men please;* *. . . and must have a good sense of humour; Don't bother to write if you smoke, because I can't stand it.* Furthermore, 18 per cent had saluations (*Hi* or *Hello*) and several had a closing (e.g. *Anybody out there?* or *Enjoy!* or *I look forward to hearing from you, soon!*), which indicate that many of the contributors see themselves more as communicators writing a letter than as 'advertisers'.

In all five regions studied the classic virtues such as honesty, reliability, tolerance, respect toward others, faithfulness, and seriousness are frequently mentioned, but more important in the US, India, and West Africa are emotional values (e.g. warm-hearted, loving, caring, kind, cuddly), while such virtues as a good sense of humour and fondness for laughter are noticeably more present in the ads from the UK.

The Western emphasis on outer appearance continues to play a central role. In India education remains dominant. In West and East Africa social and family status are also relatively more prominent than in the West, though not so distinctly as in India. In India this manifests itself chiefly in terms of education and caste. Only 2 of the 10 Indian Internet ads studied were placed by family members for another, an indication that arranged marriages are perhaps less popular for Indian Internet users. While in the West religion is only a minor note (one out of 20), it shows up more frequently in Africa and Asia (8 out of 30).

Exercise 8.7: Word formation in Internet English

The Internet has contributed its share of new word formations with perhaps more emphasis on play on words (*netiquette, netizen, snail mail, knowbot, nagware*) and widespread employment of acronyms and abbreviations. The combining form {cyber-} is highly productive: *cybernetics, cyberspace, cyberpunk,*[11] *cybershopping, cybercrime, cybercrooks* (and *net police*), *cyberdoctors* (and *telemedicine*), *cyberian, cyberporn, cyberdate, cybercreep,* etc.

That communication has become easier does not mean that it has necessarily become friendlier. Otherwise there would be no *flaming* ('acrimonious or hostile response from a user', possibly leading to a *flame war*) or *spamming* (a kind of *flamage*) or *flooding* (of the net with inappropriate off-topic messages), which may be combated by *mailbombing* (multiple answers), nor would there be so many *viruses* or the need to refer to an application as *user-friendly*.

---

11 Cyberpunk fiction: 'razor-edged, near-future visions of an urbanized world in which megacorporations have replaced governments, data has become the most valued commodity, and the boundary between humans and machines has been blurred' (Flexner and Soukhanov 1997: 69).

The following are examples of new words. Your task is to explain what they mean and identify the word formation processes involved.

	Meaning	Process
1. bit		
2. braino		
3. chat room		
4. database		
5. cursor		
6. floppy disk		
7. freeware		
8. hacker		
9. HTML		
10. Infobahn		
11. Internet		
12. log in/out		
13. mouse		
14. modem		
15. navigate		
16. RAM, ROM		
17. snail mail		
18. upload		
19. virtual reality		
20. www/WWW		

Sources you might use: a good desk dictionary, or Flexner and Soukhanov (1997).

Exercise 8.8: Abbreviations in Internet English

In the following exercise, identify the abbreviations used by the *digiterati* by giving the phrases they stand for:

1. AFAIK		10. IRL	
2. AFK		11. IYKWIM	
3. BRB		12. LOL	
4. BTW		13. OTOH	
5. FAQ		14. PMFJI	
6. FWIW		15. ROTFL(L)	
7. GIGO		16. RTFM	
8. IMHO		17. TTFN	
9. IMNSHO		18. WAG	

Sources you might use: *Acronymania* or Flexner and Soukhanov (1997).

Exercise 8.9: Emoticons

In §2.2.1 we looked at iconic meaning, which was limited to onomatopoeia and sound symbolism. As we turn to the Internet, we find that there are other possibilities of employing iconic meaning. Since the Internet is visual, graphic symbols of one sort or the other can be utilized. When graphic icons are used as a part of the communication system, we are not dealing specifically with words, of course, but with symbols which stand for a conventionalized meaning suggested by the graphic representation. Computer screens make wide use of such icons (which, however, only take on meaning once they have been explained and used). Despite the non-verbal character of graphic icons, a short foray into the field is not misplaced since icons play such a prominent role in windows-type applications and in e-mail.

One of the limitations of writing is that everything you want to say must, quite literally, be spelled out. Since this is a relatively time-consuming process, Internet communicators have eagerly turned to short cuts. Among these we have just looked at abbreviations. A second type has developed within the medium of e-mail: the emoticon, 'possibly the most original feature of online communication, neatly and creatively solving the problem of being unable to see facial expressions or hear tones of voice in typed correspondence' (Flexner and Soukhanov 1997: 75). An emoticon (the word itself is a blend of *emotion* and *icon*) offers a way out of wordiness. It is a combination of characters (for the most part punctuation marks) which produce a stylized head, always seen from the side and embellished to indicate something about the author. The best known of these is the smiley, consisting of colon, hyphen, and closing parenthesis, :-). In fact it is so frequent that it is available on computers as a fully-fledged icon: ☺, which is intended to indicate that the author means what he/she says in a friendly way or in good spirits. Analogously, there is the sad icon, :-(or ☹. Emailers seem to have had a good time manipulating the resources on their keyboards, giving us such variations as ;-), which is a winking smiley or (-:, which is a left-handed one.

Give an interpretation of each of the following emoticons. If you don't already know them, use your imagination!

Emoticon	Meaning	Emoticon	Meaning
1. :-/		7. :-o	
2. :-x		8. :-)X	
3. :-})		9. :-){	
4. (:-)		10. {:-)	
5. B-)		11. :-)))	
6. 8:-)		12. :-)8	

Sources you might use (besides your imagination): Ask some of your email correspondents or look in Flexner and Soukhanov (1997).

8.4.2 Youth culture

Just how international is the English used by young people all over the world? The fact that certain areas and activities are widely imitated leads one to wonder how much of the language of these areas is also shared. In this section we look at two such areas, drugs and music.

Case study 8.9: The language of the drug culture

In looking at terms for drugs and drug consumption, no implication is intended that drug abuse is typical of young people. It is, however, among young people that we are more likely to find a familiarity with the language of this 'subculture'. In surveys conducted with informants from Scotland, the USA (Zimmer and Hillebrand 1999), Canada and South Africa (Yilmaz 2000), and England (both), the respondents were asked among other things about slang drug names familiar to them. Furthermore, they were also asked about where they had, in their own opinion, picked up the terms.

The respondents in the two surveys were young people up to 30 years of age:

Americans	16	(m: 8; f: 8)	Scottish	17	(m: 5; f: 12)
Canadians	11	(m: 7; f: 4)	South Africans	20	(m: 5; f: 14)
English	13	(m: 9; f: 4)	Total	77	(m: 34; f: 42)

The results show a clear tendency for young people in these five countries to share the slang terms they use for drugs (see Table 8.9).

Dictionaries trace the origins of many of these words to America, thus indicating relatively great influence of American usage in the subculture of drugs. Yet

Table 8.9. Slang terms for drugs

Drug	USA No.(%)	Canada No.(%)	England No.(%)	Scotl. No.(%)	S.Afr. No.(%)	Total No.(%)
Cocaine:						
Coke	8 (50)	11 (100)	11 (8)	12 (70)	19 (95)	61 (79)
Snow (White)	6 (37)	4 (36)	1 (8)	1 (6)	4 (20)	16 (21)
Heroin						
H	7 (44)	8 (73)	3 (23)	2 (12)	7 (35)	27 (35)
Smack	8 (50)	2 (18)	3 (23)	11 (65)	1 (5)	25 (32)
Junk	3 (19)	7 (64)	1 (8)	1 (6)	7 (35)	19 (25)
Brown sugar	1 (6)	3 (27)	2 (15)	1 (6)	10 (50)	17 (22)
Horse	2 (12)	3 (27)	1 (8)	1 (6)	– (0)	7 (9)
LSD						
Acid	9 (56)	10 (91)	9 (69)	10 (83)	14 (70)	52 (67)
Trip(s)	1 (6)	1 (9)	5 (38)	2 (12)	8 (40)	17 (22)
Marijuana						
Pot	9 (56)	11 (100)	6 (46)	3 (18)	10 (50)	39 (51)
Weed	9 (56)	11 (100)	5 (38)	2 (12)	10 (50)	37 (48)
Ganja	1 (6)	8 (73)	6 (46)	6 (35)	16 (80)	37 (48)
Grass	7 (44)	1 (9)	3 (23)	5 (29)	1 (5)	17 (22)
Maryjane	8 (50)	4 (36)	– (0)	– (0)	2 (10)	14 (18)
Hash	2 (12)	– (0)	4 (31)	14 (82)	– (0)	20 (26)
Herb	1 (6)	6 (54)	3 (23)	– (0)	7 (35)	17 (22)

the results of these two surveys also make it clear that despite widespread agreement across national borders, there is some evidence against the international nature of this subculture. At least the following three points may be noted:

- many of these terms are – despite their somewhat slangy nature – simply part of GenE, i.e. they are no longer markers of in-group membership
- a number of terms are used which are restricted in their currency. *Maryjane* is largely North American, probably because the word *marijuana* is used more in the Americas while *hashish* is the preferred European word. *Brown sugar* is chiefly South African; *trip* is not commonly used in North America for marijuana. Furthermore, additional terms such as *skag* (3) for heroin is only attested in the UK; *dagga* (3) for marijuana, only in South Africa.
- the sources given are frequently books and songs, but especially the movies *Pulp Fiction* (e.g. *stash*) and *Trainspotting* (*gear*, *skag*, *shit*). Inasmuch as these sources are familiar everywhere, so too are the terms – independent of whether the subculture of drugs is international or not.

Case study 8.10: Rap and reggae

The kind of music a person likes or is familiar with is a further potential medium for the internationalization of English. Music fans can frequently be heard using a phrase from the lyrics of a song currently popular. Since the music culture is so international, it would not be surprising to find that a certain amount of its vocabulary is also internationalized. An example of this is the verb *diss* mentioned above in §8.2. It originated in American Black English and was popularized by way of rap music and the hip hop culture, as in Text 8.7.

Text 8.7. Rap lyrics (Bilal Bashir, 1995)

'Personal'

Emcee's no time out, it's time to rhyme out.
You've dug your own grave, now you must climb out.
Dig out, crawl out, hide from the fallout,
'Cause when I get mad I go all out!
. . .
Syndicate boy, I don't fool out.
You're full grown, school's out.
You try to *diss*? I think you better cool out.
'Cause your butt is smoke, if we ever duel out.
. . .
I never *diss* an emcee, I wish 'em all good luck,
But if you *diss* me to my face, duck!
. . .

Now the words I speak to some may sound radical,
But I'll explain, it's simply mathematical.
You *diss*, I *diss*, this creates an equal.
You reply to my *diss*, this is called a sequel.
I reply to your *diss*, this is called a battle.

According to *The Oxford Dictionary of New Words* (Tulloch 1993) other words introduced to a broader, but young public along the lines of *diss* are *bad* 'good, cool'; *def* 'cool, great' (from *definitive* or from *death,* West Indian pronunciation); *fresh* 'new, cool, hip'; *rare* 'cool, hip' – all words of approval. (See Text 8.8.)

Text 8.8. What's 'Cool'? (Interview in *jetzt* 40, *Süddeutsche Zeitung*, 4 Oct. 1999, p. 23)

Interviewer: What is currently the coolest way for saying something is 'cool'?

Ice-T: There's 'fly', 'chill', lots of ways of saying that shit. Hard bringing them out of my head now. You can't say something that's old like 'funky fresh', and 'maxin' is pretty old, too. But now hip hop is so retro, you can use any word, [sic] that was ever used. So some rappers say 'groovy', which was already old slang back in the seventies. That's a challenge to the rappers who think, 'I am so cool I won't use "groovy"'. But I say: you motherfuckers will like it.

And, of course, the same music-culture background that brought us these words also familiarized us with *boom boxes* or *ghetto blasters*. But there are limits to how far the influence of song lyrics goes. In-group usage may encourage us to adopt 'the latest', but there is probably a fairly narrow limit to how far speakers continue to use this language in the wider public.

The lyrics of reggae, like those of rap, are often a rejection of white culture, which may make understanding not only linguistically but also politically and culturally more difficult. Winer (1990) reports that English speakers without any knowledge of Jamaican Creole had a hard time understanding reggae lyrics. This is impressively shown in the following renderings of the lines given from 'Uptown Top Ranking' by Althea and Donna:

Na pop no style, I strictly root

This may be standardized and interpreted as follows:

I don't pop any style ('put on airs, show off')
I'm strictly roots ('real, unpretentious, working class')

This line was understood in the following ways:

> My partner's style are strictly roots.
> No pot, no style, I'll strenth me roots. [*sic*]
> I have no style, I'm strictly roots.
> I stick the rules, not want no style.
> Now partner style, I strike me roots.
> No got no style, I's strictly roots.
> No pot, no style, I's strictly roots.
> No partner's style, ah, strickly roots.
> Now I've got no style, I'll stick with roots. (Winer 1990: 49)

'The results demonstrated clearly that general cultural knowledge and specific linguistic knowledge are related but separate factors, and illustrated ways in which inappropriate or inadequate top-down or bottom-up processing, or interaction between them, could lead to misinterpretation' (Winer 1990: 50).

8.4.3 English for Special/Specific Purposes (ESP)[12]

An important part of the international character of English is its widespread use as an important language of learning. In many fields scholarly and technical literature is published in English by authors who want to be accessible to as wide a readership as possible. In order to appreciate this aspect of the language better, we will look, in the concluding section of this chapter, at *English for Special/Specific Purposes (ESP)*.

Users of ESP, be they ENL, ESL, or EFL users, do not employ the language in its full potential of words, forms, text types, and so on. The *register* of ESP is characterized by a range of topics and of stylistic variation that is highly restricted. Generally speaking, only one thing is of importance: communication of clearly ordered information (often technical or scientific) by means of unambiguous terminology and unequivocal grammatical structures. The ordering of information is regulated by conventions. For example, journal articles generally have the following five divisions:

- an introduction, in which the purpose pursued/hypothesis investigated is presented
- a review section, in which previous work is summarized or evaluated
- a methods section, in which procedural sequences, criteria, etc. are evaluated
- a results section, in which the findings are presented

---

12 The older term is English for Special Purposes. Since the late 1970s, the term 'English for Specific Purposes' has largely displaced it. 'Special' implies restricted languages, while 'Specific' focuses on the purposes of the learner, which are specific, viz. 'to perform a task in English' (Robinson 1989: 396).

■ a discussion section, in which the findings are evaluated in the framework of the initial hypothesis: cf. Hopkins and Dudley-Evans (1988); Dudley-Evans (1989); see below for ordering conventions in the language of air traffic control (Case study 8.12)

Field of discourse is perhaps the most characteristic aspect of ESPs. However, the number and the size of the fields are a matter more of convenience than of agreement in principle. A broad division gives us major areas such as science, technology, law, medicine, the social sciences, business and economics. Science can be subdivided into biology, chemistry, and physics; the latter into astrophysics, biophysics, nuclear physics, etc.

Functional tenor or *purpose* leads, in addition, to a division according to functional types, which include English for Occupational Purposes (EOP), English for Academic Purposes (EAP), or the **English of Science and Technology (EST)**. Furthermore, ESP communication may revolve around a single *rhetorical function* such as description, report, exposition, instruction, or argumentation.

Personal tenor or *style* in ESP aims at neutrality, lack of emotion, and objectivity in tone, which are supposed to be characteristic of scientific and academic prose. Of course, even in ESP there are degrees of variation. An article in a peer-reviewed journal is likely to be different in style from one in a popular science magazine or a science feature in a newspaper.

Medium or mode are typically writing but speech may also be included, and may vary from a formal scholarly lecture to a technical training class to teacher–student consultations in the teacher's office or in the cafeteria.

In the following sections our attention turns to some of the linguistic characteristics of ESP, especially the field of vocabulary.

8.4.3.1 ESP and GenE

Despite its restrictions (see fn. 12 above) ESP has the whole of English grammar, morphology, and word formation processes at its disposal. The differences which may be observed include the frequencies of use of syntactic structures and morphological processes. By its very nature the vocabulary of any given field will also show frequencies which differ from those of English as a whole. In addition, ESPs are characterized by the use of terminologies, i.e. standardized sets of terms which have been created for the sake of absolute clarity of reference. This includes the use of symbols (e.g. Σ, $\leq$, $\forall$, $\pm$, $=$, μ, $°$, π, $®$) and other attributes of written texts such as graphs, tables, and illustrations. Many written texts are highly conventionalized in the way they are structured.

Since we are more interested in vocabulary, we will skip over grammatical aspects of ESP (and especially of EST) such as the greater use of the passive, of non-defining relative clauses, and rhetorical devices such as anaphora, parallelism, parenthetical elements, emphatic inversion, rhetorical questions, and ellipsis (Gerbert 1970: 40; Kok Lee Cheon 1978: 132; Huddleston 1971: 259; Gläser 1979:45–9). Instead we will point out that pronouns are used in different frequencies: *we*, *this/these* are more common; *I* and *he* are less common; and *she* and *you* are much less common (cf. Johansson 1975: 6ff., 17; Brekke 1989: 259f.). There is also a greater use of 'new plurals', e.g. *fats, oils, greases* etc. (Gerbert 1970: 40), as well as Latin and Greek plurals (*mitochondrion/-ia; bacterium/-ia*).

One of the things, besides the content and terminology, that makes an ESP text hard for an 'outsider' to read and understand is its concentrated nature, especial what is known as **nominal style**. This includes the fact that EST has a higher proportion of nouns (but also prepositions and adjectives). Sager *et al.* (1980: 234) found that this was 44 per cent of all words in EST vs. 28 per cent in GenE texts. 'As a result of strong nominalization, verbs have less communicative value and are only half or a third as frequent as in general language.'

Nominal style also refers to a higher degree of **nominalization**, the process in which whole clauses are replaced by nominal phrases, e.g. *because the surface of the retina is spherical* → *because of the sphericity of the retinal surface*; or: *[s.th.] is near the nucleus* → *[s.th.] occupies a juxtanuclear position* (examples quoted from Gerbert 1970: 36). Another feature of nominal style is the tendency to combine a function verb and a noun instead of using a simple verb. A function verb is a 'general purpose' verb of low communicative value such as *do, make, take, have*, or *give* (see Table 8.10).

8.4.3.2 Words and their frequencies in ESP

'. . . the lexicon of special languages is their most obvious distinguishing characteristic' (Sager *et al.* 1980: 230). For one thing, ESPs are sure to contain words never or hardly ever found outside a given area. There are said to be several million words for chemical compounds alone. It is impossible to say how many special words there are; however, numerous dictionaries, terminological clearing houses, databases, etc. indicate that the number is high. One general dictionary of science, for example, *The Longman Dictionary of Scientific Usage*, contains 1300 terms basic to all branches of science and 8500 technical terms from biology, chemistry, and physics.

Technical words are more frequent in EST texts (approx. 25 per cent according to Beier 1980: 40). The 1000 most common words in EST contained, in one

Table 8.10. Function verbs in nominal style

Simple verb		Function verb + noun
to work	→	to do some work
to investigate	→	to make an investigation
to photograph	→	to take a photograph
to hypothesize	→	to have (or make) a hypothesis
to report	→	to give (or make) a report

count, 339 words which do not show up in the 1000 most common words of GenE. Furthermore, cohesive devices like *this/these*, *above*, *below*, *preceding*, or *following*, for reference within a text, are more frequent, as are such relatively formal adverbs as *moreover*, *overall*, *primarily*, *therefore*, and *however* (Johansson 1975: 24,17ff., 11). Words associated with formal written discourse such as semi-technical or sub-technical words are also more common in EST:

■ exposition (e.g. *discussion, argument, result, conclusion*)
■ procedure (*analysis, experiment, measurement, observation, test*)
■ statistics (*sample, probability, distribution, significance*)
■ classification (*class, type, group, species, item, unit*)
■ relational words (*similar, distinct, average, relative, normal*)   (cf. Johansson
1975: 22)

In addition, EST prefers longer, more formal words to shorter, everyday words (Table 8.11).

The special vocabulary of ESP, but especially of EST, is international, and morphologically based on Greek and Latin elements; it is standardized and unambiguous; it is neutral (not emotive); it favours some word-formation processes over others; and it makes use of symbols. In the following section on terminologies we will look more closely at these features.

8.4.3.3 Terminologies and ESP

Terminologies, sometimes called ***nomenclatures***, are set by convention.[13] They are needed to avoid ambiguity due to regional or non-standardized meanings and so to ensure the success of scientific and technological processes including manufacturing, and also to safeguard health and safety. The criteria for terminologies (see Beier 1980: 31f.) require that the individual terms be:

■ exact: designate a particular meaning
■ unambiguous: exclude confusion with the meanings of other terms
■ unique: make available one and only one term

Table 8.11. Stylistic variation: EST vs. GenE (Johansson 1975: 25f.)

EST	GenE	EST	GenE
also	too	large	big
certain	sure	obtained	got
determine	decide	thus	so

---

13 The terminological clearing house Infoterm was established within UNESCO in 1971 for the coordination of work on terminology on an international basis; it cooperates with the International Organization for Standardization (ISO). EURODICAUTON is an on-line data-bank service for up-to-date terminology available for the use of translators using EU languages.

■   systematic: form part of a larger, ordered system of terms, preferably in a clearly structured terminological hierarchy

■   neutral: offer orientation toward cognition and objective processes without including aesthetic or emotive elements

■   self-explanatory or transparent: include elements which reflect the important features of the concept designated

These features are ideals which are not always realized. Economy may be sacrificed to the greater need for exactness, lack of ambiguity, and uniqueness. In face-to-face communication scientists and technicians may use vocabulary which is more informal. This might include metaphors from everyday language like *juice* for *electrical current* and clippings such as *streps* for *streptococci, mag sulf* for *magnesium sulphate* (examples from Beier 1980: 35f.).

8.4.3.4 Word formation in ESPs

The examples of metaphor and clipping just given indicate that ESPs draw on the same reservoir of semantic shift and word formation processes as GenE. A further example of metaphor is *memory* for *computer storage capacity*. In addition there are the usual derivational processes of GenE, e.g.

■   prefixing (*anti-, in-, mis-, non-, semi-, un-*)

■   suffixing (*-ar, -al, -ed, -er, -less, -ment, -ness*)

■   conversion/zero derivation (*to dimension < dimension*)

■   back formations (*to lase < laser*)

■   clippings (*lab < laboratory*)

■   abbreviations (*FBR < fast breeder reactor*)

■   acronyms (*laser 'light amplification by stimulated emission of radiation'*)

■   blends (*pulsar 'pulsating radio star'*)

■   composite forms (*aeroplane*).

What is more prominent in many fields, however, is the creation of terms by borrowing from Greek or Latin (e.g. *apparatus, matrix*, or *phenomenon*) and by using Greek and Latin combining forms (*aero-, astro-, baro-, cryo-, ferro-, gyro-, hydro-*, etc.) and suffixes (*-gram, -graph, -ology, -scope, -tomy*, etc.). Where there are extended systematic terminologies, as in chemistry, the order and status of roots and affixes are strictly defined:

> Thus *eth + an + ol* signifies, in that order, a structure with two carbons, simply linked together and with one of these linked to a hydroxyl (-O-H) group, and no other combination of these morphemes describes that structure. (Dermer *et al.*, quoted in Beier 1980: 32)

In addition, compounding is especially frequent as indicated above when discussing nominalization (§8.4.3.1). In ten 2000-word texts Salager found the frequencies of compound nominal phrases shown in Table 8.12.

Table 8.12. Percentage frequencies of compound nominal phrases (Salager 1984: 138f.)

General English	0.87
Medical English	9.76
Technical English	15.37

In the final two sections we will look at concrete examples of ESPs which illustrate both the special terminology involved and grammatical, morphological, and information packaging phenomena.

Case study 8.11: Example of military jargon

Military jargon is the subject of suspicion because there have been very noticeable tendencies to hide (politically or humanly) unpleasant truths behind euphemistic phrasing. In the context of the Vietnam War, to be in battle was to be 'in a combat situation'; a helicopter assault was a 'vertical envelopment'; an M-14 rifle a 'hand-held, gas-operated, magazine-fed, semiautomatic shoulder weapon' (Caputo, *A Rumor of War*, p. 14). This practice is one related to the bureaucratic tendency to use **gobbledegook** reinforced by a bias toward **PC** ('politically correct') **language**. The term *gobbledegook* (a.k.a. **bureaucratese**, **officialese**) is pejorative and is aimed both at making people aware of and at combatting pretentious, opaque, and vague language. The term *PC language* is somewhat dubious. Its positive aspect is its intention to replace insulting and demeaning language as used in ethnic, racial, sexual, and other slurs or in derogatory reference. Its negative aspect is its widely criticized programmatic nature, often motivated by unthinking lack of tolerance and perspective (cf. §8.1.5).

A second quotation from Caputo (see Text 8.9) provides us with a sample of military language in the sense of an ESP or, as labelled in the heading to this section, jargon. *Jargon* is a fitting designation because of its multiple connotations: the term is often pejorative, indicating inpenetrable language. As McArthur has it: 'Jargon . . . allows the speaker to make fairly simple ideas appear complicated, if not profound' (1996). For in-group users it is a convenient, clear, and precise way to make reference; furthermore, it may serve as a sign of group membership.

Text 8.9. Military jargon (Caputo, *A Rumor of War*, p. 14)

Enemy sit. Aggressor forces in div strength holding MLR Hill 820 complex gc AT 940713-951716 w/fwd elements est. bn strength junction at gc AT 948715 (See Annex A, COMPHIBPAC intell. summary period ending 25 June) . . . *Mission*: BLT 1/7 seize, hold and defend obj. A gc 948715 . . . *Execution*: BLT 1/7 land LZ X-RAY AT 946710 at H-Hour 310600 . . . A co. GSF estab. LZ security LZ X-Ray H minus 10 . . . B co. advance axis BLUE H plus 5 estab. blocking pos. vic gs AT 948710 . . . A, C, D cos. maneuver element commence advance axis BROWN H plus 10 . . . Bn tacnet freq 52.9 . . . shackle code HAZTRCEGBD . . . div. tacair dir. air spt callsign PLAYBOY . . . Mark friendly pos w/air panels or green smoke. Mark tgt. w/WP.

Case study 8.12: The English of air traffic control (ATC)

Many international organizations depend on English as their lingua franca to ensure safe international communication. Seaspeak, for example, was developed in the 1980s to faciltate clear communication in maritime shipping. It regulates ways of speaking (including pronunciation of numbers, times, or positions) and the order in which information is given, such as identification of speaker and type of message to be sent (advice, information, request, warning, etc.).

Much the same thing is true of the English as the language of ATC. Although English is not yet the official language of ATC it is *de facto* the international standard as adopted by the International Civil Aviation Organization (ICAO).[14] What this means is that agreement is necessary on:

1. the order of priority governing the different types of message;
2. the spelling code for letters and figures;
3. call-sign details for ground stations and aircraft;
4. message structure (call-sign followed by content), call-sign rules, acknowledgements, corrections, receptions and endings;
5. distress and emergency measures;
6. conventional expressions;
7. the phraseology itself, i.e. a set of compulsory skeleton messages for use in ATC exchanges (Philps 1991: 109).

In addition, vocabulary is chosen to avoid potential phonetic or semantic ambiguity (Table 8.13).

The syntax of ATC English is so restricted as to be a subgrammar of English. For example, a high degree of nominalization is used: 'START UP AT (time)' does not have an underlying imperative, but is telegraphic for *(Your) START UP (is) AT (time)* (ibid.:110). There is a high frequency of imperatives (42.5 per cent), but they come from the tower exclusively. There is no room for modal and

---

14 World civil aviation is regulated by the ICAO, set up in 1944 at the Chicago Convention. Linguistic regulations for radiotelephony are to be found principally in ICAO Annex 10, vol. 2 (*Communication Procedures*), and in the PANS-RAC 444-RAC/501-11 document. In particular, the International Standards and Recommended Practices for Aeronautical Communications (Annex 10, vol. 2) stipulate that 'in general, the air ground radiotelephony communications should be conducted in the language normally used by the station on the ground'. But 'pending the development and adoption of a more suitable form of speech for universal use for aeronautical radiotelephony communication, the English language should be used as such and should be available on request from any aircraft station' (Philps 1991: 104). Plans to adopt English as the official language are currently being pursued by the ICAO.

Table 8.13. The vocabulary of air traffic control

Natural English (GenE)	ATC
Yes, Of course	Affirm
Authorized, Go ahead	Cleared
No, Of course not	Negative
I'd like to, Could I	Request
Repeat, Sorry? What?	Say again
Clear, Empty	Vacated

interrogative formulations such as *I would like you to. . .; would you mind. . .?* (Philps 1991: 113).

There is systematic deletion of determiners; but reconstruction is clear since the missing item is virtually always the definite article or a possessive, cf.

WHEELS APPEAR UP
RESUME OWN NAVIGATION (Philps 1991: 116)

Subject pronouns are regularly deleted when reference is to pilot or tower. Auxiliaries are also systematically deleted:

LEAVING FREQUENCY (I am LEAVING the FREQUENCY)
CLOSING FROM LEFT (you are CLOSING FROM the LEFT)

The ICAO phraselogy and its procedures are a type of ESP and are characterized by ellipsis and exact phraseology (Philips 1991: 122).

8.5 SUMMARY

In Chapter 8 we investigated four major areas which reveal how English users, both native and non-native, employ the language. In doing this we looked at different levels of style, including formulaic language, formulaic texts, and jargon; slang appeared as an example of group language, especially as the result of processes of metaphor and metonymy. This was rounded out with a look at euphemism and rhyming slang. Some aspects of language contact (why, how, in what domains borrowing takes place) were examined with a focus on relations to Dutch, German, French, and Spanish. The international English of youth culture (especially music and drugs), of the Internet, and of English for Special/ Specific Purposes was treated with an eye to similarities and differences across national varieties Throughout the chapter we were observing the diatypical categories of tenor, field, and medium.

9 Convergence or Divergence?

English Spoken – American Understood (sign seen in Paris after the Second World War)

Americans and Britons are two peoples divided by a common language. (Marckwardt and Quirk 1960)

9.1 ENGLISH IN ONE GLOBAL WORLD

As the twenty-first century begins, one of the most prominent words bandied about is *globalization*. As the world grows into more and more of an economic unit, the need for as universal a medium of communication as possible is continually growing as well. People want growth. Growth demands cooperation. Cooperation requires communication. So aren't we getting what we want and need? This is surely nothing new. For haven't we seen the preeminence of Latin in pre-modern Europe come (and go)? Haven't we witnessed the ascendency of French (and its eclipsing)? This time it is English which is filling the role of motor for more and better cross-regional and transnational communication.

So why is it that so many voices are also being raised which warn that this increasing linguistic uniformity is a threat? For many people, English represents the greatest present-day threat to cultural and linguistic diversity. And as in the past, there are forces trying to mobilize opinion to dam in the rising tide of English words that seems about to inundate so many 'smaller' languages.

These are two views of the role of English in the present-day world, and there are elements of truth on both sides. Numerous languages with relatively few speakers have, indeed, fallen victim to this process of globalization, which itself goes back generations. How many of the Amerindian languages have survived the swamping of North America by English? What is the survival rate of the Aboriginal-Australnesian ones? How well is Irish doing? What about Maori? With each loss of a language, cultural heritages are also irrevocably lost: folk sayings, religious rites, oral histories, the collected wisdom of generations – an enormous cultural disruption. Are we, mankind, losing linguistic-cultural diversity (just as we are losing bio-diversity as more and more species become extinct), diversity that we can never win back again?

On the other side of the ledger, we must also recognize that while much of this can be chalked up to perhaps short-sighted goals, it is willed change on the part of the people directly affected, and it is the result of processes of modernization which would surely sacrifice traditional cultural values even if there were no linguistic consequences. Inevitably, in other words, there has been and will continue to be cultural change and loss.

A further possibility, but one hard to demonstrate convincingly, is that there is more continued diversity than many people want to see or are able to see. The whole point of this book is that English is a diverse language. It has a relatively uniform centre: StE, with its polycentric native-language national varieties and an increasingly diverse outer circle of New Englishes as well as a periphery of Other Englishes. Within any one of these there is a further diversity of speaker groups marked by age, gender, education, ethnicity, vocation, and much more.

In other words, it seems to be mistaken to take these two sides and try to make a balance sheet of credits and debits. Nor does it do justice to a complicated question to say that the answer is some kind of compromise. Both sides represent legitimate interests and have cogent arguments to make. If there is a solution to the dilemma of a necessary shared basis and of desirable diversity, it can, I think, only be reached in demanding more: more language. We need to be multilingual, multidialectal, multicultural. Only in this way can we ensure not only tolerance of the different (a minimum) but the much more necessary appreciation of virtues of other ways of living, thinking, working, playing, worshipping ... .

In Chapters 2–4 we concentrated on ENL varieties, and the diversity in vocabulary their geographical spread and social innovations have brought about. In Chapters 5 and 6 we saw how many underlying ESL linguistic and cultural values have contributed to a re-formation of English, changes also dependent on the domains in which English is used and on substrate influences. In Chapter 7 a variety of ENL and ESL norms were dealt with, whether part of the underlying social structures (power and solidarity in regard to social status, kinship, and the like) or social values (as manifested in pragmatic idioms). And Chapter 8 featured a selection from the enormous diversity that exists in textual forms, styles, slangs, code languages, in-group ways of expression, and so on.

9.2 LINGUISTIC RELATIVITY

One of the important ideas developed in this book is that language mirrors culture. But how far can this be carried? In its strong version this says that people's thoughts are determined by the categories present in their language. In the words of Sapir (1949: 162):

> We see and hear and otherwise experience very largely as we do because the language habits of our community predispose certain choices of interpretation. . . From this standpoint we may think of language as the *symbolic guide* to culture.

One of the consequences of this would be that the lens each language or variety of a given language applies to our view of the world is inescapable. Certainly, the prospect of finding a common neutral metalanguage to which we can relate all the languages and varieties of languages is pretty faint.

Within the framework of this book we might ask the more modest but still difficult question: is there a one-to-one relationship between language and culture? The existence of one single English language would suggest that this question must be answered with an emphatic No. For the cultures we have seen reflected' in the varieties of English explored here – differing natural worlds, differing political, educational, legal, technological, social, and familial ones – are sometimes more and sometimes less distinct from each other. Just as the kind of English used in each of them is also sometimes more and sometimes less similar.

So what about the opposite question? Does a one-to-many relationship between English and its cultures indicate that English is at the beginning of a process which will eventually lead to a multiplicity of daughter languages – just as Latin developed into French, Spanish, Italian, Romanian, Catalan, etc.? While we cannot give a definitive answer to this, it seems unlikely. The division of Latin into its daughter vernaculars was facilitated by isolation, a lack of communication beyond the local and regional communities. Furthermore, the development of the nation-state with its individual language as one of its central programmatic points also pushed developments in this direction.

Currently the English-speaking communities around the world are exposed to the more prominent varieties such as AmE, BrE, or AusE on a level that ensures mutual intelligibility – despite all the sometimes amusing and occasionally irritating misunderstandings that can and do occur. Furthermore, there seems to be a fairly strong will to accept a common denominator of StE/GenE which varies only peripherally within educated English-speaking communities everywhere.

Today more than ever before, technological developments in the field of communication as well as the ever-increasing presence of the news and entertainment media make once distant and strange Englishes ever more accessible to all of us, whatever our own variety may be. The introduction of new technologies is taking place on a global scale and occurring with great rapidity. The necessary new words often just seem to be there, wherever they may have come from. Differentiation is less and less national. As the global culture grows, new words are limited less and less by the older linguistic boundaries. This, clearly, is a tendency toward convergence.

Yet at the same time we are witnessing an increasing fragmentation of target groups, of markets, of cultures. The new groups are better labelled not by nation but by sports activities, fan clubs, tastes in music, professional interests, political persuasions, and so on. While more and more of these groups share more and more language (especially English, as we have seen in the chapter on International English), they may be speaking a unified language less and less as they find it easier to communicate with their interest-peers and harder and harder to exchange ideas with a wider but often uninterested general public. This, clearly, is a tendency toward divergence.

9.3 VOICES SPEAKING FOR CONVERGENCE, FOR DIVERGENCE

There is no more convincing way to illustrate this delicate balance of views, perhaps, than to quote from some of the many voices which see now increasing divergence, now more convergence.

Nowadays it is not impossible to find BrE and AmE words which speakers of the other variety will not understand, but these words are less likely to be part of GenE and more likely to be part of an ESP or an in-group language.

> The process of interpenetration of the lexical units of the American and British variants is undoubtedly quite intensive. Nor is there any doubt that on the lexical-semantic level both variants are considerably closer to each other than they were in the 19th century and even early in the 20th century. (Svejcer 1978: 160)

But Svejcer thinks a levelling of many long-standing differences in the future is hardly likely (p. 161).

> New technicalities bring new variation but multinational manufacturers tend to work against regional variation. The same is true of the media, where, especially in broadcasting, prestige models tend to be American . . . (Turner 1994:326)

One prominent scholar of World English believes that linguistic change is leading to a levelling of speech toward forms closer to the standard, and cites CarE and Hawaiian English as evidence for this. But new national norms are developing as well, as seen in Nigeria (Görlach 1988: 23). Because of the preponderance of the oral in WAVE, Bokamba feels it is less constrained by the written and more standardized code:

> What actually distinguishes WAVE from other non-native varieties of English is its lexicon, including the occurrence of certain types of code-mixing and regionally-bound idiomatic expressions . . . WAVE, therefore, is more likely to continue its course towards divergence from, rather than convergence into, what I have referred to as an educated native variety of English. (Bokamba 1991: 503, 506)

Even though English is seldom a first language in Singapore, it is the first school language of practically everybody who has entered Singapore schools since the early 1980s. It has also grown to be the language of national identity, of work, and of inter-ethnic (and even some intra-ethnic) communication. Yet Bokamba's view is substantiated by Platt for SingE:

> Unless there is a radical change in policy it can be assumed that the use of English will continue to increase. ... the use of Colloquial Singapore English can be expected to continue. Paradoxically, the higher the proportion of Singaporeans with English-medium education, the more a colloquial subvariety will develop. (Platt 1988: 1387)

From a more positive perspective, this can be seen as affirming the importance of local values:

> The use of a standard or informal variety of Singaporean, Nigerian, or Filipino English is thus part of what it means to be a Singaporean, a Nigerian, or a Filipino. (Richards 1982: 235)

The last word goes to the very realistic assessment of Ferguson and Heath 20 years ago:

> The trends projected over a long enough period suggest a relatively uniform international English as a new Latin, with increasingly different local vernacular Englishes, and English-based, pidginized, informal lingua francas in a number of Third World countries. (Ferguson and Heath 1981: pp. xxxviif.)

In sum, the diversity of English in today's world offers hope. There can be the specialization which is needed for international trade and travel, for the old and the new media (the press, radio, TV, the Internet), for science, for world markets, for air traffic control, and much more. Most especially, the increasing fragmentation of the postmodern world is making room both for enough convergence to guarantee worldwide communication and for enough tolerance and diversity to allow local and worldwide groups to mark their identity and in-group solidarities with their own Englishes. No single variety need dominate this process. English can and should remain varied.

Solutions to the Exercises

2.1 Doublets

1. *anger*	*angst*	native English + German loan	2. *belly*	*bellows*	doublet with differentiation
3. *crown*	*corona*	nativized via French + Latin	4. *kirk*	*church*	Scots + English
5. *plane*	*piano*	Latin + Italian	6. *raid*	*road*	Scots + English
7. *royal*	*regal*	French + Latin	8. *scoot*	*shoot*	Norse + English
9. *school*	*shul*	English + Yiddish loan	10. *shoal*	*school*	Dutch/Low German + English/Dutch
11. *wake*	*watch*	doublets from OE			

2.2 IrE expressions

1. His leg's always at him	His leg hurts
2. There's a cuttin' on him	He's very hungry
3. She let a scrake out of her	She screamed
4. If he didn't take the legs from in under me	He knocked me down
5. There not a pick on her.	She's very thin.

2.3 Animal calls

a. *baah*	→	sheep	→	j. *Blök* (German)	d. *oink*	→	pig	→	i. *Grunz* (German)
b. *cluck*	→	chicken	→	g. *glouglou* (French)	e. *peep*	→	bird	→	k. *pío pío* (Spanish)
c. *neigh*	→	horse	→	l. *hinnn/hiii-hiii* (Spanish)	f. *quack*	→	duck	→	h. *cua cua* (Spanish)

2.4 Toponyms

UK	USA	Australia
1. the governmental executive (government or administration)		
Whitehall	*inside the Beltway*	*Canberra*
2. the legislative (Parliament or Congress)		
Westminster	*Capitol Hill*	*Parliament House*
3. the head of government (prime minister or president)		
Downing Street	*the White House* see preceding/ *the Oval Office*	*Kirrabilli house* (not widespread usage)
4. the head of state		
Buckingham Palace		*Government House/ Admiralty House*
5. the world of finance		
the City/ Lombard Street	*Wall Street*	*Pitt St; Collins St* (Melbourne Sydney business streets)
6. an imaginary remote place		
Mummerset/ Zummezet, Timbuktu, Watford	*Slippery Rock Hicksville, Podunk*	*Bullamakanka* (a.k.a. *Bandy-wallop, Woop Woop, Back of Burke*) SAE: *Blikkiesdorp*

2.5 First exercise on antonomasia

1. a *macintosh*   'a raincoat'; after Charles Macintosh (19th century)

2. to *hoover*   'vacuum-clean'; from the British trademark (20th century)

3. *wellies*   'rubber/gum boots, Wellingtons'; after the Duke of Wellington (19th century)

4. to *boycott*   'refuse to buy, patronize'; after Captain Boycott, English estate manager in Ireland (19th century)

5. a *cardigan*   'a sweater open in the front'; after the 7th Earl of Cardigan (19th century)

6. to *bowdlerize* 'to expurgate' after Thomas Bowdler, editor of Shakespeare (19th century)

7. a *bobby*   'police officer'; after Sir *Robert* Peel, founder of the London Metropolitan Police (19th century)

8. a *sandwich*   'bread with other food on it or between slices'; after the 4th Earl of Sandwich (18th century)

2.6 Second exercise on antonomasia

Benedict Arnold (1741–1801), a Revolutionary War (1775–1783) Patriot (= American) officer who went over to the enemy (Loyalist, British) side for purportedly opportunistic reasons; stands for treason.

Horatio Alger (1832–99), author of numerous 'rags to riches' novels for boys; stands for success and wealth as a result of honesty and hard work.

John Hancock (1737–93), the first signatory to the American Declaration of Independence (1776), who signed with an especially large signature and purportedly said, 'This is so John Bull can read without his spectacles'; stands for a person's signature.

Emily Post (1873–1960), author of *Etiquette: The Blue Book of Social Usage* (1922); stands for the ultimate authority on etiquette.

Rambo, hero of the movies *First Blood* (1982) and (eponymous hero of) *Rambo: First Blood Part II* (1985), a Vietnam veteran whose extravagant courage and violence symbolically redeemed the lost power and pride of the United States after defeat in Vietnam; stands for machismo and violence.

Uncle Sam, by dress (red, white, and blue) and origin an early 19th-century (Yankee) figure; originally used derisively by Americans opposed to the War of 1812 (against Great Britain); symbol of the US (compare the initials), its government or people.

Uncle Tom, eponymous hero of Harriet Beecher Stowe's novel *Uncle Tom's Cabin* (1851–2); a slave, he was pious, deferential, and loyal to whites, the 'ideal' 'white man's black'; stands for abject servility to whites.

Noah Webster (1758–1843), first American dictionary-maker, or lexicographer, author of *American Dictionary of the English Language* (1828); he also proposed numerous spelling reforms such as *color* for *colour* or *center* for *centre*; stands for authority in language (meaning, spelling, pronunciation).

2.7 British and American terms for schools

Terms	UK	USA	Features
1. *grammar school*	b, e	b, d	(a) state-run
2. *high school*	b, e, f	b, e	(b) private or state
3. *kindergarten*	c, d	b, d	(c) private only
4. *middle school*	b, d+e	b, e	(d) pre-secondary
5. *prep school*	c, d	c, e	(e) secondary
6. *public school*	c, e	a, d+e	(f) esp. Scottish

3.1 Expressions for 'zero'

1. *nothing* (both), *zip* (AmE), *nil* (BrE)		6. *love* (both)	
2. *oh* (both)		7. *null*, *non-entity* (both), *cipher* (AmE)	
3. *zero* (AmE), *nought* (BrE)		8. *nothing* (both), *nix*, *zilch* (AmE)	
4. *oh point eight* (both), *nought point eight* (BrE)		9. *null*, *empty* (both)	
5. *zero* (both)		10. *duck* (BrE only)	

3.2 Units of measurement

Unit	Type of unit	Typically used in	Unit	Type of unit	Typically used in
1. *buck*	money	USA	7. *fortnight*	time	esp. Britain
2. *bob*	money	Britain	8. *gill*	liquid	Britain
3. *cent*	money	USA, Aust., Canada	9. *perch*	length, surface; volume of stone	Britain
4. *crore*	number	Pakistan, India	10. *quarter section*	surface of land	USA
5. *dime*	money	USA, Canada	11. *quid*	money	Britain
6. *dram*	liquid, esp. liquor	Britain esp. Scotl.	12. *stone*	weight	esp. Britain

3.3 Analogues

US institution/term	UK analogue	US institution/term	UK analogue
1. President of the USA	Prime Minister	8. AFL-CIO	TUC
2. Secretary of the Treasury	Chancellor of the Exchequer	9. CIA	MI6 (SIS: Secret Intelligence Service)
3. Attorney-General	Lord Chancellor	10. Federal Reserve Bank	Bank of England
4. Secretary of State	Foreign Secretary	11. Medicare and Medicaid	National Health Service
5. Supreme Court	House of Lords, Law Lords	12. Social Security	old age pension
6. US Constitution	Magna Carta		
7. Republican Party	Conservative Party		

3.4 The semantic features of *pie*

	AmE	BrE
Feature 1	[+baked]	[+baked]
Feature 2	[+pastry crust]	[+pastry crust]
Feature 3	[±pastry covering]	[+pastry covering]
Feature 4	[+sweet filling; usu. fruit]	[±savoury filling; usu, meat]

Feature 1 implies the use of an oven and distinguishes pie from stove-top cooked food (fried, boiled, sautéed, etc.) i.e. items like pancakes, stews, soups, noodles, and sauces.

Feature 2 distinguishes pies from cakes, lasagnes, and casseroles, but includes quiches, flans, tarts.

Feature 3 indicates that an American pie may but need not have a top; a British-Irish one does have a top. This makes *pie* and *tart* virtually synonymous in America if filled with fruit.

Feature 4 is most decisive, since pies are regularly understood as sweet (with fruit, creams, and custards) in North America. For instance, anyone promising to bring along a pie to a picnic would be expected to be contributing to the *dessert* (in BrE also: *sweet, pudding,* or *afters*). One containing meat would have to be explicitly named, e.g. *meat pie* or *chicken pie*.

3.5 Who eats dessert?

Usage labels: A check of various dictionaries shows that class labels are not usual. *Afters* is frequently given the stylistic label: *colloquial. RHWCD* (AmE) does not list *afters; pudding* and *sweet* are labelled as *Brit.*

Content differences: None discernible.

3.6 Heroes

	RHWCD	Flexner and Soukhanov (1997)
1. *bomber*	–	upstate NY
2. *Cuban sandwich*	–	Miami, Tampa
3. *grinder*	New England/Inland North	Boston; New England
4. *hoagie*	NJ/PA	Philadelphia; NJ
5. *po'* (= poor) *boy*	New Orleans	New Orleans
6. *spuckie*	–	Italian Boston
7. *sub*(*marine*)	Northeast/Northern Midlands	generalized
8. *torpedo*	[listed without reg. label]	NJ
9. *wedge* (or *wedgie*)	Coastal CN + RI	downstate NY, CN, RI
10. *zep* (< *zeppelin?*)	–	NJ

3.7 Cooking utensils

	A/B/C	AusE		A/B/C	AusE
can opener	AmE	tin-opener	cooker	BrE	stove
dish towel	AmE	tea-towel, tea-cloth	draining board	common	draining board
faucet	AmE	tap	fish slice	BrE	fishslice
fridge	BrE	fridge, frig (colloquial)	spatula	AmE	fishslice
refrigerator	AmE	refrigerator	sink	common	sink
stove	AmE	stove	tap	BrE	tap
tea towel	AmE	tea-towel, tea-cloth	tin opener	BrE	tin-opener

Clearly AusE is more closely oriented toward BrE in this area, with some evidence of independence as well as a small affinity to AmE.

3.8 Regional cuisine

1. bannock	pancake of barley or oatmeal	Scotland
2. butty	sandwich	northern England
3. cornbread	bread	US South
4. cruller	doughnut	US Northeast (NY)
5. half-round	slice of bread, sandwich	Britain, Australia
6. hushpuppies	deep-fat-fried dough	US South
7. johnny cake	pancake	US North
8. soda bread	yeastless bread	Ireland, Scotland, Australia

3.9 Drinking collocations

1. heavy drinker
2. blind -, dead -, stinko drunk
3. hold (your) liquor
4. cold -, stone sober
5. take a swig
6. wet your whistle
7. drunk as a deacon
8. full as a fiddler's fart, - to the scuppers, - as a tick
9. dead drunk
10. high as a kite
11. sober as a deacon
12. swill beer, - booze

3.10 Collocations and idioms

	Collocation/idiom	Translation	A/B/C
1. *be cheesed off*	I	bored, fed up	B
2. *cheese it*	I	look out, run away	A
3. *chew out*	I	scold	A
4. *chew up*	I	scold	B
5. *chug-a-lug*	I	drink in one draught	A
6. *cook out*	I	picnic, barbecue	A
7. *freshen a drink*	C	add to, fill up (cf. 17)	A
8. *get one's teeth into something*	I	deal with firmly, enjoy	C
9. *grab a bite*	C	eat on the run, in a hurry	C
10. *greasy spoon*	C	cheap restaurant	A
11. *hot up*	I	warm up	B
12. *lay the table*	C	set out plates, flatware, etc.	C
13. *local pub*	C	bar	B
14. *pig out*	I	eat voraciously and gluttonously	A
15. *plump out*	I	get plump	C
16. *slim down*	I	get thinner, diet	B
17. *top up a drink*	C	fill up a glass (cf. 7)	B
18. *tuck in* (to food)	I	attack food, eat with an appetite	B
19. *wash up*	I	wash the dishes	B
		wash oneself (hands, face)	A
20. *wipe up*	I	wipe a table, etc. clean of liquid	C
		dry dishes	B

4.1 Indigenous animals

1. *armadillo*	USA	from Spanish
2. *cockabully*	NZ	from Maori (anglicized)
3. *gemsbok*	S.Afr.	from Afrikaans
4. *ground hog*	USA	native compound
5. *hedgehog*	GB	native compound
6. *Illawarra shorthorn*	Aust.	native compound using place name from Aboriginal language
7. *kiwi*	NZ	from Maori (anglicized)
8. *koala*	Aust.	from Aboriginal language
9. *Manx cat*	GB	native compound using place name from Norse
10. *meerkat*	S.Afr.	from Afrikaans
11. *numbat*	Aust.	from Aboriginal language
12. *pipi*	NZ	from Maori
13. *platypus*	Aust.	neologism out of Greek elements
14. *prairie dog*	USA	native compound
15. *quagga*	S.Afr.	from Hottentot
16. *roedeer*	GB	native compound
17. *taniwha*	NZ	from Maori 'mythical monster'
18. *waterbuck*	S.Afr.	from Afrikaans (loan translation)
19. *woodchuck*	USA	from Algonquian (Native American)
20. *wild boar*	GB	native compound

4.2 Loan words and loan translations

1. *aardwolf*	< Afk. *aard* 'earth' + *wolf*; hyena (loan word + loan translation)
2. *bandicoot*	< Telugu *pandikokku*; -*kokku* probably changed to -*coot* on the model of *coot* (a type of bird); in Southern Asian English (India, Sri Lanka) *bandicoot* is a type of rat; borrowed into AusE for a rat-like marsupial animal (loan word)
3. *camelthorn (tree)*	< Afr. *kameeldoring (boom)*; a kind of desert acacia (loan translation); also used in the Afrikaans form as a loan word
4. *dallgyte*	< Nyungar (Aboriginal language) *talkatj*; the greater bilby (loan word)
5. *elephant's food*	< Afr. *olifantskos* (also *spekboom*; portulacaria); succulent shrub (loan translation)
6. *kai*	< Maori; food (loan word)
7. *marae*	< Maori; courtyard of a Maori meeting-house; the focus of social life in a Maori community (loan word)
8. *yallera*	< from an Australian Aboriginal language for a kind of (rabbit-eared) bandicoot (loan word)

4.3 Compounds with *bush* and with *tucker*

Depending of the provenance of your dictionary you will find only some of these. No single dictionary checked contains them all. We used the *Macquarie* as the major source for the AusE terms. It listed many items not included in the exercise as did *ACOD*. Items found in the *Macquarie* are given in *italic*; those found in *ACOD* are given in SMALL CAPS.

	Provenance	Meaning	If AusE: 1, 2, 3
1. BUSHBABY	SAE	a small lemur	
2. *bush carpenter*	AusE	rough, amateur carpenter	(3)
3. BUSHCRAFT	AusE	ability to live in the bush with little equipment and help	(1)
4. *bush cure*	AusE	a household remedy	(3)
5. *bush-faller*	NZE	lumberjack (also: *bush-feller, ~falling*)	
6. *bush farm*	NZE	farm cleared from the forest (also: *~er, ~ing*)	
7. BUSHFIRE	GenE	fire in forest or scrub country	
8. BUSH LAWYER	AusE NZE	a type of prickly, trailing plant	(1)
	AusE	someone who pretends to know the law	(3)
9. BUSH LEAGUE	AmE	minor league; amateur, inferior, mediocre	
10. *bush-line*	AusE	timberline, tree line	(1)
11. BUSHMAN	AusE	pioneer; someone with bushcraft	(1)
	NZE	bush-faller	
	SAE	San, a racial-ethnic group in South Africa	
12. *bush-pilot*	AusE	small aircraft pilot serving the outback	(2)
13. *bushrat*	AusE	Australian species of rat	(1)
14. BUSH WEEK	AusE	fictitious festive week when country people come to town	(2)
15. BUSHWHACKER	AusE	bushie; a native (Aboriginal) person	(3)
	NZE	bush-faller	
	AmE	backwoodsman; guerrilla, outlaw	

4.4 The ending {-y, -ie}

If the items are listed in *ACOD* or the *Macquarie* (*M*), they are marked.

	1, 2, 3, or 4	meaning
1. *bikkie, bickie* (*M*)	1	biscuit; also word for 'dollar'
2. *bluey* (*ACOD, M*)	2	bushman's bundle; summons; a cattle dog (*M*); red-headed person (*ACOD*)
3. *brassie* (-)	1	bra < brassiere (endearing) (Baker 1966: 372); in *ACOD* + *M*: brass-like; cheeky; type of golf club (GenE)
4. *Brizzie, Brissie* (*ACOD, M*)	1	Brisbane (endearing)
5. *broomie* (*ACOD, M*)	3	sweeper in (sheep-) shearing shed
6. *cozzie, cossie* (*ACOD, M*)	1	swimming costume (NSW) (endearing)
7. *darkie, -y, -ey* (*ACOD, M*)	4	racially offensive: a dark-skinned person, esp. in Australia an Aboriginal; faeces (*M*); moonless night; night shift (Baker 1966: 370)
8. *hottie* (*ACOD, M*)	2	hotwater bottle; tall story; 'hot' story; sharp business practice (Baker 1966: 370)
9. *kookie* (*ACOD, M*)	2	AmE crazy; also AusE kookaburra (Baker 1966: 370)
10. *maty, -ey* (*ACOD, M*)	2	mate (endearing; depends on tone of voice)
11. *milky* (*ACOD, M*)	3	NZE milkman; AusE has milko (*ACOD, M*)
12. *swaggie, -y* (*ACOD, M*)	3	swagman, vagabond, itinerant worker; (NZE) swagger
13. *truckie, -y* (*ACOD, M*)	3	truck driver, trucker
14. *weirdy, -ie, -o* (*ACOD, M*)	2	strange person (= AmE weirdo) (disparaging)
15. *wharfy, -ie* (*ACOD, M*)	3	semi-skilled worker (< wharf labourer)

4.5 Dialect and standard

1. *billy*	c. can or pail	7. *larrikin*	g. rowdy
2. *bonzer*	j. terrific	8. *lurk*	f. racket, scam
3. *cobber*	e. mate	9. *nong*	d. idiot
4. *crook*	h. sick	10. *shout*	i. stand a round of drinks
5. *dag*	k. unkempt, untidy person	11. *swag*	a. tramp's bundle
6. *dinkum*	b. genuine		

4.6 Semantic shift

1. *bachelor flat*	a small flat or apartment, cf. NZE *bach* 'vacation house'	distinctive
2. *black stump*	beyond the pale, outside civilization	narrowing
3. *block*	section of land	narrowing
4. *bush*	woods, forest	broadening
5. *duplex*	a house with a flat or apartment on each floor	narrowing
6. *flatette*	bachelor flat (q.v.)	distinctive
7. *granny flat*	garage apartment	distinctive
8. *home unit*	condominium, condo (AmE)	distinctive
9. *homestead*	ranch house	narrowing
10. *never-never*	ultima Thule	narrowing
11. *outback*	backwoods, boondocks	distinctive
12. *(own your own)*	home unit (q.v.)	distinctive
13. *paddock*	field	broadening
14. *project house*	standard design (series) house	distinctive
15. *scrub*	barrens	narrowing
16. *squatter*	large landowner	narrowing
17. *the suburbs*	suburbia (dreary, philistine)	narrowing
18. *station*	ranch	broadening
19. *township*	small town or townsite; cf. (North America) an administrative unit within the county; (in Britain) a division within a parish usu. with its own church; (in South Africa) an area formerly set aside for black Africans	broadening
20. *villa homes*	row or terrace houses connected by garages	distinctive

4.7 The sources of the vocabulary of transportation

AmE	BrE	AusE
AUTOMOBILES		
1. fender	mudguard	mudguard
2. hood	bonnet	bonnet
3. trunk	boot	boot
4. carburetor	carburettor	carburettor
5. bumper	bumper	bumper bar
6. (house) trailer	caravan	caravan
7. gas(oline)	petrol	petrol
STREETS AND ROADS		
1. interstate, freeway, expressway, etc.	motorway	expressway, freeway
2. asphalt, macadam, blacktop road	asphalt, bitumen, tarmac road	asphalt, bitumen, blacktop, macadam, tarmac(adam), tarseal (NZE)
3. speed bump	speed bump, sleeping policeman	speed bump/hump (NZE: jandal)
4. parking space	parking place	(car) park
5. sidewalk	pavement	footpath (also NZE)
6. shoulder, verge	verge	nature strip, verge, shoulder
TRAINS		
1. (train) engineer	train-/engine-driver	(engine-)driver
2. conductor	guard	conductor/guard
3. cow catcher	–	cow/roo catcher (of a train); bull bar (of a car)
4. bumper	buffer	buffer
PLANES		
1. airplane	aeroplane	aeroplane
2. runway	tarmac/runway	runway/ tarmac

4.8 Euphemisms

Taboo	Euphemism	Taboo	Euphemism
1. bloody	blooming	2. damn	darn, durn
3. goddamn	doggone	4. God	gosh
5. fuck	fudge	6. Jesus	jeez
7. shit	shoot, sugar	8. son of a bitch	son of a biscuit eater

4.9 Southern hemisphere terms for non-whites

1. *Abo*	AusE: an Aboriginal, colloquial and often derogatory
2. *blackbird*	AusE: (formerly) a Kanaka kidnapped and transported to Australia as a slave labourer
3. *boong*	AusE: an Aboriginal, derogatory
4. *coloured*	GenE: belonging wholly or in part to some other racial group than white
5. *darkie*	AusE *Colloq.* 1. a dark-skinned person, esp. an Aborigine (older usage); also: 2. faeces; *drop* or *choke a darkie*, to defecate; 3. luderick (kind of fish)
6. *hori*	NZE: derogatory for Maori (from around 1900), connotations of stupidity, naivety, primitiveness, laziness, dishonesty, pleasure-seeking and irresponsible, bad manners
7. *Indigenous Australian*	AusE: politically correct for an Aboriginal
8. *Kaffir*	SAE: derogatory for any South African black
9. *koori*	AusE: an Aboriginal: if used among Aboriginals, not necessarily objectionable; derogatory when used by others
10. *nigger*	GenE: derogatory for a Negro or any black person

4.10 Generic names as euphemisms

1. *dick*	use 1: (euphemism, tabooed) penis	GenE
	use 2: (colloquial) a detective	GenE
	(colloquial) a foolish person	AusE
2. *fanny*	use 1: (euphemism) female genitals	AusE, BrE
	use 2: (colloquial) bottom, rear end	AmE
3. *jack*	use 1: (euphemism) venereal disease	AusE
	use 2: (colloquial) a man, a buddy or mate	GenE
	(colloquial) policeman	NZE
	(slang) money	AmE
4. *jock*	use 1: (slightly tabooed) athletic supporter for the male genitals	GenE
	use 2: (slang) an athlete	AmE
5. *john*	use 1: (euphemism) a toilet	GenE
	(euphemism) penis (a.k.a. *John Thomas*)	AusE, BrE, NZE
	use 2: (slang, slightly euphemistic) a prostitute's customer	AmE
	(slang, somewhat derogatory) a Chinese	GenE
	(rhyming slang) a cop (< *Joe Hop*)	AusE
6. *peter*	use 1: (euphemism) penis	AmE
	use 2: (colloquial) till, cash register	AusE
	(colloquial) a prison cell	AusE, BrE
7. *willy*	use 1: (euphemism) penis	AusE, BrE
	use 2: (colloquial) a wallet	AusE
	(colloquial) sudden outburst of emotion	AusE

4.11 Tabooed animal names

1. *ass*	'bottom' (cf. *arse*)	→	donkey, jackass (burro) (US)
2. *bitch*	'malicious or lewd woman'	→	a she(-dog) (etc.) (general)
3. *cock*	'penis'	→	rooster (chiefly US)
4. *coney*	'female genitals' (cf. *cunt*)	→	bunny, rabbit, jackrabbit (general)
5. *pussy*	'female genitals'	→	kitten (general)

6.1 Word formation

Item	Meaning	Word formation process	Further example
1. *big big* (Holm 1994: 359)	huge	reduplication + calque cf. Yoruba *nlá nlá* or Kongo *múpátipáti*	*Stevie-Weevie*
2. *boy-chil'* (Holm 1994: 359)	son	calquing (<Bambara *dén-ce*)	*loan word* (<German *Lehnwort*)
3. *cow-itch* (Görlach 1989)	climbing herb that causes an itch	folk etymology from Hindi *kewanch*	*crayfish* from French *écrevisse*
4. *destool* (Bokamba 1991: 501)	dethrone	prefixation	*de-brief*
5. *die man* (Pemagbi 1989: 22)	embezzlement using vouchers of people who who have died	compounding (verb + noun)	*cry baby*
6. *goondaism* (Görlach 1989)	rowdyism	suffixation	*statement*
7. *han elbo* (Holm 1994: 362)	elbow	pleonasm	*refer back*
8. *to safe* (Holm 1994: 358f).	be safe	conversion (adj→verb)	*to wet*
9. *shoe-bite* (Görlach 1989: 300)	blister	compounding (noun + verb/noun)	*car park*
10. *Tanzingereza* (Schmied 1985a)	Tanzanian English	loan word + blend <*Tanzania* + Kiswahili *Kiingereza* 'English'	*Spanglish*

6.2 Identifying cases of PkE word formation

The sentences in this exercise were taken from Baumgardner (1998).

1. In another incident a young girl Rabia Bibi (d/o) Karim jumped into Lower Jhelum Canal. = abbreviation

2. Then the self-righteous dictator Gen Ziaul Haq was the perpetrator of the biggest rigging in the referendum, popularly called ('refraudum'.) = blend, specifically a sandwich word

3. Political and social sectors have demanded the Government provide shelter to (poors.) = adjective → noun conversion + pluralization

4. Sindh inspector general of police has (deconfirmed) 23 inspectors who were promoted out of turn. = prefixation

5. ... Mr Shahid Aziz, commissioner in Karachi, said that all the (affectees) would be paid compensation. = suffixation

6. The district police launched a ... drive against ((a) cattle-lifting) and recovered stolen ((b) cattle heads) worth about Rs 2.5 lakh .... = (a) noun + noun compound; (b) rank reduction

7. A youth who was taunted repeatedly by his ((a) kins) for ... for having ((b) love-married) his girl-friend, shot and injured his aunt, ... = (a) pluralization of an uncountable noun (not listed in Table 6.2); (b) noun + verb compound

8. To (character assassinate,) demean and belittle the other seems to be a necessity for our politicians. = back-formation

9. A large number of parents also visited the college but left ... without collecting (admit cards) ... for the coming examination. = clipping (< *admittance cards*)

6.3 Characterizing proverbs

1. *Pretty is as pretty does.* (a, c, d, e, f, g)	'It's what you are that counts, not appearances'
	'Appearances are deceptive'
2. *You can take the boy out of the country, but you can't take the country out of the boy.* (a, c, d, e, f, g)	'A leopard can't change his spots'
	'Once a loser, always a loser'
3. *Idle hands lead to mischief.* (a, d, e, f, g)	'Busy people have no time to make trouble'
4. *If you can't beat them, join them.* (a, c, d, e, f, g)	'It's better to be on the winning side'
5. *If it ain't broke, don't fix it.* (a, d, e, f, g)	'Let good enough alone'
6. *Garbage in, garbage out.* (a, b, c, d, e, f, g)	'If what you put into something is substandard, what you get out of it won't be better'
7. *The more, the merrier.* (a, b, c, d, e, f, g)	'Come join in!'

6.4 Fixed expressions: binomials and trinomials

The resources (learner's dictionaries, *BBI*, Seidl and McMordie 1988) are not very satisfactory; among the three of them most of the items can, however, be found.

Bi-, trinomial	Principle	Gloss	Class
1. *kith and <u>kin</u>*	alliteration	friends and relatives	noun
2. *assault and <u>battery</u>*	word field	criminal attack	noun
3. *<u>hook,</u> line, and sinker*	meronymy	completely	noun
4. *left, right, and <u>centre</u>*	adversative	everywhere	adjective
5. *huff and <u>puff</u>*	rhyme, word field	be annoyed; breathe loudly	verb
6. *from fruit to <u>nuts</u>*	word field	the whole works	noun+prep.
7. *<u>make</u> or break*	rhyme, adversative	all or nothing	verb
8. *forgive and <u>forget</u>*	alliteration	let bygones be bygones	verb
9. *<u>head</u> over heels*	alliteration	headlong; completely, impulsively	noun
10. *hire and <u>fire</u>*	rhyme	*literal*	verb
11. *from <u>rags</u> to riches*	alliteration	be successful	noun+prep.
12. *<u>high</u> and dry*	rhyme	alone, helpless	adjective
13. *<u>footloose</u> and fancy-free*	alliteration	carefree	adjective

6.5 Explicit 2nd person plural pronouns

Pronoun	Where used	Level of usage
1. *all you (aa-yu)*	Eastern Caribbean	decreolized Creole
2. *una/unu*	Caribbean, West Africa	basilect Creole
3. *y'all*	American South	colloquial
4. *yiz*	Scotland, N. Ireland	dialect
5. *you guys*	general, esp. America	colloquial
6. *youse ones*	Scotland, N. Ireland	dialect
7. *yous(e)*	Scotland, Ireland, NY, NZ	colloquial
8. *you'uns*	Scotland, N. Ireland	dialect

6.6 Personal pronouns and grammatical categories

Bodine (1975) has made the interesting point that none of the grammatical categories of the English personal pronouns, namely number, person, and gender, are strictly observed in actual usage.

(a) Number. It is, for example, well known that *we* may be used singularly in the so-called 'royal we' (e.g. Queen Victoria's *We are not amused*) or the editorial *we* (see the first paragraph of this chapter: *In this chapter we will be looking at* . . . ; also a case of inclusive person, see next). For singular *they* see Gender, below.

(b) Person. *We* is used inclusively to refer to the addressee as well, presumably, as the speaker (cf. example above under Number). Impersonal *you* is regularly used as a 3rd person form (*How do you* [= anyone] *get from here to the airport?*), but sometimes also as a 1st person form (cf. *As tired as I am, you* [= I] *can't stand any extra noise*). The *you* is never stressed when used in this way.

(c) Gender. *She* is often used for the neuter. Bauer mentions 'the use of *she* as a neutral or non-referring pronoun: *She'll be right!*' (1994: 400), which many of us know from the use of *she* for cars, ships, and countries when there is a measure of positive emotional attachment involved.

He is the traditional default pronoun and therefore includes both male and female referents when the gender of the referent is not known. (*Ask your professor and see what he thinks.*)

On the basis of the rather loose and pragmatic application of grammatical categories in English, Bodine argues for the use of singular *they* as a non-sexist indefinite generic pronoun. This not only works (*Ask anyone; they'll agree*) but is also natural to most speakers when they refer to indefinite antecedents such as *anyone, someone, no one*. This also makes logical sense since such pronouns, while grammatically singular, are notionally plural because *anyone*, for example, means 'all people'.

This exploration of actual usage suggests that rather than adopting some new and unnatural 3rd person singular generic pronoun, we would do better to resort to the double pronoun, *he or she*, or the use of *they*. Singular *they*, after all, is natural enough with indefinite antecedents. In writing, at least, it is only a small step to use a plural antecedent, such as *students* or *writers*, which then allows the use of sex-neutral but plural *they* without violating number concord.

6.7 Multiple negation

1. *He don't hardly know what to do.*	GenE: *He hardly knows what to do.*
2. *It is not unlikely that they will come.*	StE: *Probably they will come.*
3. *Ain't nobody at home.*	BAE: *There isn't anybody at home.*
4. *You definitely cannot not go to her party.*	StE: *You definitely must stay home.*
5. *Nobody didn't do nothing.*	BAE: *Nobody did anything.*
6. *The teacher didn't go nowhere.*	GenE: *The teacher didn't go anywhere.*
7. *She don't believe there's nothing she can't do.*	GenE: *She doesn't believe there is anything she can't do.*
	BAE: *She doesn't believe there is anything she can do.*
8. *We don't think they won't come.*	StE: *We think they will come.*

6.8 Tag questions

1. *My mother hasn't arrived yet, has she?* (Unproblematic)

2. *The drill sergeant can help us, can't he?* (Wild assumption: the drill sergeant is a man.)

3. *John's dog bit him, didn't he/she/it?* (Are dogs masculine, feminine, or neuter?)

4. *Neither Jack nor Jill fetched the water, did they/he/she?* (What determines the number of a subject in an *(n)either-(n)or* construction? The normative StE rule says: the part nearest the verb, which is *Jill = she*.)

5. *My aunt may come, mayn't she?/may she not?/don't you think?* (Some varieties, esp. AmE, have difficulties with *mayn't*.)

6. *Nobody told him, did they/he/he or she?* (Singular *they* vs. generic *he* vs. inclusive *he or she*.)

7. *Leave us alone, won't you?* (Imperatives presuppose some kind of volition, possibly expressed by *will*.)

8. *Let's go early, shall we?* (*Shall* in questions ask what the addressee considers desirable; cf. Case study 2.5).

9. **Did you see that . . .* (Questions cannot be tagged!)

10. *I'm afraid to speak up, am I not?/aren't I?/ain't I?* (There is no actual contraction of *am* and most people avoid the awkward-sounding *am I not*; *aren't I* will do in its place, but many people feel it is inappropriate for the 1st person singular of the verb *be*; although *ain't* is a widely used GenE form, it is considered to be a sign of lack of education and is not StE.)

Rules 1–3 are hard enough for non-native speakers to apply even in clear cases. Native speakers themselves frequently have difficulties, as you have surely seen. For this reason it is no wonder that invariant forms such as *is it?* or *isn't it?* have been so widely adopted: they are formally parallel to the grammatical tags (auxiliary + personal pronoun + (usually reversed polarity) even though they do not observe the rules of grammatical concord of StE.

7.1 Generic names

Generic name	Reference	Used in
1. *Paddy*	Irishman (also *Mick, Mack*)	BrE, general
2. *Sandy*	Scotsman (also *Jock*)	general
3. *Pedro*	Mexican/Chicano	AmE
4. *Sambo*	African	AmE/BrE
5. *Bruce*	Australian	BrE
6. *Sheila*	young woman	AusE
7. *Jim Crow*	African American	AmE
8. *Mac*	any man	AmE
	Irishman	BrE
9. *Ikey*	Jewish man	AmE
10. *Jim*	a (non-white) man	SAE

7.2 Appropriate vocatives

Rank/office	Formal address	Informal alternative
1. Judge	*Your Honour/My Lord*	*Judge*
2. Bishop	*Your Excellency*	−
3. General	*General* + LN	*General*
4. Professor	*Professor*	*Prof*
5. Pope	*Your Holiness/Holy Father*	−
6. Ambassador	*Your Excellency*	*Ambassador*
7. Governor	*Your Honour*	*Governor*
8. King	*Your Majesty*	−
9. Mayor	*Your Honour*	*Mayor*
10. Medical doctor	*Dr* + LN	*Doc*
11. Abbess	*Mother Superior*	−

7.3 Region

Term	Evaluation	Used for
1. *Tassie*	neutral	a Tasmanian
2. *Groper*	slightly disparaging	a Western Australian
3. *Tar Heel*	neutral	a North Carolinian
4. *Paki*	disparaging	a Pakistani in GB
5. *Rooi Nek*	disparaging	a white S. African
6. *Brit*	slightly disparaging	an inhabitant of GB
7. *Kiwi*	neutral	a NZer
8. *Reb*	disparaging	a US Southerner
9. *Pakeha*	neutral	a NZ white
10. *Sooner*	neutral	an Oklahoman

7.4 Choosing appropriate forms of address

1. For a customer in a department store: *sir*; Amer. South: *honey*; elsewhere in America: *dear*; BrE: *love*

2. For a general in the army: *sir*

3. For your mother: *Mom/Mum*

4. For your boyfriend: all of above (multiple naming)

5. For your greying teacher: none of above (unless given permission)

6. For your colleague: *James* or *Jamey*; in BrE possibly: *Sutherland*

7. For the taxi cab driver: *Thank you, mack*; *Ta, guv* is BrE, would be used by the driver, and is older usage

8. For your grandmother: *Grandma*; *Granny* (slightly old-fashioned); *Nanna* (esp. AusE); *Ouma* (esp. SAE)

9. For someone female dear to you, a male: *kitten*; BAE possibly: *bitch*

10. For someone male dear to you, a female: *bear*

7.5 Choosing appropriate addressees

1. *Brother* is possible to

    (a) a male pal, if a 'Soul' brother (esp. African American)

    (b) a male sibling, but FN is usual

    (c) a member of a (Catholic) order

    (d) a member of your (Protestant) church

2. *Miss* is possible to

    (a) any female school teacher in BrE

    (b) a young female (polite form)

    (c) a spinster, but really only + LN; today *Ms* is often preferred

    (d) the winner of a beauty contest, but + geographical origin (e.g. *Miss Georgia*)

3. *Doc* is possible to

    (a) an egghead (may sound ironic)

    (b) an MD (informal)

    (c) a PhD (rare and slightly off)

    (d) any man (informal, friendly: *What's up, Doc?*)

4. *Mate* is possible to

    (a) an associate in AusE or BrE (friendly, jocular)

    (b) an officer on a ship: under no circumstances, not even the First Mate, who would be addressed as *sir*

    (c) a skilled worker: under no likely circumstances

    (d) a spouse: under no likely circumstances

5. *Operator* is possible to

    (a) a devious, possibly dishonest person: no, even though he or she may be a 'slick operator'

    (b) a person who runs a machine: no, even though a machine operator

    (c) a person who runs a telephone switchboard

    (d) a surgeon: no, even though an operator

6. *Yank(ee)* is possible to

    (a) an American if the speaker is not American

    (b) a New Englander (= the actual original Yankees)

    (c) a North American: not to Canadians

    (d) a Northerner if you're a Southerner (American South)

7.6 Interpreting power and solidarity

(a) mother ↔ child: *Mommie* ↔ *Honey*/FN

Mother gives FN (or diminutive); child gives relation name (or diminutive)

non-reciprocal, + solidarity, + power: quadrant II: factors: age, kinship

(b) teacher ↔ student: TLN / honorific ↔ FN

teacher gives FN; student gives TLN or respect form, *sir/ma'am/miss*

non-reciprocal + solidarity, + power: quadrant II: factors: age, hierarchy, gender (for the choice of honorific)

(c) boss ↔ employee: TLN ↔ TLN + *sir/ma'am*

reciprocal, − solidarity, + power: quadrant I: boss gives TLN; employee gives TLN, possibly respect form

sir/ma'am factors: hierarchical status (possibly age)

(d) colleague ↔ colleague: TLN ↔ TLN (mutual TLN)

reciprocal, - solidarity, - power: quadrant III: factor: hierarchical status + lack of acquaintance

(e) sports club member ↔ sports club member: FN ↔ FN (mutual FN)

reciprocal, + solidarity, − power: quadrant IV: factors: shared hierarchical status, age, gender, interests

(f) waitress ↔ customer: *waitress*/zero ↔ *sir/ma'am*/zero

waitress gives *sir/ma'am* (or zero); customer gives function name (*waitress*) or zero

non-reciprocal, − solidarity, + power: quadrant I: factors: hierarchical status, gender + lack of acquaintance

7.7 Fun naming

1. I'll be back, Jack.
2. Alright, Dwight.
3. No way, José.
4. That's the truth, Ruth.
5. Here's the money, Honey.
6. Like your tail, Nightingale.

7.8 Opening and closing formulas

1. business letter	c.	*Dear Madam, dear Sir*
2. fairy tale	i.	*Once upon a time*
3. formal speech	g.	*Ladies and Gentlemen!*
4. funny story	a.	*A funny thing happened to me on the way to . . .*
5. joke	d.	*Have you heard the one about . . .*
6. prayer	h.	*Oh Lord, . . .*
7. parliamentary session	f.	*The meeting is called to order.*
8. telephone call	e.	*Hello!*
9. West Indian folk tale	b.	*Cric . . . crac* (in the French Creole influenced territories: story-teller says *Cric*; audience replies *Crac* (Roberts 1988: 149))

7.9 Greetings and leave-taking formulas

GREETINGS

1. *Good morning!*	(formal)	5. *Hi*	(neutral)
2. *Morning!*	(neutral)	6. *Hi there!*	(informal; variant: *Hiya!*; a more informal variant: *Hey!*)
3. *Hello!*	(distant, to a superior)	7. *Howdy!*	(informal, rustic)
4. *Hello, X*	(polite)	8. *Kia ora*	(Maori) 'salutation'

INQUIRY ABOUT WELLBEING

1. *How's it going?*	(neutral)	4. *How are ya?*	(neutral)
2. *Are you rightly/bravely?*	(IrE)	5. *What's up?*	(informal)
3. *How's tricks?*	(informal)	6. *Is it well with you?*	(literary, East African English; response: *It is well*)

LEAVE-TAKING

1. *See you/ya (later).*	(very common, informal)	5. *So long.*	(AmE)
2. *Bye.*	(very common, neutral)	6. *Hooray!*	(NZE)
3. *Goodbye.*	(common, a bit formal)	7. *I will go ahead of you.*	(PhilE patterned on Tagalog)
4. *Cheerio.*	(BrE)		

GETTING RID OF SOMEONE

1. *Beat it.*	(impolite, to a stranger; also *Buzz off* + verbs with *off*; see below)
2. *Can you <u>please</u> go away.*	(polite)
3. *Fuck off.*	(vulgar, impolite; less vulgar *Screw off*)
4. *Get lost.*	(esp. to younger sibling)
5. *Get the hell outa here.*	(impolite, very emphatic)
6. *Git.*	(Southern US; mild because regional)
7. *Hamba.*	(SAE; abrupt; 'get you gone!' < Zulu)
8. *Piss off.*	(somewhat vulgar, BrE)
9. *Scram.*	(impolite; cf. Pig Latin *amscray*, Exercise 8.2)
10. *Vamoose.*	(out of date, AmE; from Spanish *vamos* 'Let's go')
11. *Voetsak.*	(SAE; to dogs, sometimes to people < Akrikaans *Voort seg ik!*)

7.10 Cultural misunderstanding

Jim:	*Would you like a cup of coffee?*
Mbunwe:	*Thank you.* (meaning 'No' but interpreted as 'Yes')
Jim:	*How do you like it?*
Mbunwe:	*Like what?*
Jim:	*How do you like your coffee?*
Mbunwe:	*Very well indeed.*

The basic difficulty lies in the use of *thank you*. Perhaps most usually in situations like this one it is taken to mean *yes*. If the intended answer is *no*, then the usual strategy is to prefix *thank you* with a *no* (*No, thank you*). Mbunwe is using *thank you* to say *no*, a strategy found in numerous languages. In German, for example, both *yes* and *no* might be indicated by *danke* ('thank you'); however, the former would be spoken with high falling intonation and the latter with low falling intonation. In Afrikaans a simple *thank you* means 'No, thank you.'

Jim's following question is, of course, puzzling to Mbunwe, i.e. it is a non sequitur. This forces Mbunwe to undertake a repair, in which he takes it to be a question about the degree of liking (*How <u>much</u> do you like your coffee?*). Of course, on the basis of an original *yes*, Jim was asking about manner: *Do you like it black or with milk and/or sugar?*

8.1 Stylistic evaluation

	Johnson	COBUILD			Johnson	COBUILD
1. doughty	ironic, burlesque	old-fashioned	6.	piss	[neutral]	informal, rude
2. expropriate	not in use	formal	7.	stout (n.)	a cant word	[neutral]
3. far-fetch(ed)	ludicrous	[neutral]	8.	tiny	a burlesque word	[neutral]
4. hussy	[neutral]	offensive	9.	topping (adj.)	a low word	informal, old-fashioned
5. lingo	a low cant word	informal	10.	width	a low word	[neutral]

8.2 Metaphor and metonymy

BLACK WORDS FOR BLACKS:

1. *booger, boogie* 'Uncle Tom' (see text) metaphor via contractions of *Booker T. Washington*, a black leader in the period 1890–1915, who conformed to white expectations; or a Southern variant of bogey 'Devil'

2. *charcoal* 'black like . . . '; metaphor

3. *cloud* 'dark as associated with clouds'; metonymic

4. *crow* 'black like a . . . '; metaphor

5. *Cuffee* < African word for Friday, used as a day-name for blacks born on a Friday; hence metonymic

6. *ink* 'black like . . . '; metaphor

7. *jig, jigaboo, zigaboo,* 'a Negro (esp. in connection with music)'; probably metonymic from the jig (dance) which Negroes were traditionally supposed to have been good at

8. *Russian* 'a Southern black, one who came "rushin" up north'; play on words

9. *suede* 'nappy surface, i.e. one with short fuzzy fiber ends'; hence metonymic

10. *shine* 'reflected light on a "shiney" surface'; metonymic

11. *spade* 'black as a . . . '; metaphor

12. *spagingy-spagade* 'spade'; Hog Latin: first consonant(s) (<sp-> plus the element <aginy> plus reduplication of the <sp> with the element <agade>; secret language

BLACK WORDS FOR WHITES:

1. *fay, ofay* 'foe, white person'; Pig Latin; first consonant is moved to the end; <-ay> is added; secret language.

2. *fagingy-fagade* 'foe'; Hog Latin for *fay* (see *spagingy-spagade*); secret language

3. *Mister Charlie* 'a white man'; one name (TFN!) for all white men; metonymy

4. *pink, pinktail* 'white person'; from the skin colour; metonymy

8.3 Euphemisms for 'toilet' or 'toilet room'

1. *can*	AmE, slang, slightly vulgar
2. *cloakroom*	BrE, euphemistic (also *cloaks*)
3. *comfort station*	AmE, AusE, public use
4. *convenience*	BrE, AusE, public use (also *public ~*)
5. *gents*	BrE, colloq. (< *gentlemen's room* by shortening)
6. *the geography*	general, colloq. 'the location in a private house of the "facilities"')
7. *head*	nautical (< originally from position at the head or bow of a ship)
8. *jerry*	BrE, AusE slang for *chamber pot*
9. *john*	AmE, colloq. or slang
10. *ladies' (room)*	BrE, AusE (AmE), public use
11. *latrine*	military; *latrine* is of restricted use in GenE
12. *lavatory*	general, public use
13. *loo*	BrE, AusE, colloq. (not to be confused with *loo-blowing* (IndE) from the Hindi word for a warm, dry, dusty wind in northern India)
14. *powder room*	general, polite usage, for women
15. *restroom*	esp. AmE, public use
16. *thunderbox*	esp. AusE, colloq.
17. *washroom*	AmE, public use
18. *WC*	esp. BrE, AusE, colloq., slightly old-fashioned; abbrev. (< *water closet*); also: *closet* arch. 'outhouse'(< *private closet, privy*)

8.4 Rhyming slang

1. *babbling brook*	crook	2. *blood blister*	sister
3. *bottle and stopper*	policeman (copper)	4. *ducks and geese*	police
5. *holy friar*	liar	6. *John Hops*	policemen (cops)
7. *mutton shanks*	Yanks	8. *pot and pan*	man (father, husband)
9. *septic tanks*	Yanks	10. *twist and twirl*	girl

8.5 Spanish words in English

Term	Gloss	Source	Spanish Meaning
1. *bronco*	mustang, esp. unbroken	shortening of *potro bronco*	wild foal
2. *buckaroo*	cowboy	vaquero	cowboy
3. *calaboose*	jail, prison	calabozo	dungeon
4. *chaps*	leather leggings	chaparajos	covering
5. *cinch*	saddle girth	cincha	cinch
6. *corral*	enclosure for horses, cattle	corral	enclosed area
7. *hoosegow*	jail	juzgado	court
8. *lariat*	noosed rope to catch cows, etc.	la reata	the rope
9. *lasso*	lariat	lazo	noose
10. *mustang*	(type of) horse	mestengo	stray horse
11. *palomino*	golden horse with white-tail and mane	palomino	resembling a dove
12. *pinto*	mottled horse	pinta	spot
13. *ranch*	cattle, sheep farm	rancho	mess room
14. *rodeo*	show of cowboy skills	rodeo	cattle ring
15. *sombrero*	broad-rimmed straw hat	sombrero	(sun) hat
16. *stampede*	frenzied flight of frightened herd	estampida	stamp (past participle)
17. *ten-gallon hat*	cowboy hat	galón	braid (around hat rim)
18. *wrangler*	cowboy in charge of the horses	calballerango	groom, stable boy

8.6 English words in Spanish

1. *la ley*	the law, 'police'	semantic extension
2. *lechuga*	lettuce, 'money'	semantic extension (metaphor)
3. *jonrón*	'home run'	borrowing + phonological adaption
4. *fullar*	'fool around'	borrowing + shortening
5. *daime*	'dime'	borrowing
6. *bombo*	'a drunk'	borrowing + adaption from *to be bombed*
7. *shopear*	'to shop'	borrowing
8. *mopear*	'to mop up'	borrowing + shortening
9. *embarrassar*	'embarrass' ≠ *embarazar*	
	'to become pregnant'	semantic shift
10. *croseando la calle*	'crossing the street'	semantic extension (Hendrickson 1985: 208–11)

8.7 Word formation in Internet English

	Meaning	Process
1. *bit*	**b**inary dig**it**	blend; cf. also *byte*, of uncertain origin, which combines with {kilo-, mega-, giga-}
2. *braino*	a *brain fart*, the result of a *glitch* or a *thinko*, an unintentional error in thinking	shortening + derogatory suffix; cf. *typo* (Flexner and Soukhanov 1997: 78)
3. *chat room*	virtual area for communication among people sharing an affinity (cf. *chat group*), or *SIG* (special interest group)	compound
4. *database*	collection of information by computer	compound
5. *cursor*	movable, blinking indication on a screen of where input activity is possible	semantic broadening from 'sliding object on a scale, as on a slide rule'
6. *floppy disk*	portable computer disk, originally flexible	institutionalisation (cf. *hard disk*)
7. *freeware*	software available free	one of many combining forms with {-ware}; cf. *hardware*, *software*, *shareware*, *brochureware*, *vaporware* ('announced but never shows'), *nagware* ('reminder to pay for shareware taken')
8. *hacker*	expert programmer	derivation from *haque* 'elegant hacking'; cf. related words from field of computers: *geek* ('nerd'), *wannabe* (aspires to hacker lifestyle), *internauts*, *net potatoes*, *robot*, *bot*, *knowbot*
9. *HTML*	hypertext mark-up language	abbreviation
10. *Infobahn*	Information superhighway	blend + borrowing (from German; cf. *Autobahn*)
11. *Internet*	global network linking computers	shortening + compound of **Inter**national **Net**work
12. *log in/out*	gain access to a computer system, to terminate access	phrasal verb formation (also: *log on/off*)
13. *mouse*	device to point at and select items on a screen via analogous movement	metaphor (based on appearance whereby the wire is like a tail)
14. *modem*	**mod**ulator-**dem**odulator	blend
15. *navigate*	to browse or surf through the Internet	metaphor

16.	*RAM,*	Random Access Memory,	acronyms
	ROM	Read Only Memory	
17.	*snail mail*	conventional (= slow) mail	word creation by rhyme with *e-mail*, which itself is an abbreviation of *electronic mail*
18.	*upload*	to transfer data to network, bulletin board or the like	derivation (prefixation); cf. the reverse, *download*
19.	*virtual reality*	computer simulation of the 'real' world	semantic shift (broadening from meaning 'implicit')
20.	www/ WWW	World Wide Web	abbreviation

8.8 Abbreviations in Internet English

1. *AFAIK*: As far as I know	2. *AFK*: Away from keyboard
3. *BRB*: Be right back	4. *BTW*: By the way
5. *FAQ*: Frequently asked questions	6. *FWIW*: For what it's worth
7. *GIGO*: Garbage in, garbage out	8. *IMHO*: In my humble opinion
9. *IMNSHO*: In my not-so humble opinion	10. *IRL*: In real life
11. *IYKWIM*: If you know what I mean	12. *LOL*: Laughing out loud
13. *OTOH*: On the other hand	14. *PMFJI*: Pardon me for jumping in
15. *ROTFL(L)*: Rolling on the floor laughing (loudly)	16. *RTFM*: Read the fucking manual
17. *TTFN*: Ta ta for now	18. *WAG*: wild-assed guess

8.9 Emoticons

1.	:-/	sceptical	5.	B-)	horn-rimmed glasses	9.	:-)}	wearer of beard
2.	:-x	my lips are sealed	6.	8:-)	little girl	10.	{:-)	wearer of toupee
3.	:-{)	wearer of moustache	7.	:-o	shocked	11.	:-)))	double chin
4.	(:-)	bald-headed	8.	:-)X	wearer of bow tie	12.	:-)8	big girl

Comments on the Projects

We have not included comments on all the projects, but have rather selected from among them in order to give you an idea of some of the problems which can crop up and some of the kinds of results which can be found.

2.1 Toponyms

Remember

- the names of particular schools often carry associations which are due to the social or ethnic type of students who stereotypically attends them ('*an Eton type*'; '*a Yalie*');
- historical events or public institutions may be connected with others;
- in many areas the name of the local or regional mental hospital is frequently used as a derogatory *epithet* for disliked people or undesirable features of people.

2.2 Non-British systems of education

Here are likely answers in an American and an Australian context.

Terms	USA	Australia
1. *A-levels*	high school diploma	certificate II
went up	went (to), attended	went up
read	studied .	studied
2. *tutorials*	small seminar	individual or small-group teaching
don	prof	head, fellow, tutor
quadrangle	quad	court, quadrangle
3. *went down*	left, went home	left
vac	vacation	vacation, vac
4. *Greats*	(senior year) finals	final examinations
first	4.0 average	first-class (degree)
5. *DPhil.*	PhD, doctor's degree	DPhil., PhD, doctoral degree
prize fellow	graduate assistant	postgraduate

2.3 The negation of *Have*

Usage in BrE seems to have changed in the last generation or so. Direct negation of lexical *have* may have been considerably more frequent earlier in the last century. For this reason a contrastive survey of present-day and earlier BrE might be more rewarding.

3.1 Prototypical meaning

The author (from the American South) answers: yellow (=cheddar) cheese, chicken, green beans, peaches, ice tea.

3.3 The eating day

Tip: *The Australian Phrasebook*, 2nd edn. (Lonely Planet, 1998) features a page on the Australian eating day.

4.1 Results of the Vocabulary of World English survey

In many cases there is a great deal of agreement in the area of taboo expressions. Here are the results of answers from 19 Americans and 17 Australians. Responses given by only a very small number of informants (usually by only one or two) have not been listed unless they appear elsewhere; e.g. *wee* was given as the taboo word for urine by only one American, but it appears below because the same word is a commonly accepted Australian euphemism.

Taboo	Amer.	Aust.	Euphemism	Amer.	Aust.
shit	18	14	*poo/poop/poo-poo*	17	13
piss	16	15	*pee/pee-pee*	17	3
wee	1	–	*wee*	–	13
fart	17	16	*gas*	12	3
gas	1	–	*wind*	–	8
cock	7	8	*peter*	1	–
dick	12	12	*dick*	2	4
willie	–	1	*willie*	–	3
penis	1	1	*penis*	4	9
			peepee	4	–
cunt	8	11	*vagina*	–	10
pussy	9	6	*poopoo*	1	–
fanny	–	2	*pussy*	–	1
vagina	–	1			
tits	15	16	*tits*	–	2
boobs	2	2	*boobs/boobies*	10	8
breasts	–	1	*breasts*	4	8

Among other things these findings show that, despite a great amount of agreement, there is a certain degree of variation in the judgement of how appropriate certain expressions are. This is evident from the fact that a number of expressions show up as both taboos (for some speakers) and euphemisms (for others).

Despite the widespread agreement we can observe a clear regional split in the euphemisms for urine (AmE favors *pee(pee)*; AusE favours *wee(wee)*) and for intestinal gas (AmE *gas*; AusE *wind*).

Among the euphemistic terms reduplication (doubling), as in *poopoo*, *peepee*, and *weewee*, is notable, as it is a feature of baby talk and indicates that these forms are probably used when talking to children. Whether *boobies* belongs here is more doubtful. The use of generic male names for *penis* is perhaps similar and is remarkable in its diversity.

In addition, a couple of items show such diversity or, indeed, lack of answers that we can conclude that there is no conventionalized euphemism. This is the case with *penis*, where most answers were the neutral term itself. The situation is similar for *vagina*, where the degree of tabooization is so strong that, once again, there is no common euphemism, but only the taboo words themselves and the neutral term.

Finally, we can also observe that the existence of taboos has apparently led to a blurring of categories: the words *poopoo*, *peepee*, and *weewee* are used as euphemisms both for excrement and, by a few speakers, for body parts.

What expressions are used to make exclamations of disgust, despair, etc.?

There are two major sets of expressions: religiously oriented ones and bodily parts/functions:

Taboo	Amer.	Aust.	Euphemism	Amer.	Aust.
The deity					
Christ	–	5	*Christ*	–	1
Jesus Christ	1	4	*jeez/Geez*	–	2
(oh)(my) God	2	5	*(my) God*	–	2
			gosh (darn)	2	–
Damnation					
damn (it)	6	4	*damn*	–	3
goddamn	6	–	*darn*	7	4
(oh) hell	6	3	*doggone (it)*	2	–
(blazing/bloody/fucking) hell	2	4	*hell*	3	2
go to hell	3	–	*heck*	3	–
Bodily part/function					
(oh/go) fuck (you)	8	10	*fudge*	1	–-
mother fucker	1	–	*fuzzy duck*	1	–
			f-you	1	–
			freekin'	1	–
oh shit/shithead	3	1	*oh shit*	–	1
			shoot	2	–
			shucks	1	–

5.2 Dictionary usage labels

The *Random House Wester's College Dictionary*, with a strong orientation towards AmE, has the following:

- REGION (examples): *Australian, Brit*[ish], *Canadian; Chiefly New England, South Midland US*. What is unlabelled is 'in general use in the US'.
- STYLE (complete list): *Baby Talk, Disparaging, Eye Dialect, Facetious, Informal, Literary, Pron*[unciation], *Spelling, Offensive, Slang, Vulgar*
- FIELD (examples): *Baseball, Chem*[istry], *Law, Math*[ematics], *Music, Zool*[ogy]
- CURRENCY: *Archaic, Obs*[olete], *Older Use, Older Slang*
- OTHER: *Dial*[ect] ('with a somewhat rural flavour'); *Chem*[ical] *Symbol* (e.g. *Au* for gold); *AmerSp* (American Spanish), *French, Latin* for borrowings from other languages.

7.6 Greeting and leave-taking

Here are sample answers collected from 20 American informants. Note that there are not many distinctions between a good friend and a superior, but the use of a vocative form is more likely with a superior (in 5 out of 25 answers given). With a good friend the marker of informality *there* is added three times and a question about how the addressee is occurs five out of 25 times.

Greeting a good friend

How are you?	1	*Hi*	7	*Hi yah*	1
Hi, how are you?	2	*Hey*	3	*Hey there!*	1
Hi there	2	*How's it going?*	1	*Howdy!*	1
What's up?	3	*Hey, How are you*	1	*Good morning*	1
Morning	1				

Greeting a superior

Good morning/afternoon +		*Hello Ms/Mr/Dr +* LN	2	*Hey, Dr+* LN	1
Dr/Mr/Mrs + LN	2	*Hi*	5	*Hi, how are you?*	1
Good morning/afternoon/	4	*morning!*	1	*Hello*	6
evening	4	*How's it going?*	1	*Hi! How are you?*	1
What's happening?	1				

In leave-taking the slightly more formal *Goodbye* predominates over the more informal *Bye* for a superior as compared to a good friend. *See you later* (and its variants) are clearly the favoured informal forms.

Taking leave from a good friend		Taking leave from a superior	
See you/ya later	9	*Goodbye*	10
Bye	8	*Bye*	5
Goodbye	3	*Good night* (at end of work day)	2
See ya	2	*See you/ya tomorrow/afterwhile*	2
Later!	1	*See you later!*	1
Take care	1	*See yah*	1
		Have a good day	1
		Take care	1

7.8 Acknowledging compliments

Herbert found that 'the best predictor of this response type [appreciation] is the male sex of the complimenter, with almost one-half (48.76%) of male compliments receiving this textbook response [*thank you*] as opposed to 13 percent of compliments by females' (1990: 212).

Typical male responses were nos. 8 and 11; but they avoided 6 (to other males).

8.3 Expressions of approval and disapproval

What colloquial expression(s) might you use to indicate that you find something to be:

(a) very good (e.g. Super! Groovy!)? Twenty American informants gave the following responses:

awesome	2	*cool*	4	*excellent*	3
fantastic	1	*great*	8	*outa sight*	1
super(b)	4	*terrific*	1	*wonderful*	2

(b) very bad (e.g. *That's the pits*)?

awful	1	*(very) bad*	2	*bummer*	1
damn	1	*Darn!*	1	*horrible*	3
lousy	1	*shifty*	1	*shit*	1 ('depending on who's around')
Shoot!	1	*That stinks*	3	*it/that sucks*	4
terrible	4				

8.4 English in French

In one study (Baumes 2000) job offers in a specialized weekly paper, *Carrières, Emplois* (the leader in its field in France), were examined. The sample base (492 ads, 626 job offers) is statistically sound. Each page contains an average of five to six ads. The positions are mostly for middle and upper management positions.

Five areas of employment were selected. In a total of 80 pages 60 English words (types) were found, which with their multiple use represent 196 'hits' (tokens). On an overall basis there are 0.68 English types and 2.23 tokens per page of ads.

A reader will discover a higher penetration of English in the hi-tech/computer job offers (1.5 'single' words per page) than, for instance, in job offers in production.

Eight words (types) represent over two-thirds of the English words used. French-speakers could with little effort find – most of the time – elegant substitutes for direct English loans such as *leader, manager, e-commerce* (= 50 per cent of the multiple hits!) and eliminate some of the more obvious loans.

The question can be asked whether the French are adhering to the legislation regarding the exclusion of foreign expressions in the French language. Legal requirements have been introduced regarding publications. The job advertisements investigated suggest that the French authorities apply leniency in the interpretation of the law and accept deviations from the rule. Most of the loans are fairly straightforward borrowings of English words and are commonly used by businessmen and women. They are not likely to hurt French national feelings, as a great number of the ads are placed by international employers. Furthermore, in a Europe which is growing together any attempt to enforce these legal requirements would be unpopular.

Looking at some of the ads and words, it seems that observation of the legal requirements is not always taken seriously. On a humorous note, it looks as if some advertisers are taking advantage of the obligation to put an asterisk on foreign-language expressions. Sometimes the translation of the foreign expression has some added personal flair or wit to it, thus giving very 'free' interpretations of the original text (a sort of phenomenon creation). This is the upside to an otherwise stern regulation.

Dictionaries, Thesauruses and Encyclopedias

Below is a selection of mainly modern works. They are cited in the text by title. Other reference works can be found in the main Bibliography.

Acronymania: A Celebratory Roundup of Nomenclature Yielding Mischief: Abbreviations, Neologisms, Initialisms, Acronyms! (1993), by D. Hauptman. New York: Dell.

Africanisms in Afro-American Language Varieties (1993), ed. S. Mufwene. Athens, GA: UGAP.

American Heritage College Dictionary, 3rd edn (1993), ed. R.B. Costello. Boston: Houghton Mifflin (+CD-ROM).

American Place-Names: A Concise and Selective Dictionary for the Continental United States of America. (1970), by G.R. Stewart. New York: OUP.

And Now for Something Completely Different: Dictionary of Allusions in British English (1977), by R. Sampson and C. Smith. Munich: Hueber.

Australian Concise Oxford Dictionary (1987), ed. G.W. Turner. Melbourne: OUP.

Australian National Dictionary: A Dictionary of Australianisms in Historical Perspective (1988), ed. W.S. Ramson. Melbourne: OUP.

Barnhart Dictionary of Etymology, The (1995), ed. R.K. Barnhart. New York: HarperCollins.

BBI Dictionary of English Word Combinations, 2nd edn (1997), by M. Benson and R. Ilson. Amsterdam: Benjamins.

Britain: An Official Handbook. (yearly edns). London: HMSO.

British English for American Readers: A Dictionary of the Language, Customs, and Places of British Life and Literature (1992), by D. Grote. Westport, CT: Greenwood.

Cambridge International Dictionary of English (1995), ed. P. Procter. Cambridge: CUP.

Cambridge International Dictionary of Phrasal Verbs (1997), ed. E. Walter. Cambridge: CUP.

Cassell Dictionary of Clichés, The (1998), ed. N. Rees. London: Cassell.

Chambers Dictionary, The (1995), ed. C. Schwarz. Gütersloh: Bertelmann.

Collins COBUILD English Dictionary, 2nd edn (1995), ed. J. Sinclair. London: HarperCollins.

Collins English Dictionary, 4th edn (1998), ed. M. Makins. Glasgow: HarperCollins.

Compact Scottish National Dictionary (1986), ed. W. Grant and D.D. Murison. 2 vols. Aberdeen: Aberdeen UP.

Concise Oxford Dictionary of Current English, The, 8th and 10th edns (1990, 1999), ed. R.E. Allen. Oxford: OUP. (+CD-ROM).

Concise Scots Dictionary (1985), ed. M. Robinson. Aberdeen: Aberdeen UP.

Concise Ulster Dictionary (1996), ed. E.I. Macafee. Oxford: OUP.
>http://www.dictionary.com/<

Dictionary of Africanisms, A (1982), by G.M. Dalgish. Westport, CT: Greenwood Press.

Dictionary of Americanisms on Historical Principles, A (1951), ed. M.M. Mathews., 4 vols. Chicago: University of Chicago Press.

Dictionary of American English on Historical Principles (1936, 1944), ed. W.A. Craigie and J.R. Hulbert. 4 vols. London: OUP.

Dictionary of American Regional English (1985, 1991, 1996), ed. F. Cassidy, Vols. i-iii (up to O). Cambridge, MA; Belknap Press of Harvard UP.

Dictionary of Australian Colloquialisms, A, 4th edn (1996), ed. G.A. Wilkes. Oxford: OUP.

Dictionary of Bahamian English (1982), ed. J.A. Holm with W.A. Shilling. Cold Spring, NY: Lexik House.

Dictionary of Canadianisms on Historical Principles (1991), ed. W.S. Avis. Toronto: Gage.

Dictionary of Caribbean English Usage (1996), ed. R. Allsopp, with French and Spanish supplement by J. Allsopp. Oxford: OUP.

Dictionary of Confusing Words and Meanings (1985), by A. Room. London: Routledge & Kegan Paul.

Dictionary of Jamaican English, 2nd edn (1980), ed. F.G. Cassidy and R. LePage. Cambridge: CUP.

Dictionary of Prince Edward Island English (1988), ed. T.K. Pratt. Toronto: Toronto UP.

Dictionary of South African English, 4th edn (1991), ed. J. Branford. Oxford: OUP.

Dictionary of South African English on Historical Principles (1996), ed. P. Silva. Oxford: OUP.

Encarta World English Dictionary (1999), ed. A. Soukhanov. New York: St. Martin's Press. (+CD-ROM).

Euphemisms: Over 3,000 Ways to Avoid Being Rude or Giving Offence (1993), by J. Ayto. London: Bloomsbury.

Guinness Book of British Place Names, The (1993), by F. McDonald and J. Cresswell. Enfield, UK: Guinness.

Heinemann New Zealand Dictionary, 2nd edn (1989), ed. H.W. Orsman. Auckland: Heinemann.

Idioms: Their Meanings and Origins (1996), by G. Jarvie. London: Bloomsbury.

Krio-English Dictionary (1980), by C.N. Fyle and E.D. Jones. Oxford: Oxford UP and Sierra Leone: Sierra Leone UP.

Longman Dictionary of American English, 2nd edn (1997), ed. D. Summers and A. Gadsby. White Plains, NY: Addison Wesley Longman.

Longman Dictionary of Contemporary English, 3rd edn (1995), ed. D. Summers. Harlow: Longman.

Longman Dictionary of English Language and Culture, 2nd edn (1998), ed. D. Summers. Harlow: Addison Wesley Longman.

Longman Dictionary of the English Language, 2nd edn (1991) [no editor]. Harlow: Longman.

Longman Lexicon of Contemporary English (1981), by T. McArthur. Harlow: Longman.

Longman Pronunciation Dictionary, 2nd edn (2000), by J.C. Wells. Harlow: Longman.

Macquarie Dictionary (1981), ed. A. Delbridge. St Leonards, NSW: Macquarie University.

Merriam-Webster's Collegiate Dictionary, 10th edn (1993), ed. F.C. Mish. Springfield, MA: Merriam-Webster.

New Zealand Dictionary, The (1995), ed. E. Orsman and H.W. Orsman. Auckland: New House Publishers.

NCT's American English Learner's Dictionary: The Essential Vocabulary of American Language and Culture (1998), ed. R.A. Spears. Lincolnwood, IL: NTC.

NTC's Dictionary of Quotations (1994), compiled by R. Hyman. Lincolnwood, IL: NTC.

Orkney Wordbook: A Dictionary of the Dialect of Orkney (1995), by G. Lamb. Birsay, UK: Byrgisey.

Oxford Advanced Learner's Dictionary of Current English, 4th and 6th edns (1989, 2000), ed. A.P. Cowie and J. Crowther. Oxford: OUP. (+ CD-ROM).

Oxford Dictionary of Foreign Words and Phrases (1997), ed. J. Speake. Oxford: OUP.

Oxford Dictionary of New Words, The, 2nd edn (1998), by E. Knowles with J. Elliott. Oxford: OUP.

Oxford English Dictionary, The (1884–1928), ed. J.A.H. Murray, H. Bradley, W. Craigie, C.T. Onions *et al.* 12 vols. Oxford: Clarendon Press. (+ supplements).

Oxford English Dictionary, The, 2nd edn (1988), ed. J.A. Simpson and E.S.C. Weiner. 20 vols. Oxford: OUP (+ CD-ROM).

Oxford Guide to English Grammar (1994), by J. Eastwood. Oxford: OUP.

Oxford Spelling Dictionary, The (1995), ed. M. Waite. Oxford: OUP.

Random House Dictionary of the English Language, The, 2nd unabridged edn (1987), ed. S.B. Flexner. New York: Random House.

Random House Dictionary of Popular Proverbs and Sayings (2000), by G.Y. Titelman. New York: Random House.

Random House Webster's College Dictionary, 2nd edn (1999), ed. R.B. Costello. New York: Random House. (+ CD-ROM),

Roget's Thesaurus of English Words and Phrases (1966 [1852]), ed. R.A. Dutch. Harmondsworth: Penguin.

Shetland Dictionary, The, 2nd edn (1993), by J.J. Graham. Lerwick: Shetland Times.

Shorter Oxford English Dictionary on Historical Principles, 3rd rev. edn (1978), ed. G.W.S. Friedrichsen, C.T. Onions *et al.* 2 vols. Oxford: Clarendon Press.

Slang: The Authoritative Topic-by-Topic Dictionary of American Lingoes from All Walks of Life, 2nd edn (1998), by P. Dickson. New York: Pocket Books.

Slang Thesaurus, The (1986), by Jonathon Green. Harmondsworth: Penguin.

Tassie Terms: A Glossary of Tasmanian Words (1995), compiled by M. Brooks and J. Ritchie. Melbourne: OUP.

Times-Chambers Essential English Dictionary, 2nd edn (1997), ed. E. Higgleton, V.B.Y. Ooi *et al.* Singapore: Times Publishing Group.

21st Century Manual of Style (1993), ed. Princeton Language Institute and B.A. Kirfen. Princeton, NJ: Laurel.

Webster's New World College Dictionary, 3rd edn (1997), ed. V. Neufeldt. New York: Simon & Schuster.

Webster's New World Dictionary of American English, 3rd college edn (1988) ed. V. Neufeldt and D.B. Guralnik. New York: Webster's New World.

Webster's New World Dictionary of Media and Communications (1996), ed. R. Weiner. New York: Macmillan.

Webster's Third International Dictionary of the English Language (1971), ed. P.B. Gove *et al.* Springfield, MA: Merriam Webster.

Words Apart: A Dictionary of Northern Ireland English (1990), by L. Todd. Gerrards Cross, UK: Smythe.

Words from the West: A Glossary of Western Australian Terms (1994), compiled by M. Brooks and J. Ritchie. Melbourne: OUP.

Bibliography

Titles which offer a useful introduction to or overview of particular themes are marked with an initial asterisk. Only a minimum of dictionaries have been included; see Chapter 1, Tables 1.1–1.5 for further titles and the preceding list.

Abdulaziz, M.H. (1972) 'Triglossia and Swahili–English Bilingualism in Tanzania'. *Language in Society* 1, 197–213.

—— (1988) '150. A Sociolinguistic Profile of East Africa'. In U. Ammon, N. Dittmar, and K.J. Mattheier (eds), *Sociolinguistics Soziolinguistik*. Berlin: de Gruyter, 1347–53.

—— (1991) 'East Africa (Tanzania and Kenya)'. In J. Cheshire (ed.), *English Around the World: Sociolinguistic Perspectives*. Cambridge: CUP, 391–401.

Adekunle, M.A. (1972) 'Sociolinguistic Problems in English Language Instruction in Nigeria'. In D.M. Smith and R. Shuy (eds), *Sociolinguistics in Cross-Cultural Analysis*. Washington, DC: Georgetown UP, 83–101.

Adetugbo, A. (1979a) 'Appropriateness and Nigerian English'. In E. Ubahakwe (ed.), *Varieties and Functions of English in Nigeria: Selections from the Proceedings of the Ninth Annual Conference of the Nigerian Studies Association*. Ibadan: African Universities Press, 137–66.

—— (1979b) 'Nigerian English and Communicative Competence'. In E. Ubahakwe (ed.), *Varieties and Functions of English in Nigeria: Selections from the Proceedings of the Ninth Annual Conference of the Nigerian Studies Association*. Ibadan: African Universities Press, 167–83.

Agheyisi, R.N. (1988) 'The Standardization of Nigerian Pidgin English'. *English World-Wide* 9, 227–41.

Akere, F. (1982) 'Sociocultural Constraints and the Emergence of a Standard Nigerian English'. In J. Pride (ed.), *New Englishes*. Rowley, MA: Newbury House, 85–99.

*Akmajian, A., R.A. Demers, A.K. Farmer and R.M. Harnish (1990) 'Semantics: The Study of Meaning and Denotation'. Ch. 6 in *Linguistics: An Introduction to Language and Communication*. 3rd edn. Cambridge, MA: MIT Press, 193–228.

Algeo, J. (1988) 'The Tag Question in British English: It's Different, I'n't?' *English World-Wide* 9, 171–91.

—— (1989) 'British–American Lexical Differences: A Typology of Interdialectal Variation'. In O. García and R. Otheguy (eds), *English across Cultures, Cultures across English: A Reader in Cross-Cultural Communication*. Berlin: Mouton de Gruyter, 219–41.

Allsopp, R. (1996) *Dictionary of Caribbean English Usage*. With a French and Spanish supplement by J. Allsopp. Oxford: OUP.

Angelo, D. *et al.* (1998) *Australian Phrasebook*, 2nd edn. Hawthorn, Vic.: Lonely Planet.

Angogo, R. and I. Hancock. (1980) 'English in Africa: Emerging Standards or Diverging Regionalisms'. *English World-Wide* 1, 67–96.

Augustin, J. (1982) 'Regional Standards of English in Peninsular Malaysia'. In J. Pride (ed.), *New Englishes*. Rowley, MA: Newbury House, 249–58.

Baker, S.J. (1966) *The Australian Language*. 2nd edn. Sydney: Currawong.

Bamgbose, A. (1983) 'Standard Nigerian English: Issues of Identification'. In B.B. Kachru (ed.), *The Other Tongue: English Across Cultures*. Oxford: Pergamon, 99–111.

Barltrop, R. and J. Wolveridge (1980) *The Muvver Tongue*. London: Journeyman.

Barry, M.V. (1984) 'The English Language in Ireland' In R.W. Bailey and M. Görlach (eds), *English as a World Language*. Cambridge: CUP, 84–133.

Barton, H.D. (1980) 'Language Use Among Ilala Residents'. In E.C. Polomé and C.P. Hill (eds), *Language in Tanzania*. Oxford: OUP, 176–205.

Baudet, M.M. (1981) 'Identifying the African Grammatical Base of the Caribbean Creoles: A Typological Approach'. In A. Highfield and A.Valdman (eds), *Historicity and Variation in Creole Studies*. Ann Arbor, MI: Karoma, 104–17.

*Bauer, L. (1983) *English Word-Formation*. Cambridge: CUP.

—— (1994) 'English in New Zealand'. In R. Burchfield (ed.), *The Cambridge History of the English Language*, vol. V: *English in Britain and Overseas: Origins and Development*. Cambridge: CUP, 382–429.

*Baugh, A.C. and T. Cable (1993) *A History of the English Language*. 4th edn. London: Routledge.

Baumes, A. (2000) 'English in French'. Bielefeld University seminar paper.

Baumgardner, R.J. (1998) 'Word-Formation in Pakistani English'. *English World-Wide* 19, 205–46.

—— and A.E.H. Kennedy (1994) 'Measure for Measure: Terms of Measurement in Pakistani English'. *English World-Wide* 15, 173–93.

Beier, R. (1980) *Englische Fachsprache*. Stuttgart: Kohlhammer.

Benson, M., E. Benson and R. Ilson (1986) *Lexicographic Description of English*. Amsterdam: Benjamins.

—— (1997) *The BBI Dictionary of English Word Combinations*. 2nd edn. Amsterdam: Benjamins.

Bennett, T.J.A. (1988) *Aspects of English Colour Collocations and Idioms*. Heidelberg: Carl Winter.

Berlin, B. and P. Kay (1969) *Basic Color Terms*. Berkeley: University of California Press.

Blair, D. (1981) 'Words and the World'. In A. Delbridge (ed.), *The Macquarie Dictionary*. St Leonards, NSW: Macquarie Library, 34–6.

Bodine, A. (1975) 'Androcentrism in Prescriptive Grammar: Singular "They", Sex-Indefinite "He or She"'. *Language in Society* 4, 129–46.

Bokamba, E.G. (1983) 'The Africanization of English'. In B.B. Kachru (ed.), *The Other Tongue*. Oxford: Pergamon, 77–98.

—— (1991) 'West Africa'. In J. Cheshire (ed.), *English Around the World: Sociolinguistic Perspectives*. Cambridge: CUP, 493–508.

Branford, J. (1991) *A Dictionary of South African English*. 4th edn. Oxford: OUP.

Branford, W. (1994) 'English in South Africa'. In R. Burchfield (ed.), *The Cambridge History of the English Language*, vol. V: *English in Britain and Overseas: Origins and Development*. Cambridge: CUP, 430–96.

Brann, C.M.B. (1988) '159. West Africa'. In U. Ammon, N. Dittmar and K.J. Mattheier (eds), *Sociolinguistics Soziolinguistik*. Berlin: de Gruyter, 1414–29.

Brekke, M. (1989) 'The Bergen English for Science and Technology (BEST) Corpus: A Pilot Study'. In C. Laurén and M. Nordman (eds), *Special Language*. Clevedon, Avon: Multilingual Matters, 253–64.

Britain: An Official Handbook (annually) London: HMSO.

Brosnahan, L.F. (1963) 'Some Historical Cases of Language Imposition'. In J. Spencer (ed.), *Language in Africa*. Cambridge: CUP, 7–24.

Brown, L. and K. Henke (1983). 'Problems of English Usage: Number'. *Bielefelder Beiträge zur Sprachlehrforschung* 12, 1–135.

*Brown, P. and S.C. Levinson (1987) *Politeness: Some Universals in Language Usage*. Cambridge: CUP.

Brown, R. and M. Ford (1964) 'Address in American English'. In D. Hymes (ed.), *Language in Culture and Society*. New York: Harper & Row, 234–44.

—— and A. Gilman (1972) 'The Pronouns of Power and Solidarity'. In P.P. Giglioli (ed.), *Language and Social Context*. Harmondsworth: Penguin, 252–82.

Bruthiaux, P. (1996) *The Discourse of Classified Advertising: Exploring the Nature of Linguistic Simplicity*. Oxford: OUP.

Buckle, R. (ed.) (1978) *U and Non-U Revisited*. London: Debrett.

*Burchfield, R. (ed.) (1994) *The Cambridge History of the English Language*, vol. V: *English in Britain and Overseas: Origins and Development*. Cambridge: CUP.

Burling, R. (1973) *English in Black and White*. New York: Holt, Rinehart & Winston.

Burridge, K. and J. Mulder (1998) *English in Australia and New Zealand: An Introduction to Its History, Structure, and Use*. Melbourne: OUP.

Cannon, G. (1987) *Historical Change and English Word-Formation*. New York: Lang.

Cashman, S.D. (1984) *America in the Gilded Age*. New York: New York UP.

Cassidy, F.G. (1967) 'Some New Light on Old Jamaicanisms'. *American Speech* 42, 190–201.

Charteris-Black, J. (1999) 'The Survival of English Proverbs: A Corpus Based Account'. In *DeProverbio: An Electronic Journal of International Proverb Studies* 5(2). http://www.deproverbio.com/DPjournal/DP,5,2,99/BLACK/SURVIVAL.htm

Chick, J.K. (1991) 'Sources and Consequences of Miscommunication in Afrikaans English–South African English Encounters'. In J. Cheshire (ed.), *English Around the World: Sociolinguistic Perspectives*. Cambridge: CUP, 446–61.

—— (1996) 'English in Interpersonal Interaction'. In V. de Klerk (ed.), *Focus on South Africa*. Amsterdam: Benjamins, 269–83.

Collins, P. (1989) 'Divided and Debatable Usage in Australian English'. In P. Collins and D. Blair (eds), *Australian English: The Language of a New Society*. St Lucia: University of Queensland Press, 138–49.

*——and D. Blair (eds) (1989) *Australian English: The Language of a New Society*. St Lucia: University of Queensland Press.

Conrad, A.W. and J.A. Fishman (1977) 'English as a World Language: The Evidence'. In J.A. Fishman, R.L. Cooper and A.W. Conrad (eds), *The Spread of English*. Rowley, MA: Newbury House, 3–76.

Coupland, J., N. Coupland and J.D. Robinson (1992) '"How Are You?" Negotiating Phatic Communion'. *Language in Society* 21, 207–30.

Craig, D.R. (1983) 'Toward a Description of Caribbean English'. In B.B. Kachru (ed.), *The Other Tongue: English Across Cultures*. Oxford: Pergamon, 198–209.

*Cruse, D.A. (1986) *Lexical Semantics*. Cambridge: CUP.

Crystal, D. (1997) *English as a Global Language*. Cambridge: CUP.

—— and D. Davy (1969) *Investigating English Style*. London: Longman.

Dabke, R. (1976) *Morphology of Australian English*. Munich: Fink.

Das, S.K. (1982) 'Indian English'. In J. Pride (ed.), *New Englishes*. Rowley, MA: Newbury House, 141–9.

De Klerk, V., and G.P. Barkhuizen (1998) 'English in the South African Defence Force: A Case Study of 6SAI'. *English World-Wide* 19, 33–60.

Delbridge, A. (1981) *The Macquarie Dictionary*. St Leonards, NSW: Macquarie Library.

*Dillard, J.L. (1973) *Black English: Its History and Usage in the United States*. New York: Vintage.

Divakaruni, C. (2000) 'Uncertain Objects of Desire'. *Atlantic Monthly* (Mar.).

Dixon, R.M.W. (1980) 'The Role of Language in Aboriginal Australian Society Today'. In *The Languages of Australia*. Cambridge: CUP, 69–96.

D'souza, J. (1997) 'Indian English: Some Myths, Some Realities'. *English World-Wide* 18, 91–105.

Dubois B. and I. Crouch (1975) 'The Question of Tag-Questions in Women's Speech: They Don't Really Use More of Them, Do They?' *Language in Society* 4, 289–94.

Dudley-Evans, T. (1989) 'An Outline of the Value of Genre Analysis in LSP Work'. In C. Laurén and M. Nordman (eds), *Special Language*. Clevedon, UK: Multilingual Matters, 72–9.

Dutch, R.A. (1966) *Roget's Thesaurus of English Words and Phrases*. Harmondsworth: Penguin.

Eco, U. (1979) *A Theory of Semiotics*. Bloomington: Indiana UP.

Ehret, R. (1997) 'Language Development and the Role of English in Krio'. *English World-Wide* 18, 171–89.

Ekwall, E. (1970) *The Concise Oxford Dictionary of English Place-Names*. 4th edn. Oxford: Clarendon Press.

Emihovich, C.A. (1981) 'The Intimacy of Address: Friendship Markers in Children's Social Play'. *Language in Society* 10, 189–99.

Ervin-Tripp, S. (1974) 'Sociolinguistics'. In B.G. Blount (ed.), *Language, Culture and Society*. Cambridge, MA: Winthrop, 268–334.

Falkenhagen, M. and I. Hanke (1999) 'Slang in Different Varieties of English: A Survey'. Bielefeld University term paper.

Fannie Farmer Boston Cooking School Cookbook, The All New (1970) 10th edn. New York: Bantam.

Ferguson, C.A. (1964) [1958] 'Diglossia'. In D. Hymes (ed.), *Language in Culture and Society: A Reader in Linguistics and Anthropology*. New York: Harper & Row, 429–39.

*—— and S.B. Heath (1981) 'Introduction'. In *Language in the USA*. Cambridge: CUP, pp. xxv–xxxviii

Fishman, J.A. (1977) 'The Spread of English as a New Perspective for the Study of "Language Maintenance and Language Shift"'. In J.A. Fishman, R.L. Cooper and A.W. Conrad (eds), *The Spread of English*. Rowley, MA: Newbury House, 108–33.

Fishman, R.A., R.L. Cooper and Y. Rosenbaum (1977) 'English Around the World'. In J.A. Fishman, R.L. Cooper and A.W. Conrad (eds), *The Spread of English*. Rowley, MA: Newbury House, 77–107.

Flexner, S.B. (1960) 'Preface' and 'Introduction to the Appendix'. In H. Wentworth and S. Flexner (eds), *Dictionary of American Slang*. London: Harrap, pp. vi–xv and 596–608.

*—— and A.H. Soukhanov (1997) *Speaking Freely: A Guided Tour of American English*. New York: OUP.

Follett, W. *Modern American Usage*. London, 1966.

Franklyn, J. (1960) *A Dictionary of Rhyming Slang*. London: Routledge & Kegan Paul.

Friel, B. (1981) *Translations*. London: Faber & Faber.

Fussell, P. (1984) *Class*. London: Arrow.

García, O. and R. Otheguy (eds) (1989) *English across Cultures, Cultures across English: A Reader in Cross-Cultural Communication*. Berlin: Mouton de Gruyter.

Gerbert, M. (1970) *Besonderheiten der Syntax in der technischen Fachsprache des Englischen*. Halle: Niemeyer.

Gläser, R. (1979) *Fachstile des Englischen*. Leipzig: Enzyklopaedie.

Gonzalez, A. and M.L.S. Bautista (1985) *Language Surveys in the Philippines (1966–1984)*. Manila: De La Salle.

Gopinathan, S. (1980) 'Language Policy in Education: A Singapore Perspective'. In E.A. Afendras and E.C.Y. Kuo (eds), *Language and Society in Singapore*. Singapore: Singapore UP, 175–202.

Görlach, M. (1988) 'English as a World Language: The State of the Art'. *English World-Wide* 9, 1–32.

—— (ed.) (1989a) [Texts] *English World-Wide* 10, 135–49.

—— (1989b) 'Word-Formation and the ENL:ESL:EFL Distinction'. *English World-Wide* 10, 279–313.

Graham, A. (1975) 'The Making of a Nonsexist Dictionary'. In B. Thorne and N. Henley (eds), *Language and Sex*. Rowley, MA: Newbury House, 57–63.

*Gramley, S.E. and K.-M. Pätzold (1992) *Survey of Modern English*. London: Routledge.

Green, J. (1986) *The Slang Thesaurus*. Harmondsworth: Penguin.

Greenbaum, S. (1974) 'Problems in the Negation of Modals'. *Moderna Språk* 68, 244–55.

Gregory, M. and S. Carroll (1978) *Language and Situation*. London: Routledge & Kegan Paul.

Grimshaw, A.D. (1971) 'Some Social Forces and Some Social Functions of Pidgin and Creole Languages'. In D. Hymes (ed.), *Pidginization and Creolization of Languages*. Cambridge: CUP, 427–45.

*Grote, D. (1992) *British English for American Readers: A Dictionary of the Language, Customs, and Places of British Life and Literature*. Westport, CT: Greenwood.

Gumperz, J.J. and E. Hernández-Chavez (1972) 'Bilingualism, Bidialectalism, and Classroom'. In D.B. Cazden, D. Hymes and V.P. John (eds), *Functions of Language in the Classroom*. New York: Teachers College Press, 84–108.

Hawkins, P.A. (1986) Supplement of Indian Words. In J. Swannell (ed.), *The Little Oxford Dictionary*. 6th edn. Oxford: Clarendon Press.

Hendrickson, R. (1987) *American Talk: The Words and Ways of American Dialects*. New York: Penguin.

Herbert, R.K. (1990) 'Sex-Based Differences in Compliment Behavior'. *Language in Society* 19, 201–24.

*Holm, J.A. (1988) *Pidgins and Creoles*, vol. I. Cambridge: CUP.

*—— (1989) *Pidgins and Creoles*, vol. II. Cambridge: CUP.

—— (1994) 'English in the Caribbean'. In R. Burchfield (ed.), *The Cambridge History of the English Language*, vol. V: *English in Britain and Oversea: Origins and Development*. Cambridge: CUP, 328–81.

Hook, D.D. (1984) 'First Names and Titles as Solidarity and Power Semantics in English'. *IRAL* 22, 183–9.

Hopkins, A. and T. Dudley-Evans (1988) 'A Genre-Based Investigation of the Discussions Section in Articles and Dissertations'. *ESP Journal* 7, 113–21.

Horstmann, K. (2000) 'English Loan Words in German Fashion Catalogues'. Bielefeld University term paper.

Huddleston, R.D. (1971) *The Sentence in Written English: A Syntactic Study Based on an Analysis of Scientific Texts*. Cambridge: CUP.

Hughes, S.E. (1992) 'Expletives of Lower Working-Class Women'. *Language in Society* 21, 291–303.

Jibril, M. (1982) 'Nigerian English: An Introduction'. In J. Pride (ed.), *New Englishes*. Rowley, MA: Newbury House, 73–84.

—— (1991) 'The Sociolinguistics of Prepositional Usage in Nigerian English'. In J. Cheshire (ed.) *English Around the World: Sociolinguistic Perspectives*. Cambridge: CUP, 519–44.

Johansson, S. (1975) *Some Aspects of the Vocabulary of Learned and Scientific English*. Gothenburg: Gothenburg Studies in English.

Jones, B.M. (1990) 'Constraints on Welsh English Tags: Some Evidence from Children's Language'. *English World-Wide* 11, 173–93.

Joos, M. (1961) *The Five Clocks: A Linguistic Excursion into the Five Styles of English Usage.* New York: Harcourt, Brace, World.

Kachru, B.B. (1966) 'Indian English: A Study in Contextualization'. In C.E. Bazell (ed.), *In Memory of J.R. Firth.* London: Longman, 255–87.

—— (1978) 'Code-Mixing as a Communicative Strategy in India'. In J.E. Alatis (ed.), *International Dimensions of Bilingual Education.* Washington, DC: Georgetown UP, 107–25.

—— (1984) 'South Asian English'. In R.Bailey and M. Görlach (eds), *English as a World Language.* Cambridge: CUP, 353–83.

—— (1985) 'Standards, Codification and Sociolinguistic Realism: The English Language in the Outer Circle'. In R. Quirk and H.G. Widdowson (eds), *English in the World.* Cambridge: CUP, 11–30.

—— (1986a) *The Alchemy of English.* Oxford: Pergamon.

—— (1986b) 'The Indianization of English'. *English Today* 6, 31–3.

—— (1988) 'India'. In U. Ammon, N. Dittmar and K.J. Mattheier (eds), *Sociolinguistics Soziolinguistik.* Berlin: de Gruyter, 1282–87.

Kok Lee Cheon (1978) *Syntax of Scientific English.* Singapore: Singapore UP.

Kramer, C. (1975) 'Sex-Related Differences in Address Systems'. *Anthropological Linguistics* 17, 198–200.

Kuo, E.C.Y. (1980) 'The Sociolinguistic Situation in Singapore: Unity in Diversity'. In E.A. Afendras and E.C.Y. Kuo (eds), *Language and Society in Singapore.* Singapore: Singapore UP, 39–62.

Kytö, M. (1991) *Variation and Diachrony, with Early American English in Focus: Studies on 'Can/May' and 'Shall/Will'.* Frankfurt: Peter Lang.

*Lakoff, G. and M. Johnson (1980) *Metaphors We Live By.* Chicago: U. of Chicago Press.

Lakoff, R. (1976) *Language and Woman's Place.* New York: Harper & Row.

*Lipka, L. (1992) *An Outline of English Lexicology.* 2nd edn. Tübingen: Niemeyer.

Llamzon, T.A. (1969) *Standard Filipino English.* Manila: Ateneo UP.

The Longman Dictionary of English Language and Culture (1998) 2nd edn, ed. D. Summers. Harlow: Longman.

The Longman Dictionary of Scientific Usage (1979). Harlow: Longman.

McArthur, T. (ed.) (1981) *Longman Lexicon of Contemporary English.* Harlow: Longman.

*—— (ed.) (1996) *The Oxford Companion to the English Language.* Abridged edn. Oxford: OUP.

McClure, M. (2000) 'Youth Language–School Language'. Bielefeld University term paper.

McIntire, M.L. (1972) 'Terms of Address in an Academic Setting'. *Anthropological Linguistics* 14, 286–92.

MacKay, D.G., and T. Konishi (1980) 'Personification and the Pronoun Problem'. In C. Kramarae (ed.), *The Voices and Words of Women and Men.* Oxford: Pergamon, 149–63.

Marchand, H. (1960) *The Categories and Types of Present-Day English Word-Formation.* Wiesbaden: Harrassowitz.

Marckwardt, A.H. (1980) *American English,* rev. by J.L. Dillard. New York: OUP.

—— and R. Quirk (1960) *A Common Language: British and American English.* London and Washington, DC: BBC and VOA.

Martyna, W. (1980) 'The Psychology of the Generic Masculine'. In S. McConnell-Ginet, R. Borker and N. Furman (eds), *Women and Language in Literature and Society.* New York: Praeger, 69–78.

Mehrotra, R.R. (1982) 'Indian English: A Sociolinguistic Profile'. In J.B. Pride (ed.), *New Englishes*. Rowley, MA: Newbury House, 150–73.

Mencken, H.L. (1963) *The American Language*. 4th edn. and 2 supplements, abridged by R.I. McDavid, Jr. New York: Knopf.

Mesthrie, R. (1987) 'From OV to VO in Language Shift: South African Indian English and Its OV Substrates'. *English World-Wide* 8, 263–76.

Morris, E.E. (1972) [1898] *A Dictionary of Austral English*. Sydney: Sydney UP.

Muysken, P. (1988) 'Are Creoles a Special Type of Language?' In F.J. Newmeyer (ed.), *Linguistics: The Cambridge Survey*, vol. II: *Linguistic Theory: Extensions and Implications*. Cambridge: CUP, 285–301.

Nair, R.B. (1992) 'Gender, Genre and Generative Grammar: Deconstructing the Matrimonial Column'. In M. Toolan (ed.), *Language, Text and Context: Essays in Stylistics*. London: Routledge, 227–54.

Nihalani, P., R.K. Tongue and P. Hosali (1979) *Indian and British English: A Handbook of Usage and Pronunciation*. Delhi: OUP.

Odlin, T. (1991) 'Irish English Idioms and Language Transfer'. *English World-Wide* 12, 175–93.

Ogden, C.K. and I.A. Richards (1949) [1923] *The Meaning of Meaning: A Study of the Influence of Language upon Thought and of the Science of Symbolism*. 10th edn. London: Routledge & Kegan Paul.

*Opie, I. and P. Opie (1959) *The Lore and Language of Schoolchildren*. Oxford: OUP.

Orkin, M. M. (1971) *Speaking Canadian English*. London: Routledge & Kegan Paul.

Partridge, E. (1984) *Dictionary of Slang and Unconventional English*. 8th edn. New York: Macmillan.

Pascasio, E.M. (1988) 'The Present Role and Domains of English in the Philippines'. In A. Gonzales (ed.), *The Role of English and Its Maintenance in the Philippines*. Manila: Solidaridad, 114–24.

Pemagbi, J. (1989) 'Still a Deficient Language?' *English Today* 17, 20–24.

Philipsen, G., and M. Huspek (1985) 'Bibliography of Sociolinguistic Studies and Personal Address'. *Anthropological Linguistics* 27, 94–101.

Philps, D. (1991) 'Linguistic Security in the Syntactic Structures of Air Traffic Control English'. *English World-Wide* 12, 103–24.

Platt, J.T. (1984) 'English in Singapore, Malaysia, and Hong Kong'. In R. Bailey and M. Görlach (eds), *English as a World Language*. Cambridge: CUP, 384–414.

—— (1988) 'Singapore'. In U. Ammon, N. Dittmar and K.J. Mattheier (eds), *Sociolinguistics Soziolinguistik*. Berlin: de Gruyter, 1384–88.

—— (1991) 'Social and Linguistic Constraints on Variation on the Use of Two Grammatical Variables in Singapore English'. In J. Cheshire (ed.), *English Around the World: Sociolinguistic Perspectives*. Cambridge: CUP, 376–87.

—— and H. Weber (1980) *English in Singapore and Malaysia*. Kuala Lumpur: OUP.

Pollard, V. (1989) 'The Particle *en* in Jamaican Creole: A Discourse-Related Account'. *English World-Wide* 10, 55–68.

Poynton, C. (1989) 'Terms of Address in Australian English'. In P. Collins and D. Blair (eds), *Australian English: The Language of a New Society*. St Lucia: U. of Queensland Press, 55–69.

Prator, C.H. (1968) 'The British Heresy in TESL'. In J.A. Fishman, C.A. Ferguson and J. Das Gupta (eds), *Language Problems of Developing Nations*. New York: Wiley, 459–76.

Pride, J. (ed.) (1982) *New Englishes*. Rowley, MA: Newbury House.

Quirk, R., S. Greenbaum, G. Leech and J. Svartvik (1985) *A Comprehensive Grammar of the English Language*. London: Longman.

Ramson, W.S. (1981) 'The Historical Study of Australian English'. In A. Delbridge (ed.), *The Macquarie Dictionary*. St Leonards, NSW: Macquarie Library, 37–42.

Random House Dictionary of the English Language, 2nd edn. (1987) ed. J. Stein and L. Urdang. New York: Random House.

Random House Webster's College Dictionary. 2nd edn. (1997) ed. R.B. Costello. New York: Random House.

Richards, J.C. (1982) 'Rhetorical and Communicative Styles in the New Varieties of English'. In J. Pride (ed.), *New Englishes*. Rowley, MA: Newbury House, 227–48.

—— and M.W.J. Tay (1977) 'The *La* Particle in Singapore English'. In W. Crewe (ed.), *The English Language in Singapore*. Singapore: Eastern UP, 141–56.

Ridder, S. (1995) 'English in Dutch'. *English Today* 44, 44–50.

Roberts, P.A. (1988) *West Indians and Their Language*. Cambridge: CUP.

Robinson, P.C. (1989) 'An Overview of English for Specific Purposes'. In H. Coleman (ed.), *Working with Language: A Multidisciplinary Consideration of Language Use in Work Contexts*. Berlin: Mouton de Gruyter, 395–427.

Ross, A.S.C. (1959) 'U and Non-U: An Essay in Sociolinguistics'. In N. Mitford (ed.), *Nobless Oblige*. Harmondworth: Penguin, 9–32.

Rubin, R. (1981), 'Ideal Traits and Terms of Address for Male and Female College Professors'. *Journal of Personality and Social Psychology* 41, 966–74.

*Saeed, J. (1997) *Semantics*. Oxford: Blackwell.

Sachs, J. (1987) 'Preschool Boys' and Girls' Language Use in Pretend Play'. In S.U. Philips, S. Steele and C. Tanz (eds), *Language, Gender and Sex in Comparative Perspective*. Cambridge: CUP, 178–88.

Sager, J.C., D. Dungworth and P.F. McDonald (1980) *English Special Languages*. Wiesbaden: Brandstetter.

Salager, F. (1984) 'Compound Nominal Phrases in Scientific-Technical Literature: Proportion and Rationale'. In A.K. Pugh and J.M. Ulijn (eds), *Reading for Professional Purposes: Studies and Practices in Native and Foreign Languages*. London: Heinemann, 136–45.

Sandefur, J.R. (1983) 'Modern Australian Aboriginal Languages: The Present State of Knowledge'. *English World-Wide* 4, 43–68.

Sapir, E. (1949) *Selected Writings in Language, Culture and Personality*, ed. D.G. Mandelbaum. Berkeley, CA: University of California Press.

—— (1970) [1921] *Language*. London: Granada.

de Saussure, F. (1972) [1916] *Course in General Linguistics*. Chicago: Open Court.

*Schiffrin, D. (1994) *Approaches to Discourse*. Oxford: Blackwell.

Schmied, J.J. (1985a) *Englisch in Tansania*. Heidelberg: Groos.

—— (1985b) 'Attitudes Towards English in Tanzania'. *English World-Wide* 6, 237–69.

Schulz, M.R. (1975) 'The Semantic Derogation of Woman'. In B. Thorne and N. Henley (eds), *Language and Sex*. Rowley, MA: Newbury House, 64–75.

Searle, J.R. (1976) 'The Classification of Illocutionary Acts'. *Language in Society* 5, 1–23.

Seidl, J. and W. McMordie (1988) *English Idioms*. 5th edn. Oxford: OUP.

Shnukal, A., and L. Marchese (1983) 'Creolization of Nigerian Pidgin English: A Progress Report'. *English World-Wide* 4, 17–26.

Sibayan, B.P. (1988) 'Social Engineering Strategies for the Maintenance of English'. In A. Gonzalez (ed.) *The Role of English and Its Maintenance in the Philippines*. Manila: Solidaridad, 91–6.

Simpson, J. (ed.) (1992) *The Concise Oxford Dictionary of Proverbs*. 2nd edn. Oxford: OUP.

Spencer, J. (ed.) (1963) 'Introduction'. In *Language in Africa*. Cambridge: CUP, 1–5.

Sridhar, K.K. (1983) 'English in a South Indian Urban Context'. In B.B. Kachru (ed.), *The Other Tongue: English Across Cultures*. Oxford: Pergamon, 141–53.

—— (1991) 'Speech Acts in an Indigenised Variety: Sociocultural Values and Language Variation'. In J. Cheshire (ed.), *English Around the World: Sociolinguistic Perspectives*. Cambridge: CUP, 308–18.

Stanley, J.P. (1977) 'Paradigmatic Woman: The Prostitute'. In D.L. Shore and C.P. Hines (eds), *Papers on Language Variation*. Birmingham: U. of Alabama Press, 303–21.

Stewart, G.R. (1970) *American Place-Names: A Concise and Selective Dictionary for the Continental United States of America*. New York: OUP.

Sure, K. (1991) 'Language Functions and Language Attitudes in Kenya'. *English World-Wide* 12, 245–60.

Svartvik, J. (1968) 'Plotting Divided Usage with *Dare* and *Need*'. *Studia Neophilologica* 40, 130–40.

Svejcer, A.D. (1978) *Standard English in the United States and England*. The Hague: Mouton.

Tay, M.W.J. (1982) 'The Uses, Users, and Features of English in Singapore'. In J. Pride (ed.), *New Englishes*. Rowley, MA: Newbury House, 51–70.

Taylor, B. (1989) 'American, British and Other Foreign Influences on Australian English since World War II'. In P. Collins and D. Blair (eds), *Australian English: The Language of a New Society*. St Lucia: U of Queensland Press, 225–54.

Tingley, C. (1981) 'Deviance in the English of Ghanaian Newspapers'. *English World-Wide* 2, 39–62.

Todd, L. (1982) *Cameroon*. Heidelberg: Julius Gross.

—— (1984a) 'The English Language in West Africa'. In R.W. Bailey and M. Görlach (eds), *English as a World Language*. Cambridge: CUP, 281–305.

—— (1984b) 'By Their Tongue Divided: Towards an Analysis of Speech Communities in Northern Ireland'. *English World-Wide* 5 (1984), 159–80.

—— (1989) 'Cultures in Conflict: Varieties of English in Northern Ireland'. In O. García and R. Otheguy (eds), *English Across Cultures, Cultures Across English: A Reader in Cross-Cultural Communication*. Berlin: Mouton de Gruyter, 335–55.

—— and I. Hancock (1986) *International English Usage*. London: Croom Helm.

Tongue, R. (1974) *The English of Singapore and Malaysia*. Singapore: Eastern Universities Press.

Traugott, E. (1972) *A History of English Syntax: A Transformational Approach to the History of English Sentence Structure*. New York: Holt, Rinehart & Winston.

Trudgill, P. (1999) 'A Window on the Past: "Colonial Lag" and New Zealand Evidence for the Phonology of Nineteenth Century English'. *American Speech* 74, 227–39.

Tulloch, S. (ed.) (1993) *The Oxford Dictionary of New Words: A Popular Guide to Words in the News*. Oxford: OUP.

Turner, G.W. (1972) *The English Language in Australia and New Zealand*. London: Longman.

—— (ed.) (1987) *The Australian Concise Oxford Dictionary*. Melbourne: OUP.

—— (1989) 'Some Problems in Australian English Etymology'. In P. Collins and D. Blair (eds) *Australian English: The Language of a New Society*. St Lucia: U. of Queensland Press, 214–24.

—— (1994) 'English in Australia'. In R. Burchfield (ed.), *The Cambridge History of the English Language*, vol. V: *English in Britain and Overseas: Origins and Development*. Cambridge: CUP, 277–327.

Tzankow, M. (2000) 'A Discourse on Language and Social Variation in Personal Ads in the Internet'. Bielefeld University term paper.

Valdés, G. (1988) 'The Language Situation of Mexican Americans'. In S.L. McKay and S.C. Wong (eds), *Language Diversity: Problem or Resource? A Social and Educational Perspective on Language Minorities in the United States*. New York: Newbury House, 111–39.

Verma, S.K. (1982) 'Swadeshi English: Form and Function'. In J.B. Pride (ed.), *New Englishes*. Rowley, MA: Newbury House, 261–86.

Wales, K. (1994) 'Royalese: The Rise and Fall of "The Queens's English"'. *English Today* 39, 3–10.

*Wardhaugh, R. (1986) *An Introduction to Sociolinguistics*. Oxford: Blackwell.

Watson, S. (1995) *The Harlem Renaissance: Hub of African-American Culture, 1920–1930*. New York: Pantheon.

Webster's Third New International Dictionary of the English Language (1971) ed. P.B. Grove *et al.*

*Wells, J.C. (1982) *Accents of English,* vol. I: *An Introduction*. Cambridge: CUP.

Wentworth, H. and S. Flexner (eds) (1960) *Dictionary of American Slang*. London: Harrap.

Willmott, M.B. (1978/9) 'Variety Signifiers in Nigerian English'. *English Language Teaching* 33, 227–33.

Winer, L. (1990) 'Intelligibility of Reggae Lyrics in North America: Dread ina Babylon'. *English World-Wide* 11, 33–58.

Wolfson, N. (1984) 'Pretty Is as Pretty Does: A Speech Act View of Sex Roles'. *Applied Linguistics* 5, 236–44.

Wright, P. (1981) *Cockney Dialect and Slang*. London: Batsford.

Yilmaz, T. (2000) 'Survey on Drug Language'. Bielefeld University term paper.

Yule, H. (1969) [1903] 'Preface'. In *Hobson-Jobson,* 2nd edn. ed.W. Crooke. London: Routledge & Kegan Paul.

Zentella, A.C. (1981) 'Language Variety among Puerto Ricans'. In C.A. Ferguson and S.B. Heath (eds), *Language in the USA*. Cambridge: CUP, 218–38.

Zimmer, D. and H. Hillebrand (1999) 'Comparison of American and Scottish Drug Slang: A Quantitative Approach'. Bielefeld University term paper.

Zuengler, J.E. (1983) 'Kenyan English'. In B.B. Kachru (ed.), *The Other Tongue: English Across Cultures*. Oxford: Pergamon, 112–24.

Glossary and Index

This Glossary serves both as a glossary and an index. The numbers refer to sections where further clarification of the term can be found.

Symbols and conventions

{. . .} braces (AmE) or curly brackets (BrE) are used to enclose morphs and morphemes. The former are given in lower-case (small) letters; the latter are given in capitals.

/. . ./ slant or slanted lines are used to enclose phonemes (phonemic transcriptions).

[. . .] brackets (AmE) or square brackets (BrE) are used to enclose phonetic transcriptions such as allophones; they are also used to enclose semantic features.

'. . .' quotation marks or inverted commas (BrE) are used, among other things, to enclose glosses of meanings.

Note: Words printed in bold italic type within Glossary entries cross-refer to other entries

abbreviation (1.4.3.2; 4.3.2.5; 6.1.6; Exercise 8.8) a word consisting of the first letters of what it stands for, each pronounced by its letter name, e.g. *NZ* /enzed/ for New Zealand

Aboriginal English (4.4.2) a range of non-standard varieties of English spoken chiefly by Australian Aboriginal peoples and sometimes marked by features borrowed from Aboriginal languages

acrolect see *creole*

acronym (4.3.2.5; 8.4.1.2, 8.4.3.4) a word consisting of the first letters of a phrase whose meaning it takes on, e.g. *wowser* (*we only want social evils remedied*)

address, modes of (7.2) the *pronouns* and *vocatives* (including *kinship terms*, *names*, *honorifics*, *titles* and *descriptors*) used for someone when talking to them

adjacency pair (7.3.1, Project 7.8, 7.3.2.5) a *pragmatic idiom* which consists of two members, the first demanding the second, e.g. *Thank you - You're welcome.*

adstrate language (3.7; 5.1.2.5) a language with which a given language is in contact and from which it borrows features, esp. vocabulary; see also *substrate*, *superstrate*

affix (4.3.2.3–4; Exercise 4.4; 6.1.1; 6.1.1.2; 8.4.3.4) the addition (*affixation*) of a *prefix* (before a word, e.g. *do > redo*) or a *suffix* (after a word, *help > helpless*); also *infixes* (within a word, e.g. (esp.) AusE *19-fuckin'-86*)

Afrikaans (Case studies 2.5, 3.6; 4.1, 4.3.1.1–2, 4.3.2.4; 6.4.2.2; Case study 7.1; 8.1.1) one of the languages of South Africa, which developed out of Dutch

age (2.2; 3.7, Case study 3.5; Projects 4.1, 4.2; 5.2, 5.3.1, 5.3.1.1; 7.0, 7.2.1.1, Case study 7.1, 7.2.3, 7.2.4.1, Project 7.5, Exercise 7.6, 7.3.1, Exercise 7.8; 8.1; Case 8.4, 8.5, Project 8.3) a variable in *sociolinguistics*

ambiguity (2.2.3.2; 3.1.1, 3.3.3; 8.4.3: passim) the state of being interpretable in more than one way, e.g. the word *bird* is a case of lexical ambiguity in BrE because it can mean 'animal of class Aves' or 'girl'

AmE: American English (1.1.1–2, 1.4.2–3, 1.4.5; Chs. 2–4; 5.1.2; 6.3.1, 6.3.3, Case study 6.6; 7.2.3, 7.2.4.1, Project 7.8; 8.1.2.1, 8.1.3–4, Case study 8.4, Project 8.3, Exercise 8.3, 8.3.2, Case study 8.7, 8.4.1.1, Case study 8.9) the varieties of English spoken in North America; AmE can be understood as designating the the English of the USA and that of Canada (see also *CanE*)

amelioration (a.k.a. *melioration*) (4.5.2, 4.6; 6.2) the case in which a word takes on a more positive meaning or association; cf. *pejoration*; see also *broadening of meaning, narrowing of meaning, connotation, denotation, semantic shift*

analogue (3.2.1, Exercise 3.3) institutions which serve a similar purpose or have a similar status in different countries, e.g. the analogues of Oxford and Cambridge in Britain might be said to be Harvard and Yale in the USA

antonomasia (Exercises 2.5, 2.6) a process in which a proper name serves as a common noun designating a characteristic associated with the proper name; adj.: *antonomastic*

antonymy (a.k.a. *gradable antonymy*) (1.4.4; 3.1.1.2; 6.3.3), two words which form the end-points of a scale with intermediate points, e.g. *big–small* with intermediate *biggish, middle-sized, smallish*, etc. See also *complementary pair, converses, reverses*

aphasia (1.4.1) impairment to the brain due to injury; aphasias can be of various sorts depending on the area damaged; the resulting impairment differs accordingly

apologies (7.3.2.2) a type of (expressive) *speech act*

arbitrariness (2.2) the lack of any reason for the attribution of a meaning to a word form which might be explained by the nature of either the word form or the meaning, e.g. the animal of the class Canis can with equal justice be called *perro, chien, Hund,* or *dog*

article (2.2.4.1; 5.1.2.5) one of two types: *definite* (*the*) or *indefinite* (*a/an*), the latter including no article (zero article: ø); Articles serve to identify individual countable nouns (indefinite: *a dog/ø dogs*) and to specify them (definite: *the dog/the dogs*); see also *determiner*

aspect (5.1.2.5) a grammatical category of the verb; progressive aspect is used for ongoing activities and processes (*he's reading*); non-progressive aspect is expressed in the simple form and is used for characteristic acts and events (*he shaves every morning*) or singular punctual acts or events (*he left at ten*)

AusE: Australian English and *Australia* (1.1.1, 1.4.2; Exercise 2.4, Case study 2.5; 3.1.1.2, Case study 3.3, Exercise 3.3, 3.4.3, 3.6.1.3, 3.6.2, 3.7; Ch. 4; Case study 6.5; 7.2.2.2, 7.2.3, 7.2.4.1; Case study 8.5, Exercise 8.4)

autochthonous language (5.1.2.2, 5.2.1.1; 6.1.1) language native to a particular country, e.g. Igbo in Nigeria; contrast *exogenous languages*

auxiliary verb (2.2.4–4.1) a grammaticalized verb used with a full or lexical verb to form complex verbal expressions; there are two types: (1) primary auxiliaries (*be*: used to form the progressive and the passive; *have* for the perfect; *do*: for questions and negations when no other auxiliary is present) and (2) *modal auxiliaries* (particularly *can, could, will, would, may, might, shall, should, must*)

back-channel behaviour (5.3.2.3; 7.3.1) the non-verbal nods, smiles, etc., the murmured *uhuh*'s, *mmhm*'s, etc. as well as interjected *oh yeah*'s, *I see*'s, etc. which a listener performs to signal active listening.

back-formation (6.1.6) the formation of a new word by deleting what is assumed to be a suffix, e.g. deriving *televise* from *television* by deleting the {-ion} in analogy to pairs like *create:creation*

back slang (Exercise 8.2) a secret language in which words are spelled backward (*niwt* 'twin'); see also *Pig Latin*

base (4.3.2.2, 4.3.2.4, Exercise 4.4; 6.1.4) any single *morpheme* or combination of morphemes to which an *affix* may be added, e.g. *tell* is a base to which *fore-* may be added; *foretell* itself is a base to which an *-s* may be added

BAE: Black American English (Case study 6.6, Exercise 6.7; 7.2.2.2; 8.2, 8.2.1, Case study 8.7, Case study 8.10) an ethnic variety of AmE spoken mostly by African Americans, but by no means by all of them

basilect see *continuum*

bilateral local markedness see *local markedness*

bilingual dictionary (1.4.2) a dictionary with entries in one and explanations or definitions in another language

binomial (a.k.a. *irreversible binomial*) (Exercise 6.4) two lexemes of the same word class (nouns, verbs, adjectives) which occur together in a fixed (irreversible) order and frequently with idiomatic meaning, e.g. *part and parcel* e.g., but not always, *moan and groan*

blend (a.k.a. *portmanteau word*) (Case study 3.2; 4.3.2.2, 4.3.2.5; 6.1.6, Case study 8.6; 8.4.1.4, 8.4.3.4); the combination of part of one word with part or the whole of another to form a new word which combines aspects of the meanings of both, e.g. *heliport* < *helicopter airport* (see also *loan blend*)

borrowing (2.1: passim; 3.2.4, 3.7; 4.3.1: passim; 4.5.5, 4.6.2; 5.1.2.5, 5.2.1.1; 6.1 passim; 7.2.2.3, Case study 7.3, 7.3.2.1; 8.3: passim, 8.4.3.4) the process of taking lexical items from other languages; this includes *folk etymology*, *loan blend*, *loan translations*, *loan words*

BrE: British English (1.4.2; Ch. 2; 3.2.1, 3.6.2; 4.5.4, 4.5.6; 7.2.3; 8.1.2.1, Case study 8.1, Case study 8.2, Case study 8.5, Exercises 8.3, 8.4/8.4.1.1, Case study 8.9)

broadening (extension) of meaning (4.5.1; 6.1.1; 6.1.8; 8.3.6) a widening of the extent of meaning as when fewer *semantic features* (q.v.) are necessary to determine the sense of a word, e.g. when *hat* no longer necessarily includes the feature [+ brim] and can, consequently, refer to caps; see also *semantic shift*

bureaucratese (a.k.a. *gobbledygook*, *jargon*, or *officialese*) (8.1.5, Case study 8.11) the obscure diction of bureaucrats and the government, esp. characterized by *acroynms*, *abbreviations*, and *euphemisms*

calque see *loan translation*

camaraderie form see *semantic inversion*

CamE: Cameroon English and *Cameroon* (5.1.2.3, 5.2.1.1, Case study 5.1; 8.4.1.1)

CanE: Canadian English and *Canada* (2.2.4; 3.5.2; 5.1.2; Case study 8.9) see also *AmE*

CarE: Caribbean English (3.1.2; 3.7; 6.1.4–5, Case studies 6.5, 8.10)

case (2.1.3; 6.4.1.1; 8.3.2) a grammatical category realized in English as a pronoun in the subject or nominative (*I*, *they*), the object or accusative (*me*, *them*), and possessive or genitive case (*mine*, *theirs*).

Celtic see *Gaelic*

central phase (7.3.1) the phase of a *conversation* in which the 'business' is transacted

change of meaning see *semantic shift*

class, social (2.1.2.1, 2.1.4.1, 2.2.3.7; 3.3.9–10, 3.4.1–2; 5.1.2.4–5, 5.2.1.4, 5.2.2.1, 5.3.1, 5.3.1.1; 7.2.1.2, Case study 7.2; 8.1.4: passim, 8.2) a variable in *sociolinguistics*

clipping (a.k.a. *shortening*) (4.3.2, 4.3.2.4, Exercise 4.4; 6.1.4, 6.1.6; 8.3.2, 8.4.3.3–4); a shortened form of a word, in which the beginning, the end, or the both may be cut (clipped) out, cf. *bus* < Latin *omnibus*; *ad* < *advantage* (AmE < 'advantage in tennis') *van* (BrE < 'advantage in tennis').

closing (7.3.1, Exercise 7.8) of a *conversation*, also *ending*; the phase in which a conversation is terminated

closing (8.1.2.1, Project 8.1, 8.4.1.1) of a *letter* (cf. *salutation*) the formula used to sign off, e.g. *Yours sincerely* or *Love*

Cockney English (Exercise 8.4) the traditional (East End working-class) dialect of London; see also *rhyming slang*

code-mixing (5.2.1.1, 5.2.2.1; 8.3.7, Case studies 8.7, 8.8) the use of words or phrases from one language in discourse which is basically conducted in another, e.g. *Tengo la waist twenty-nine, tengo que reduce*

code-switching (5.2.1.1, 5.2.2.1; 8.3.7, Case studies 8.7, 8.8) the movement between one or more languages or varieties within a single communicative encounter (including *code-mixing*) *Dijo mi mamá que I have to study*, or: *Sí, sí, él habla mucho, pero cuando llegó la hora no se atrivió a bring it up at the meeting* (Yes, sure, he talks a lot, but when the time came he didn't have the guts to bring . . .)

co-hyponym see *hyponymy*

collocation (lexical) (1.4.2; 3.5.1–2, Exercise 3.9, Exercise 3.10) a usual combination of lexical words of differing classes in syntactic rather than morphological relationship (not compounds), relatively fixed, and usually transparent (non-idiomatic) in meaning, e.g. *foregone + conclusion*. There are also syntactic collocations such as an infinitive and the marker *to*; see also *fixed expression*

colloquial English (1.1.2, 1.4.3, 1.4.5; 3.1.1.2, 3.3.8, 3.4.7, 3.5.2; 4.4.2, 4.6, 4.6.4; 5.3.2.3–4; Exercise 6.5, Case study 6.6; 8.2, 8.2.5) informal English as it is spoken or written in relaxed, familiar atmosphere

colonial lag (4.2) the observation made that colonial societies are sometimes slower in changing linguistically

colonial language (2.1.4.2) varieties (here: of English) which came into existence in colonial societies, e.g. in Australia or India

combining form (8.4.1.2, 8.4.3.4) a base form which does not normally stand alone (though they may do so as *clippings*) but enters into componds, e.g. {*auto-*}, an initial combining form or {*-archy*}, a final one

common noun (Case study 2.2) a noun which refers to a whole class of concrete entities (*book*) or to a general abstraction (*listlessness*); see *proper noun*

complementary distribution (5.1.2.3) the distribution of forms in such a way that the differing forms (phonetic, syntactic) do not occur in the same environment or under the same conditions; in 5.1.2.3 *StE* is used under different (complementary) conditions from *Pidgin English*

complementary pair (a.k.a. *simple antonymy*) (3.1.1.2) two words which form a set of mutually exclusive terms; a bipolar relationship: either the one is appropriate or the other, with no half-way states, e.g.: *dead/alive*; *male/female*. See also *antonymy*, *converses*, *reverses*

complementizer (3.6.1.5) a grammatical marker used to introduce a clause embedded in another, e.g. *that* or *for* as in *We said that it was late*; *they asked for him to come*

complex item see *multi-word item*

compliment (7.3.2.3–4, Projects 7.7, 7.8, Case study 7.4) a type of (expressive) *speech act*

componential analysis (Case study 3.4) the process by which the unitary meaning of, for example, a word is divided up (i.e. analysed) into its smaller units (i.e. components). The components are referred to as *semantic features* and conventionally written in square brackets, *boy* consists of [+human], [+male], [+young]

composition (a.k.a. *compounding*, *compound*)

compositionality (4.3.2.1) the principle observed when the meaning of the whole (a word, a sentence) can be understood as the sum of its parts, e.g. a *lawn-mower* is a mower for lawns

compound (4.3.2, 4.3.2.1; Exercise 4.3; 6.1, 6.1.4) a complex word consisting of more than one free form (or *free morph*) combined, usu. with a more specialized meaning than that componentially indicated by the sum of its parts (also: *compounding*) e.g. *black* + *bird* > *blackbird*; compounds may be written as one word, as two words (*dining room*), or with hyphenation (*twenty-two*)

concept (2.0, 2.2.2.1, 2.2.3, 2.2.3.2, 2.2.4; 3.1–4) meaning as *mental representation*; see *theories of meaning*

conceptual gap (3.4.4) the lack of a concept in a speech community and, consequently, the lack of a lexeme to express it. Sometimes the focus is not on the missing concept, but on the missing referent, hence referential gap.

conditional (form) (7.1, 7.3.2.4) the past tense form of *modal auxiliaries* used to express distance, including the tentativeness of *politeness*, e.g. *would, could*

connotation (3.1.1; 4.5.2, 4.6.1, 4.6.3; 6.2) meaning not covered by denotational semantic features. Connotation can thus include regional, stylistic, text-typical, evaluative distinctions, e.g. the varying connotational meanings of *gazette, journal, rag, newspaper*. See also *amelioration, pejoration, broadening of meaning, narrowing of meaning, denotation, semantic shift, cultural literacy*

constant reference (2.2.3.1) the unique reference typical of proper nouns, e.g. *Chicago* always refers to the same particular city

continuum (1.1.2; 3.6.3; 5.1.2.3, 5.1.2.3, 5.2.1.2; 6.4.1.1) a series of gradually differing varieties of a language stretching from the low, powerless, non-standard extreme, the *basilect*, via intermediate *mesolects* to the establishment language StE, the *acrolect*; typical where English coexists with English-oriented *pidgins* or *creoles*, also between *traditional dialects* and *StE*

conversation (7.3.1) consisting of *opening, central phase*, and *ending*

converses (1.4.4; 3.1.1.2) involve the reversal of a mutual relationship, e.g. *buy/sell* (*x buys y from z* is the converse of *z sells y to x*); *mother/child* (*a* is mother of *b*; *b* is child of *a*); see also *antonymy, complementary pair, reverses*

conversion (a.k.a. *zero derivation*) (4.3.2, 4.3.2.2; 6.1.4) the change of the part of speech/word class of a word without any changes in the word form, e.g. *down* (adv.) becomes a verb as in *to down a drink*; see also *derivation*

countability (1.4.4; 5.1.2.5) a grammatical category of the noun; countable nouns have singulars and plurals, for they refer to things which occur in single (and therefore countable) instances. *Non-countable nouns* (mass nouns, abstract nouns) cannot normally be pluralized (e.g. *water, plausibility*)

count noun see *countability*

creole, creolized (1.1.2, 1.4.3; 3.6.1.3, 3.7; 4.2.3; 5.1.2.3, 5.1.2.5, 5.2.1.1–2; 6.1.1, 6.1.4–5, 6.1.8, 6.4, 6.4.1, Case study 6.5; 8.4.2.2) a *pidgin* which has become a mother tongue and therefore has re-expanded in the dimensions of its social use and its linguistic repertoire

cultural literacy (1.4.5) encyclopedic knowledge about a culture such as historical events and persons, institutions, and customs. It is intimately connected with the linguistic community's language, contributing proper names and connotations of meaning

dative alternation (3.6.1.1) the switch in position of an *indirect object* between occurrence immediately after the verb (with no preposition) and occurrence after the direct object (preceded by *to*), cf. *him* in *give him the key* vs. *give the key to him*

definite article see *article*

denotation, **denotational meaning** see *theories of meaning*

denotatum see *referent*

derivation (4.3.2, 4.3.2.2–4; 6.1.4; 8.4.3.4) *word formation* by means of *affixation* and/or phonological change (vowels, consonants, stress) or *shift*, e.g. *kindness* derives from *kind*; *truth* from *true*; or *a read* from *to read*

descriptors (7.2.1.1) vocatives which designate the addressee by activity or appearance, e.g. *Operator*, *Waiter* or *Slim*, *Red*

desk dictionary (1.4.2.3) a monolingual dictionary intended for a native speaker; cf. *learner's dictionary*; see also *dictionary*

determiner (2.2.3.1) one of a group of form or grammatical words used in front of nouns to specify or quantify them. They include the *article*, but also demonstrative (*this*, *that*), indefinite (*some*, *any*), and possessive (*my*, *your*) determiners

dialect (1.1.2, 1.4.3.2; 2.1; 3.1.1.2, 3.1.2, 3.4.4, 3.7; 4.1, 4.2, 4.4.1–2; 5.1.2.4, 5.3.1, 5.3.2.4; Case study 6.5, Exercise 6.5; 7.1; 8.1) language variation by user characteristics such as age, class, ethnicity, gender, region; unmodified dialect is usually understood as regional dialect, but *lects* also include *social dialect* (a.k.a. *sociolect*), *genderlect* and *ethnic dialect* (a.k.a. *ethnolect*)

diatype (5.3.2) language variation according to features of the situation of use; adj. *diatypical*; see also *register*, *field of discourse*, *medium*, *functional tenor* (purpose), *personal tenor* (*style*)

dictionary (1.1.2, 1.3, 1.3.3, 1.4.2–5; 2.2.3; 3.1.1.2, 3.2.4, 3.4.2; 4.3.2.2, 4.3.3.1–2; 5.3.1.2, 5.3.2.3–4; 6.1.2, 6.3.3; 8.1.4, 8.2, Case studies 8.9, 8.10, 8.4.3.2) a book listing words or phrases in some kind of alphabetical order and providing various types of information about them; see also *desk dictionary*, *historical dictionary*, *learner's dictionary*, *special dictionaries*

diglossia (5.1.2.2–3, 5.2.1.4, 5.2.2.1–2) the use of two languages or distinct varieties of one language, the one for high purposes (esp. written literature, state institutions, established religion), the *H(igh)* language and the other for everyday purposes (esp. the *vernacular*), the *L(ow)* language; see also *triglossia*

diminutive (suffix) (4.3.2.4, Exercise 4.4), abbrev. D; renders what the words refer to more familiar and/or endearing, e.g. suffix {-*y*}: *Stephen* by shortening to *Steve* and by diminutive to *Stevie*

discourse marker (7.3.1, Case study 7.3) a word inserted into discourse with little denotative meaning but largely to organize turn-taking (*well*), to structure topics (*now*, *okay*), and to appeal to shared knowledge (*you know*)

disjunctive (6.4.1.1) the 'strong' form of a personal pronoun, identical with the object/accusative form; used esp. when standing alone (or 'disjoined') in word order, e.g. *me* in *Who said that? Me!*

ditransitive verb (3.6.1.1) a verb with two objects, such as a direct and an indirect object, e.g. *she told him a lie*

Dog Latin see *Pig Latin*

domain (5.1–2; passim; 8.3.3, 8.3.7) area in which a language is used, e.g. family, work, administration; cf. also the *diatypical* category of *field of discourse*; see also *word field*

do-**periphrasis** (Case study 2.4) the use of the auxiliary *do* to form questions and negations, e.g. *Did she come? No, she did not.*

double negation see *multiple negation*

doublet (2.1.1.3, 2.1.2.1) pair of words similar in their origin (*lexical doublet*) or in their meaning (*semantic doublet*); see also *triplet*

Dutch (1.2.2; 4.3.2.1, 4.3.3.2; 8.3.1)

economy (3.3.5) the use of the fewest necessary *semantic features* in order to achieve a distinctive matrix.

education (2.2.3.7; 4.6.6; 5.1.2.2, 5.2, 5.2.1.2–4, 5.2.2.1–3; 7.2.1.1, Exercises 7.2 and 7.8; 8.1.4) a variable in *sociolinguistics*

EFL (English as a Foreign Language) (1.1.1, 1.4.2; 5.0, 5.1, 5.1.2.4; 8.3, 8.4.3) English when it is taught in countries and used in situations in which some other language(s) has (have) official status; e.g. English is (and has the status of) a *foreign language* in Italy, where it is taught in schools and used instead of Italian in situations where the speakers do not have English as a *first* or *second* language

emoticon (Exercise 8.9) icons used in Internet communciation to convey something about the writer, e.g. the *smiley* ☺)

encyclopedia (1.4.5) a reference work oriented toward thematic areas of knowledge rather than linguistic items; cf. *dictionary*, *thesaurus*

ending (7.3.1) of a *conversation*; also *closing*; the final phase in a conversation

ENL (English as a Native Language) (1.1.1, 1.4.2; 5.0, 5.1, 5.1.2.5, 5.3.1; 6.1.6, 6.2.1, 6.3.6, 6.4.1, 6.4.2.1–2, 6.4.2.4; 7.2, 7.2.3, 7.3.2.1, 7.3.2.2; 8.1.1, 8.1.2.1, 8.2.3, 8.4.3; 9.1) English acquired as the *first language* which a person learns in his or her life, a.k.a. mother tongue; ENL countries are those with a significant proportion of native speakers of English, esp Australia, Canada, Jamaica, New Zealand, South Africa, the UK, and the USA. Note: the use of English as someone's main language although it is not their *native language* is its use as a *primary language*, for which the term *first language* is also sometimes used

entry (1.3, 1.4.2–5; 4.3.3.2, 4.5.7; 5.3.2.3; 7.2.4.1) the *headword* in a dictionary, thesaurus, or encyclopedia, the form looked up

eponym (2.2.3.1) the name of one person which serves to designate whole sets of similar persons, e.g. *stetson* from the name of the hatter John Stetson; abstract concept: *eponymy*

ESL (English as a Second Language) (1.1.1, 1.4.2; 5.0–1, 5.1.2.3, 5.1.2.5, 5.2, 5.3.1; 6.1, 6.3.6, 6.4.1; Case study 7.1; 8.1, 8.1.1, 8.1.2.1, 8.4.3; 9.1) English learnt in addition to a *native language*, esp. when it has the status of an official language in a given country. Note that English and French are the official languages in Canada, i.e. its legally prescribed languages; English is referred to as a *second language* from the perspective of a mother tongue speaker of French

ESP: English for Special/Specific Purposes (1.4.3.2; 8.4.3) the special(ist) language of a particular field such as law, chemistry, or linguistics; see also *field of discourse*

EST: English of Science and Technology (8.4.3) an *ESP*

ethnicity (2.2.3.7; 3.3.9–10, 3.4.1; 4.6.6; 5.3.1 passim; 7.1, 7.2.1.2, 7.2.4.2) a variable in *sociolinguistics*

ethnolect (a.k.a. *ethnic dialect*) (5.3.1) language variation typical of a particular ethnic group, e.g. *Black American English*; see also *dialect*

etymology (1.4.2) the study of the history and origin of words

euphemism (1.4.3.2; 4.6, Exercises 4.8, 4.10 and 4.11, Project 4.1; 6.1.4; 8.1.5, Exercise 8.3) mild or inoffensive substitute for an offensive, harsh, blunt, or tabooed word

exogenous language (5.1.2.) a language not native to a country, as English in Nigeria; contrast *autochthonous*

extension of meaning a.k.a. *broadening of meaning* see also *semantic shift*

face see *politeness*

face-threatening act (FTA) see *politeness*

feature matrix (Case study 3.4) the set of semantic features which describe the meaning of a word via *componential analysis*

field of discourse (5.3.2, 5.3.2.4; 7.2.1.1; 8.4.3) variation based on the vocabulary of a subject area, e.g. the English of science, technology, law, etc.; part of *diatypical* variation, which includes *register*, *medium*, *functional tenor* (purpose), *personal tenor* (*style*); see also *domain*; *word field*

first language (1.1.1; 5.1.1, 5.1.2.5, 5.2.1.1; 6.0) the official language of a country or region, the default language in relation to which various second languages may be added

fixed expression (a.k.a. *routine formula*) (3.5; 6.3, 6.3.7; Exercise 7.7); a combination of words which regularly occur together, e.g. *binomials*, *idioms*, *proverbs*; see also *syntagmatic*

folk etymology (3.7; 4.3.1.3) a reinterpretation of a borrowed word so as to offer a plausible though not historical explanation, e.g. French *crevice* 'freshwater crustacean' > *crayfish* (or in some dialects *craw(l) fish* – since crawfish crawl)

foreign language (1.1.1–2, 1.3.3, 5.1.1; 8.3) a language learnt in addition to one's first or native language, often in a school context and one which has no official status in the country one lives in

formality see *style*

form word see also *grammatical word*

four-letter word (4.6; Case study 8.4) a taboo or swear-word, typically, but not necessarily consisting of four letters, e.g. *shit*, *hell*, but also *bitch*

free morph (4.3.2.1) a lexeme which can occur as an independent word (often equivalent to a simplex)

French (1.1.1, 1.3.3; 2.1.2.1, 2.1.4.1, 2.2.1.2; 3.7; 5.1.2, 5.1.2.5, 5.3.2.4; 8.2.6, 8.3.1, Project 8.4)

full verb see *lexical verb*

functional tenor (5.3.2.2–3; 8.4.3) the purpose pursued in a *speech act* or a text viewed under the aspect of *diatypes*; see also *register, field, medium, personal tenor (style)*

fun naming (Exercise 7.7) the use of a rhyming name with no reference to the addressee after a commonplace remark, e.g. *jeez Louise*

Gaelic (2.1.1.1, 2.1.6; 6.3.2) see *Irish*

Gambia (5.1.2.3, 5.2, 5.2.1.1)

GenAm: General American (1.4.2) the most widespread standard of pronunciation in the USA and Canada

gender (2.2.3.7; Case study 3.5, 3.4.1; Project 4.1; 5.2, 5.3.1, 5.3.1.1, Project 5.2; 6.4.2.2; 7.0, 7.1, 7.2.1.2, 7.2.3.1, 7.2.4, 7.2.4.2, Exercise 7.6, Case study 7.2, 7.3.1, Exercise 7.8, Project 7.6; 8.1) a variable in *sociolinguistics*

gender (2.1.3; 6.4.1, 6.4.1.4+6) a grammatical category realized in English by means of the personal pronouns *he, she,* and *it*

genderlect see *dialect, gender*

GenE: General English (1.1.2) both standard and non-standard forms of English, but excluding *traditional dialects* and English-oriented *creoles*. The widespread use of *double* or *multiple negation* or 3rd person *don't* (*he don't like it*) are GenE, though not StE

German, Germany (1.1.2, 1.4.2; 2.2.1.1–2; 3.3.3; 4.3.2.1, 4.3.2.3; 5.1.2.5; 6.3.6; Case study 8.6)

Germanic (2.1, 2.1.1.1, 2.1.1.2–3, 2.1.2.1–2, 2.1.4.1; 4.3.2.2, 4.6; 6.1.6)

Ghana (5.2.1.1; 8.4.1.1)

gobbledygook see *bureaucratese*

gradable antonym see *antonymy*

grammatical preposition see *preposition*

grammatical word or *form word* (1.3; 2.1.3, 2.2.2.1, 2.2.4; 3.6.1.2; Exercise 6.6; 8.1.5) a word which does not have real-world referents (cf. *non-referring expression*). Such words are highly grammatical (e.g. closed class items such as articles and determiners, auxiliary verbs, and pronouns). Cf. *lexical words*

grammaticalization (3.6.1.2) the process by which a lexeme is associated with grammatical meaning, e.g. the development of *to* from a preposition into a marker of the infinitive (*to be*)

Great Vowel Shift (2.1.2) a change in the phonetic value (pronunciation) of the long vowels of English in the late ME/early ModE period, e.g. /eː/ became /iː/ as in *seon* to *see*

Greek (1.4.4; 2.1.4.1; 4.6; 8.4.3.1–2, 8.4.3.4)

greetings (7.3.2.1, Exercise 7.9, Project 7.6) a type of (expressive) *speech act*

hard word see *learned word*

headword see *entry*

heteronym (a.k.a. *incompatibility* or *heteronymy*) (3.1.1.2) a set of words (*taxonomic sisters*) which share one or more elements of meaning, but are mutually exclusive: *Monday, Tuesday, Wednesday* . . .; *red, blue, green* . . .

hierarchical relationships (3.1.1.2) meaning relationships in which a more general (*superordinate*) term such as *vehicle* includes a *subordinate* term (*hyponym*) such as *car* or *bus*; see *hyponymy*

High language (5.1.2.2–3 + 5, 5.2.1.4, 5.2.2.1–2) the prestigious language of education and power in the sense of *diglossia*

Hindi (5.1.2.1; 5.2.2.1; 6.1.3)

historical dictionary (1.4.3) a dictionary which documents the use of words from their earliest recorded occurrences; see also *OED*

Hog Latin see *Pig Latin*

homographs see *homonymy*

homonymy (1.4.2; 3.1.1.1, 3.3.8) identity of form but two (or more) different lexemes (= *homonyms*). Spelling and pronunciation can be identical (*hind* 'rear (end)' vs. *hind* 'deer'. If only the spelling is identical (n. *tear* /tiːr/ vs. v. *tear* /ter/) we speak of homographs; we speak of homophones if only the pronunciation is identical (/naɪt/ for *night* and *knight*); see also *polysemy*

homophones see *homonymy*

honorifics (7.1, 7.2.1.2, 7.2.2.3, Exercises 7.2, 7.6) a respectful vocative, e.g. *sir, ma'am*

hybrid see *loan blend*

hyponymy (3.1.1.2) a vertical ordering of words in a word field terms such that a *superordinate term* is a generic or cover term for all the terms ordered under it, which are its *hyponyms*, e.g. *vehicle* is a superordinate term for its hyponyms *car, truck, plane, boat, train*, etc., all of which are *co-hyponyms*. Hyponymy is a transitive relationship. This means that if a Rolls-Royce is a car and a car is a vehicle, then a Rolls-Royce is a vehicle. It is also a case of entailment or inclusion: if something is a Rolls it is necessarily a car; but if something is a car, it is not necessarily a Rolls

icon (Exercise 8.9) a representation which stands for something else by virtue of some resemblance or similarity between the icon and that thing, esp. the graphic symbols used on computer screens; see also *emoticon*

iconic meaning see *theories of meaning*

idiom, idiomatic expression (1.4.2–3, 1.4.5; 2.1.6; 3.5.3, 3.5.3–4; 6.1.5, 6.3, Exercise 6.3, 6.3.3, Exercise 6.4; 7.3.1, 7.3.2: passim) a composite expression whose meaning cannot be reconstructed from the sum of its parts; see *compositionality*, also *metaphorical idiom, phrasal verb, pragmatic idiom*

illocutionary act (5.3.2.2; 7.3.1) the act that a speaker intends to carry out when performing a *speech act*, e.g. *representatives, directives, commissives, expressives, declaratives*

immigrant language (2.1.4.3) a language spoken by immigrants to a country where their language is not a native language, e.g. Urdu in the UK or Chinese in Australia

imperative (Case study 2.1, Case study 2.5; 7.1; Case study 8.12) the grammatical form of the verb used in making a direct command, e.g. *Close the door!*

inclusion see *hyponymy*

incompatibility see *heteronym*

IndE: Indian English (5.1.2.4–5; 6.1.2, Projects 6.2, 6.4.2.1, Case study 6.6, 6.4.2.2; Case study 7.1, 7.2.3; 8.1.1, 8.1.2.1, 8.4.1.1)

indefinite article see *article*

indefinite pronoun (6.4.1.2) one of the members of the set including *some* and its compounds (*someone, somewhere, sometime,* etc.); ditto of *any*; also *all, none, every, each, both, (n)either*; see also *determiner*

indirect object (3.6.1.1) the recipient of giving, addressee of telling, the audience of demonstrating, e.g. *give/tell/show someone something*; see also *dative alternation*

indirect speech (a.k.a. *reported speech*) (Case study 2.5; 3.6.1.1; 7.1) the communication of something said or thought in a clause after a verb of speech or thought, e.g. *They remarked/felt (that) she was unfair*

indirect speech act (7.1) the performance of a *speech act* by implication, e.g. remarking *Those cookies are mighty good* instead of saying *Please offer me another cookie*

Indo-European (2.1) a family of historically related languages including most of the European languages such as English, French, German, Italian, Polish, Russian, Spanish

infinitive marker to (3.6.1.3) a *grammaticalization* of the preposition *to*

infix, infixation see *affix*

Internet, the (1.1.1, 1.3.2–3, 1.4.2; 3.2.3; 4.2; 8.4, 8.4.1, 8.4.1.1, Exercises 8.7, 8.8, 8.9)

interruption (7.3.1) a change in speaker turns in which the new speaker does not take the floor in an ordered way

IPA: International Phonetic Alphabet (1.4.2) a widely accepted transcription system using symbols such as /ʃ/ for 'sh'

Irish a.k.a. (Irish) *Gaelic*

IrE: Irish English, Ireland (2.1.4.2, Case study 2.1, Exercise 2.2, 2.2.4.3; 3.2.1, 3.3.8, 3.3.11, 3.7; 5.1.2; Case study 6.4, 6.3.3, 6.4.2.1; 7.2.4.2)

Jamaica see *CarE*

Jamaican Creole (Case study 6.5) the vernacular of Jamaica, in *basilect* and *mesolect* forms which stand in a *continuum* with *StE* at the *acrolect* end

jargon (5.3.2.3; 8.1.5, 8.2, Case study 8.11) a specialized or technical language, esp. of a particular trade or profession, e.g. the jargon of linguists; see also *bureaucratese, legalese*

Kenya (3.2.3; 5.0. 5.1.2.1, 5.1.2.5, 5.2.1.3–4; 8.4.1.1)
Kiswahili (5.1.2.1, 5.2.1.3–4)
Krio (5.2.1.1; 6.1.4) a West African English-based creole
Kriol (4.4.3; Case study 6.5) an Australian English-based creole
KTs: kinship terms (7.2.1.2, 7.2.2–3) vocatives and terms of reference for relatives, e.g. *Dad, Auntie, Uncle Bill*

language contact (5.1) the influence of languages on each other as a result of being used by the same set of speakers, esp. *borrowing*
Latin (1.3.3; 2.0, 2.1.1.2, 2.1.4.1; 3.6.1.1; 4.3.3.4, 4.3.3.6, 4.6; 5.1.2.4; 6.1.6; 8.3.1, 8.4.3.1–2, 8.4.3.4)
learned word, a.k.a. *hard word* (1.4.3; 2.1.4.1; 4.6; 8.1.5) a word of Latin or Greek origin, often bookish rather than colloquial in style, *avarice* rather than more everyday *greed*
learner's dictionary (1.4.2.3) a *dictionary* intended for foreign learners or users of a language and restricted to more frequently used words, which are defined in a lexically accessible way
lect see *dialect*
legalese (8.1.5) the language of the law, characterized by archaic words and grammatical constructions and therefore difficult to understand; one of the targets of reform of the *Plain English movement*
lemma, (plu. *lemmas* or *lemmata*) see *entry*
lexeme (1.3; 2.0; 3.1.1.1–2, 3.3.10; 4.3.3, 4.3.3.1, 4.3.1.6; 4.4.1) a word as a lexical unit; lexemes may be single words or complex phraseological units such as *phrasal and prepositional verbs* and other *idiomatic expressions*
lexical change see esp. *borrowing, derivation, semantic shift*
lexical doublet see *doublet*
lexical field see *word field*
lexical gap (3.2, 3.3, 3.3.5; 5.2.2.1; 8.3.6) the lack of a *lexeme* for a familiar concept, e.g. while a reddish-brown horse is a *chestnut*, there is no single word for a white horse
lexicalization (4.3.2.1) an aspect of word formation in which (a) a newly formed word is accepted more widely and is therefore not merely a *nonce word* or (b) a word which has been institutionalized in use to such an extent as no longer to be *transparent* in meaning, but more specialized, e.g. *demo* (< *demonstration*) but used only for publicity
lexical morphology see *word formation*
lexical preposition see *preposition*
lexical semantics (5.0) the branch of linguistics dealing with word meaning, which includes *semantic/word fields*, *sense relations* such as *antonymy*, *homonymy, hyponymy, polysemy, synonymy*, see also *semantic features/components* and *componential analysis*
lexical unit (1.3) a combination of one *lexeme* and one distinct meaning

lexical verb (Case study 2.4) a full verb (e.g. *see*, *think*, *write*) as compared to an auxiliary verb (*can*, *have*, *will*); see *lexical word* and *grammatical word*

lexical word (1.3; 3.6.2; 8.1.5) a word which has a real-world referent (be it ever so abstract). Also *referring expression*; cf. *grammatical word* or *non-referring expression*

lexicography (1.4) the branch of word study dealing with the making of *dictionaries*, *thesauruses* and the like

lexicology (1.3.2; 3.1.1.2) the branch of linguistics which is devoted to the study of words and consisting of such branches as *etymology* (*lexical change* in the form and meaning of words, *borrowing*), *word formation/lexical morphology*, (*composition*, *derivation*), *word meaning/lexical semantics*, *dictionaries/lexicography*, and *complex* or *multi-word items*

lexicon (1.2, 1.4; 2.2.3; 8.4.3.2) all the words, i.e. *lexical units* of a language. See also *grammatical word*, *lexeme*, *lexical word*, *mental lexicon*, *word*, *word form*

lexifer language (3.7) the language from which a pidgin or a creole draws the major portion of its vocabulary

Liberia (5.1.2.3, 5.2, 5.2.1.1, Case study 5.2)

linguistic relativity (9.2) the view that the categories present in any particular language influence the way people view the world, e.g. languages with tense may lead their speakers to a greater propensity to see the world in terms of time

loan blend (a.k.a. *hybrid*) (Case study 8.6) a compound consisting of an element from another language, e.g. English-German *Fleece-Jacke* 'jacket with a soft fleece-like nap'; see also *blend*, *loan shift*, *loan translation*, *loan word*

loan translation (a.k.a. *calque*) (3.7; 4.3.1.2, Exercise 4.2; 6.1.1, 6.1.4, 6.3.6; 8.3.1–2, 8.3.6) a word translated element by element from another (source) language and then adopted into the target language, e.g. the word *loan translation* is a translation of German *Lehnübersetzung* (*Lehn* 'loan' + -*übersetzung* 'translation'); see also *loan blend*, *loan word*

loan word (a.k.a. *borrowing*) (4.3.1.1; Exercise 4.2; 6.1, 6.1.1–4; 8.3.2, 8.3.5–6) the adoption of words from another language, usually with a modification in the pronunciation so that they will conform more to the sound patterns of the target language, e.g. *kindergarten* (sometimes *kindergarden*) < German *Kindergarten*. Sometimes the terms *transference/transfer* are used; see also *loan blend*, *loan translation*

local markedness, unilateral (or bilateral) (3.4.1) the term for a word which is current only in one (local) variety in addition to a shared word for the same thing. If only one variety has a local marked word, the relation is unilateral; if both have a local word, it is bilateral

Low language in the sense of *diglossia*

Maori (4.1, 4.3.2.1–2; 6.4.1.1; Case study 7.1) the aboriginal population of New Zealand

malapropism (2.1.4.1) the mistaken use of a word for a similar sounding one of completely different meaning, often with an amusing effect, e.g. *compensation* for *complications,* as in *After the accident compensations set in*

manmade artefact (4.1) a *referent* which is subject to arbitrary voluntary change because it is the product of human industry; cf. also *natural kind*

matrix (3.3.2, 3.3.5–6; 4.5.7) of *semantic features*; the array or list of features which collectively make up the meaning of a word

meaning see *theories of meaning*

meaning change see *semantic shift*

meaning component see *semantic feature*

medium (of discourse, of language) (1.1.1, 1.3.2; 2.2.4.4; 5.3.2.1, 5.3.2.3–4; 7.2.1.2; 8.1, Case study 8.1, Exercise 8.9, 8.4.3) one of the modes in which language is transmitted: writing and speech are the major means of transmission. Tactile means include braille and the finger alphabet. Other visual means besides writing include signing (sign language); see also *field, functional tenor, register, style*

melioration see *amelioration*

member-collection see *meronymy*

mental lexicon (1.4.1) vocabulary as structured and stored in any given user's brain

mental representation see *theories of meaning*

meronymy (1.4.4.; 3.1.1.2; 6.3.7) a part–whole relationship, such as *petal–flower.* Meronymy is not always precise since it is not always clear what the necessary parts of a whole are. In addition, this relationship is only sometimes transitive (a petal of a flower is also a petal of a plant), but not always (the leg of a chair, the chair of a suite, but not the leg of a suite). Member–collection is somewhat similar to meronymy. Examples are *student–class* or *person–crowd.* Portion–mass is also similar, where a substance is individualized via the name for a unit, e.g. *bar of chocolate* or *flake of snow.*

mesolect see *creole*

metaphor (1.4.5; 2.2.2.1–2; 3.1.1.1, 3.5.3; Exercise 4.8; 6.3.4, 6.3.6; 8.1.1, Case study 8.2, 8.4.3.3–4) a comparison which sets one thing as equal to another, e.g. *He's an ass* 'stubborn as an ass/donkey'

metaphorical idiom (3.5.2) a figurative or colourful idiom such as *go jump in a lake* 'get lost, go away, leave (me) alone'; see also *idiom*

metonymy (2.2.2.1–2; Exercise 4.8; Exercise 8.2) the replacement of one term by another which it is associated with, e.g. *noses* 'people' as in *to count noses*

Middle English (2.1.2–3; 6.4.1.6) English in the period 1150–1500

modal auxiliary verbs (2.2.4, 2.2.4.3; 3.6.1.3; 5.2.1.2; 7.1; 8.4.3.6) verbs like *must, shall, should,* and *will,* which share certain morphosyntactic characteristics and express personal attitudes towards the likelihood of what is predicted

mode see *medium of discourse*

mode of address see *vocatives*

Modern English (2.1.4) English in the period since 1500

monolingual dictionary (1.4.2) a dictionary in which entries and definitions are in the same language

morph (4.3.1.3, 4.3.2.1, 4.3.2.3) the actual form (phonetic or orthographic) which realizes a *morpheme* such as the plural {-s} in *books* or the prefix {de-} in *debrief* (see *affix*) or the lexemes {black} and {berry} in the *compound black-berry*

morpheme (1.4.1; 3.6.1.1; 4.3.1.3, 4.3.2.2; 5.3.1.1; 8.2.2, Case study 8.6, 8.4.3.1, 8.4.3.2, 8.4.3.4) a minimal meaningful unit of grammatical-lexical analysis; the meaning can be grammatical, e.g. the plural morpheme, {-S} or lexical, e.g. a *base*, *prefix*, or *suffix*, e.g. *plurals*, *unbased*, *prefix*, *suffixation*; see also *morph*

multiple naming (7.2.3) the practice of freely changing back and forth between a variety of forms of address, e.g. addressing Susan Ann Lewis as *Susan* (first name), *Susy* (diminutive), *Susan Ann Lewis* (full name), *Lewis* (last name), or *Honey Bun* (nickname); a sign of intimacy

multiple negation (a.k.a. *double negation*) (6.4.2.2–3) the use of more than one element indicating negation for its reinforcing effect, widespread in GenE, e.g. *they don't want none*

multi-word item (1.3, 1.4.2; 3.5) a lexical unit such as a *compound*, *idiom*, *collocation*, *phrasal verb*, etc. consisting of two or more words, e.g. *grandfather clock*, *pick-me-up*

name (1.3.2, 1.4.3.2; 2.1.1.1, 2.1.1.3, 2.2: passim; 3.2, 3.2.6; 4.2, 4.3.3.6, 4.3.3.8, 4.5.2, 4.5.4, 4.6.4; 7.2: passim, 7.3.1; 8.1.2.1, 8.2.4) the designation given to persons, places, and things, including *proper names* (a.k.a. *proper nouns*), which are used as *vocatives* and are usually capitalized, because unique. The Greek element {-onym}, which means 'word' or 'name', crops up again and again in the terminology used in this book, e.g. *antonym*, *epononym*, *homoym*, *metonymy*, *synonym*, *toponym*

narrowing of meaning (4.5.1, 4.5.3; 6.1.1, 6.1.8) the process by which a lexeme gains one or more *semantic features*, thus narrowing the *referents* to which it may be applied, e.g. *corn* 'grain' is narrowed in AmE to 'grain of the species *Zea mays*'; see also *amelioration*, *broadening of meaning*, *connotation*, *denotation*, *pejoration*, *semantic shift*

native language (1.1.1, 1.1.3; 1.4.2; 2.2.4; 3.7; 4.1; 5.3.1; 7.2.3; Ch. 8) the first language a person learns as a child employing the human ability to acquire language (cf. *first*, *primary*, *second*, and *foreign language*)

natural kind (4.1) a *referent* which occurs in nature and is not subject to arbitrary human change; often included in major taxonomic classifications such as the Linnaean system or the period table of elements. Birds, for example, include chickens, crows, ducks, penguins, and sparrows; cf. also *manmade artefact*

negation (Case study 2.4, Project 2.3; 6.4.2.1, Case study 6.6, Exercise 6.7) morphologically marked change in the polarity of a word or statement, e.g. the negative of *kind* is *unkind*; the negative of *I'm tired* is *I'm not tired*

neologism (2.1.4.1) a newly created lexeme or the use of one in a new sense. The term is also sometimes used in much the same way as *nonce word*

NigE: Nigerian English (4.4.1.1; 5.1.2.2–4, 5.2.1.1–2, 5.3.2.4)

nomenclatures see *terminologies*

nominalization (2.1.6; 8.4.3.1, 8.4.3.6) part of *nominal style*, i.e. the use of nouns rather than verbs or adjectives, e.g. *the apple is red* becomes *the redness of the apple*; *to walk for three hours* becomes *a three-hour walk*

nonce word (4.3.2.1; Case study 8.6) a newly coined word or a new use of a familiar word which does not go into wider use (*an once*[-used] *word* > *a nonce word*), e.g. momentarily referring collectively and pejoratively to teachers as *teacherdom*

non-count noun see *countability*

non-referring expression see *grammatical word;* cf. *referring expression*

non-standard English (1.1.2; 3.6.1.3, 3.6.2; 4.4, 4.4.3; Case study 6.6; 8.4.3.3) types of English not conforming to the vocabulary or grammar of *StE*; this can be *GenE, a (traditional) dialect*, or an English-oriented *creole*

non-U see *U*

noun (1.3, 1.4.2, 1.4.4–5; 2.1.1.1, 2.1.6, 2.2.2. 2.2.2.1, 2.2.3, 2.2.3.1, Project 2.2, 2.2.4; 3.1.2, 3.5.3; 4.3.2.2–4, 4.5.1; 5.2.5; 6.1.6, 6.3.7; 8.4.3.1) one of the *parts of speech*, variously defined, e.g. 'the name of a person, place, or thing'; also defined by position in a sentence, inflection, or function in the phrasal units of a sentence

number, grammatical (1.4.4; 2.1.3; 6.4: passim) a grammatical category realized in English by means of singular and plural

number of users (of *English***)** (5.1.2)

NZE: New Zealand English and *New Zealand* (1.1.1, 1.4.2; Case study 2.3; 3.2.3, 3.7; Ch. 4; 6.4.1.1; Case study 7.1; Exercise 8.4)

OED: *Oxford English Dictionary* (1.4.3) the major historical dictionary of English

officialese see *bureaucratese*

Old English (2.1.1, 2.1.3; 6.4.1.6) English in the period 450/550–1150

Old Norse (2.1.1.3)

onomatopoeia (2.2.1.1–3) the formation or use of words which may be said to be imitative in the sound of what they designate, e.g. *moo* (of a cow), *boom* (of an explosion), adj. *onomatopoeic* or *onomatopoetic*

opaque (3.5.2; 4.3.2.1) hard to understand; the converse of *transparent*

opening (7.3.1, Exercise 7.8) the initial phase of a *conversation*

opposites (3.1.1.2) a way in which word meanings can be seen as related to each other, see also *antonymy, complementary pair, converses, meronymy, reverses*

overlap (7.3.1) in *turn-taking* in a *conversation*

PakE: Pakistani English (3.2.4–5; 5.2.2; 6.1.6)

palatalization (2.1.2.1) a change in the place of articulation to a tongue position closer to the palate, e.g. /s/ to /ʃ/ with the stress change from *society* to *social*

paradigmatic (3.1.1.2) a relationship between words in which one may replace the other in the same position within a construction, e.g. *car* and *auto* stand in a paradigmatic relationship in *He's a(n) ____ saleman*; see also **syntagmatic**

part of speech (a.k.a. *word class*) (1.4.2; Case study 2.2; 3.1.1.2, 3.5.1; 4.3.2.2; 6.3.7) one of the eight or nine traditional divisions of words according to morphosyntactic behaviour, viz. noun, pronoun, verb, adjective, adverb, preposition, conjunction, interjection, and determiner/article

past tense (a.k.a. *simple past*) (1.4.2; 2.2.4.1; 7.1) one of the two morphological tenses in English (the other being the present)

PC (politically correct) language (Case study 8.11) a choice of terms so as not to derogate, insult, or demean anyone because of group membership. PC language is applied esp. to racial-ethnic, sexual, age, and ability categories, e.g. the use of <u>human</u>kind because <u>man</u>kind may be considered sexist

pejoration (4.5.2, 4.6: passim; 6.2) the case in which a word takes on a more negative or derogatory meaning, e.g. *bitch* as an insulting word for a female has undergone pejoration from its originally neutral meaning of 'female dog'; see also **amelioration, broadening of meaning, connotation, narrowing of meaning, semantic shift**

perfect (Case study 2.4, Project 2.3) an aspectual category of English indicating an act, event, or state which transpired or existed previous to another, e.g. *he <u>had gone</u> before I arrived*

person (6.4) a grammatical category consisting of 1st, 2nd, and 3rd persons, as with *I/we, you,* and *he, she, it/they*

personal pronoun system (2.1.3; 6.4) a closed system of pronouns used to designate 1st person (speaker), 2nd person (address), or 3rd person (neither of above), e.g. *I, you, he/she/it*

personal tenor see *style*; see also **diatype, register, field, medium, functional tenor**

phatic behaviour/communion (7.2.1) communication serving to maintain social contacts more than to exchange information, sometimes played down as small talk; it includes greetings like *How's it going?*

phenomenon creation (Case study 8.6) a word which by appearance seems to be borrowed from another language, but in reality is a new, independent creation on the foreign model, e.g. German *Handy* on the model of English {hand} + {y} for *cell* or *mobile phone*

Philippine English and the Philippines (5.1.2.1, 5.2.2.3; 6.3.6)

phonesthetics (a.k.a. *phonesthesia*) see **sound symbolism**

phrasal verb (1.4.3.2; 3.5.2) a **multi-word item** consisting of a verb and a particle with idiomatic meaning, e.g. *pig out* 'eat gluttonously'

pidgin, Pidgin English (3.6.1.3, 3.7; 5.1.2.3, 5.1.2.5, 5.2, 5.2.1.1–3; 6.1.1, Case study 6.5) a language made up of elements of more than one other language and which is normally no one's native language, e.g. *West African Pidgin English (WAPE)*, which is widely used throughout West Africa for communication among speakers who may share no other language; Pidgin Englishes typically draw on English as the ultimate source of much of their vocabulary even though their grammar may differ greatly from that of StE

Pig Latin, a.k.a. *Hog Latin, Dog Latin* (Exercise 8.2) one of many thousands of secret languages, in this case based on the transposition of sounds and the addition of syllables, e.g. *Latin > Atin + l + ay = Atinlay*; see also *back slang*

Pilipino (5.1.2.1, 5.1.2.3, 5.2.2.3) the national language of the Philippines derived from Tagalog

Plain English movement (8.1.5) a number of different movements in various of the ENL countries directed chiefly against obscure bureaucratic language (see *bureaucratese*)

pleonasm (6.1.4) a redundant use of words, e.g. *refer back (to something)* for *refer (to something)*

polite form also *tentative form* (Case study 2.5; 7.1) a form which shows distance and hence respect for another's *face*, e.g. a *past tense* or *conditional form* such as *would you ...* or *I thought ...*

politeness (7.1, 7.2.3, 7.2.4.1, 7.3.1, 7.3.2.4) social behaviour, often highly conventionalized, governed by considerations of positive (building someone up) and negative face (not intruding on someone's territory as with a *face-threatening act (FTA)*); see also *indirect speech act*

politically correct language see *PC language*

polysemy (1.4.2; 3.1.1.1) the existence of two or more distinct meanings of one single lexeme, e.g. *bed* (to sleep in, of a river, for flowers) (adj. *polysemous*); see also *homonym(y)*

portion-mass see *meronymy*

portmanteau word see *blend*

power (7.2.1.1, Exercises 7.6 and 7.7, 7.2.3, 7.3.1, 7.3.2.1, Exercise 7.9, Case study 7.6) a relationship of relative distance. It is one of the basic dimensions regulating social relations, esp. as seen in modes of address; see also *solidarity*

pragmatic idiom (3.5.2; 7.3.1 + 2) conventionalized expressions used in connection with certain acts, e.g. *Goodbye* + the act of leaving

pragmatics (5.3.2.2; 7.0, 7.3) the branch of linguistics which deals with 'speaker meaning', i.e. intentions, but also the speaker's knowledge and beliefs

prefix, prefixation see *affix*

preparatory conditions (7.1) the conditions necessary for the successful (or felicitous) accomplishment of a *speech act*, e.g. a request that somebody do something presupposes that that person is able to carry out the act requested, hence making ability a preparatory condition

preposition (3.6) incl. *grammatical preposition* (3.6.1) and *lexical preposition* (3.6.2) a functional word class or part of speech which typically expresses relationships of place, time, cause, etc., sometimes highly grammaticalized, e.g. *in, at, on, for, to*

prepositional verb (3.5.3–4) a verb + preposition combination with a more or less idiomatic meaning often paraphrasable by a single verb, e.g. *look at (TV)* = *watch (TV)* or *go into* 'investigate'

present perfect see *perfect*

primary language (5.1.1) the language used most frequently by any given speaker. It may be his or her *native* or *first language* or a *second* or *foreign language*

pronouns (7.2.1.2, 7.2.3) as vocatives, e.g. addressing someone as *Hey, you!*; see also *personal pronouns*

proper name see *name*, *proper noun*

proper noun (Case study 2.2, 2.2.3.1) the name of a specific person, place, time, and capitalized, e.g. *Richard, Detroit, Tuesday*

prototype theory see *theories of meaning*

proverb (1.4.3.2; 6.3: passim) a statement of (conventional) wisdom consisting of a whole sentence, e.g. *Cleanliness is next to godliness*

race see *ethnicity*

rank reduction (Case study 6.1) the use of the designation for a container for the thing contained, e.g. *coffee cup* for *cup of coffee*

reciprocity (7.2.1.1, Exercise 7.6) the use of equivalent forms of address between two people, e.g. both use first names or both use title and last name for each other

reduplication (6.1.1, 6.1.4) the doubling of a word, in English usually for emphasis; reduplication may be exact (*yum-yum*), rhyming (*higgledy-piggledy*), with the prefixed consonants /ʃm/ as a replacement of the original initial consonant (*luck-schmuck*) (typically Yiddish-influenced English), with vowel change (Ablaut) (*ding-dong, mishmash*)

redundant feature/redundancy (3.3.3) the unnecessary and uneconomical (see *economy*) use of semantic features where a more general feature would serve: the presence of one general feature as a component of the meaning of a word implicitly guarantees the presence of more basic features, e.g. [+HUMAN] entails [+ANIMATE]

reference (or *denotation*) see *theories of meaning*

referent (a.k.a. *denotatum* or *significatum*) (2.2.2; 3.1.2, 3.2) the entity (person, place, thing, idea, event, etc.) referred to by a word

referential gap see *conceptual gap*

referring expression see *lexical word*

region (2.2.3.7; 3.1.1.2, Project 3.3, 3.4.1, 3.4.8; 4.6.4–6; 5.2, 5.3.1.2; Case study 6.4; 7.2.1.1; Exercise 7.3; 8.1) a variable in *sociolinguistics*

regional dialect see *dialect*

register (5.3; 6.4.2.2; 8.4.3) diatypical variation or variation according to use (*diatype*); sometimes including dialectal variation or variation by user as well (*dialect*)

religion (3.3.9; 5.1.2.2, 5.2, 5.3.1, 5.3.1.1–2; 6.3.2; 7.2.1.1, 7.2.4.2, Project 7.4) a variable in *sociolinguistics*

reported speech see *indirect speech*

representational meaning see *theories of meaning*

reverse dictionary (1.4.3) a dictionary organized alphabetically according to the final element of a word, e.g. *statement* not under 's', but under 'm' for *-ment*

reverses, (a.k.a. *reversives*) (3.1.1.2) involve an identical type of movement in opposite directions, e.g. *come/go*, *in/out*; or processes which can be reversed, e.g. *separate/mix*; *freeze/thaw*. See also **antonymy, complementary pair, converses**

rhetorical functions (8.4.3) the ultimate purpose of a text, viz. description, report, exposition, instruction, argumentation

rhyming slang (Exercise 8.4) a pair of words, the second of which rhymes with the word meant, but unspoken, e.g. *Joe Blake* 'a snake'

ritual insult see *semantic inversion*

routine formula see *fixed expression*

RP: Received Pronunciation (a.k.a. Oxford English) (1.4.2) the prestige pronunciation of England

SAE: South African English and *South Africa* (1.1.1; 3.2.3, 3.6.3, 3.7; Ch. 4; 5.1.2, 5.2.1, 5.2.1.1; Case study 7.1, 7.2.3, 7.2.4.2, 7.3.2.4, Case study 7.4; 8.1.1, 8.4.2)

salutation (8.1.2.1, Project 8.1, 8.4.1.1) the greeting phrase of a *letter*, e.g. *Dear Madam* or *Hi!*; see also *closing*

San (4.1) one of the languages of South Africa

sandwich word (6.1.6) the insertion of one word into another with some overlap, e.g. *fascinating* + *sin* > *fas-sin-ating*, a kind of *blend*

Scots (1.1.2, 1.4.2; 2.1.1.1, 2.1.2.2, 2.1.6, 2.2.3.4–5, Case study 2.5; 3.7; 4.5.1; 6.3.2; Case study 8.5, Project 8.3, 8.4.1.1, Case study 8.9)

second language (1.1.1, 1.3.3; 5.0, 5.1, 5.2; 6.1.8) (a) a language learnt after and in addition to a native language by any given speaker; (b) on the other hand, a second official language in a given country, e.g. in Singapore the national language is Malayan, but each of the languages Mandarin Chinese, Tamil, and English are second languages

secret language (Exercises 8.2 and 8.4) a language expressed in a code which serves to disguise it, e.g. *back slang*, *Pig/Hog Latin*, *rhyming slang*

semantic broadening see *broadening of meaning*

semantic change see *semantic shift*

semantic derogation (Exercise 4.8) effectively the same as *pejoration*

semantic doublet see *doublet*

semantic feature or *component* (a.k.a. *meaning component*) (3.3.1: passim; 4.5.1, 4.5.7) an element of meaning which together with other such elements constitutes the distinctive meaning of a lexical unit, often given in square brackets and small caps with a + or − sign, indicating its presence or absence e.g.

[+ROUND] of a circle, which also would take [+GEOMETRIC FIGURE], [+PLANE], [+EQUIDISTANT FROM CENTRE]. Semantic features are a useful means of defining meaning, as a look at any dictionary will immediately show, but theoretically they are difficult, as there is no way to determine how many there are or what their ontological status is. For example, if the concept 'dog' consists ultimately of a distinctive semantic feature such as [+canine], what then is the meaning of [+canine]? see also *matrix*

semantic field see *word field*

semantic inversion (Case study 7.2; 8.2, 8.2.4) the use of a negative form of address to mark particular solidarity, e.g. *How're ya doin', ya old bugger!* Includes taboo or derogatory expressions (*old bugger*), which are then *ritual insults* and/or *camaraderie forms* (*mate, buster, mac*); largely restricted to male use

semantic narrowing see *narrowing of meaning*

semantic shift (1.1.1; 3.1.1.1; 4.5.1; 6.1.1–2, 6.1.5; 8.3.9, 8.4.3.4) change in meaning involving processes such as *amelioration, broadening of meaning, pejoration, narrowing of meaning*

semiotics (3.1) the discipline that deals with symbols used to communicate. Language is especially prominent, but systems of non-verbal symbols also serve this purpose, such as visual behaviour (e.g. eye contact), kinesics (body movement), facial expression, gestures, and style of dress

semiotic triangle (a.k.a. the 'triangle of signification' or 'referential triangle') (1.4; 3.1.1) a figure used to indicate the relationship between a referent and a word, which is indirect and is mediated by the language user's concept of the referent

sense relation see *theories of meaning*

shift see *semantic shift*

shortening see *clipping*

Sierra Leone (5.1.2.3, 5.2.1.1–2)

simple past see *past tense*

SingE: Singapore English (1.4.2; 3.2.3; 5.1.2.4–5, 5.2; 6.1, 6.1.3, 6.3.6, 6.4.2.1–2; 7.1, 7.2.3, Case study 7.3, 7.3.2.1)

slang (1.1.2, 1.4.3.2; 3.1.1.2, 3.4.2, 3.5.2; 5.3.2.3–4; 8.1.4, Case study 8.2, 8.2, Case study 8.9) vocabulary, often colourful, typical of groups marginalized in some fashion, e.g. schoolboy slang

sociolect (a.k.a. *social dialect*) (1.1.2, 1.2, 1.3.2–3; 2.1; 3.4.2; 5.2.5, 5.3.1.1–2; 6.1.1; Ch. 7; 8.1.4) language variation typical of a social class; see also *dialect, U and non-U*

sociolinguistics (Ch. 7; 8.1.4) branch of linguistics dealing with the relationship between social features of users and features of their language variety; see also *dialect*

solidarity (7.2.1.1, 7.2.3., Exercises 7.6 and 7.7, Case study 7.3, Project 7.6, Case study 7.4) a relationship of relative intimacy; one of the basic dimensions regulating social relations, esp. as seen in modes of address; see also *power*

sound symbolism (a.k.a. *phonestheticslphonesthesia*) (2.2.1.2) the suggestion of meaning by some sound combinations, e.g. *-ash* /æʃ/ as in *bash, crash, clash, dash, flash, gash, gnash, mash, rash, slash* for sudden or violent movements

Spanish (2.2.1.2; 4.6.2; 6.4.2.4; 8.3.1, 8.3.3, Exercises 8.5, 8.6, Case studies 8.7, 8.8)

special dictionaries (1.4.3) dictionaries restricted to such entries as *abbreviations*, clichés, colloquialisms, *dialect*, *ESP*, *euphemisms*, *hard words*, *idioms*, *names*, new words, *phrasal verbs*, phrases and quotations, *proverbs*, *slang*; also *reverse dictionaries*; dictionaries of spelling, pronunciation, grammar, *etymology*, usage

speech act (1.3.2; 5.3.2.2; 6.4.2.1; 7.1, 7.3.1) consisting of the types representatives or assertives, e.g. as statements and assertions; directives, e.g. requests and questions; commissives, e.g. promises, threats, and offers; expressives, e.g. thanking, apologizing, congratulating; declaratives (a.k.a. performatives) (pronouncing someone husband and wife). See also *illocutionary act, preparatory conditions*

spoken English (1.1.2; 2.2.4.2; 5.3.2.1, 5.3.2.4; 7.2.1.1; 8.2, 8.4.3) one *medium* of language; see also *written English*

spoonerism (1.4.1) the exchange of sounds or words within a sentence, e.g. *slow and sneet* 'snow and sleet'

standard (language) see *StE*

status (7.2.4.1) a variable in *sociolinguistics*

StE: Standard English (1.1.2; 3.7; 4.4; 5.1.2.3–4, 5.1.2.5, 5.2.1.2; 6.4, 6.4.1, Case studies 6.5, 6.6, Exercise 6.7; 8.1.4, 8.2, 8.2.4) the type of English associated with better education and often with middle-class manner (avoidance of *slang* and *swear words*); standards vary, however, from country to country and region to region

style (a.k.a. *personal tenor*) (1.1.1–2, 1.3.2, 1.4.2; Exercise 3.5; 5.3.1.2, 5.3.2.3; 7.2.3, 7.3.1.2; 8.1: passim, 8.2.6, 8.3.2, 8.4.1.1, 8.4.3, 8.4.3.1) involves a choice between two or more words, structures, pronunciations, etc. in which the choice is dictated by the relationship between the people communicating and motivated by the reaction it is likely to evoke in the addressee; see also *diatype, register, field, medium, functional tenor*

style calque (8.1.1) a linguistic expression chosen according to the style dictates of a non-English language, e.g. the expression of extreme deference in IndE where not called for in ENL

subjunctive form/mood (Case study 2.5) the uninflected form of the finite verb (e.g. *I, you, helshe be*) used in clauses after a small set of predicates such as *demand, be necessary*, etc.

substrate language or *substratum influence* (2.1.6; Case study 3.6, 3.7; 5.1.2.5; 6.4, Case study 6.5) the language or variety of a language with less prestige whose influences are sometimes seen as creating changes in the structure of the standard language (see *superstrate*) as with Irish on IrE, African languages on English pidgins and creoles, or Chinese, Tamil, or Malay on SingE; see also *adstrate*

suffix, suffixation see *affix*

superordinate see *hyponymy*

superstrate language (3.7; 5.1.2.5) the more dominant of two languages or of two varieties of one language, i.e. the one more likely to influence the other; the prestige language or *lexifer language* which supplies a *pidgin* or *creole* with the mass of its vocabulary; see also *adstrate*, *substrate*

swear word see *taboo word*

synonymy, synonym (1.4.1, 1.4.4; 2.1.4.1; 3.1.1.2, 3.4.2–3; 8.1.5) words which mean the same thing and can be exchanged for each other (theoretically in any context), e.g. *tap* and *spigot*. Sometimes meaning is restricted to *denotational meaning* such as might be covered by an identical set of semantic features. In this case differences in *connotational meaning* are not affected, e.g. the fact that *tap* is BrE for Southern AmE *spigot*

syntagmatic (3.1.1.2) a relationship between words in a sequence, esp. when the combination is (relatively) fixed, as with *collocations*, *idioms*, and *proverbs*, e.g. *merry + Christmas*

taboo word (a.k.a. *swear word*) (1.1.2; 4.6, 4.6.1, 4.6.5–6; 5.3.2.3; 7.2.4.10; 8.2, 8.2.4., 8.2.6–7) a word considered strongly inappropriate when used under polite circumstances, e.g. *goddam(n)* (profanity), *fuck* (obscenity), *shit* (dirty word)

Tagalog see *Pilipino*

tag question (5.1.2.5; 6.4.2.2, Exercise 6.8) words added on to statements to make them emphatic or change them into questions. Tag questions can be invariable (*Let's go, okay!*) or grammatical and varying, e.g. *She went, didn't she? He should, shouldn't he?*

Tamil (5.1.2.1, 5.2, 5.2.2.1–2; 6.1.3)

Tanzania (3.2.3; 5.0, 5.1.2.1, 5.2.1.3–4; 6.1.5; 7.3.2.1; 8.4.1.1)

tautonyms (3.3.4) words that are the same, but have different meanings, e.g. *corn* (in England: 'wheat'; in Scotland: 'oats'; in America: 'maize')

taxonomic sisters (3.1.1.2; 4.3.1.3) closed sets of mutually exclusive terms, all of which are 'opposites' of all the others, e.g. the months of the year or days of the week; see also *heteronym*

tentative form (Case study 2.5) a form indicating uncertainty by means of a form showing distance such as a past modal auxiliary, e.g. *I might go*; see also *polite form*

terminologies (a.k.a. *nomenclatures*) (8.4.3) systematic and conventionalized sets of designations in technical areas, e.g. the Linnaean system in biology

thanking (7.3.2.5) a type of (expressive) *speech act*

theories of meaning (2.2) some of the various explanations of meaning include:

  (a) *iconic meaning* (2.2.1), in which there is an analogy or other type of relationship between the word and what it designates (as in *phonesthetics, onomatopoeia*)

  (b) *reference theory* (*denotational meaning*) (2.2.2; 3.1.1.2, 3.4.2; 4.5.1; Case study 8.6), in which the actual thing is the meaning

(c) *representational (mentalist) meaning* (2.2.3), in which the meaning of a word lies in the mental concept associated with it, which itself may be defined by *semantic features* (note: *prototype theory* (2.2.3.2; 3.3) is a psychological approach to conceptual meaning which implicitly involves semantic features; *sense relations* (3.1.1.2) such as *homonymy*, *synonymy*, or *antonymy* may be understood as part of representational meaning); and

(d) *use theory* (2.2.4), in which meaning is determined by the function of a word in an utterance

thesaurus (1.4.4; 8.2.6) a dictionary of synonyms (and antonyms) organized by field

title, abbrev. T (7.1, 7.2.1.2, 7.2.3, 7.2.4.1, Project 7.6) vocative or term of reference which generally confers status, e.g. *Dr*, *Prof*, *Capt*, *Col*, etc. *Mr*, *Mrs*, *Ms*, and *Miss* often count as titles

token (6.3.3) instances of use of a word, e.g. the definition just given has two tokens of the word *of*; while the abstract word *of* is called a *type* (8.6.2.4)

toponym (Case study 2.2, Exercise 2.4, Project 2.1) a place name, e.g. *Central Park*, *Boston*

traditional dialect (1.1.2) a non-standard regional dialect which derives directly from the dialects of Old English and which does not stand in a one-to-one phonological, syntactic, and lexical relationship to GenE, e.g. one of the Lowland Scots dialects

transparency (3.5.3; 4.3.2.1; 8.4.3.4) clear in meaning; see *compositionality*, cf. *opaque*

triglossia (5.1.2.2) a diglossic situation with two *H(igh)* languages; see *diglossia*

trinomial (Exercise 6.4) a fixed and usually irreversible combination of three items of the same part of speech (three nouns or three adverbs, etc.) e.g. (*every*) *Tom, Dick, and Harry* or *left, right, and centre;* see also *binomial*

triplet (2.1.4.1) three words in a lexical-semantic set which combines a *semantic doublet*, e.g. *bower* (Germanic origin) and *arbour* (French origin), and a *lexical doublet*, e.g. *arbour* and Latin *herbarium*.

turn-taking (7.3.1) the interchange between participants in *conversation* determining who has the floor; it includes *interruption* and *overlap*

type see *token*

U and *non-U* (8.1.4, Case study 8.2) upper-class (and non-upper-class) speech

Uganda (3.2.3; 5.0, 5.2.1.2, Case study 5.2; 8.4.1.1)

Ulster (2.1.6–7; 6.3.2; 7.1)

unilateral local markedness see *local markedness*

United Kingdom see *BrE*

United States see *AmE*

usage label (a.k.a. *style*, *status*, *descriptive label*) (1.4.2; Exercise 3.5, Project 5.2) indication of restricted currency of lexemes. Usage labels may indicate *region*(al dialect), (vocational) *field*, *style*, less seldom *class*

use see *diatype*

user see *dialect*

use theory of meaning see *theories of meaning*

utterance act (7.3.1) the act of producing sounds, syllables, words, sentences independent of communicative purpose

vagueness (2.2.3.2; 3.1.1.1) meaning characterized by openness about the nature of the features involved, esp. typical of prototypes, which vary from person to person, e.g. my *giant* (always bearded) is different from yours (never bearded)

variable reference (2.2.3.1) reference to whole classes of things, say, tables, in which actual reference may be now to this table, now to that one

vernacular (5.1.2.1–4, 5.2.1.2, 5.2.2.1–3) the everyday language of communication, often the diglossically *Low language*

vocabulary addition see *borrowing, derivation, semantic shift*

vocabulary loss (4.2) a process in which words go out of use

vocation (3.3.9; 5.3.1, 5.3.1.2; 7.2.1.1, 7.2.4.1, Exercise 7.2) a variable in *sociolinguistics*

vocatives (7.2) expressions used to address someone, e.g. *Steward, sonnie, sir, Grampa, Ms Lewis*; see also *address, descriptor, diminutive, honorific, kinship term, name, pronoun, title*

vulgar (1.1.2; 3.4.2; 4.6; 5.3.2.3–4; 8.1.4, 8.2.7) impolite, rude, or even taboo usage (see also *taboo word*)

WAPE: West African Pidgin English see *pidgin*

WAVE: West African Vernacular English (5.2.1.1–2)

Welsh, Welsh English, Wales (2.1.1.1, 2.2.3.4; 6.4.2.4; Case study 8.5)

word (1.3) the term used for a lexeme under any and all of the grammatical guises it may appear in, such as the singular, plural, and possessive forms of the single lexeme *child, children, child's, children's*

word class see *part of speech*

word field (a.k.a. *lexical* or *semantic field*) (1.2, 1.4.4; 3.1.1.2, 3.2.4, 3.3.1, 3.3.6–8, 3.4.4, 3.5; 4.5.5–6; 5.0, 5.3.1.2, 5.3.2.4; 6.2, 6.3.7; 8.3.2, 8.4.2, 8.4.3.1) a set of words used for the same general extralinguistic ('real world') area. The members of a field share a number of *semantic features*; see also *domain* (area of use) and *field of discourse* (an aspect of *diatypes*)

word finder, word/language activator, word menu see *thesaurus*

word form (1.3 ; 2.0, 2.2; 3.1.1.1, 3.5.2; 6.1.4) the physical word independent of its meaning as a sequence of sounds or of letters

word formation (a.k.a. *lexical morphology*) (1.1.1, 1.3.2; 3.7; 4.3.2: passim, 4.5.2; 5.0; 6.1: passim, 6.3.6; 8.2.2, 8.3: passim, Exercise 8.7, 8.4.3.4) the processes by means of which new words are formed in a language using the resources of the language itself rather than borrowing; see also *abbreviation, acronym, affixation, blend, borrowing, clipping, composition, compound(ing), derivation, folk etymology, onomatopoeia, reduplication*

word meaning see *theories of meaning*

written English (1.1.1–2; Projects 2.3, 2.4; 3.2.4; 5.1.2.2, 5.3.2.1, 5.3.2.4; Exercise 6.5; 7.1; 8.1.2.1, 8.1.3, Case study 8.1, 8.3.2–3, 8.4.1, 8.4.1.1, Exercises 8.8, 8.9, 8.4.3, 8.4.3.1–2) one *medium* of language; see also *spoken English*

Xhosa (4.1, 4.3.1.1) one of the languages of South Africa

yes/no, use of (6.4.2)

zero article see *article*

zero derivation see *conversion*

Zulu (4.3.1.1; 5.1.2) one of the languages of South Africa